DECONSTRUCTION

DECONSTRUCTION

An American Institution

GREGORY JONES-KATZ

The University of Chicago Press   CHICAGO AND LONDON

PUBLICATION OF THIS BOOK HAS BEEN AIDED
BY A GRANT FROM THE BEVINGTON FUND.

The University of Chicago Press, Chicago 60637
The University of Chicago Press, Ltd., London
© 2021 by The University of Chicago

Published 2021
Printed in the United States of America

30 29 28 27 26 25 24 23 22 21   1 2 3 4 5

ISBN-13: 978-0-226-53586-9 (cloth)
ISBN-13: 978-0-226-53605-7 (paper)
ISBN-13: 978-0-226-53619-4 (e-book)
DOI: https://doi.org/10.7208/chicago/9780226536194.001.0001

Library of Congress Cataloging-in-Publication Data

Names: Jones-Katz, Gregory, author.
Title: Deconstruction : an American institution / Gregory Jones-Katz.
Description: Chicago : University of Chicago Press, 2021. | Includes
bibliographical references and index.
Identifiers: LCCN 2020056566 | ISBN 9780226535869 (cloth) |
ISBN 9780226536057 (paperback) | ISBN 9780226536194 (ebook)
Subjects: LCSH: Deconstruction. | Criticism—United States.
Classification: LCC PN98.D43 J66 2021 | DDC 801/.950973—dc23
LC record available at https://lccn.loc.gov/2020056566

♾ This paper meets the requirements of ANSI/NISO Z39.48-1992
(Permanence of Paper).

TO LAURA—
WITHOUT YOU, I'D BE HOMELESS.

CONTENTS

INTRODUCTION

Has any approach to reading texts ever attracted such rancorous attention? It was a Trojan Horse, esteemed literary critic and scholar René Wellek warned in 1977, that would "destroy literary studies from the inside."[1] Because its practitioners argued that no text existed, Reagan-appointed head of the National Endowment for the Humanities William Bennett cautioned in 1982 that it threatened the basis of humanistic inquiry.[2] *Newsweek* imparted it with dramatic and destructive power, reporting in 1981 that its champions, who drew "heavily on Modern European theories of language and have a decidedly nihilistic philosophy of life," waged an "all-out war" with "partisans of the humanist tradition who believe that the purpose of [literary] criticism" should, "in Matthew Arnold's words, . . . 'propagate the best that is known and thought in the world.'"[3] In his unexpected 1987 bestseller, classicist Allan Bloom memorably observed: "The school" that disseminated it "is the last, predictable, stage in the suppression of reason and the denial of the possibility of truth in the name of philosophy."[4] And in 1991 screeds on the state of the American academy, social critic Camille Paglia caustically referred to it as a "bookworm affectation by tunnel-vision careerists" that "systematically trashes high culture by reducing everything to language and then making language destroy itself."[5]

"It" was deconstruction. Yet "it" was also a whack-a-mole, a lure of sorts; enemies found "it" difficult to define. For rather than a fixed method of reading, deconstruction was a set of sophisticated reading techniques that identified the rhetorical dimensions of a text, often a contradiction that subverted the text's own value-laden hierarchies, such as form/meaning, literal/metaphorical, or original/imitation. In such conceptual paradoxes, a key term struggled and failed to unite incompatible implications, or a peripheral phenomenon was disclosed as repressed and in fact at stake. Pinning down what deconstruction was required stressing terms or reading tactics as central and essential to deconstruction and making other terms or procedures secondary. Doing this downplayed the figural character of language and the consequences of using value-laden hierarchies of meaning—precisely what deconstructive reading procedures were meant to identify and show as self-subverting. Such a dilemma could easily be viewed as a brilliant and devious game of obfuscation or, more positively, as a way to motivate readers to actually read deconstructive interpretations of texts. But more often the media and other scholars, too, became frustrated and sometimes openly hostile to deconstruction, with their resulting representations of it unfortunately generating far more heat than light.

It turns out that what most readers in America came to understand as deconstruction was initially formulated not, as commentators on the right frequently claimed, by leftist radicals but by midcareer university professors, proponents of and contributors to the speculative tumult that shook literary-critical circles and humanities departments at East Coast universities in the second half of the 1960s. Above all, it was the writings and teachings during the 1970s and early 1980s of the "Hermeneutical Mafia"—a cadre of literary critics, theorists, and philosophers of literature based at Yale University—that helped put the word "deconstruction" into the mouths of the intellectually hip and onto the pages of culture war polemics. Composed of Harold Bloom, Paul de Man, Geoffrey Hartman, J. Hillis Miller, and, in a complicated fashion, French philosopher Jacques Derrida, the Yale School was the group around and through which the most influential forms of deconstruction in America initially pulsed. By 1990, with the number of partisans and opponents of the intellectual movement having grown exponentially, a kind of deconstruction, if not exactly the rhetorical reading techniques formulated by the Yale School, had spread like kudzu across departments and fields throughout the humanities and social sciences and from there throughout American life, reaching architecture, fashion, music, theater, and the law.

Still, our picture of how deconstruction developed in America remains remarkably incomplete.[6] Many see it—along with other innovative interpretive perspectives and discourses, including Saussurean linguistics, Lacanian psychoanalysis, Althusserian Marxism, and various (post)structuralisms—as having been airlifted out of Parisian cafés to American ivory towers.[7] In this version of the story, a paper that Jacques Derrida presented at a now famous 1966 Johns Hopkins international symposium launched the stunning invasion. Relatedly, literary critics au courant with intellectual advances in Europe often emphasized the sheer and exhilarating newness—that is, the introduction—of deconstruction to the American academy. Sometimes, these portrayals highlighted the French contingent aligned with Derrida's philosophical project, focusing on the crew associated during the late 1960s and early 1970s with the avant-garde literary magazine *Tel Quel*—Roland Barthes, Michel Foucault, and Julia Kristeva—and a younger faction linked in the late 1970s to the Parisian publishing house Flammarion—Sylviane Agacinski, Sarah Kofman, Philippe Lacoue-Labarthe, and Jean-Luc Nancy. We've also heard of how deconstruction changed after crossing the North Atlantic; François Cusset, for example, deployed Pierre Bourdieu to convincingly explore the "structural misunderstandings" that accompanied this voyage of French thought.[8]

Other narratives have more subtly pushed the foreignness of deconstruction. That 1981 *Newsweek* article held that the Yale School members had "bent deconstruction to their own individual—and practical—purposes."[9] This implies that Derrida's deconstruction came first; the Yale School ostensibly only extended or adopted the French philosopher's insights. To be sure, there were observers of academic trends who did see deconstructionist literary criticism as a series of attempts to domesticate Derrida's work.[10] Deconstruction as it existed in America, for these observers, was hardly radical; it simply chanted earlier methodological developments and intellectual traditions in literature departments in a French key. Even these sympathetic exegetists would have readers believe that deconstructionists' meticulous studies of the linguistic devices and figural language in prose and poetry brought established critical approaches to their logical limits.[11] A string of broadsides in high-profile, middlebrow publications during the early and mid-1980s—the *New York Times* here; the *Wall Street Journal* there—solidified the view that deconstruction was of foreign provenance.[12]

Long-standing intimations that deconstructionists dismantled the Arnoldian imperative to learn from the "best that has been thought and known in the world"[13] took on explosive power in 1987 with the discovery of Paul de Man's writings—169 review essays and articles, most on literature and music—for collaborationist journals in his native Belgium under Nazi occupation at the beginning of the Second World War. De Man's willing proximity to the Nazi propaganda machine convulsed American humanist circles. Here, for many, was the smoking gun that proved the bankruptcy of deconstructionists' foreign-born antihumanist skepticism and nihilism toward life and literature. After all, de Man, dead for four years, had been Derrida's most prominent friend in American intellectual life. He also had been *capo di tutti capi* of the by then defunct Hermeneutical Mafia. The ensuing de Man Affair made it difficult—nigh impossible—to continue to conduct inquiries into deconstruction.[14] For, as logically fallacious as it may be, guilt by association was a very effective tactic used to not simply discredit de Man's mature work but stain any attempt to put the deconstructive community into perspective, historical or otherwise.

But the deconstruction that has been portrayed as a European import had been misunderstood in other ways as well, conflated with (1) postmodernism, a perspective that underlined, in a playfully self-referential medley of ironic modes, the provisional and plural nature of knowledge claims and value systems; and (2) "theory," perhaps best described as either "works that succeed in challenging and reorienting thinking" through their "novel and persuasive accounts of signification" or the examination of problems about the structure and components of discourse and their relations and our transactions with them.[15] Jonathan Culler has helpfully pointed out that overlap existed between deconstruction and what most nonacademics today would call postmodernism. This is undeniable; questioning the assumed difference between language and metalanguage, deconstructionists and postmodernists both aimed to demonstrate that philosophies of narrative were narratives, philosophies of writing were writing, and philosophies of repression required repression. Overlap existed between deconstruction and theory as well, as proponents of both uncovered the hidden principles, expectations, and norms that undergirded texts and arguments. However, these tendencies to conflate deconstruction with postmodernism or theory have blurred and in some cases nearly erased the key institutional sites, persons, and intellectual networks that laid the groundwork for and produced deconstruction in America.[16] What's more, deconstruction has been implicated in narratives about the fracturing of American scholarly life across a range of disciplines—economics, political science, anthropology, philosophy, and so on.[17]

There are certainly difficulties to telling this story. Deconstructionists' multiplicity of interpretive styles and convictions appear to prohibit a tidy and coherent narrative of their lives and works. And a skilled deconstructionist could highlight how rhetorical elements in the texts used throughout the following narrative subvert themselves, thereby undermining the structure of this story before it even began and well after it has finished.[18] Further, a compelling case can be made that what we routinely call deconstruction today contains only distant echoes of Derrida's or de Man's versions of deconstruction. In fact, the word "deconstruction" has been and is often used, without drawing on its fund of pedigreed knowledge, to denote simply "analysis" or "breakdown."[19] In a 2007 *New York Times* article, for example, baseball slugger Barry Bonds was said to have "spent Thursday afternoon . . . deconstructing video of his swing and taking extra batting practice," while the titular character of Woody Allen's *Deconstructing Harry* (1997) skidded out of focus, decentered and blurred like one of his own fictional characters.[20] Deconstruction has even been co-opted into the terrifying vernacular of the far right; Norwegian terrorist Anders Breivik narrated, in his fifteen-hundred-page manifesto, that "deconstruction" arrived in America "from France" in the 1970s to help "cultural critics" remove "traditional meaning" and replace it with "the Political Correctness that infests society today."[21] A number of former president Donald Trump's cabinet picks and advisers employed the word to describe their aims. "The deconstruction of the administrative state," Steve Bannon chillingly declared, necessitated deregulation and massive cuts in discretionary federal spending.[22]

That we today can so readily talk of the deconstruction—however the term is defined—not just of literary works and philosophical tomes but of recipes and menswear is quite remarkable, especially amid all the talk and hand-wringing about the social irrelevance of the humanities. The ubiquity of deconstruction in our cultural vocabulary perhaps, then, points to a distinctive turn or, rather, a distinctive trope, meaning, in the ancient Greek fashion, "a manner, style, turn, way." For deconstructionists' diverse projects, over approximately forty years, displaced metaphysical assurances about the nature and reliability of meaning by revealing the contradictions or logical disjunctions that undid assumed ahistorical binaries that shaped not just literary texts and literary criticisms but cultural concepts like "the author," "art," "history," "politics," "the social," and "identity." Actually, maybe deconstruction is today less a way of reading texts than, pinching from W. H. Auden's poem (1940) on Freud, "a whole climate of opinion" that "quietly surrounds all our habits of growth."[23]

Grasping how this mood orients our different ways of being in the world—understanding how deconstruction became a meme—requires above all an intellectual and institutional history of the aforementioned Yale School. And to understand the members of this group's professional trajectories and intellectual output necessitates inquiry into precisely what all of those portrayals of deconstruction as a European import, as equivalent to postmodernism and/or theory, or as part of a more general fracturing of society and culture, have largely overlooked: the domestic institutions, publications, classroom experiences, conferences, pedagogical programs, and philosophical and literary-critical practices that *instituted*—not merely *adopted*—deconstruction in the United States. One scholar's suggestion that "the history of deconstruction in America is a history of journals and journal publications" therefore misses the mark.[24] Another scholar of the deconstructive event in America is motivated by a theoretical sensibility that merges to a degree with that of Yale School members; this is philosophically bracing, but such an approach diminishes his study's value as a history.[25]

For better or worse, this book intends to remain analytically and rhetorically detached from deconstructionist thought, intervening in the historiographical mainstream by identifying the American institution of deconstruction, searching for its processes of descent, emergence, and execution.[26] This goal could be construed as succumbing to the transcendental desire for origins, thus manufacturing a strict separation between America and Europe and placing the key locales and events wholly on one side of the North Atlantic.[27] Yet this history is not one of "American exceptionalism."[28] While accounting for transatlantic exchanges and without denying the importance of certain continental lineages, the primary aim here is to explore the complex intellectual-institutional matrix in America—the sites, settings, situations, individuals, groups, and traditions—from which deconstruction emerged and how particular conditions of possibility helped it become a distinct practice in its own right. Much, though not all by any means, of this institutional history occurred at Yale, whose "peculiarities" facilitated the development and implementation of deconstruction as a pedagogical-intellectual project of the Yale School.[29] No other faction of so-called postmodern theorists, critics, or philosophers taught and wrote in such close institutional quarters, sometimes literally the same classroom. Because the Yale School, its students, and its interlocutors were subject to conspicuous nationwide changes in intellectual and academic life, such an inquiry also offers a clearer understanding of the history of theory and the cultural perspectives of postmodernism in America. Moreover, because de Man and company highlighted the rhetorical elements of texts, their works provide potent historical indexes of the linguistic turn, the stress in the discourses of the humanities and social sciences during the 1970s on the power of language in human meaning making.[30] This history of deconstruction also aims to give a close-up look at the desacralization of American academic culture in the last decades of the twentieth century.[31] Finally, since deconstruction does not conform to a straightforward politics of right/left, this history complicates and thus contributes to attempts to place deconstruction squarely within an established political lineage.

It was a group of daring professors of literature—Peter Brooks, Alvin Kernan, and Michael Holquist—who designed a groundbreaking pedagogical program at Yale that cultivated favorable conditions for the American institution of deconstruction there. Yale proved such a fertile setting for this trio partly because the school, since the beginning of the postwar period, boasted leading departments of English, French, and comparative literature. Brooks, Kernan, and Holquist continued the university's tradition of literary-critical innovation by aiming to reform literary education. To varying degrees, they responded to undergraduates' rising antiformalist interests in the "extraliterary"—these students were baby boomers, top of the class yet also raised by TV, for whom participating in consumer culture was second nature. Dominant in literature departments since the midcentury rise of the New Criticism, formalism was a way of reading that focused on a literary work's internal, structural purposes. Often, such a focus was to show the harmony between the text's form, the arrangement of words and spaces on the page, and the words' meanings, as well as that literature was a unique, sometimes sacred, kind or use of language; indeed, the work of many New Critics gave the impression that poetry was the only available substitute for the lost authority of and security provided by (Christian) metaphysics.

But Brooks, Kernan, and Holquist's reformation of literary education at Yale also responded to fellow professors' belief, expressed across the country, that professional overspecialization, by emphasizing national literary traditions and interpretive schools of thought, had undermined the sacrosanct uniqueness of literature and threatened the "prestige of literary culture." On the heels of the sixties, Brooks, Kernan, and Holquist implemented their pedagogical endeavor, hoping to reverse students' indifference to literature and answer scholars' anxious questions about the purpose of literary education, with their experimental undergraduate course Literature X "(eks, not ten)," which served as the basis for a literature major.[32] The program of Lit X, first taught in 1970, and the lit major, inaugurated in 1973, instructed undergraduates to interrogate the metaphysical hierarchical oppositions that traditional literary study erected between high and low, prose and poetry, and literary and nonliterary texts, so as to recognize all cultural products as a kind or aspect of fiction. By training undergraduates to question conventional modes of literary education, though, Lit X and lit major curricula struggled to realize a pedagogical agenda that recouped the uniqueness of literature at Yale and the power of literary culture more generally. For, by the early 1970s, the end of the postwar prosperity that built the golden age of higher education and had placed the humanities at the forefront put pressure on intellectual and institutional networks, leading to the displacement of literary study as the organizing principle of the university's cultural mission.

Though Lit X and the lit major were inspired in part by the writings of European thinkers, Brooks, Kernan, and Holquist's institutionalization of an experimental program of literary education was informed by the upheavals of the late 1960s and early 1970s—that is to say, the sixties—more than anything else. Not simply the sway that popular culture, the counterculture, and mass media exerted on undergraduates or even the diversification of student populations but political challenges, such as the one launched by a New Left contingent of English professors and graduate students against the New Critics' formalism, fueled fears among scholars and critics that the status of literature was in irreversible decline, that sociohistorical forces threatened the hallowed autonomy and metaphysical unities of literary works, and that the teaching of prose and poetry was increasingly pedagogically ineffective. While the architects of Lit X and the lit major sought to allay these anxieties, some Yale professors felt their program actively undermined literary education. The quixotic and discordant goals of Lit X and the lit major, these professors charged, capitulated to the sixties-inspired demands made by a literary-critical vanguard for novel and persuasive interpretive techniques, veering too far toward a reading style that destroyed the harmonic singularity and autonomy of literature. But last-ditch efforts to derail the adoption of the lit major— attempts that aimed to protect conventional (biographical, historical, or formalist) ways of studying literature from the sixties, or, rather, from theory—failed. By 1975, Lit X and the lit major were themselves Yale traditions. Yet the coincidence between the establishment of the lit major and the crises that ended the golden age of higher education marked the reputation of Brooks, Kernan, and Holquist's bold experiment. It was but a short step for opponents, such as René Wellek, who had established in 1946 and chaired until 1972 Yale's Comp Lit Department, from charging the lit major with subverting humanistic literary education to accusing the rhetorical reading techniques soon known as deconstruction of "destroying literary studies."

This was not the only substantial transformation of literary criticism and education at work in America or even at Yale, however. The prismatic adventures of deconstruction in America are often described as commencing at the 1966 Johns Hopkins symposium, which provided the avenue for the import from France of not only deconstruction but postmodernism and theory as well, a triumvirate frequently accused across the political spectrum of relativism, subjectivism, and nihilism, of reducing metaphysical truth to a question of opinion and superficial political expediency. The proximate stimulus for this shift in the American academy is in turn often attributed to the sixties, that exceptional noun that encompasses a chain of "highly visible, contentious movements and events that dominated public life."[33] The sixties apparently catapulted relativism, subjectivism, and nihilism into universities (and supposedly provided the foundation for our posttruth era) by providing energy and a rebellious attitude to tenured radicals who dismantled the hierarchies of gender, race, class, sexual identity, and age that the Greatest Generation, by way of law, tradition, and religion, had upheld since the Second World War.[34] Emphasizing the roles played by contemporary French thought and the raucous, rowdy, and TV-ready sixties, though, has helped to overshadow the important "protodeconstructive" work undertaken at elite American universities by a group of vanguard literary critics, three of whom—Paul de Man, Geoffrey Hartman, and J. Hillis Miller—later constituted the Yale School. Supported by a range of domestic institutions built during and bolstered by the prosperity of the postwar period, and drawing from an array of intellectual traditions, these vanguard critics, at key academic conferences and symposia during the 1960s, moved their work beyond literary formalism. This meant revising the philosophical (metaphysical) grounds of as much as cultivating alternatives to accepted literary-critical practice. By the early 1970s, this postformalist work, which largely grew out of the unresolved interpretive problems of the New Criticism, instituted deconstruction in America.

That the vanguard critics' training, entrance, and acclimatization to the profession occurred during the halcyon days of the welfare state funding regime decisively shaped their postformalist projects. Throughout those ostensibly golden years, public monies had funded the expansion of tertiary institutions and the tenured teaching corps, as well as, more broadly, "the academic revolution."[35] Keeping the demands of capital at bay, the academic revolution granted relative autonomy to humanistic education and made "the graduate school departments of liberal arts" the benchmark for intellectual respectability for colleges and universities.[36] The New Critics' quasi-scientific literary formalism was ideally suited for the postwar massification of higher education as well as its academic revolution and bureaucratization of culture; it achieved such outstanding success in literature departments partly because it helped undergraduate students, who often entered college without much literary-historical or poetic knowledge, appreciate the linguistic complexity of literary works; it also provided teachers of literature with a solution to the problem of how to coordinate their profession's teaching and research legs. Even after the New Critics withdrew from promoting and elaborating the intricacies of their interpretive techniques in the early 1960s, however, the ongoing academic revolution would stoke new fires of critical transformation, making European intellectual influences accessible and supporting work inspired by them, such as the vanguard critics' protodeconstructive projects. Symposia, conferences, visiting professorships, research centers, and new journals devoted to exploring innovative thought soon followed. Meanwhile, graduate programs—newly established at public and expanded at private universities—in modern languages and literatures spawned a notable increase in the sheer volume of writing about literature. Because graduate students were more than ever educated in the writing of criticism and "professional professorial critics embraced the notion that their primary task was research and publication," these programs gradually underscored questions about interpretation.[37] The growing professional demand for cutting-edge critical approaches—soon known as theory—helped to create a critical clerisy, positioning the literary critic as the most sophisticated, if not always the most respected, member of humanities faculties. Along with jobs, funding, and prestige, the growing stress on complex accounts of signification also provided stimulus and support for vanguard critics' adjustments and appropriations of novel interpretive possibilities that subverted the New Critics' literary formalism. Importantly, unlike many New Critics, whose careers had started outside the university and only gradually and sometimes reluctantly bonded with it, the vanguard critics began and ended their professional lives in the university; their postformalist techniques remained within, even as they undermined, settled literary-critical practices.

It was René Wellek, "dean of historians of criticism," who first charged Yale's literature major with destabilizing literary education and then condemned deconstruction for annihilating literary studies. Such a leap required conflation and confusion, but a link there was: the Yale School. Harold Bloom, Paul de Man, Geoffrey Hartman, J. Hillis Miller, and, often cast as a supplement, Jacques Derrida formed a group that was unified in trying to understand the demand that literature placed on readers to be viewed as language irreducible to, yet of essential import for, all discourses, particularly humanistic ones. During the 1970s and 1980s, the Yale School's responses to the literary imperative not only produced vibrant and revealing interpretations of canonical writings but also revived/created a discipline of rhetorical reading. Teaching was central to this reflexive endeavor, and not simply for propagation to graduate students and by extension undergraduates. In classrooms, the Yale group formulated parts of important publications and presentations that launched their discipline of rhetorical reading into the literary-critical world and onto the national stage. With great élan and to great effect, de Man and company drilled two related Yale quarries. The first was graduate seminars in French, English, and comp lit departments. These programs' stellar reputations lent gravity to every lecture, every assignment, and every apprenticeship between adviser and student, especially in the case of de Man and his advisees. Second, the Yale School mined undergraduate courses, most notably those in the lit major, whose core pedagogical sequence included, by 1977, not just a revamped Literature X (and Literature Y), but de Man and Hartman's groundbreaking Literature Z.

The formation of the Yale School did roughly coincide with an explosion of countercultural expressions in popular culture, various crises that followed the sixties in rapid succession, among them Watergate, the oil embargo, and stagflation, as well as a thickening atmosphere of skepticism toward authority of all types. Focusing on these, though, directs attention away from more local reasons for the Yale group's achievements. Yale, since the 1950s, boasted "The Best English Department in the World," housing several prominent New Critics. While never dominating its literature departments, these professors did dominate the school's external reputation, promulgating their commitment to reading literary works as complex linguistic objects and a poetic-historical narrative wherein modernists deflated the (mostly British) Romantics' idealist delusions, which had ostensibly undermined the literary achievements of Renaissance poets by effectuating a "dissociation of sensibility," a deleterious separation of poetic thought from poetic feeling.[38] The New Critics also nationally distributed the view that poetry was a kind of secular scripture and that it was in the classroom where the worldly literature professor should train the favored to discover how the value to be identified in literary works, "if not identical with moral and religious values, is very close to these."[39] After the mid-1970s departures of several of these New Critics from Yale, Bloom, de Man, Hartman, and their graduate students developed a strong sense of a communal effort to repudiate those metaphysical views, turning the European Romantics from undisciplined poets of nature into sages of reflexive literary vision and insight. Under the specter of a holy literary formalism at Yale, de Man's, Hartman's, and Bloom's overlapping rhetorical reading projects can undoubtedly be read as an Oedipal rebellion against the false aesthetic gods of the New Critics. Their teachings on the Romantics developed along different paths and with different emphases and tones, but all deepened the New Critical–like attention to literary language by highlighting the rhetorical dimensions of the text, while at the same time underlining and undermining the ontological/theological foundations of literary education—foundations that the New Critics, who had earlier attracted the best students to New Haven, helped strengthen as the terms of reference for literary study in America.

For example, Bloom began in the 1970s to rewrite the established story of the cheerful growth and progress of English literature, portraying this history instead as a gigantic intertextual battle waged by strong poets—Bloom's exemplars were Milton and Blake—against their elders, with the former attempting to make space for their poetic voice by cunningly dis-*figuring*, by slyly hiding their rhetorical debts to, the latter. Hartman, at Yale since 1967, commenced his trailblazing interpretation of Wordsworth's poetry during the mid-1960s. While allying himself with a Derridean philosophical response to the demands of literature in the mid-1970s, Hartman highlighted how the creative linguistic powers of the critic subverted the metaphysical trust in the strict division between artwork and commentary, outfoxing interpretive rivals and offering the most talented of critics the chance to claim the title and authority of "poet-artist." But, really, it was de Man, arriving from Johns Hopkins in 1970, who stood at the center of the Yale School's rhetoricized challenges to literary humanism and accepted literary-critical practice. His deconstructions—most conspicuously of Wordsworth's poetry, Rousseau's writings, and Nietzsche's philosophical essays—pinpointed the linguistic conflicts that undermined texts' value-laden, metaphysical hierarchies of meaning. By interpreting the Romantics as self-divided poets of chiaroscuro—poets who, because of the nature of literary language, mechanically subverted their own stated beliefs, ideas, and truths—de Man tunneled through the established role the Romantics played in literary studies. When Derrida joined the Yale Comp Lit Department as a visiting professor in 1975, Bloom's, Hartman's, and de Man's endeavors were well under way, and Derrida's own "philosophical" project became, to the regret of a fair share of fellow travelers, aligned with this Yale School's revivified discipline of rhetorical reading that identified the linguistic contradictions—the "undecidables" as both de Man and Derrida flagged them—that undermined direct paths between the form and the meaning of prose and poetry.

De Man and company's texts and teachings deconstructively wrestled with the metaphysical—in other words, the ontological/theological—substructure of postwar criticism, but Yale deconstruction was not entirely revolutionary. It actually possessed a conservative thrust, sustaining itself on and thus in a manner reinforcing established formalist reading protocols. Furthermore, while sixties activists believed that healing the wounds of American culture and society would lead to personal authenticity and a feeling of wholeness, deconstructive reading perpetually sought to expose the flaws in any claim to purity or oneness.[40] And, of course, occurring and being practiced primarily within academia at one of the most prestigious private universities in the world, deconstruction was to a large extent restricted to but a privileged few. Regardless, members of the Yale School received substantial attention on the American literary-critical scene in part because their work, including their "anti-manifesto" (1979), high-profile appearances at conferences, and touted articles and books, bore the trappings of a new major critical movement. This movement inherited not only the authority of theoretical innovation that previously rested with a literary avant-garde but also the mantle of the New Critics. To their supporters, de Man and company defended their profession's integrity during a wider post-sixties crisis in literary education by offering a comprehensive science of rhetorical reading that protected the autonomy and status of the literary text as well as rigorously reinvigorating the practice of literary criticism. But for opponents of deconstruction, who often cherry-picked phrases from de Man's and Derrida's readings that appeared to advance negative and nihilistic views of life and literature, the Yale School contributed to the crisis in literary studies and demonstrated just how much damage had been done by the university's bureaucratization of culture. Their coterie criticism, it was felt, furthered the divide, fostered by expectations for writing and publishing set after the academic revolution and exacerbated by the ratcheting up of competition for jobs and grants in the 1970s, between the profession's research and teaching arms. De Man and company's deconstructions may have been intellectually edifying and professionally useful for members of the literary-critical *savant garde* at, say, Yale, Hopkins, or Cornell, but critics believed they were ineffective at best, dangerous at worst, for undergraduates' consumption. For a number of these detractors, an odd group that included as many liberals as cultural conservatives, deconstruction represented the hazards posed to the bedrock of humanistic education and the tenets of "American ideology" by fashionably foreign logics of signification. However, in an irony worthy of the gods of intellectual history, such accusations ignored the deep debt Bloom, de Man, Hartman, and Miller owed not least to the traditions of and opportunities fostered by the postwar university. This group's professional life and intellectual yield was greatly motivated by a desire to devise alternatives to established literary-critical praxis that rigorously responded to literature's demand to be read first and foremost as literature, as literary language, and it was out of this context that deconstruction in America productively emerged during the 1970s, at and through Yale.

Journalistic and academic representations of deconstruction, above all those devoted to the star-studded enclave at Yale, have been gravely remiss in understanding the range and diversity of the American institution of deconstruction. Such depictions have consistently disregarded "The Brides of Deconstruction and Criticism."[41] This cadre of feminist-deconstructive critics (and one philosopher) comprised Judith Butler, Margaret Ferguson, Shoshana Felman, Margaret Homans, Barbara Johnson, Mary Poovey, Jack Winkler, Eve Sedgwick, and Gayatri Spivak.[42] The existence and legacy of the Brides and their innovative expansions of the discipline of rhetorical reading shatters the image of the Yale group as solely comprising middle-aged men, for far from a *supplément* to what Johnson wittily called the "Male School," feminist deconstructionists were central to the story of deconstruction at Yale and in America. Local and national factors both profoundly informed Yale's feminist moment. Inspired by second-wave feminism and the cultural politics of the women's and gay liberation movements during the early to mid-1970s, professors, administrators, and students at the university struggled against "Male Yale," which, despite going coed in 1969, continued patterns of female effacement and marginalization. Feminist deconstructionists prominently contributed to overturning these patterns of erasure. By the 1980s, their overlapping, though distinct, feminist responses to literature's imperative moved rhetorical reading techniques away from a postformalist focus on paradoxes of English, French, and German prose and poetry toward gender, sexual difference, race, and psychoanalysis in a range of texts. Subverting the control that masculine metaphysics exerted on literary humanist education by alerting readers to how figural language disrupted texts' gendered and sexed hierarchies of meaning, feminist deconstructionists transformed fields of inquiry, including Mary Shelley studies, Romantic studies, Lacan studies, and Subaltern studies, and founded others, such as trauma studies, queer theory, and gender studies. Besides their groundbreaking publications, though, the Brides' classrooms and their participation in Yale's Women's Studies Program, launched in 1979, helped propel feminist-deconstructive cultural politics into American academic life and beyond.

Johnson and company thus accomplished far more than a contribution to the enlargement of the demographic and cognitive boundaries of the humanities at Yale. This was in part due to how these feminist deconstructionists' undertakings and the progressive principles they advanced were implicated in the contemporary loss of disciplinary authority and in the widespread subversions of the metaphysical underpinnings of literary studies. This erosion and these subversions resulted partly because of the increased stress placed on professionalism and the loss of institutional standards for the study of literature following the post-sixties proliferation of theoretical perspectives and discourses. Feminist deconstructionists not only broke out of the formalist impasse that the vanguard (and then Yale) critics earlier aimed yet failed to surpass but also offered paths out of the methodological cul-de-sac that the procedures of rhetorically reading texts formulated by the "Male School" presented for literary education. Because they undermined the masculinist onto-theological (philosophical) infrastructure of postwar criticism, Johnson and company's publications and teachings were at once social and political interventions that developed tactics of interpretation indispensable to proponents of deconstruction and helped pave the way for cultural studies during the 1980s. Indeed, if an idea's influence is measured by the extent to which it has affected nonacademic life, then a strong case can be made that the Brides' intellectual-cultural work outstripped that of the "Male School"; their feminist extensions of the discipline of rhetorical reading were dispersed throughout and beyond colleges and universities, with discourses in the last decade of the twentieth century about the deconstruction of gender binaries but one striking consequence. That members of the extreme political right in France today read "gender theory" as "American" should give pause to pundits who ignore the achievements of and reasons for the initial emergence and later successes of feminist deconstruction at Yale and in the United States.[43] By the mid-1980s, in fact, the Brides of Deconstruction and Criticism penetrated the highest echelons of the American theoretical revolution, just as academics and journalists bestowed deconstruction the rare honor of being the target of a smear campaign. The ensuing minor media sensation was part of the so-called theory wars, a series of attacks waged by a grab bag of partisans who nominally defended literary humanism from the antihumanist scourge of cultural theory.

One central avenue for the development and dissemination of theorists' subversions of the metaphysical dichotomies that controlled the reading of texts was the School of Criticism and Theory (SCT). In 1976, two English professors at the new University of California, Irvine, took advantage of the absence of institutional traditions, the encouragement of administrators, and the financial support (still sometimes) offered for cutting-edge programs and research, to found the SCT. In addition to broadly trying to satisfy the desire among graduate students and professors in the humanities for ever more specialized, rigorous, and varied innovative interpretive approaches, the SCT was designed to fill a perceived gap left in literary-critical circles by the closing, in 1972, of The Kenyon School of English, whose galaxy of formalists had, in the 1940s and early 1950s, shaped "responsible literary judgments" and trained "students to make critical evaluations to supplement the historical and factual knowledge they learned in graduate school."[44] Yet the SCT was not simply the latest example of a decades-long academization of literary criticism, as it trained attendees how to exploit theory so as to develop homegrown styles of postformalist reading techniques. Strange as it might be to those with jaded ears, SCT attendees were also entrusted with using theory to highlight the worth of literature and the criticism dedicated to it to undergraduates in order to provide cohesion and purpose to the humanities, solving the "crisis of humanities" that, though it originated in the late nineteenth century, had intensified by the end of the golden age of higher education in the mid-1970s. While this initial call for the reintegration of the humanities via a brand of refurbished literary education was quickly set aside, the SCT helped to nurture an environment at UC-Irvine favorable to deconstruction and its cross-pollination with theory.

This next chapter in the American institution of deconstruction dawned on the West Coast after de Man's death in 1983, when Miller and Derrida decamped for UC-Irvine in 1986, and the dissolution of the Yale School per se. But soon thereafter the shocking 1987 discovery of de Man's articles for collaborationist newspapers threatened to discredit the entire deconstructive enterprise. *L'affaire Heidegger* in France, which reignited debate over the German philosopher's relationship to Nazism; the turn in the critical revolution in America away from attention to a text's internal purposes and linguistic forms toward "history," a turn instigated in part by young critics' fears about limited career opportunities; a new academic appreciation in Europe and America of the relationship between memory and history; and an increasing public interest in heritage all contributed to the ensuing paroxysms over de Man. The revelations raised anew questions about de Man's reflexive discipline of rhetorical reading and the interpretations it produced. The reason for his intense debunking of literary humanism's onto-theological underpinnings, his dogged stand against sociohistorical approaches for understanding texts, his rejection of the view that literature expressed an author's inner thoughts, and his single-minded stress on the contradictions that undermined a text's meaning appeared clear. This all was undeniable evidence of his deviousness—for how, if one subscribed to de Man's supposedly comprehensive discipline of rhetorical reading, could interpretive decisions be decisively made about his pro-Nazi writings? How could moral judgments be made about him and his work, prewar as well as postwar? De Man's friends and colleagues sprang to his defense, most (in)famously Derrida, who published a spectacularly controversial deconstruction of de Man's thirty-five years of silence and his wartime writings.

Little clarity was gained during the 1987–89 debate, such as it was, over de Man. Deconstructionists were reticent to explain the desacralizing logic behind their mind-bending readings of de Man's wartime articles as subversive of the official language of the Nazi regime. And questions, dating from the 1970s, about the differences among deconstructionists' projects, such as those between de Man's and Derrida's, were not satisfactorily answered. More broadly missing during the heated debates was a historical perspective on the relationship between the academic revolution and the shifting fortunes of the "intellectual" in American life, the humanities disciplines, and the loss of esteem once accorded to literary culture. Such a conversation could have gone a long way in explaining the role that professional regard for advanced literary-critical thought played in ensuring an unbridgeable divide. On one side were the deconstructionists, specialists who called for ever more complicated readings of de Man and his postwar work that did not fit the right/left political grid. On the other were frustrated critics, many generalists who denounced deconstructionists as obfuscators and requested a rational, "commonsense" return to traditional humanistic inquiry and styles of interpretation. The de Man Affair, in the end, reinforced views of deconstruction as a relativist, albeit sophisticated, method of reading that licensed the interpreter to exercise a kind of ahistorical, nihilistic will to misread texts. It actually became a matter of course to lay the decline of literary education at the feet of deconstruction or theory (with de Man serving as a nice synecdoche for either or both); the apparent Nazi origin of deconstruction was deemed proof positive of a fifth column who used the critical revolution to infiltrate the sacred halls of American humanities departments. As for the other camp: a number of de Man's former students and colleagues kept the flame alive at UC-Irvine and elsewhere, and Derrida took his celebrated ethical and political turns during the late 1980s, though his media presence, voluminous writings, and globetrotting lecture series contributed to his enemies' determination to erase (the memory of) Yale deconstruction. The Hermeneutical Mafia's discipline of rhetorical reading, certainly, continued to be practiced and taught—in part because de Man and company had been so effective in imparting the deconstructive arts to students—though its prominence in literary studies was much diminished.

While intending to revise the conventional history of deconstruction, this narrative of the American institution of deconstruction also aims to illuminate facets of the recent past in order to help counter the disillusion that permeates our intellectual atmosphere in the academic humanities. Things might seem hopeless. A heroic age of theory will, alas, not return; nor will the golden age of higher education and its attendant academic revolution, both having nurtured the New Criticism in literary studies, the dominance of which helped open the gate to all those powerful interpretive styles and discourses that transformed humanistic investigation. Furthermore, the demographic and intellectual diversification of tertiary institutions during the last half century divested the cultural authority once ascribed to a group of critics or a way of reading; because this authority will (thankfully) not be reconstituted, literature can no longer be taught as secular depositories of the sacred. There is also an increasing awareness of the Anthropocene, a period suggested to have begun around the mid-eighteenth century during which humans began to exert a significant influence on Earth's geology and ecosystems, that has rightfully directed attention to the environmental catastrophe we all face. And thanks to the all-encompassing logic of neoliberalism within university walls and college classrooms that foreground corporate values and privilege market forces, persuasive arguments in favor of supporting the arts and letters or, perish the thought, funding permanent teaching positions and research in the humanities are difficult to make to a public unwilling to listen. It looks grim. That the ideological spirits that breathed life into intellectual and pedagogical agendas of the traditional liberal arts have largely departed, however, will not mean the complete demise of humanities departments. At the wealthiest and highest-tiered institutions like Yale, academic humanists will survive, perhaps flourish to an extent, not least because the feverish quest for cultural prestige still makes space for the kinds of self-consciousness cultivated in humanists' classrooms. But those humanists' work may not reach more than a very elite cohort. Despite all the long-standing accusations of nihilism, the Yale School's pedagogical success in focusing readers' and students' attention on how rhetorical elements undermined a text's value-laden hierarchies serves as an example—however imperfect, however possible only due to the eccentricities of Yale and its intellectual culture—of the power that the humanities can effectuate within and beyond the academy.

This type of institutional project could—and according to some should—be possible not only at one particular moment at one peculiar wealthy institution of higher education. In a May 12, 1780, letter to Abigail Adams, John Adams wrote: "I must study Politicks and War that my sons may have liberty to study Mathematicks and Philosophy. My sons ought to study Mathematicks and Philosophy, Geography, natural History, Naval Architecture, navigation, Commerce and Agriculture, in order to give their Children a right to study Painting, Poetry, Musick, Architecture, Statuary, Tapestry, and Porcelaine."[45] No deconstructionist worth his or her salt would blithely agree with Adams's narrative of cultural progression and of generations that culminates in the study of poetry, painting, and porcelain. For Adams, though, the humanities symbolized the finest conceivable future for his descendants. As Adams's figurative offspring, we might do well to again struggle to realize his vision, with the guarantees that all citizens have robust access to the study of the humanities alongside all other branches of knowledge.[46]

1
A CRISIS IN UNDERGRADUATE LITERARY EDUCATION AT YALE

Lit X and the Literature Major

By subtly linking, in a 1966 article, postformalist reading techniques to the atmosphere of protest then gripping the nation, Geoffrey Hartman, newly ensconced in Yale's English Department, troubled William K. Wimsatt, philosopher-elect of the New Critics and expositor of the Christian verities offered by literature.[1] Wimsatt's distress, to be sure, had some legitimacy, as sixties turmoil hit New Haven hard. Anti–Vietnam War sentiment reached a fever pitch in 1969, and Yale's ROTC program came under fire that May. In June, an actual fire, likely set by students, gutted the school's Brutalist Art and Architecture building, its "harsh cement slabs with broken corrugations" and "bleak expanses of glass" felt by many students to be the very incarnation of faceless "modernist" oppression and repression.[2] One year later, following the Kent State shooting in May 1970, Yale seniors planned a "counter-commencement" that would benefit antiwar political candidates.[3] Then the New Haven Black Panther trials, which became a national cause célèbre, brought more than ten thousand protesters, from disaffected students to speakers such as Abbie Hofmann, Dr. Benjamin Spock, even Jean Genet, France's "Black Prince of Letters," to the New Haven Green. "We were the center of the universe for a few moments," one protester gleefully recalled.[4] Indeed, during the May Day protests, the National Guard was called in, police fired tear gas canisters, bombs exploded in a stairwell at Ingalls Rink, and tanks rolled down streets. While his university went "on strike," the Kennedyesque president Kingman Brewster Jr., instrumental in helping enroll more minority students and opening undergraduate admission to women, expressed doubts to faculty that the Black Panthers could get a fair trial anywhere in the United States. But "the [revolutionary] forces beyond our gates," he was quoted as saying in the *New York Times*, "could destroy the internationally significant, free, private university in its present form."[5]

Many of Yale's tenured literature professors hoped to keep the sixties outside their ivory tower and away from the artworks they so revered.[6] In early 1968, Wimsatt delivered a direct response to the unholy interpretive disorder he perceived Hartman and others fomented in their writings, accusing these anti–New Critics of "battering the [literary] object" by creating a "sanctuary for the intolerable" inside criticism and the university.[7] Other professors of literature wrung their hands over the sociohistorical interests that ostensibly made literature as such immaterial to undergraduates. While enthusiastically participating in consumer culture, popular culture, and counterculture, many baby boomers, their Yale teachers feared, possessed little interest in the edification provided by the "high culture" of Homer and Shakespeare. Would students—increasingly political, diverse, and invested in the extraliterary—view the "great books" of the "Western tradition" with indifference, perhaps even hostility?[8] Sixties radicals demanded that literary education come down to earth, become more "relevant" to social and political causes. Its "irrelevance," though, had seemed to have resulted in part from the very postwar prosperity that had granted independence and awarded cultural prestige to humanities departments, particularly to literary studies programs. At Yale, an institution that housed the most prestigious departments of English, French, and comparative literature in America, this crisis in literary education was cause for concern—and perhaps collective action.

These portrayals were overwrought, certainly. But they signal an awareness acutely felt at Yale of the predicament some undergraduate teachers of literature faced during the late 1960s. Many professors were concerned that students' increasing antiformalist interests in sociohistorical matters encroached on "the interior life of the poem."[9] Professors also believed that overspecialization, fostered by the increasing need for new critical methodologies that would support research agendas, undermined their ability to effectively impart the uniqueness of literature to undergraduates. It was also feared that this academic overspecialization stripped literary culture of its cultural capital. A group of maverick professors of literature at Yale responded to both students' seeming apathy and their colleagues' real worries by implementing a pedagogical program that rethought conventional—that is, historical, biographical, or formalist—approaches to literary education. Beginning in 1970, these professors taught Literature X, an experimental course they had devised that served as the basis for a literature major, established in 1973. Bound by neither genre nor geography, as in French, English, or German departments, the lit major's curriculum revolved around having students adopt the persona of the *Homo signiferen*, who speculatively engaged humanity's universal need for and use of fictions. To consider "Man" as the *Homo signiferen* subverted the metaphysical hierarchical oppositions, upon which conventional literary studies relied, between high and low, prose and poetry, and the literary and nonliterary; at the root of these value-laden binaries, it was taught, was a shared desire for fiction, with literature but one historically determined example.[10] By clearing the institutional deck of other ways of reading and not adhering to any single approach, the program of Lit X and the lit major would nurture agreeable conditions for the American institution of deconstruction at Yale, specifically the teaching of deconstruction to undergraduates.[11] More broadly, examining the struggle to institutionalize Lit X and the lit major contributes to the understanding of how the upheavals of the sixties affected the intellectual culture at one of the most elite and oldest universities in America.[12] Because it helped students transform all cultural products into a type or facet of fiction, the lit major curriculum executed a pedagogical agenda congruent with the importance accorded literary education during the golden age of higher education. And, by jettisoning the notion that teachers of literature were secular cultural priests imparting great artworks' wisdom to students, this desacralizing teaching program unified Yale's cultural mission around the study of a worldly concept of literature, recovering the status of literature and the prestige of literary culture. But it wasn't always seen that way.

Literature X: A Homegrown Response

During the late 1960s, more than a few literature professors sought answers to questions about the worth and value of literary education. A fair share of this soul searching stemmed from the fact that campuses had become the center for New Left activity, with many academics reconsidering their professional conduct in light of their political obligations. New Leftists, for example, launched a devastating critique of English departments in a 1970 volume that emerged after the raucous protest at the 1968 Modern Language Association meeting against the organization's apolitical stance toward the Vietnam War and other hot-button issues.[13] One essay in the volume portrayed New Critical pedagogy, acknowledged as the benchmark for teaching "normal criticism" in English departments and associated with conservative and isolationist politics, as a "crude and frankly reactionary formalism," the "essence" of which was similar to "the ostrich [who] sticks his head in the sand and admires the structural relationships among the grains."[14] This was only one of many brazen intellectual attacks on literary formalism for its ahistorical and antisocial stance toward prose and poetry, particularly for its flight from Vietnam and the racist and sexist realities that bore on the condition of "modern man."

These attacks also echoed some of the now-famous critiques of structuralism in France, like that of an anonymous student who, during the massive May 1968 protests against Charles de Gaulle and his Gaullist Party, scrawled across a blackboard at the Sorbonne, "Structures don't march in the streets." Forms weren't staying formal and structures weren't staying structured for those "on the ground," it seemed. A year later, in America, a tipping point in New Leftists' attempts to reorganize the undergraduate teaching of literature was reached. Radicals gained control of the MLA and endorsed an anticapitalist agenda that aimed to reveal the hidden sociopolitical biases in literature; a line in the sand was drawn between those who upheld the conservative and "humanistic" and those who endorsed a radical way of teaching literature.[15] The former group sought to protect the sacred reserves proffered by great art; the latter group, which focused on showing how such humanistic views of art are flawed and morally dangerous, aimed to topple the adored artistic edifice.[16]

Though radicals' dramatic call did not strongly resonate at Yale, provost Charles Taylor saw the need for reform and began to consider ways to start a conversation among faculty on the issue. In the spring of 1969, Taylor helped to assemble a committee to discuss the state of undergraduate literary education. Attending faculty included thirty-one-year-old Peter Brooks, from French and Comparative Literature, who had earned his PhD from Harvard University in 1965. Brooks's first book, published in 1969, explored how four eighteenth- and early nineteenth-century French novelists used their stories to articulate different "social techniques that further[ed] this life and one's position in it"—what Brooks called "worldliness."[17] Brooks's thesis was semiformalist—he eschewed consideration of the "correspondence . . . between [his four writers'] representations and historical social realities."[18] But Brooks himself wasn't isolated with the text, having gloriously run through the streets of Paris during the May 1968 protests. Taylor's faculty meeting also included thirty-four-year-old Michael Holquist, who had received a PhD in 1968 from Yale's Slavic Department. A student of the work of Fyodor Dostoyevsky, Holquist liked to meditate on existential contradictions.[19] Also attending Taylor's meeting was self-described "tory-radical" and former associate provost Alvin Kernan, who taught English literature. Brooks, Holquist, and Kernan possessed distinct motivations and intellectual itineraries—all three, for instance, studied and primarily taught a distinct national literature. All, however, keenly felt that literary education was undergoing a crisis of desacralization that could and should be confronted in a constructive manner.[20]

Peter Brooks's thoughts on the matter had developed significantly in Normandy, at Le Centre Cultural International de Cerisy-la-Salle. Since

1952, the CCIC had served as a meeting place and conference center for French artists, researchers, teachers, students, and, generally, a public interested in cultural and scientific exchanges. Brooks went there for a 1969 colloquium that extended critical assessments of structuralists, who used the Saussurean-inspired science of "semiology" to study "the life of signs at the heart of social life" and phonology, a branch of linguistics, to describe said structures of social life as systems of binary semantic differences.[21] Unusually, the colloquium combined such deliberations with considerations of the relations between the "sciences humaines," poetry, and the teaching of literature. Contributors disagreed on a variety of issues, but attendees expressed the most differences over the meaning of literature and the goals in teaching it. Among the cited causes of dissatisfaction included the deleterious and dreaded effects of positivism— think of those dry-as-dust dissertations that scientifically verify facts about the development of prose and poetry—and the forgetting of the simple pleasures of reading literature. CCIC attendees yearned for a way to once again use aesthetic categories in their teaching. But it was French structuralist Jean Cohen's paper that really stimulated Brooks's thinking about whether, and how, to confront the crisis afflicting literary education. Cohen, Brooks recalled, maintained that "only 'science' could be taught; that logic, grammar, rhetoric, and poetics could no doubt be taught, but that 'literature,' possessing none of the characteristics of a scientifically organized body of knowledge, was a false subject."[22] In an important structuralist study published in 1966, Cohen argued that prose, chiefly concerned with the communication of facts, was exemplified by the language of science, while formal poetry and poetic language deviated from direct communication by a series of "écarts," or unusual images or examples of incongruous logic. For Cohen, poetry, by definition, thus thwarted systematization and attempts to engage it as a scientific topic. Cohen's claim vexed Brooks. Struggling to formulate a response at the 1969 colloquium, Brooks replied to Cohen that, while he may be correct that "'literature' . . . was a false subject, we could teach the *reading* of literature: we could guide an apprenticeship in the form of attention required for the study of literature."[23] And yet, Brooks later reflected, this answer did not address *what* precisely the teacher was directing students' attention toward.

"What is literature?" was in fact a question with a wide array of enshrined answers. For New Critic and Yale professor of English Cleanth Brooks, paradox shaped and provided literature with its "meaning."[24] For Roman Jakobson, a Russian American linguist and literary theorist whose work was central to the development of structuralism, "the object of literary science is not literature but 'literariness,' that is, what makes a given work a *literary* work."[25] By "literariness" Jakobson meant something akin to Anglo-American formalism, in that for him discernible "devices" of literary works highlighted their own language in meter, rhyme, and other patterns of sound and repetition. Similarly, Paul de Man, at the time working at the Johns Hopkins University, posited that Jean-Jacques Rousseau's language was literary because it flagged its own rhetorical mode.[26] Surveying a half century of debate, New Critic and founder of Yale's comparative literature program René Wellek observed in 1970 that "'literature' . . . once meant 'learning,' 'knowledge of literature.'"[27] For his part, Peter Brooks realized that earlier definitions of literature no longer carried much water, and the humanistic notion embraced by Wellek that literary study cultivated character seemed more and more questionable. Coming to refer "frighteningly" and simply to "the body of the written," some (like the structuralists, apparently) had reduced literature to a crudely materialist phenomenon, Brooks quoted Wellek.[28] Yet while he could not answer what constituted literature per se, Brooks remained committed to his belief that teachers could direct students' focus to literature itself and train them in scientific ways to interpret it.

Significantly, Brooks was not especially concerned with repairing what some, such as New Left radicals, saw as literature's severed connections to worldly human concerns and political activities—in making literature, in sixties parlance, "relevant." Brooks's pedagogical interests thus stood somewhat askew to Alvin Kernan's. By the late 1960s, Kernan had come to consider, though certainly not in a New Leftist way, that "the old regime"—that is, the kind of conventional literary education that aimed to develop students' character and capacity for critique by way of training them to recognize transcendent beauty, immutable meanings, and the creative potential of the individual genius—"had become in many ways a museum, filled with great works but removed from its human context to a world of hushed reverence."[29] Guiding undergraduates to Matthew Arnold's idea of "culture" had unintentionally rendered literary works, Kernan now believed, otherworldly, quite unimportant to students. "If literature was to be saved from oblivion," he wrote, the teaching of literature had to become "more open, less idealized," situating "the canonical works, in the middle not of perfect art but of a continuing, ever present human activity of making up stories that give meaning to events and sort out the perplexities of human life."[30] By putting canonical works in contact with the everyday—with individuals' fundamental desire and need for fictions, such as the narratives of popular films or television sitcoms—Kernan held that teachers could show students that literature and literary culture were remarkable, profound, very much alive, immediate, and proximate to their daily living and thinking.

FIGURE 1.1 Alvin Kernan at Yale in the 1960s (Courtesy of Yale University)

As a former Yale associate provost, Kernan was in demand on the national lecture circuit, and his discussions with college teachers around the country also had opened his eyes to the widespread dissatisfaction among educators with the atomization of literature into national traditions. This fission, teachers felt, placed significant obstacles in front of both the educator and pupil. For approximately eighty years, separate academic departments had been devoted to the language and literature of a single nation or, at the largest, a single culture or geographic area: Greek and Latin, French, Russian, Chinese and Japanese, Spanish, German, Italian, English. To be sure, by the late 1960s there were alternative models for the teaching of literature, such as Yale's famed "Great Books" course. Yet that, Kernan explained, was an "exclusive class for a hundred of the best and brightest freshman who wanted to grapple with the masterworks of Western art, starting with Greek tragedy and the Bible and moving by the end of the academic year to Goethe's *Faust* and Eliot's *Waste Land*."[31] Designed for a self-selected group at a highly selective college, the class hardly addressed the larger pedagogical issues around the desacralization of literary studies. In fact, Kernan believed that by emphasizing a canon, such "Great Books" courses stressed works' sacred immutability and apartness and their authors' towering genius, and thus, by default, could not possibly show undergraduates how or why literature as such directly related to their run-of-the-mill thinking and everyday acting.[32]

As it transpired, by 1970, younger faculty members in Yale's literature departments were questioning the assumptions of the regnant humanist model. In 1971, Kernan and the 1969 committee explained that literature professors at Yale thought the "proper way of managing literary study" was taking "for granted a number of increasingly questionable" conventions, "chief among them that literature is primarily, even exclusively, the product of a particular national state and the genius and language of its people; that intense specialization within this national literature was the only way to study literature; and that the teaching of language and the teaching of literature were inseparable."[33] Such probing of the reigning model likely had much to do with the contemporary eruption of critical methodologies. Those diverse interpretive approaches, part of a widespread questioning of disciplinary authority during and in the aftermath of the sixties, interrogated assumptions about the meaning and form of "the text"; such questioning of "the text" affected literary education. And it was in Yale's literature departments that the intensity of specific pedagogical issues was to manifest itself in noticeable ways.

Michael Holquist, another member of Taylor's 1969 committee, felt the atomization of literature into national traditions with particular pathos. His department, Slavic literature, closely adhered to the German philological model, focusing—Holquist believed excessively—on language rather than literature. Far from performing, teaching, and defending the kinds of formalist readings typical in Yale English, members in Slavic were more philologically oriented and were required to know, in addition to Greek or Latin, Old Church Slavonic and have at least two years of study in all three of the major Slavic language areas. This emphasis helped Holquist see, as he later wrote, that "the different national adjectives were in danger of absorbing the substantive they sought to modify." He continued: "The more each department refined its concerns or defined itself as a profession, the less they seemed to have in common with each other." Such atomization, Holquist believed, threatened to disperse the very essence of literature into parts, fine mists, narrow streams of knowledge, that had little to do with literature qua literature. Interestingly, Holquist recalled, it was not only he, thirty-four and untenured, but eminent Yale professors who yearned to orient their scholarly and pedagogical practices toward literature: "Long ago," one distinguished senior professor told Holquist, "I said I would like to be called professor of literature, just as there are professors of history and philosophy." Still, that that professor requested anonymity is noteworthy; such a longing for literature as literature was seen as naïve and ultimately "unprofessional."[34]

For these interrelated reasons—rising resistance to the dominant model of literary humanist education, teachers' anxiety about the relevance of prose and poetry to undergraduates—Brooks, Kernan, and Holquist began to view conventional teaching of literature as in crisis. They found themselves united by a desire to rethink and redesign undergraduate literary education. Launching such an endeavor would require heading off the suggestion among a vocal faction of literature professors that an expansion of the school's "Great Books" course could handily resolve this predicament. Brooks, Kernan, and Holquist argued that the "Great Books" course wrought literature into something both detached and inert, a corpus too often like a corpse. They also pointed out that, while the establishment of comp lit departments after the Second World War encouraged literary scholars and critics to question some pedagogical conventions, Yale's Comp Lit remained confined to the graduate level. The department was moreover restricted by the application of either sociohistorical methods or New Critical approaches as applied to between one and three national literatures, as in the English Department. Comp Lit encouraged probing the arbitrary divisions of national language and literature departments, therefore, but the school's undergraduate education was barely affected. So what Yale really needed, Brooks, Kernan, and Holquist stressed to their colleagues, was an undergraduate curriculum that taught literature in a way that did not presuppose what precisely needed to be "questioned, examined, and eventually—to the extent needed and in the measure possible—proved: the place and importance of literature" in the entire range of human activities and history.[35] Students needed to be shown that the demand of literature to be read as literature was the constitutive engine of what occurred all around them.

Brooks, Kernan, and Holquist also strongly advocated for working with undergraduates to answer the question of why humanity needed literature and how humans satisfied this need. This jointly pursued worldly and desacralizing pedagogical agenda would revolve around answering their initial central questions, which Brooks summarized: "Can we teach in such a way as to make literature a form of learning, without reducing it either to information (which it isn't), or to the contemplation of perfection (which is futile), or else displacing the object of our study to the sciences which speak of it? Is there a pedagogy which will lead us into the dynamics and the project of literature?"[36] Literature—an intellectual and cultural practice irreducible to bits of information or mathematical questions, resolutely anti-Platonic and thus of *this* world, always breaking free of necessary scientific models or techniques of reading. To Brooks, Kernan, and Holquist, what was most necessary was for teachers at Yale (and, optimistically, elsewhere) to encourage and provide students with the intellectual tools to uncover what to them was most obvious: the central place of literature among human activities, functions, and concerns.

Toward *Homo Signiferen* in New Haven:
Man, the Carrier of Sign Systems

The most direct and local result of Brooks, Kernan, and Holquist's discussions was the experimental course Literature X. Approved—without dissent—by Yale College faculty in February 1970 and first offered to undergraduates that fall, Lit X was these three professors' response to the widely perceived crisis in literary education.[37] Positivist approaches tended to impart information about the literary work and treat it as the product of an institution; sociohistorical methods often had readers examine the chronological development of a specific literary genre, period, or tradition; and formalist methodologies trained students to interpret literature as a self-contained, self-justified linguistic object. In distinction, the Lit X curriculum inculcated a sensitivity to literature's cross-cultural and transtemporal presence by transforming all cultural objects into a species of fiction; a film or a recipe counted as much as a Shakespearean sonnet. And by making fiction into a sort of anthropological datum, the Lit X program aimed to protect the prestige and centrality of undergraduate literary education not only at Yale but, considering Yale's clout, across the country as well; Lit X in other words would serve as an exemplar. One way the course aimed to accomplish all this—and in keeping with its goal to redraw the boundaries of literary study—was to eschew exclusive affiliation with any single department, while also being a shared venture of and staffed by teachers from all five of the university's undergraduate literature departments—English, Russian, German, classics, and French. Administratively, Lit X was a bridge between and in a way transcended departments of literature.[38]

Brooks once said that the experimental course was not born of a "superficial obsession with 'relevance,'" that "war cry of the recent past."[39] Yet sixties unrest informed Lit X itself as much as it did Yale as a whole. Undergraduates (and Americans in general) now found the future puzzling, threatening, even overwhelming. The psychological state of what Alvin Toffler called "future shock"—when rapid technological transformations trigger social paralysis—dovetailed with an increasing suspicion of institutions and authority of all kinds to influence Lit X.[40] "The late 1960s and early 1970s were strange years for the whole country," Holquist later reflected, "but one felt this with special force in New Haven, as undergraduates struggled with political and social issues, such as war in Viet Nam, and embraced a new sense of exploration of sex, drugs, and personal

behavior."[41] What's more, various local political traumas and the accelera-
tion of recruitment from "public schools"—code for non–white Anglo-
Saxon Protestant students—were beginning to relegate the homogeneous
"Yale experience" to the past. When Yale president Kingman Brewster Jr.
persuaded the institution's governing body in the fall of 1969, against the
wishes of an aggressive and loud group of alumni, to authorize the admission of women to the undergraduate ranks, Yale appeared to have become
unmoored from its history altogether, entering a new era.

Signs of these tumultuous times were legible in different registers and
areas at the school. During the late 1960s, New Haven underwent rapid
deindustrialization, and its government and the Yale administration jointly
undertook redevelopment projects that razed several neighborhoods,
aiding the significant demographic change already under way—the city's
African American population was increasing as Italians, Jews, and Irish
departed for the suburbs. At Yale, even once staid and stable cultural institutions became transformative and mind-expanding. In the fall of 1969,
a student could attend a performance of Alexander Scriabin's multimedia
"Prometheus, Poem of Fire" by the Yale Symphony Orchestra, which,
"catering to the extramusical expectations of a fun-loving audience," had
"lights . . . stationed around much of Woolsey Hall and smoke . . . released
through the floor vents to provide a kind of three-dimension screen for
the lights."[42] Those looking to tune in to and be turned on by alternative
ideas didn't need to look very far.

But for the New Critics, a long feared Romantic apocalypse had arrived, fueled by demands from students and younger professors for imagination, emotion, freedom, and social and political relevance in the reading of prose and poetry, rather than a sober and sacralizing formalism.
Endorsing an offensive politics of the French Revolution that threatened
elitists and heralded the age of the democratic, a young William Wordsworth implored in "The Tables Turned" (1798): "Up! up! my Friend and
quit your books; / Or surely you'll grow double: / Up! Up! My Friend,
and clear your looks; / Why all this toil and trouble?"[43] More than simply fearing this Romantic *Stimmung*, however, W. K. Wimsatt (English),
Cleanth Brooks (English), Robert Penn Warren (English), and René
Wellek (Slavic and Comp Lit)—all powerful and tenured professors at
Yale—viewed such uncontrolled emotion and violence as striking at the
heart of literary education and threatening to demolish literary culture.
Students' and upstart professors' vulgar Romantic demands seemed to
stridently clash with the humanist tradition that informed the proper
teaching of literature, an important strand of which was deeply influenced
by T. S. Eliot's understanding of criticism as the "elucidation of works of
art and the correction of taste."[44] Wellek vigorously contested "attacks"

against "literature," such as Louis Kampf's accusation as president of the MLA in 1971 that "the very category of art has become one more instrument of making class distinctions."[45] Unto death did secular cultural priest Wimsatt stick to his formalist convictions, writing in 1976: "When institutions are crumbling, when chaos surges at the gates, art can only record the event it has perhaps helped to bring on—sometimes with an accent of guileless impotence, sometimes pathetically, wringing its hands. Art has no remedies."[46] Literature was for literature's sake one might say. As for Cleanth Brooks, ca. 1970: though his students, and even some fellow professors, looked to him as if they had "just stepped out of a hobo jungle," he continued to wear a suit and tie to class and continued to perform his New Critical readings.[47]

Lit X did not, as Peter Brooks claimed, directly respond to the sixties, but it did aim to address the felt crisis of faith in literary education, notably through a critical-pedagogical perspective that could potentially expand the "temple" of literature. For Lit X tasked teachers and students to apply a sort of phenomenological suspension of judgment of what precisely such a course should accomplish. A "Literature *of . . .*" type of course concentrated on imparting an understanding of literature as a slice of something greater, a period, genre, movement, or whatnot; a "Literature *and . . .*" type of course treated literature as separate and in addition to something nonliterary. In contrast, Lit X would train students to dismantle the hierarchical oppositions between high and low, prose and poetry, and literary and nonliterary in order to focus on literature itself. To achieve this goal, Lit X jettisoned conventional definitions of literature, Arnoldian conceptions of culture, and the orientation of a general education class. Lit X was a "survey course without a theme," Holquist wrote, existing to raise questions "so naïve, so radical, that they had been mainly excluded from, or forgotten, in the study of literature: questions such as 'Why do we have literature?,' 'Why do we need it?,' 'Where is it?,' and 'What is it?'"[48] Crucially, Brooks explained, in order to inspire undergraduates to shed their elevated presuppositions about "literature" and literary education so as to pose these questions about the purpose of literature, these issues were not "faced head on at all times" but "posed in a variety of lateral manners," such as interrogating "literature in its own interrogation of the world" or "confront[ing] the text in its confrontations of what is not itself."[49] Lit X was a staging ground for using literature to ask all kinds of questions— philosophical, historical, sociological, psychological, rhetorical, and so on—in all kinds of ways about literature and its aims. And questioning— not definitive answers—was a central ingredient. One could perhaps say that the pedagogical strategy of Lit X was existential with a literary twist, in that, like Sartre's famous proposition that existence precedes essence, the substance of the course—literature—was its execution, an execution carried out through acts of questioning literature itself. Here, ways of knowing (epistemology) the "literary" were to be privileged over ways of being (ontology) "literary."

Such novel ways to de-idealize the meaning and place of literature resonated with the existential turbulence experienced by Yale's undergraduates. One, Laura R. Cohen, suggested that the course had "the ambitious, presumptuous, and terribly unconventional weight of trying to define itself."[50] Nonetheless, without a home department, without a theme, without even a central critical perspective, Lit X surely could have seemed to be solely intent on dismantling literary education and inspiring pupils to dismantle literature. For Kernan and Holquist, in fact, Lit X, in a theoretical sense, did not even really exist. They playfully explained that Lit X was "not a passive admiration of great fiction but an institutional fiction in itself."[51] For them, Lit X was but a humble self-aware novel, a piece of reflexive literature, as it bent back on, referred to, and affected itself. In this respect, Lit X was a part of a postmodern cultural tradition begun but a few years prior, in 1966. "The cultural products of this year," a commentator has noted, "seem, time and again, to *fold back* on themselves or to *tuck themselves back into* themselves, forming all kinds of strange loops, the equivalents of topological paradoxes such as the Klein bottles or Möbius strips—figures of *meta, meta*figures."[52]

Yet Lit X was self-consciously fictional (literary) in other ways as well. In distinction to "Great Books" classes, the course purposefully lacked a core content, and without a core content there was nothing to have either teachers or students venerate. According to Brooks, he, Kernan, and Holquist were "painfully aware . . . that any suggestion of a 'canon' of Literature X texts and categories is contradictory to the whole enterprise." Lit X thus went "wander[ing] beyond . . . traditional . . . boundaries."[53] Unlike other courses, Lit X, Kernan explained, "was contrived to a certain extent for the sake of raising issues."[54] But these issues were not only raised by professors who yearned to somehow break literature as such free of departmental boundaries. Overspecialization also haunted and hounded students. "The course's attitudes have been derived from the students' need to escape 'literary analysis,'" Kernan suggested.[55] By demystifying accepted views that sanctified specialists' scientistic interpretive nets, Lit X architects aligned the course's pedagogical strategy with undergraduates' demands for interpretive license, demands in response to the dominance of approaches in literature departments that produced hidebound readings of texts. For example, Kernan said, undergraduates understood that "before an Othello or Doctor Faustus may be excavated or even appreciated, more basic questions must be considered concerning the 'existence of imaginative lies amidst the truths of a technological society' or 'creativity per se as a vital, human drive.'"[56] The value cultivated by Lit X was in some ways derived from undergraduates' fundamental questions regarding the material practices and worldly purposes of prose and poetry. Lit X therefore aimed to give professors a platform to expand the scope of their teaching as much as give students the opportunity to break through ossified theories or ideas about literature to reveal its essential force and central role, its closeness and immediacy.

Lit X's curriculum and classroom experiences were intended to accomplish these ambitious goals by moving literary education away from studying the relation of prose and poetry to the particular context in which it was written and toward a theory of literary forms and literary discourse. With such a poetics, undergraduates would conceive literature as but a single aspect of a more universal human culture and activity: the making of fictions. In a way, Lit X intended to transform students not into literary scholars who sought meaning but into quasi-literary critics who identified a text's forms and its links to specific settings. In 1972, Brooks, Kernan, and Holquist explained that students adopted the course's approach to literary forms and literary discourse by investigating "the purposes and uses of fiction, its form and methods, and its relationship to 'reality.'"[57] A year later, the trio defined "fiction" in their textbook *Man and His Fictions: An Introduction to Fiction-Making, Its Forms and Uses* as "works which are openly or tacitly accepted by creator or audience as not being *literally* true."[58] The general poetics of Lit X was to inspire pupils to accept a variety and range of fiction making, with literature considered the most insightful, the most powerful of fictions, because literary works "question their own value even as they demonstrate it, and in this way they become simultaneously fiction and critical theory."[59] For Lit X students, then, a piece of literature was neither, as for traditionalists and general literary humanists, a timeless work free from the vicissitudes of daily life nor, as many New Critics, like Cleanth Brooks in Yale's English Literature Department, asserted, a linguistic object that joined dualisms into an organic harmony. Rather, Lit X students were habituated to the view that literature was a concentrated instance of ordinary fiction making, albeit one that, by virtue of its extraordinary manner of interrogating its own meaning, by virtue of being "meta," established its cultural importance and constituted a kind of theoretical perspective—much like Lit X itself.

To have students see fiction making as a universal human activity was, according to Holquist, the course's "philosopher's stone."[60] For once undergraduates viewed and appreciated fiction making as a common and mundane activity, they were capable of abandoning conventions and standards that arbitrarily limited literary education and could explore literary forms in a diversity of literary traditions, say, the novel in nineteenth-century Russia and eighteenth-century England or the drama in Renaissance Spain as well as ancient Greece. With such a capacious view of fiction making, Lit X students were thus encouraged to seek an understanding of the ambitions and reflexive projects of "literature" in various places and times, including their own; in this way, Lit X was not precisely opposed to literary scholars' historical approaches. Instead, Lit X's cultivation of the sensitivity to the universality of fiction making beyond the value-laden oppositions traditionally upheld between high/ low and literary/nonliterary oriented undergraduates to a way of approaching the world and its objects that saw fiction as ever present, as providing a critical theory, already central to and for use in their everyday lives. Put differently, Lit X coached students to accept the belief, which Kernan suggested they already possessed, that fiction directly affected and commented on their lives, that students exercised fictions for a myriad number of everyday aims and thoughts.[61] In Lit X, the secular temple of Arnoldian "culture" would comprise all of culture.

Teachers of Lit X refined pupils' desacralizing ability to see fiction making as the worldly source of "literature" by interrogating, just as they did with literature, the project and function of fiction. These interrogations aimed to help students become aware of the intellectual conditioning that hindered their appreciation of the "worldliness" of fiction. The questions that pupils were urged to ask included: "How is fiction making distinguishable from other human activities? For what purposes are fictions designed? What constants are there in man's fictions? What variations?" While answering these questions, students not only scrutinized and transcended hierarchies that structured literary study. The resultant larger and broader "fictional" culture was accorded the same prestige and analytical acumen once given to literary culture. Holquist found that Lit Xers' answers in the classroom stimulated fellow students to formulate such expanded definitions of "literature" and what it meant for prose and poetry to be "literary." "Canonical literature is only seen through habituation," he explained, and "where plot and eloquence are often lacking, though character 'seems to touch a nerve of perception in the imagination,' . . . students are compelled to seek more precise definition of 'what is well-written' and ultimately 'what is literary.'"[62] Lit Xers' examination of the diverse uses of literary devices—plot, metaphor, personification, simile—or simply characters in different genres of fictions often subsequently provoked them to discover that these devices or characters were employed everywhere and at all times. Kernan summarized how an expanded definition of "what is literary" facilitated students' identification of fiction's universality:

Just as all men dream, so all societies pay a good deal of attention to making up and telling stories; and they seem to tell something like the same stories, though in a variety of ways. Furthermore, these stories tend to be organized in the same way (plot), and to use the same linguistic devices: metaphor, imagery, symbol, rhyme, rhythm, puns, etc. Conceived of as one aspect of man's fiction-making powers, literature immediately loses some of its "splendid isolation," and connections begin to appear not only with other humanities—art and religious studies, for example—but with those social sciences which are engaged in the study of other kinds of human fictions. Man's fiction-making faculties are not, after all, limited to story telling and the production of poems and plays, but are employed also in the construction of the kinship patterns studied by the anthropologist, the language structures dealt with in linguistics, even the dreams explored by the psychologist.[63]

Lit X's course materials were essential to executing Brooks, Kernan, and Holquist's self-consciously "unholy" pedagogical aims. The class covered an unconventional range of texts, including texts from different national literatures (in translation) as well as texts usually not considered "literature." The inaugural fall 1970 syllabus for Lit X included several modern texts, such as Sir Arthur Conan Doyle's Sherlock Holmes stories, Vladimir Nabokov's *Lolita* (1955), Owen Johnson's *Stover at Yale* (1912), and Anne Desclos's *The Story of O* (1954). So far, so ordinary.[64] But films, such as *Frankenstein* (1910) and the twelve-part space opera *Buck Rogers* (1939), were shown as well. This examination of popular culture in literature departments was rare, and especially so at Yale, where literary study, upholding the hierarchical distinction between high cultural treasures and low, ephemeral texts, focused on "masterpieces." What was even more controversial in Lit X, though, was the opposition between modern classics and film on top of a second questioning of a binary opposition: undergraduates blasphemously read these modern texts and watched these films in juxtaposition to "perennials" such as *The Odyssey* (eighth century BCE), Euripides's *The Bacchae* (405 BCE), William Shakespeare's *The Tempest* (1610–11), John Milton's *Samson Agonistes* (1671), and Charles Dickens's *Great Expectations* (1861). In the inaugural semester, Kernan recalled, Tarzan and Rousseau were "deliberately picked not only to 'enhance the study of natural man' but to accentuate for the students, with their similar contents, the differences which historically have deemed one work literary and another 'trash.'"[65] This profane commingling of ostensibly distinct categories was meant to embolden Lit Xers to undermine the hierarchies that undergirded literary education. That Brooks, Holquist, and Kernan in their course textbook considered the category and endeavor of fiction as an anthropological datum certainly encouraged Lit Xers to embrace a subversive desacralizing spirit:

> "Fiction" can apply to everything man makes, to tools, machinery, buildings, legal systems, and daydreams, as well as to stories, poems, and plays. Such a wide range of meaning is not a disadvantage in the long run, for it serves to remind us how completely man lives in a man-made or man-arranged world, in culture and how closely connected stories and poems are to man's central business, the shaping of things to his own ideas and purposes. To see that the elaboration of a systematic philosophy, the design of an automobile, and the telling of a story are different manifestations of the same instinct to construct fictions may be a bit startling, but it does have the value of breaking down absolute divisions between things based on the *kind* of thing made and substituting a unity centering on the act and purpose of making.[66]

This conception of fiction making as a universal drive, at once mundane and profound, propelling all human activity burst apart resilient assumptions—whether philosophical, literary, or scientific—about what constituted fiction making and what fiction making constituted. Lit X would later be accused of advancing an antihumanism, but based on the agenda formulated here it really called for a radical revision of humanist precepts. For in one fell swoop, Brooks, Holquist, and Kernan cast fiction making as the foundational way of ordering and comprehending all of creation and every created object. And for teachers to accept fiction making as a universal enterprise would help invigorate undergraduates to intervene in not only others' ways of thinking but their own as well. Formulated at a time in America when everything seemed up for grabs, coming in fact five months after the riotous May Day protests at Yale, Lit X impressed on students—or, rather, encouraged students to express—that a fictional, postmodern culture was ubiquitously here and now.

Because the Lit X classroom was to no longer be a chapel of literature where cultural clerics healed the faithful or converted the faithless, pupils, it was anticipated, would feel free to challenge the conventions of literary education. Instructors, for instance, encouraged students to use a variety of styles and reading techniques. No particular approach was privileged; every week students heard lectures by professors representing different departments and different methods. "Someone from French," Holquist explained, "might take a 'Structuralist' approach to the material; the next week a teacher from German might demonstrate the strengths of philology, and the week after an instructor from the English department might use Northrop Frye's [archetypal myth] categories in his exegesis."[67]

By varying professors and changing critical methods every week, Lit X subverted the commonly held view that professors did and should possess sole and institutionally consecrated authority over the meaning of the course material. No metaphysical principle guided Lit X. "Far from sharing any 'credo' or 'philosophy' of literature," Brooks and Holquist wrote to colleagues concerned about the pedagogical radicalness of Lit X, "the course is staffed by teachers . . . united simply by the desire to . . . make the study of literature an exciting and pertinent experience for students."[68] And yet Lit X did seem designed to help undergraduates unseat the professor's sanctioned authority and place it in students' increasingly nimble interpretive hands. Brooks, Holquist, and Kernan hoped that such a reversal would demonstrate to undergraduates that "literature" (understood as both fiction and critical theory) possessed a certain worldly urgency and undeniable vitality about it, that they were already intimately in touch with "literature" and "literature" was already intimately in touch with them.

Lit X's syllabus, which Holquist at one point coyly claimed "reveal[ed] no logic," illuminated the course's secularizing teaching tactics. Lit X's introductory section—"The Story-Teller"—aimed to elevate students' understanding of the demystifying reflexivity of fiction making by having them examine "fictions which were themselves about fiction-making"; narratives about narrativization that problematized or thematized the act of storytelling.[69] Not high culture but self-conscious fictions were the first source of Lit X's pedagogical plan to raise undergraduates' postmodern awareness of their own fictional existence. The section started with stories from *The Arabian Nights* and Jorge Luis Borges's *Ficciones* (1962). These narratives highlighted the fiction maker's interpretive stance and the tale's function. The legendary queen and storyteller of *The Arabian Nights*, "Scheherazade," Brooks explained, "invents fictions ultimately to save herself, and to right the balance of a disordered reality; and the multiple narrators and narratives which fall between the first and the last nights evoke almost all the possibilities of story telling, from vicious lying to erotic arousal to the imparting of that 'wisdom' which [German Jewish philosopher] Walter Benjamin sees as the function of the storyteller."[70] Borges, too, adopted the perspective, in *Ficciones*, of a commentator on preexisting, imagined fictions. In his short story "Tlön, Uqbar, Orbis Tertius," he cleverly used the genre of memoir to mix the narrator's personal recollections so as to interrogate, parody, and in the end undermine the metaphysical oppositions between truth and falsity, reality and imagination, fact and fiction. Attributing his discovery of Uqbar to the concurrence of a mirror and encyclopedia, Borges's storyteller blended conceivably accurate events in Buenos Aires with the whimsical inventions of a fictional land (Tlön); fantastic characters with the names of Borges's real friends; real books, including the *Encyclopaedia Britannica*, with invented ones, such as *The Anglo-American Cyclopaedia* on Uqbar and *A First Encyclopedia of Tlön*; outrageous philosophical theories with selections from Benedict de Spinoza, Arthur Schopenhauer, and David Hume. If students had pretensions about receiving transparent knowledge from literature in Lit X, Scheherazade's and Borges's self-aware fabrications would release them from such naïveté.

Lit Xers were next encouraged in the course's introductory section to adopt a critical view of fiction making; students were to embrace an elaborate reflexivity about "fictionality" to ponder the human desire for order and organization. Then the question of *why* people tell stories— what were the uses and values of fiction—was asked in more concentrated samples, all of which "blasphemed" cultural authority. These impious stories included Peter Weiss's *Marat/Sade* (1963), a play within a play that dealt with the abuse of power and the significance of revolution; Norman Mailer's *Armies of the Night* (1968), a Pulitzer Prize–winning report on the Peace March on Washington in 1967, during which the author was imprisoned and fined for an act of civil disobedience; the late 1950s and early 1960s stories and novellas of Andrei Sinyavsky and Yuli Daniel, which bravely satirized Soviet rule; Sigmund Freud's early investigations of the tales told by hysterics and the countertales elaborated by the analyst in his *Studies in Hysteria* (1895), which challenged Victorian sexual morality; and Joseph Conrad's *Heart of Darkness* (1899), a novella customarily viewed as a powerful critique of colonialism. Unconventionally ranging across genres and periods, these reflexive fictions additionally encouraged Lit Xers to think of the scandalous social, intellectual, cultural, even political roles that fiction performed. The pedagogical hope was to inspire students to not merely embrace a critical attitude toward fiction making but also to cultivate an awareness of the potentially "vicious results when men mistake their fictions for myths, and begin to believe in them."[71] Take for instance Freud's surmise that the psychologically ill Fraulein Anna O's habit of storytelling during her meetings with her physician Josef Breuer, by bringing hallucinations and traumatic experiences to conscious attention, helped her overcome her debilitating condition. This kind of self-directed storytelling became known as the "talking cure." In contrast were Sinyavsky's and Daniel's satires, which mocked the Communist regime. Though smuggled abroad and published under pen names, Sinyavsky's and Daniel's fictions brought down upon them the very real weight of the Soviet system, which imprisoned the two dissidents. The advantages and disadvantages of postmodern fiction for the "writerly" and "readerly" life, students learned, were all too real.

The course syllabus's second section—"Encountering Things: Consciousness and Things"—facilitated Lit Xers' further overturning of the intellectual-institutional traditions that restricted appreciation of the foundational impulse for fiction making. Instead of using a Freudian scheme, in which humanity's yearning for stories was an expression of one's own unconscious, or a Marxist model, in which the instinct for narratives originated in the means and modes of production, Lit X used styles of reading that identified fictional forms and contents. Yielding to this imperative was meant to help students grasp Brooks, Holquist, and Kernan's belief that humanity needed and used fictions to process and shape humans' "difference" from the world; individuals fabricated fictions to understand humanity's place and identity, to define and mold the "human." "Fictions are," *Man and His Fictions* explained, "direct attempts to grapple with and transform an alien, or at least highly problematical, world. Fiction-making is thus an active earthbound force, constantly locked in struggle with the opacity of things, the endlessness of time, and the undifferentiated continuum of being."[72] Discerning the universal impulse for narratives that wrestled with and attempted to domesticate—to humanize—a persistent foreignness permitted Lit Xers to, again, examine fictions across literary traditions, genres, and periods, including those by Alain Robbe-Grillet, William Wordsworth, Jean-Luc Godard, George Herbert, John Donne, even Genesis and Cinderella. In these fictions, stress was now placed on the human desire to produce and use metaphor as a device that brought objects into relation to consciousness, as a desacralizing tactic intended to make the world cease to be "other" or "otherworldly" by giving it meaning, value, and worth. Students therefore learned interpretive techniques that various fictions used to negotiate the difference between consciousness and the realm of things. By this point in the course, any secular worship of "high culture" was not only brought low but also widened beyond precedent.

Lit Xers, for example, were guided from Robbe-Grillet's insistence that fiction ought to disjoin the human imprint from the phenomenal world to the views of British Romantics, whose poems attempted to find or make the world identifiable and inhabited by the plenitude of meaning. Though employing different writing techniques, both Robbe-Grillet and Romantics, students were taught, wrote fiction that functioned as a node within which humans situated themselves vis-à-vis unfamiliar and strange, perhaps threatening, material matters. Robbe-Grillet, according to *Man and His Fictions*, thought fiction "should seek to preserve a sense of the otherness and neutrality of the objective world."[73] For him, literature should not assign meanings to things or anthropomorphize them: "Les choses sont les choses, et l'homme n'est que l'homme."[74] Robbe-Grillet had instantiated his theory of literature in his novel *La jalousie* (1957), where he used the metaphor of the centipede squashed on the wall to allude to the problematic character of the narrator, a jealous husband who spies on his wife. In distinction to Robbe-Grillet's anti-anthropologizing fiction and critical theory, the Romantics used metaphor to perform a "transaction between contexts" by forging deep analogies between the order of things and the order of the mind. Such assimilative analogies were to be understood as being made by fictions more generally. "The process," *Man and His Fictions* clarified, "by which objects are invested by consciousness with interest, glamour, desirability—the process that Wordsworth consciously engages in with 'The Thorn' and that Keats struggles with in 'On Seeing the Elgin Marbles' and 'Ode on a Grecian Urn' . . . surrounds us in the contemporary landscape, where man-made objects are proposed to our possession, and we are solicited virtually to define ourselves through the things we acquire."[75] To recognize "the romantic heart of things"—to recognize how the Romantics' position on the meaning*ful* link between consciousness and the mundane world of things permeated contemporary culture—students subsequently examined vulgar advertisements for Pepsi-Cola, Ballantine beer, and Vita pickled herring.[76] Expressing and performing the base "desire of things," a Ballantine ad rhapsodized: "To be crisp a beer must be icily light / Smooth and delicious, precisely right / Lively golden, crystally clear / The crisp refresher, Ballantine / Ballantine beer."[77] At the end of the second section of Lit X's syllabus, students thus emerged with an amplified sensitivity to the multitude of ways in which "Man" was "*Homo signiferen*," the bearer of sign systems that are sense-making systems. Such an understanding was integral to Lit X's subversion of the inherited hierarchical oppositions that shaped the undergraduate teaching of literature at Yale and institutions like it.

After this examination of diverse efforts to place the world of things into (metaphorical) language and therefore assert human control over the nonhuman by making the realm of things absorbable by consciousness, Lit Xers considered *how* fictions were assembled. This third section was vital for the pedagogical effectiveness of the course because it trained students in how to identify the nuts and bolts of fiction, in the ways fiction or, rather, all cultural items, performed. Also key was how, despite the defiant catholicity of its contents and approaches, Lit X did not endorse impressionism, subjectivism, or relativism. Students were not given the freedom to interpret texts without constraints; there *was* form to fictions and students would learn how to recognize it. For instance, in the class's third unit, "Beginnings, Middles, and Ends: Putting Things Together," students concentrated not on particular plots or genres of stories but what Brooks, Holquist, and Kernan believed *all* plots and kinds of stories sought to realize: the bestowal of "totality" (or structure or form) on objects and events that would otherwise be unrelated or lack a definitive start and end. "Like a map," Lit Xers read in *Man and His Fictions*, "plot is an instrument of discovery. Like a clock, it is a means for measuring movement. Similar to both, plots provide an orientation."[78] By investigating the contingent mechanisms of invention that shaped countless stories, and examining how and for what ordering purposes the structures of these fictions were used, Lit Xers further oriented themselves to the root impulse for fiction making.

This demystifying section of the Lit X syllabus comprised three subsections: "The Detective Story," "Forms and Functions," and "Antiplot." The first subsection juxtaposed a Sherlock Holmes story with Sophocles's *Oedipus* (406–405 BCE) to help students classify the patterns that shaped different mystery stories, including disorder, inquest, detection, and identification. In the second subsection, Lit Xers learned how the "microstructures" of such plots and the relationships of a particular plot to a life fabricated beginnings, expanded or compressed middles, and satisfied humanity's metaphysical longing for "an ending," even though such endings, teachers stressed, were not actually locatable in "the world's time."[79] Specifically debunked were the subtle formal plot devices in a medieval quest romance, where an idealized hero-knight set out on a journey for love or adventure or some holy object; in a picaresque novel, where a mischievous hero from the lower classes outwitted an immoral society while being carried along by unexpected events; and in meticulously plotted nineteenth-century novels such as Charles Dickens's *Great Expectations* (1860), which, partly due to serialization, possessed a distinct chapter structure with an almost mathematical precision in storyline development. The form and function of this "Forms and Functions" subsection does indeed lend a certain amount of credence to the view that Lit X taught undergraduates how to use formalist or structuralist techniques to read texts. "Lit X," J. Hillis Miller reflected, "was a more or less structuralist course on fictions, using Propp's *Morphology of the Folktale* (1958), Barthes *S/Z* (1970), etc., as part of the readings."[80] However, though Holquist was taken with the work of Soviet folklorist Vladimir Propp, particularly Propp's identification of the basic plot devices of Russian folktales, and though Brooks was influenced by the structuralist studies of Roland Barthes and Tzvetan Todorov, *Man and His Fictions* did not cite these scholars' works or theories of reading.[81]

It is more accurate, as evidenced by part III of Lit X's third section, titled "Antiplot," to consider Lit X as inspiring students to see how even the most self-aware of fictions employed different kinds of plots and types of stories to organize and confer a nonmetaphysical "wholeness" on "fictional" objects and events. The basic practical details of plots' openings, midpoints, and conclusions all worked to transfer a sense of fullness and completeness. In this subsection, undergraduates wrestled with extremely self-conscious fictions produced by way of "postmodern" writing techniques, including those found in the texts of Jean-Paul Sartre, Roland Barthes, Samuel Beckett, and Vladimir Nabokov.[82] Understanding the ways in which such fictions criticized "conventional" plotting for falsifying contingency while at the same time offering interpretive conclusions oriented Lit Xers to the novel grammars that ordered contemporary fictions. In one exercise meant to impress lessons about the structures of and temporal ordering purposes in "postmodern" fiction, students cut a perforated strip of paper from *Man and His Fictions* to construct a Möbius strip. Neither formalist nor strictly structuralist, Lit Xers literarily performed the form and function of the "postmodern" fiction they read.[83]

The final section of Lit X, "Shaping the Self," pressed the unrepentantly subversive premise of the experimental course—fiction making was a profane universal activity, at the mundane heart of all human products—to its anthropological limits. This section sharpened pupils' ability to confront the difference often drawn between fiction and myth. "Fiction," as defined by *Man and His Fictions*, was a story that was "openly or tacitly accepted by creator or audience as not being *literally* true," while a "myth" was a story that creator or audience believed to be plainly real.[84] To arrive at a place from which to question the orthodox distinction between fiction and myth, Lit Xers read a number of creation stories, including the Australian Aboriginal myth *Eingana the Mother*, the Native American *The Creation of Man*, and the opening section of Ovid's *Metamorphoses*. Lit Xers were prompted to consider: "However much the stories vary we can sense behind each of them an attempt, by means of a fiction, to deal with the questions, Who and what is man? How did he come to be here? And Why and in what ways is he unlike other things?—in short, What is unique about us as men?"[85] Lit X architects understood that, while it was "probably impossible to rethink oneself back into the essentially religious framework in which myth" had an "explanatory and ritualistic value," Lit Xers' asking of these questions might complicate the established difference between fiction and myth.[86] This distinction was itself rooted in a theological assumption that fiction was purely imaginary and of human provenance and myth was extraordinary and of ontotheological provenance.

Yet this difference was of no great consequence in Lit X, undermined as it was by showing students that myths were fictions, functioning in as well as saturating the cultural landscape, and doing so in the way that Roland Barthes identified: ancient myths were actually unacknowledged fictions that operated by way of an array of signs, forms of which included advertising, sport, and design. For a fantastic example of how myths were a subset of fiction and inhabited daily lives, Brooks, Kernan, and Holquist directed undergraduates to comic-book heroes such as Superman, whose creators drew from mythological characters, most notably Samson and Hercules, as well as contemporary cinema. The overall goal of these last subversive exercises was to usher Lit Xers out of the classroom, aware that society was flush with the "fictional" products of consumer culture and images promulgated by mass media. This undermining of the fiction/myth difference capped the course with a postmodern pedagogical flourish, aiming to impress on students the simultaneous fragility and remarkable power of literature to mark reality. With any luck, Lit X students could now reflexively see themselves as having already been and forever continuing to be *Homo signiferen*.

Lit X quickly became known among Yale undergraduates as an exciting, almost avant-garde, certainly heterodox, learning experience. An early 1970s report stated that, "though the number of sections was increased from five to seven [in the 1971–72 year], it was still necessary to turn away about seventy-five students, largely freshman, who wished to take the course."[87] The enthusiasm was evident in undergraduates' testimonials. In the 1972 *Yale Course Critique*, an annual guide to class selection, Lit X was described as "stimulating," a "refreshing change of pace" from the "conventional literature course," "anything but . . . mindless," and a clear "alternative to the traditional critical approach of the Yale English class."[88] Students reflected that Lit X understood what "an increasing number of students . . . are coming to believe": "that there is more to the appreciation and understanding of literature than writing formula papers with beginnings, middles, ends, appropriately witty comments, indented quotations and meaningless concluding paragraphs—the familiar self-indulgent horseshit which is the lifeblood of the Yale English major."[89] (So much for the "The Best English Department in the World.") Yet, for these undergraduates, Lit X did not simply and excitingly explode traditional literary devices but was institutionally important, because it reframed and expanded the function and place of undergraduate literary education. Along similar lines, students wrote that Lit X ignored "the cobwebs of literary tradition" and so provided "the freedom to explore new ideas." "Creativity is encouraged." Its "reading list" was "as enormous as it" was "superb and unconventional."[90] For one student, Lit X raised issues about literature and the universal role of fiction in human history and culture so profound that they "raised questions about me as well as books." "I hope," the student continued, "when I'm 50 years old I will still be able to ask the questions 'X' raised for me as a Junior."[91] Judging from

FIGURE 1.2 A student-drawn cartoon for Literature X from the *Yale Course Critique, 1974*

these responses, Brooks, Holquist, and Kernan's desacralizing aims succeeded in eliciting existential questions and answers from undergraduates as well as subverting the institutionalized traditions and habits of reading that restricted the purview of literary study.

Lit Xers often pointed to their classroom experiences as the key evidence of their intellectual gain. The weekly lectures, undergraduates said, were "staffed by some of the most brilliant members of Yale's strongest [literature] departments."[92] "Literature X," Laura R. Cohen reported in 1971, "offers rhetorical battles instead of lectures."[93] Kernan recalled that students "took to the very idea [of the course], and it was all very lively," with "[professor of English] Howard Felperin acting out the great apes' dance of the dum-dum from Tarzan; furious discussions of whether *The Story of O* (1954) was pornography and if explicit sexual descriptions had a legitimate place in human fictions; whether there was a distinction between outright lies and fiction."[94] Lit X also resonated with students because it undermined the ostensible separation between town and gown, between the Yale haven and New Haven. Occasional visits to theme parks and professional wrestling matches surely helped as well. But Lit X classrooms echoed sixties revolution-inspired and -inspiring cultural events in town, including Joseph Heller's antiwar *We Bombed in New Haven* and the musical *Hair. Bombed*, a play that had actors pretending to be actors pretending to be airmen, figuratively bombed its fall 1968 premier at the Yale Drama School, while Yale's Shubert Theater showed a pre-Broadway presentation of *Hair*, in which politically active, long-haired hippies resisted the draft and embraced the sexual revolution, while awaiting the Age of Aquarius.[95] Though the consideration of pornography and puritan classics side by side with detective stories and commercial advertisements was certainly libidinally exciting to students, it was the synergy between the classroom setting, teachers, the course materials, and undergraduates' everyday experiences that permitted Lit X to effectively open and support a thrilling postmodern space where sacrosanct conventions of literary education were unconventionally destabilized.[96]

There was, nonetheless, a significant blind spot in this de-idealizing endeavor: the male/female hierarchical opposition remained largely unexamined. This hierarchy persisted in Yale's literature departments, a fact registered in the very subtitle of Lit X and its textbook: *Man and His Fictions*. While Lit X designers intended to build a place where students identified and appreciated the universality of fiction making, Lit X's expansive answer of how to understand literature's distinctness remained the product of cultural convention, staying within the bounds established by pedagogical traditions that sidelined women, their writings, and their achievements. Some contemporaries did challenge the course textbook's title and content. The book turned out to have been "inauspiciously named," Kernan remembered, as feminism, partly due to the influx of women undergraduates beginning in the early 1970s, was becoming a force on campus to be reckoned with. Kernan recalled: "The indignant letters poured in: 'Where do you hegemonic males get off trying to claim fiction for the phallocracy?' 'Why are there so few women writers in this dreadful book?'"[97] Indeed, *Man* included only one text by a woman: Sylvia Plath's "Lady Lazarus," a feminist poem that found Lady Lazarus committing multiple suicides and comparing herself to a Holocaust victim; as her final resurrection approached, readers were told to beware of her because she would rise from the ash and "eat men like air." The bias in Brooks, Holquist, and Kernan's "radical" reformation of the teaching of literature persisted until Lit X itself was revised later in the decade.

Before then, however, in the spring of 1972, Brooks, Holquist, and Kernan took a further step to institutionalize their postmodern pedagogical program. They developed and introduced "Literature Y: Introduction to the Theory of Literature," a course sponsored and paid for by Yale's German Department and presided over by Peter Demetz. Born in Prague in 1922, Demetz immigrated to the United States in 1952 after having been imprisoned in a concentration camp. He had studied philosophy and English literature at Charles University in Prague, and in America earned his doctorate in comp lit from Yale before joining the faculty there. Demetz found Lit Y, he wrote, to be "an exhilarating experience (at least for the instructor)."[98] This was likely because of the ways the course echoed Lit X's demystifying response to the crisis of faith in literary education. Like that course, Lit Y's classroom had guest speakers, but they were recruited not only from Yale's literature departments but from the school's philosophy, linguistics, and religious studies departments as well. And while undergraduates were encouraged in Lit X to adopt a general concept of the "fictional" character of all cultural items, students in Lit Y were given, for the first time at Yale, the elements of a more methodical critical thinking about the ontology—the way of being in the world—of art and the nature of the critical languages exercised upon it; that is to say, Lit Y offered undergraduates an anatomy of the major modern schools of criticism and interpretation, focusing on methods for reading literary works and art. These methods, Demetz explained, included "theories of meaning and interpretation (hermeneutics); questions of genre, with discussion of representative examples, the mixture of forms, and the fusions of various arts. The structure and range of literary value judgments, and a critical analysis of Marxist, psychoanalytic, formalist, and structuralist approaches to literature."[99] Yet Lit Y, like Lit X, remained a pilot course; its innovative response to literature was without an institutional home.

Demetz's eagerness to see the program of which Lit Y was a part develop to its full capabilities intersected with Brooks, Holquist, and Kernan's ambitious desacralizing plans. For the Lit X architects had begun to design an undergraduate major at Yale inspired by the premise of Lit X that fiction making was an anthropological fact. Due to factors and forces both inside and outside the university, however, the adoption of a major in literature would prove difficult indeed. Yale's departments of literature indisputably provided fertile ground for not only Lit X but also for severe opposition to its profanations against sanctuaries of "culture." This opposition came from several powerful professors of literature who, hoping to uphold hierarchy and tradition, considered Brooks, Holquist, and Kernan's pedagogical answer to the question of literature's singularity destructive in its undermining of the traditional and justifiable value-laden oppositions between literature and nonliterature. For these literary-critical clerics, the potential major was but a product of the "unholy" sixties that threatened to demolish the consecrated limits that conventional scholarship had, for good reasons, erected around the literary object; the major would also further the undoing of the humanist subject who, through the moral and intellectual lessons imparted by "great artworks," stood at the center of literary knowledge. For these opponents, the lit major's broad encouragement of undergraduates to view "Man" as the *Homo signiferen,* the self-conscious carrier of sense-making sign systems, would ultimately exacerbate the perceived emergency in literary education that Brooks, Holquist, and Kernan aimed to solve. Even Yale's celebrated place as a locus for bestowing prestige on literary culture was at risk. And when retrenchment set in at the university in the early 1970s, it became unclear to what extent Brooks, Holquist, and Kernan's experiment had itself come upon an unresolvable predicament of its own.

Campus Politics and the Challenge of Building an X-ey World: *Homo Signiferen* and the Literature Major

Though Brooks, Holquist, and Kernan repeatedly claimed that their course was unrelated to contemporary mayhem, Holquist himself noted in 1973 that "[t]he academic landscape is currently littered with the bleaching bones of experimental courses that were launched in the tumult of the 1960s. Their demise is one of the factors now contributing to the eerie silence of the '70s. A lusty exception to this trend is Yale's 'Literature X,'"[100] an unquestionable victory against "cultural" orthodoxy, even if only at one institution and only in one course. But as the semesters passed, Brooks, Holquist, and Kernan became increasingly aware that Lit X and Lit Y remained mere pilots and that if they wanted to reform the undergraduate teaching of literature around their innovative and expansive response to literature's demand to be read as literature at Yale— and perhaps elsewhere—a full-blown program and major were required. Greasing the administrative wheels, they drafted a proposal and, early in the spring semester of 1972, disseminated a tentative plan of study. "The curriculum of the interdepartmental program in literature," an application for external funding summarized, "aimed to offer an opportunity to study man as the sense-maker through sign-systems in a number of literary traditions. It offers a chance to test the belief, shared by the teachers from various literature departments who are cooperating in the program, that at this time, the most significant literary criticism is reaching out to more encompassing views and searching to formulate methods of study that transcend national boundaries and the traditional subdivisions of the field."[101] A provisional governing board was also established, which included, in addition to Holquist from Slavic and Brooks from French, representatives from Classics, German, Spanish, Italian, and English.

Lit X and Y as well as the planned lit major were in fact contemporary with a series of educational reforms undertaken partially out of necessity at American colleges and universities. The increasingly diverse demographics of higher education meant that curricula must expand. Educational reforms included the establishment of black studies and women's studies programs. These and other reforms across the United States aimed not simply to make tertiary education more inclusive but to found courses of graduate study and research programs that produced new bodies of knowledge that responded to and developed the new intellectual diversity. All of this institutionalized a democratic ideal of equality that challenged the authority once reserved for the social elite. When black students at Yale demanded the establishment of a black studies program, the university's president Brewster encouraged them to organize a national symposium to explore the matter, which they did in May 1968. Yale's faculty then quickly approved the establishment of the college's (and the nation's) first major in black studies, which the Ford Foundation awarded over $1 million to develop in 1969 and 1970. But instead of expanding the definition of humanity by focusing on marginalized groups, Brooks, Holquist, and Kernan wanted to institute a major around the de-idealized and enlarged definition of "the text" explored in Lit X. "The proposed program and major in literature," their circulated proposal stated, "would take for its field [the] extensive world of fictions and, while necessarily centering still on literary fictions, would introduce students to the variety and range of fiction-making, its universality among men, and promote investigations of some of the most basic questions about the purposes and uses of fiction, its forms and methods, and its relationship to 'reality.'"[102] As they had suggested earlier, it was Yale undergraduates as opposed to graduate students or faculty who yearned to consider the commonplace *and* profound forms and functions of fiction: "Compartmentalization of the kind represented by the traditional departments of national literatures has long ago ceased to satisfy the keen though vaguely defined desire of our students for a more universal view of their subject matter and their sense that men everywhere are the same in their basic ways of thinking and doing."[103] The lit program and major were thus pitched as a response to a "bottom-up" need; the reformist curricula actually lagged behind pupils' understanding of the worldliness of fiction (literature). And like Lit X, the lit major would replace the traditional kind of coverage found in departments of literature.

Notably, however, Lit X engineers' heady and heterodox rethinking of pedagogical tactics did not happen in other departments at Yale. Undoubtedly, the lit major's pseudoanthropological approach to the literariness of postmodern life might have made it appear to easily intersect with work in anthropology—it did not. The existential questions about literature that the lit major raised also might have made it congruent with work pursued in philosophy—it did not.[104] Instead, Yale philosophers had for the first half of the twentieth century adhered to an intellectual tradition that was committed to protecting and preserving religious and cultural orthodoxies. But by the 1970s, the department was in almost complete disarray, having become the battleground of a turf war between a group sometimes labeled "humanists" or "metaphysicians" and another group often called "positivists," "empiricists," or "analytics." The former, in the majority at Yale, pondered how to profess the ideals of "the good life," how to impart morals, ethics, wisdom, and a depth and breadth of vision to students; the analytic, an encircled and embittered minority at Yale yet ascendant since the early Cold War in Anglo-American departments of philosophy, used and honed reason, logic, and empirical evidence to determine truth. While most professional philosophers embraced the "a-political" and "a-historical" analytic atmosphere during the 1950s, Yale's humanist philosophers often saw their teaching as contributing to the school's mission to train America's future leaders, and thus "religiously" pursued "philosophical vision," constantly attacking the "dead technique" of their positivist and empiricist colleagues. The long-standing struggle between Yale's humanist thinkers and analytics more or less ensured that the department remained out of touch with the mainstream of the profession. The authors of a 1972 internal report to President Brewster expressed "universal concern" that Yale philosophy lacked even one "truly distinguished member," with "humanism" perhaps serving as a "coverup for incumbent mediocrity."[105] This strain between camps—a tension exacerbated by famous philosophers being denied tenure, such as Richard Bernstein in 1965, and controversial hires, such as that of Kenneth Mills, who scandalously turned out to already hold a tenured position elsewhere—led "Brewster [to believe] . . . that the philosophers were in disarray, not masters of their own house, and not to be trusted in their judgment."[106] Yale philosophers, it appeared, could never have designed or implemented an innovative and potentially comprehensive pedagogy like Brooks, Holquist, and Kernan's.

The state of Yale philosophy meant little enthusiastic support from colleagues and administrators for it, but the situation was otherwise for the proposed lit major: its ecumenical solution to the problem of how to read literature qua literature received a good deal of "grassroots" interest and from a variety of quarters as well. Dean of Yale College Horace Taft gave his blessing, writing to Kernan in January 1972 about his "enthusiasm and support" and wagering that "this is the way that most Literature will be taught."[107] In response, an energized Kernan sent Taft copies of letters from the chairs of the involved literature departments to show the "extensive . . . backing of the proposed program."[108] These supporters believed that the lit major might help enact a sorely needed political challenge: all who majored in literature were encouraged to question the dominance or supremacy of Western literatures over non-Western literatures; the major's courses—most drawn from existing ones—would be divided into the "History and Development of Western Literature" and "Non-Western Literatures" (the latter acknowledged as "unfortunately limited").[109] Majors were required to take five terms of classes in Western literatures, chosen from a list of more than thirty courses, and one or two terms of a non-Western literature class, a list that included "Chinese Literature," "Japanese Literature in Translation," "The Afro-American Literary Tradition," and "Anthropological Approaches to Folklore." Incorporating non-Western literatures into a major in literature meant that Brooks, Holquist, and Kernan's program ever so slightly expanded the category of literature, especially considering the extent of Eurocentrism then prevalent.[110]

But, similar to how Lit X reinforced the phallocracy, the lit major as proposed still instituted a Eurocentric vision of "culture" and its history. The placement of the Afro-American literary tradition in the category of "Non-Western Literature" undermined Brooks, Holquist, and Kernan's overarching intention to inspire students to recognize a vast array of forms and uses of fiction in different places and periods. For, according to the description of the major's requirements, "History and Development of Western Literature" clearly suggested historical growth and maturity, maybe even a telos, while such implications were absent from "Non-Western Literature." Even to have only two groupings highlighted Eurocentrism, not only because it enforced a "West and the Rest" topology but also because such groupings obscured differences within each category. Indeed, the lit major continued to uphold a hierarchical opposition between Western and non-Western literatures. And this opposition subsisted partially because the major's consideration of literature as found in all locations and all times conflicted with the institutional and intellectual resources that were marshaled for realizing this desacralizing aim. The major may have questioned, and commendably so, a number of the principles that organized literary education, yet it reinforced prejudices that were not simply held by individuals but were also structural, part of Yale's almost three-hundred-year history, a history itself shaped by the biases and prejudices enforced by "Western Culture."

Professors of non-Western literatures at Yale nevertheless saw the reformist potential of the lit major, and many supported it. In a letter to Kernan, William K. Simpson, whose *Literature of Ancient Egypt* (1972) would set a standard of expectations for the lay public interested in the topic, called the lit major an "excellent idea." Simpson also touted that enrollment in his undergraduate course, "History and Archaeology of Ancient Egypt," grew in recent years and that he looked forward to including the class as an offering in the lit major.[111] Other professors of East Asian languages and literatures backed the proposed major as well. In his own letter to Kernan, John Whitney Hall, considered one of the twentieth century's finest scholars of Japanese history, his work having "opened up the first thousand years of Japanese history to the English-speaking world," expressed his and colleagues' excitement that East Asian literatures could be "studied as examples of the universal fact of literature" rather than as "isolated phenomena approachable only by the specialist."[112] Later called the "de-exoticize[r] of the study of Japan," Hall saw the lit major as a promising avenue through which to popularize East Asian literature, which was then being opened at Yale to students with no relevant language proficiency. All told, members in Yale's Department of East Asian Literatures realized that their participation in the lit major might lead to a less marginal spot in Yale's cultural hierarchy, even if the major did not subvert the hierarchical opposition between Western and non-Western literatures vigorously enough.

Despite all this excitement about the lit major's overt and latent demystifying powers, however, institutionalizing it with sufficient financial and administrative support was going to be problematic. When the major came up for formal consideration in 1972, the end of the period of postwar prosperity was almost upon America. The Organization of Arab Petroleum Exporting Countries, in response to America's weapon deliveries to Israel during the Yom Kippur War, cut production in October 1973, tripling the price of crude oil. The subsequent spike in oil prices added to the financial instability already caused by America's abandonment of the gold standard in 1971. With Yale's legendary endowment struggling, administrators found themselves hard pressed for funds; departments and programs faced large budget shortfalls; new appointments were put on hold, and vacancies went unfilled. The opportunities for young academics suddenly dried up. "Young men and women, who a few years before could have confidently expected several job offers, found that a Ph.D. completed in 1973 got them nowhere," historian David Hollinger has explained, while cuts to the National Defense Education Act placed additional burdens on literature and language teachers.[113] In classrooms and faculty lounges at Yale and across America, professors' fears about the displacement of literature from its centrality in undergraduate education had seemingly been realized. "It is no secret," Peter Brooks noted, "that at least most of the foreign literature fields face, nationwide, a slow but fully ominous decline in numbers of students—certainly in numbers of majors, if not in numbers of students who enroll in their courses."[114] It was not just that the golden age of higher education was concluding. The balance between science and humanities in institutions of higher learning during the 1960s, achieved in part because of the academic revolution, the effects of which protected the status of the arts and letters at all college and university tiers, also appeared to have tipped.

The university was in the midst of its economic austerity moves when Brooks and Holquist requested final approval of the literature major at a Yale College faculty meeting in the spring of 1972. Despite being awarded a three-year $150,000 grant from the Mellon Foundation, which bought faculty members' teaching time, administrative time for the director of undergraduate studies, office expenses, and the employment of a half-time secretary, institutionalization was not guaranteed.[115] Faculty in Yale's departments of literature had not in other cases sanctioned innovative answers to the call of literature. For example, professor of classics Erich Segal was legendary for his cheerful mixing of high and low. He published *Roman Laughter* (1968), a seminal and serious scholarly study of the comedic works of the ancient playwright Plautus. Yet he also helped script the Beatles' *Yellow Submarine* (1968) and authored the best-selling romance *Love Story* (1970), which became a popular movie. The chair of his department questioned neither his teaching ability nor the excellence of his publications. Segal was denied tenure in 1972 nonetheless, seemingly because the powers that be frowned on the connections he drew between scholarship and pop culture, connections that encouraged the extraliterary to pollute the sanctity of Yale's hallowed halls. "Mr. Segal does other things besides teach classical literature," Yale professor of the history of art Jerome Pollitt harrumphed to the *New York Times*.[116] "It wasn't fair," recalled *Doonesbury* cartoonist Garry Trudeau, class of 1970, "but you can't dress up in tight leather pants [as Segal did] to chat with starlets on Johnny Carson Friday night and expect to be taken seriously in a classroom Monday morning."[117] A number of Yale's literature professors were in the old guard, and they clung to the belief that literary humanists should abjure politics and the social world, as such avoidance allowed the scholar to serenely study "culture" of the Arnoldian kind and effectively teach criticism that corrected students' character and taste. To the old guard, then, the "blasphemous" challenges that the lit major posed to the clear hierarchies that structured the teaching of literature appeared part of the vulgar trends inaugurated by the sixties. Segal was but one example of just how far and to what deleterious effects embracing such irrational exuberance about the expansion of culture might go.

Almost from the beginning, however, Brooks, Holquist, and Kernan anticipated disquiet—and perhaps righteous resistance—from the more pedagogically conservative among their colleagues. In May 1972, Kernan wrote to Dean Taft: "Trials [are] on the way. . . . It has been a long road to this, but it *is*, I believe the right road."[118] Four years later, Lit X had garnered quite a reputation on campus, among not only undergraduates but faculty too. "The experimental course was," Holquist reflected, "a frequent topic over the macaroni and cheese in college dining halls as well as over the sherry at faculty cocktail parties. Not everyone liked what they were hearing."[119] For the "X" of Lit X, meant by the course's architects to signal its lack of both a central content and critical-pedagogical perspective, became, for the course's skeptics as well as its enthusiasts, a descriptor applied to any lecture or seminar thought weird or bizarre. "Campus language was briefly enriched in the 1970s by a new adjective: if a course in any subject seemed slightly unusual or modish, it was said not to be 'too sexy,' but 'too X-ey.'"[120] This notoriety of the postmodern interpretive stance toward culture inculcated in Lit X informed conversations throughout the Yale community. That the course implicitly encouraged undergraduates to strike at the heart of Yale's self-definition—its myths— also ruffled feathers.

The "X-ey" reputation of Lit X continued to reinforce already skeptical faculty members' suspicions that the course condoned (and would perpetuate) the irreverent excesses of the sixties. And at the spring 1972 faculty meeting, professors from several humanities departments came out of the woodwork to oppose adoption of the lit major, charging it with threatening the efficacy of undergraduate literary education. These professors specifically questioned, Holquist recalled, "whether in the long run . . . Literature will be taught, because the word 'literature' was in quotation marks throughout the proposal."[121] These scare quotes seemed to purposefully undermine any attempt to identify the specificity or uniqueness of literature. Other professors lodged the complaint—likely made in reference to how Lit Y cycled through literary-critical approaches or perhaps Lit X's rotating cast of guest lecturers—that the lit major would place "too much emphasis on fashionable and recondite new critical schools, to the detriment of the 'primary texts' themselves."[122] Another charge, likely from a proponent of the New Criticism, was that because the lit major assimilated literature "to the search for a totalizing system of structural analysis," it "neglect[ed] . . . verbal structure and linguistic specificity." (A statement in the proposal that "men everywhere tell the same stories" lent credence to this accusation.)[123] By burying literature under interpretive models based on and technical jargon derived from Saussurean semiotics and chic structuralist theories, the lit major would, antagonistic professors suggested, undercut its stated aim: to direct undergraduates to literature. Faculty who had not objected to Lit X now resisted the lit major because it showed that Lit X was "spawning": it was a dangerous romance between structuralism and literary criticism, and it was institutionalizing before their very eyes.[124] However, not only would lit major teachers' uses of abstruse linguistic terms and figures of speech and application of anthropological tools distance students from literature itself, but such an approach ensured undergraduates' readings were "coldly scientific and anti-humanist . . . and not enough about feelings and ethics."[125] For resisting professors, the lit major, by twisting the definition and role of literature beyond what was recognizable, by making literature into an effect of self-conscious technique rather than a sincere expression of genius, spirit, and morality, hardly reformed literary education; it was more "an attack on the idea of the humanities from within."[126] To them, the major in literature was a Trojan Horse, entering from inside the intellectual fortress that buttressed Yale's revered purpose. A purpose put to the college by the Puritans that established it, to serve and protect cultural and religious hierarchies.

Adding to the hysteria surrounding Lit X was the belief that the course instituted a new vision of undergraduate literary education that facilitated political turmoil and upheaval.[127] Similar warnings were being made at the highest echelons of academe. In 1972, during the first Thomas Jefferson Lecture in the Humanities, the highest honor the US government can award for distinguished intellectual achievement in the humanities, literary critic and "culturally conservative" liberal Lionel Trilling lamented the recent rejection of the effort in literary studies to educate and impart ethical values to the whole person. He linked this rejection to the MLA's election of the radical Louis Kampf as its president. "In our time," Trilling stated, "the mind of a significant part of a once proud profession has come to the end of its tether."[128] Meanwhile, in New Haven, lurking in the background at the 1972 Yale College faculty meeting was a filiation between academic and Cold War politics. Several prominent opponents of the lit major were refugees from countries ruled by Communist governments. Though liberals in that they generally supported the ideals of liberty and equality, they were foreign policy hawks who supported the Vietnam War out of a hatred of Communism. Many backers of the lit major were leftists of a different sort, leaning toward a radical politics that supported socialism, at least in theory, and were vocally against American involvement in Vietnam.[129]

Several senior faculty members in Yale's departments of literature voiced disapproval well before the contentious 1972 meeting. These ranged from mild and formal—"The response of the English department to the projected Literature Major is difficult to summarize"—to agitated anonymous petitions circulated among faculty.[130] Professors, some attached to the idea that great artworks possessed transcendent beauty and bestowed immutable ideas, had opposed what they considered to be the needlessly fashionable texts of Lit X. "I should like," one distinguished senior professor wrote to Brooks and Holquist (Kernan had left Yale for

Princeton by this time), "to express my dismay at the pretentious, modish and haphazard list [of texts to be studied], particularly under Lit X. . . . I find it very hard to believe that it could have been approved."[131] This incredulous professor opposed the apparent and unprofessional lack of logic used to organize the proposed lit major as much as the pompousness of it. The fiercest resistance, however, came from literature professors who, Brooks reported, accurately identified that the major's "emphasis on literature in transcendence of national and linguistic boundaries, and on fictions beyond the specific institution of literature, posed a threat to the traditional curricular presentations of literature."[132] Simply put, these faculty members wanted to protect orthodox teaching models—whether sociohistorical, biographical, or formalist—that used hierarchical oppositions between high/low, literary/nonliterary, professor/student, and inside/outside the classroom to guard established secular sanctuaries for literature.

The most vocal—and, by all measures, most formidable—opponent in this mold was professor of Slavic and comparative literature René Wellek. Born in 1903 in what became Czechoslovakia, Wellek, at the age of thirty-five, left when the German army invaded in 1938. After settling at the University of Iowa, he became central to the postwar resurgence of comparative literature, helping to found the first American journal in the subject, and, in 1946, establishing as well as chairing Yale's Department of Comp Lit.[133] By the late 1960s, Wellek was often associated with Yale New Critics Cleanth Brooks and W. K. Wimsatt. However, while Brooks and Wimsatt were High Anglican in spirit and Anglo-American in taste, and while their teaching focused on undergraduates, Wellek was emphatically a product of cosmopolitan European cultural traditions whose voluminous publications amounted to a concentrated effort to formulate a coherent literary theory for reading European literature since the mid-eighteenth century; he was mind-bogglingly well-versed in the literatures of the Slavic countries, Germany, France, Italy, Spain, and England. Wellek was also known for his mentorship of graduate students; he "directed *all* comparative dissertations at Yale," including Geoffrey Hartman's.[134] By the early 1970s, Wellek's prominence in the profession was to a great degree unmatched, a stature also derived from his book, *Theory of Literature* (1947), a comprehensive presentation of formalist techniques of reading that he coauthored with Austin Warren and that laid the intellectual foundation for the discipline of comp lit in America. Though *Theory of Literature* and Cleanth Brooks and Robert Penn Warren's *Understanding Poetry* (1938) dominated the profession until the mid-1960s, Wellek and Austin Warren's text was different from Brooks and Warren's in that the former was used to teach literary theories, not criticism. Wellek and Warren, for instance, separated criticism into "extrinsic" and "intrinsic" schools, maintaining the supremacy of the latter. Wellek differed from his New Critical colleagues in other ways; he neither expounded nor promoted a strict reading technique, nor did he defend literature as principally a question of literary language or a specific region. For Wellek, the literary critic-scholar must conceive of literature's universality, at least in Europe, and, as he wrote in 1961, "isolate . . . the literary work of art" and "evaluate it by criteria derived from, verified by, buttressed by, as wide a knowledge, as close an observation, as keen a sensibility, as honest a judgment as we can command."[135] Such an approach gelled with conventional literary study in America, though it did not necessitate jettisoning biography and sociological settings as New Critic formalists had. Rather, Wellek's critic-scholar "must deploy all of literary theory, criticism, and history to bear upon the evaluation of a work."[136]

This notwithstanding, Wellek passionately played the part of the cultural cleric. He was still a traditionalist—really a Kantian; he considered the "New Criticism" not really as new but as largely restating the German Idealists' precepts. And, unlike some archformalists, Wellek was unafraid of aesthetically judging literary works *and* of forcefully claiming that the study of the history of criticism was a study of values. This second belief guided his epic *A History of Modern Criticism, 1750–1950*. As he wrote in the foreword to volumes 3 and 4 (1965): "I keep, and want to keep, a point of view and am convinced of the truths of several doctrines and the error of others."[137] To write criticism, for Wellek, was to meditate on the aesthetic feelings expressed in the artwork, while literary theory helped to convey this independent beautiful realm. Wellek's Kantian view also informed his support of the idea that literary history was significant only if structured around a sequence of periods or epochs, each representing a specific system of values.[138] Wellek's Kantianism deeply shaped his support of the literary canon; he later claimed that he "always defended the need of [aesthetic] judgment in literary criticism and analyzed and appreciated the great writers of the past."[139] Accounting for Wellek's view that interpreting literature was equivalent to worshipping at a secular chapel, helps, in turn, explain why he so snugly fit into the intellectual culture of Yale's literature departments; it clarifies the form and content of his response to the proposed lit major as well. For Wellek emerged as a vocal defender of conventional pedagogical approaches and the aesthetic autonomy of art, both of which he correctly viewed the lit major as subverting. He was certainly prepared for a fight; in reference to the winds of change that the archetypal myth criticism of Northrop Frye and the philosophical existentialism of Sartre blew against comparative literature, he had written already in 1965: "The whole enterprise of aesthetics and art is being challenged today; the distinction between the good, the true, the beautiful, and the useful known to the Greeks but most clearly elaborated by Kant, the whole concept of art as one of the distinct activities of man, as the subject matter of our discipline, is on trial."[140]

In similar terms Wellek stated his conservative opposition to the postmodern unorthodoxies instituted in the lit major to Alvin Kernan a half decade later; he then formally explained himself and his positions in a letter to Peter Brooks in 1972. And yet, in a March 14, 1972, letter to Professor Robert L. Jackson in Slavic literature, Wellek struck a more diplomatic tone, clarifying that, while he "supports the general idea of a literature major, . . . [he] believes that the course Literature X as now devised has no coherent rationale, as it includes day-dreaming and kinship relations under literature and teaches complete trash such as Tarzan, James Bond and the 'The Story of O' to undergraduates who should spend their time reading the great works of literature."[141] Wellek therefore did not, in principle, object to the lit major—he even stressed his support for the major's goal of identifying the literariness of literature beyond national boundaries. However, he questioned the proposed lit major's internal coherence and its choice of texts, and he opposed the major's use of works in translation because he considered only the original language of a text as capable of conveying the text's aesthetic emotions and complexities. Holquist, a former graduate student of Wellek's, "loved him," but thought his former teacher "an utter elitist, especially when it came to languages."[142] And of course Wellek found Lit X's undermining of the oppositions that structured literary education to be poorly conceived, rash, and ultimately unsound. This was not simply snobbishness on Wellek's part, though there was some of that. "Coming from the Continent to England and the United States," Wellek recalled in a different context, "I felt strongly that there is a particular need of theoretical awareness, conceptual clarity and systematic methodology in the English-speaking countries, dominated as they are by the tradition of empiricism."[143] Moreover, Wellek, as J. Hillis Miller has recalled, similarly did not think Yale undergraduates were "up to doing serious theoretical reflection about literature."[144] In fact, Wellek had, in 1963, identified the condition of American comparative literature as one of perennial "crisis," due to "an artificial demarcation of subject matter and method, a mechanistic concept of sources and influences, a motivation by cultural nationalism," and he believed that this crisis could not be effectively taught to undergraduates.[145] It was for this very reason that Wellek restricted Yale's Comparative Literature Department to graduate students. In the end, he viewed Lit X as frittering away students' time and energy, as it degraded teaching by providing an anemic notion of literature: "It seems to be a pedagogical sin," he wrote to Professor Robert L. Jackson.[146]

Fortunately for Brooks and Holquist, Wellek retired in 1972 and did not fully participate in the discussions and deliberations about the lit major at the contentious faculty meeting. Wellek's culturally and pedagogically conservative views nevertheless reflected and likely influenced those of a number of faculty members in Yale's departments of literature. This was the situation in Slavic, a department established at Wellek's urging in 1946, and that began its rise to national prominence after he assumed its chair in 1948 and successfully recruited important faculty members during the early 1950s. Alexander M. Schenker, a younger member of the Slavic Department, had reported in a February 28, 1972 letter to Dean Taft that "the view of all of us [in Slavic was] that both Literature X and Literature Y represent stimulating contributions to the general curriculum of the study of literature."[147] One week later, though, Robert L. Jackson, a "big voice in Slavic," and Victor Erlich, departmental chair and doyen of American Slavists, drafted a letter to Taft that forcefully reiterated and dilated Wellek's concerns. Jackson and Erlich explained to Taft that they objected to "the credo or philosophy of the new program," which, as they had already stated in a previous letter, "seemed geared almost entirely to 'Man and his Fictions.'"[148] Like Wellek, Jackson and Erlich opposed the current lit major proposal's regrettable repetition of Lit X's concentration on fiction, a sign that the major's courses would not teach students how to understand literature's demand in a broader sense. If this was accurate, Jackson and Erlich stressed to Taft, then the rationale for affixing the word "literature" to "major" was flawed; the proposed major should more accurately be called the fiction major. Though such a cosmetic change might have soothed some anxieties about its pedagogical program, to change the name of the major would have only superficially leapfrogged over the true point of contention: the major's wide-ranging desacralizing stance.

Jackson and Erlich were also troubled by the danger that the lit major's interpretive perspective had developed in disciplines outside of literature departments. By doing so, the major would weaken the value and the edifying purpose of literary education at the very moment when it should be safeguarded. Lit Xers' orientation toward "anthropological and extraliterary interests" must likely have worried Erlich in particular, not simply because his department adhered to the German philological model, the historical study of language in oral and written sources, but because he had experienced Communists' and Fascists' ideological uses of sociopolitical externalities to warp the meaning of literature during his formative years and early adulthood. Born in Petrograd, Russia, in

1914, Erlich was the son of a scholarly Russian Jewish family who enjoyed only a short respite from the upheavals of the Russian Revolution after moving to Poland; when the Nazis invaded in 1942, Erlich, his mother, wife, older brother, and extended family escaped both the Nazis and the Soviet NKVD, wandering through Russia and Japan to eventually make their way to New York. He subsequently returned to Europe as a soldier in the US Army and was seriously wounded by sniper fire. After the war, Erlich, on the GI Bill, earned his PhD at Columbia under the direction of Roman Jakobson.[149] In 1951, Erlich was recruited by Wellek for Yale's Slavic Department and became an influential critic of modern Russian literature. Erlich's disapproval of the application of anthropological and extraliterary interests to literary study had informed his pioneering *Russian Formalism: History—Doctrine* (1955).[150] While there was no historical link between the two groups, Russian and New Critical formalists both rejected impressionistic responses to literature and aimed to identify the internal laws of literary form and literary language.

In their letter to Dean Taft, Jackson and Erlich specifically charged the critical vocabularies taught in Lit X with damaging students' ability to appreciate, even summarize, what literature was. Light-years away from correcting undergraduates' taste or improving character, the course cultivated undergraduates' decadent interpretive inclinations; Jackson and Erlich reported: "'What is literature,' a recent student of Literature X was asked. 'Literature,' he responded immediately and comfortably, 'is but an island in a sea of fictions.' 'Literature,' remarked another student of X, 'is marginal.'"[151] Taking these students' responses to the claim of literature at face value, Jackson and Erlich overlooked Brooks and Holquist's pedagogical goal of inspiring students to view "Man" as *Homo signiferen*, a self that redefined literature as a reflexive fiction and a critical theory that recognized the universality of fiction making among human activities. Lit X's architects likely viewed these student responses as evidence of their educational triumph, but for Jackson and Erlich they demonstrated that the lit major would "compound the very crisis" that the architects of Lit X felt "called upon to resolve."[152] Thus, though Jackson and Erlich recognized that Yale students were "impatient with rigid 'compartmentalization' in the study of literature," and that "there [was] some desire for 'a more universal view of their subject matter,'" the two Slavists insisted that the lit major would exacerbate the deteriorating situation.[153] "It was by no means certain," they wrote, that the "'universal' concerns and theoretical interests of the architects of Literature X respond to the problem."[154] Jackson and Erlich agreed that a crisis in the undergraduate teaching of literature existed, but, for them, this predicament was due to a "lack [in] a basic concern with man."[155] Reverberating with Yale's self-conception as stalwart defender of humanistic inquiry, Jackson and Erlich held that the antihumanistic—because too scientistic—strategy of Lit X aggravated the acute emergency plaguing literary education. "Disturbing . . . is the arid scientism . . . that imbues the concerns of those who would 'isolate the central fact of "literature,"'" the pair wrote to Dean Taft, though Erlich's general mistrust of using externalities to determine the worth and meaning of literature also resounded in the letter.[156]

As some of the big voices brought out the big guns to derail the lit major, Brooks and Holquist penned an anxious letter on March 15, 1972 to Jackson and Erlich. Their letter—which had special importance to Holquist as Erlich *was* his chair, advised his dissertation, and was the very reason he was retained at Yale after earning his PhD in 1968—clarified their pedagogical views and vision for the lit major. The two even invited Jackson and Erlich to look at Lit X's reading list or attend a lecture and discussion section, as familiarization might disabuse them of the belief that Lit X students and teachers pursued "anthropological and extra-literary" interests or that Lit X teachers advanced an "arid scientism." Lit X, Brooks and Holquist stressed, was "not operated under a superintending theoretical view of what literary study ought to be," but "lead[s] the student to think critically about the role and function of literature and man's fictionmaking activity, to ask fundamental questions about why we have and need fictions—questions which most more advanced and specialized literature courses cannot, by their nature, address directly."[157] One could have argued, after all, that Brooks and Holquist's innovative teaching agenda was actually consistent with Yale's self-understood cultural mission; to argue as much, though, required overcoming Jackson and Erlich's strong resistance to recognizing Lit X's enlarged notion of "fiction" and incorporating it into such an established undertaking.

To no avail: Brooks and Holquist were unable to persuade Jackson or Erlich. While the precise minutes recording who said what during that April 1972 faculty meeting are lost, Wellek, Jackson, and Erlich had laid much of the groundwork for the criticisms lodged there and then. Some opposition, though, was unexpected, as when an unidentified faculty member "emphasized the need for a greater concern with non-western literature in the major."[158] The ensuing debate between supporters (quite numerous) and detractors (a vocal group that included those on the political left who felt that "The course isn't weird enough!" and on the political right who believed that "It's too weird!") made Yale professors in the hard sciences—astronomy, biology, chemistry, physics, geology, and the like—"shake their heads" at the overblown antics of their humanist colleagues.[159] During the meeting, Holquist recalled, he and Brooks tried "acquainting critics with the actual workings of Lit X as a course." "It was pointed out," he remembered, "that the rumors were exaggerated—X, after all, was the creation of their own colleagues, the men who also taught, say, French 54a, English 33, or Russian 45."[160] The lit major, notes record Brooks emphasizing, would not destroy but "foster creative interplay among [literature] departments";[161] such cultural chemistry *did* come from within but would *contribute to*—not *destroy*—Yale's outward-looking pedagogical aims. Passions ran higher and higher, yet once debate ended, the literature major passed by a large margin.

Living in an X-ey World

By the mid-1970s, Kernan, Brooks, and Holquist's fictional major had become an actuality, reaching beyond itself to other departments and disciplines, not only reinforcing Yale's reputation for innovation in literary studies but also affecting its own and other universities' curricula. The end of the golden age of higher education, compounded by the upheavals and changes that followed in the wake of the sixties, pushed the crisis of undergraduate literary education to a breaking point; many teachers everywhere felt compelled to rethink their pedagogical tactics as Brooks, Kernan, and Holquist had done. Following Brooks's publication in 1973 of an article on Lit X in *College English*, the official publication of the National Council of Teachers of English, requests for information on what was happening at Yale poured in. None other than Harvard sent a committee, which tried to recruit Brooks and advised colleagues in Cambridge to create a literature concentration.[162] Though the structure of the eventual Harvard program was different, the inspiration and purposes were largely the same. Yale's lit major inspired the reform of undergraduate literary education abroad as well. When lecturing at the Australian National University in Canberra in the mid-1970s Holquist stumbled upon a lit major modeled on Yale's at Murdoch University in Perth. He recalled how "exotic a find" the program was, as Murdoch was the "'new' university" and "about as isolated as could be, even in Australia." While Down Under, Holquist even bought a secondhand copy—"much marked up"—of *Man and His Fictions*.[163] Still, these postmodern efforts at other schools, though reaping their own specific rewards, lacked the particular subversive charge that coursed through Yale's lit major, framed and informed as it was by the school's humanizing mission and metaphysically inclined interests.

Back in New Haven, the lit major's popular courses resonated with undergraduates, whose post-sixties suspicions of the "establishment" and its hierarchies intensified with the end of the Vietnam War, the widening

Watergate scandal, and the rescinding of federal support for the humanities. In a July 3, 1975, letter to Dean Taft, Brooks reported: "In 1974–75, we enrolled 73 majors. . . . Total enrollments in courses sponsored by the lit major for 1974–75 numbered 340."[164] During the next academic year, the lit major enrolled sixty-five students, making it one of the largest humanities majors at Yale. The fortunes of undergraduate literary education seemed to be reversing.

The lit major was attracting a sizable number of students, but the early 1970s economic downturn strained its long-term viability nonetheless. These stressors helped change the atmosphere permeating the major from one of a wild, desacralizing experimentation to a subdued, almost placid, character. "Cuts in faculty ranks over the past few years," Brooks wrote to Taft in 1975, made it "most difficult to secure the services of good faculty for an inter-departmental program without paying a realistic figure in return."[165] Due to retrenchment, the lit major was in fact only able to operate—which it did by providing portions of salaries of faculty members, some of whom put a third to a half of their teaching time into its courses—by acquiring outside funds, such as those from the Pew Charitable Trusts, which supported the major from January 1, 1976, to June 30, 1977.[166] Another not insignificant factor in the major in literature's toning down was that the roster of professors who designed, administered, and taught its classes changed. Not young junior professors but some of the most respected literary critics and scholars of literature at Yale (and in the entire profession) would helm the major. This group included not only key figures in the American institution of deconstruction Paul de Man, J. Hillis Miller, and Geoffrey Hartman but also John Freccero (Italian), Emir Rodriguez-Monegal (Latin America), Marie Borroff (English), and George May (French).

Despite financial obstacles, the major expanded, offering increasingly diverse and de-idealizing seminars. For example, the 1975 senior seminar, "The Nature of Metaphor," "examined the topic through the use of different theories of metaphor on the one hand and texts which use metaphor in these different ways on the other."[167] More generally, though, the lit major provided a home for courses that junior and untenured instructors wanted to offer but department heads felt were too broad or experimental. "A seminar on the pun, for instance," Holquist explained, "would have to draw on material from widely differing fields (psychology and anthropology) and languages (German and French for Freud and Levi-Strauss)."[168] "Even if all the texts were read in English," Holquist continued, "such a curriculum would have some difficulty fitting into any of the existing departmental programs for undergraduates."[169] The lit major provided a sanctioned space where faculty could

FIGURE 1.3 Michael Holquist at Yale after his return in 1986 (Courtesy of Yale University)

develop curricula that moved answers to the literary imperative beyond established disciplinary boundaries. This "curriculum wind tunnel," as Holquist described it, would never have been able to let courses through if not for the ground broken by Lit X and, of course, the institutionalization of the lit major itself, both of which helped to change what was tolerated and permitted as culture in the undergraduate teaching of literature at Yale.[170]

At the end of the 1970s, the translation of the (in)famous letters of lit major courses into more administratively acceptable numbers—Lit X became Lit 120; Lit Y became Lit 300; Lit Z became Lit 130—signaled the final stage of the major's ascension and normalization. Much like the way the political radicalism of the sixties eventually came to reinforce the liberal individualism of the mainstream culture, the lit major, from the perspective of administrators and on the paper of the course catalog, no longer seemed contrary to Yale's cultural strategy. This transition to respectability coincided with Lit X architects turning to other pursuits. Peter Brooks began work on a narratology project that grew out of Lit X, as the class, he explained, aided his movement "towards a course that would talk about narrative as a large literary kind in a—how shall I put it—quasi-anthropological context."[171] Brooks still hesitated to portray Lit X as anthropological in approach, though he did credit it with helping to activate his own interest in the structural figures and linguistic features of narrative by overlaying diverse types of stories. By contrast, Holquist's career initially suffered from his not having published enough and from "resentment . . . among some of [his] senior colleagues," and he was, after being denied tenure, forced to leave Yale in 1975, becoming chair of the Slavic Department at the University of Texas and then Indiana University.[172] In 1977, Holquist published his first book, *Dostoevsky and the Novel*; he then spent years examining the work of Russian philosopher and literary critic Mikhail Bakhtin, coauthoring the first complete account of Bakhtin's life and works in 1984. Holquist was eventually called back to Yale in 1986 to chair the lit major. In stark contrast to Brooks and Holquist, who both always spoke fondly of their "X-ey" achievements at Yale, Alvin Kernan later regretted his part in the story of Lit X. Leaving for Princeton in 1973, Kernan considered the class to have opened a Pandora's box; Lit X's democratizing desacralizations went too far, as they may have helped show fiction's relevance to students but—as Wellek and others had warned—undermined undergraduates' abilities to know what constituted "great literature."[173]

Kernan's attachment to traditional conceptions of culture aside, Lit X and the lit major, by encouraging students to adopt the persona of the *Homo signiferen* in order to question the hierarchical oppositions between high/low, prose/poetry, and the literary/nonliterary, facilitated the transformation of acceptable pedagogical practice in undergraduate literature courses at Yale. By probing the orthodox binary oppositions that structured literary humanist education, this once-experimental response to the literary imperative challenged the school's self-understanding as a champion of cultural and religious tradition. While its expansive postmodern politics of "the text" threatened the cultural authority claimed by the select few, Kernan, Brooks, and Holquist's major also produced circumstances congenial for the teaching of deconstruction to undergraduates at Yale. Paul de Man, Geoffrey Hartman, and J. Hillis Miller exploited these conditions in the 1970s, amending Lit X and developing their own courses in the lit major. Yet it was exactly the growing profile of this "Yale School" during the late 1970s that helped to obscure how Brooks, Holquist, and Kernan's "X-ey" curricula assisted the institution of American deconstruction. In fact, by the early 1980s, conservative and liberal commentators were routinely accusing the advanced postmodern techniques of rhetorical reading formulated and promulgated by de Man and company of causing—or at least significantly hastening—the decline in enrollments in literature classes and literature majors across the United States. These charges concealed the larger post-sixties crisis in literary education that the pedagogical experiment of Lit X and the lit major confronted. Instead of experimental courses, programs, or majors, a confluence of factors—the decrease in support provided to the humanities, the waning of undergraduates' interest in literature qua literature, and the changing place of literary study in university life—contributed to the lessening of the status that literary education enjoyed during the postwar period. This fading of the literary light was addressed by the lit major, which, in the twilight of the New Criticism in New Haven, demystified the secular chapel of literature with the hopes of rejuvenating the teaching of prose and poetry. For, while the old guard saw destruction and decay, it seemed to the converted that literary study's "golden age was about to dawn."[174]

2
EVOLUTION BY SUBVERSION
Vanguard Critics and Protodeconstruction

It's a fairly tidy and commonly told tale: the 1966 international symposium on structuralism at Johns Hopkins University gave birth, in one fell swoop, to deconstruction in the United States of America. This story has some validity: in Baltimore, not only did Jacques Derrida's eleven-page deconstruction of the anthropological and ethnological writings of structuralist Claude Lévi-Strauss seize the American literary-critical avant-garde imagination. The puckish French philosopher's compatriots' delivery of structuralism and its heretical offspring at Hopkins also generated an enormous amount of energy and excitement that had far-reaching effects in both the American academy and the larger society. But ascribing too much credit to foreign titans of intellect and their involvements in the then most powerful mode of thought in Paris or, as often happens in popular representations, overemphasizing the sixties and their ostensibly harmful effects on higher education, skews the record. Narratives about the importation of French intellectual products often tend to obscure the foundational contributions that a group of vanguard literary critics made to the history of deconstruction. Due as much to their personal backgrounds as their professional training, interests, and academic positions, these vanguard critics, while deeply receptive to and immersed in Continental influences, ably navigated domestic intellectual and institutional networks during the 1960s to constructively subvert the parameters of established literary-critical practice.

"Constructive" is central here for dispelling the myth of deconstruction's transfer to America, because it was not so much sixties turmoil as a virtual shelter from the emerging cultural and political storms—eventually labeled postmodern—that facilitated vanguard critics' challenges to the chief mode of "normal" criticism since midcentury: the literary formalism of the New Critics. The New Critics' professional achievements were strongly linked to the fortunes of and opportunities provided by the bounties of American postwar prosperity, which built the edifice of the modern higher education system. Meeting new pedagogical demands, the New Critics' quasi-scientific commitment to read literary works as self-enclosed linguistic objects was at once eminently teachable to undergraduates and a "rigorous" defense of literary education against charges of analytical weakness; literary studies, it was heavily implied, could be as "hard" as the hard sciences, then achieving a rising dominance in American universities.[1]

To some extent, the evolutionary stage instituted by vanguard critics by way of subverting New Critical formalism therefore required textually piggybacking on their predecessors' successes. Solely concentrating on texts, however, misses a broader history that not only revises the popular view of deconstruction as having come ashore in 1966, but also helps in the understanding of how aspects of the post-sixties fracturing of intellectual life into postmodern pieces stretches back at least to the late 1950s and early 1960s. For vanguard critics' entries into the discipline of literary studies as rising stars in their fields at the beginning of the decade occurred in an academic environment that provided avenues for professional advancement. Stabilized by a postwar institutionally supported intellectual ecosystem in which their disciplines enthusiastically received European thought and its representatives, the vanguard critics, while affiliated with elite East Coast universities, would become leading voices in literary studies by decade's end. Able and more than willing to use their clout during academic conferences and in high-octane publications to attract the attention of the like-minded professionally ambitious, the vanguard critics would develop reading techniques that both extended and critiqued New Criticism and its commitment to rigorously focus on texts' linguistic forms. In aggregate, vanguard critics' research and writing programs launched a largely homegrown literary-critical movement that amounted to protodeconstruction. When three of these vanguard critics—Paul de Man, J. Hillis Miller, and Geoffrey Hartman—further evolved their postformalist work alongside one another in the 1970s at Yale, an American institution of deconstruction was truly born.

The Postwar University and Postwar American Criticism

Before tracing the twists and turns of vanguard critics' reformist subversions of the substructure of postwar academic literary criticism, just how the latter was erected requires consideration. During the late 1950s and 1960s, America continued to reap the benefits of "the great compression," begun in the early 1940s when unequal wealth and income distribution were reduced; the country became an "affluent society."[2] Inequality and anxiety dogged this era of plenty nonetheless. Sputnik, sent into low elliptical orbit on October 4, 1957, prompted a hysteria among policy makers about an education gap with the Soviets. Congress responded by investing in human capital. The redistribution of funds helped bankroll what became known as the golden age of higher education. Lasting roughly from 1945 to 1975, this expansion of American colleges and universities was largely due to the GI Bill, a federal law that earmarked millions of scholarship dollars for two million veterans to attend college or trade schools, and then the baby boom. The number of undergraduates in the decade after World War II rose to 3.1 million; enrollments more than doubled in the 1960s, moving from 3.5 million to just under 8 million. The teaching corps expanded as well; during the 1960s, not only did the number of doctorates conferred triple yearly but, by decade's end, more faculty were hired than during the past 325 years.[3] In this massively expanded, multilayered academic ecosystem, soon replete with grants, visiting professorships, and symposia, the expectations and rewards of research were deeply transformed and in some ways revolutionized.[4]

The fortunes of the American literary critic and literary scholar were implicated in these nationwide changes. Since the 1930s, the old quarrel between the scholar, who used sociohistorical methods to determine the meaning of prose and poetry, and the critic, who made aesthetic judgments about the value or worth of literary works, had more or less entered a ceasefire.[5] A fair share of responsibility for the decades-long intellectual fisticuffs can be attributed to the New Critics.[6] Orienting the reader away from extratextual realities to a poem's complex linguistic forms, such as the length of a poem's lines, rhythms, or systems of rhymes and repetitions, New Critical formalist reading techniques arose partly in response to two late nineteenth-century modes of interpreting art: positivism, which aimed to verify facts about an artwork, and impressionism, which aimed to capture a feeling about or an experience of a work of art. Generally speaking, for the New Critics, impressionists' notion that poetry was merely beautiful language and positivists' crass empiricism avoided accounting for the power and distinctiveness that the intricate linguistic forms of literature took; and the twin dangers posed by subjective impressionism and brute empiricism to literature reinforced harmful patterns for understanding artworks that reverberated in the present. While New Critics' pursuits of interpretive precision generated enough ammunition and methodological justification to help them outflank interpretive rivals in the 1940s and into the early 1950s, it was not until the middle decades of the twentieth century that New Critics genuinely ruled academic literary criticism.

This dominance hinged on meeting the pedagogical needs of the precipitously expanding student population in postwar America. New Critics Cleanth Brooks and Robert Penn Warren shrewdly understood that, in order for undergraduates to reap the complicated cultural harvest of great literature, teachers new and old required rigorous methods of instruction easy to teach and learn from. Brooks and Warren's *Understanding Poetry* (1938), a textbook and teaching guide that shaped two generations of college (and high school) students, fit this educational bill.[7] *Understanding Poetry* trained students to consider good poetry as an autonomous linguistic object in which the supreme richness of meaning was lucidly organized into a unified whole often achieved by way of ironies and tense paradoxes. Brooks and Warren's pedagogical project was buttressed by their account of English literary history, which elevated the seventeenth-century Renaissance metaphysical poets and denigrated the eighteenth-century Romantic poets. Metaphysical poets, through a "conceit," an extended metaphor, united a text's form and content, such as by comparing dissimilar things, like the spiritual aspect of lovers and the physicality of a compass, in a lofty and clever way. The Romantics, on the other hand, allegedly due to a childlike excessive and uncontrolled emotion, clumsily disjoined a text's form and content.[8] When Brooks and Warren wanted a model of how not to write poetry, for example, they often conjured a hapless British Romantic: Percy Bysshe Shelley. For Brooks (who did admittedly on occasion write respectfully of the Romantics) and Warren, the meter—the rhythmic form—of a poem should fit the topic, a rule, they charged, egregiously violated by Shelley's poem "Death is here and Death is there, / Death is busy everywhere."[9] Their point was that Shelley's buoyant meter (form) struck a dissonant chord with the gravity of his topic.

Understanding Poetry became popular during the massification of literary education because it offered millions of college students thorough techniques for reading literature that required only the most elementary background knowledge of an author or a text and encouraged little serious contextual analysis. The textbook outmaneuvered insensitive positivist approaches to literature as well, training the student in a quasi-scientific, noninterventionist way to highlight a literary work's linguistic forms. The overarching aim of such an approach was to leave the world behind, promising access to the closed system of literature, to its formal aspects. As such, it schooled readers to put the modern world as represented by "hard" science, the Romantic notion of the author as the subjective source of their work, and the audience aside; the New Critical reading style trained students to sideline political, historical, and social questions about class and power that had earlier dominated discussions of literature, as in New Humanism and Stalinized Marxism. Such conservative interpretive habits also fit snugly with the Cold War–inflected shift, observable across disciplines, away from historicism and the concomitant withdrawal from politics. Indeed, for Brooks and many of his fellow New Critics, poetry did not espouse a "message"—it did not contain a specific, exalted content; nor did it make grand political or historical statements. Instead, as if lifted into a transcendental realm of ideas, the meaning of poetry was irreducible—it could not be paraphrased. Such summarizing was to commit "heresy" against the sacred word—because a great poem was a self-referential aesthetic object. For these formalists, poetry existed as a monadic, self-enclosed, hermetic linguistic form; the subject or theme of literature was irrelevant for critical consideration. To think otherwise might in fact lead the reader down the false interpretive paths of impressionism, maybe even empiricism. Nevertheless, in an apparent contradiction, for some New Critics, the harmonious resolution of conflicts within poetry was analogous to how they believed society and culture should also function. These New Critics saw the modern industrial world, often represented by the east coast of the country, as preventing or destroying the agrarian harmony of the American south, even as New Criticism thrived at Yale.

Yet, as Chesterton wittily wrote, there is nothing that fails like success. By the late 1950s, though the New Criticism was stupendously successful with undergraduate teachers of literature *and* flourishing in academic journals, the movement was moribund. For a couple of decades, an entire intellectual machine had woven New Critics' ideas into the discourse of the professional critic. It accomplished this through publications in and editorial work at influential quarterlies, teaching at summer institutes, and vigorous publicity efforts at the Modern Language Association, which, in 1951, revised its constitution to include "criticism" alongside "study" and "research in modern languages and their literatures."[10] American academic literary critics even came to view the tenets and claims to rigor of the New Critics as constituting not just the spirit but the respectable parameters of criticism itself. That is, the New Criticism became an ideology, if not precisely a species of propaganda, and then a norm.

But just as the laurel wreaths of victory could be laid upon the New Criticism, Brooks and similarly formalist-minded colleagues removed themselves from the battles in the academic agora where they had fought to establish unique reading procedures, a heavily anti-Romantic history of literature, and particular tastes and preferences. John Ransom Crowe had long ago—in 1937—rejected "moral studies" of literature, such as those of the New Humanists, and advocated for a "criticism" that was "more scientific, or precise and systematic."[11] W. K. Wimsatt and Monroe Beardsley had already identified, in 1946, the "intentional fallacy," a "romantic . . .

fallacy" that derived from confusion between the poem and its origins and led the reader away from the internal evidence of the words of the poem.[12] Wimsatt and Beardsley then cautioned, in 1949, against the "affective fallacy," which referred to the "confusion between the poem and its *results*," as the latter "ends in impressionism and relativism."[13] True, Wimsatt and Brooks published, in 1957, a substantial formalist contribution to literary theory that, besides advancing their by then typical assessment of the work of art as a linguistic object that married warring dualisms owing to its organic unity, emphasized metaphor as the concept that united these oppositions.[14] After all these successes, though, the New Critical movement had more or less sputtered by the early 1960s, even while New Critical attitudes and activities became so deeply embedded within the armature of literary study that most failed to recognize the movement's conservative legacy.[15] A New Critical formalist rigor toward prose and poetry was still de rigueur for most American critics, but for the group who initially gave life to these ideas rigor mortis had set in.

Reform in the Midst of Plenty: The 1965 Yale Colloquium on Literary Criticism

The sixteen academics who gathered at the "Colloquium on Literary Criticism" in late March 1965 at Yale University were well placed to develop interpretive possibilities that challenged reigning New Critical shibboleths. The school was certainly a conspicuous place to institute this subversive effort. Sometimes christened the "Yale theorists," four nationally recognized critics—Cleanth Brooks, W. K. Wimsatt, Robert Penn Warren, and René Wellek—called the university home; they were responsible for making the school nationally known as the center of the New Critical revolution; they were also the frequent target of hushed complaints about "Yale hegemony." The vanguard critics who met at the 1965 Yale colloquium kept it strictly professional, however. Though largely retaining New Critics' quasi-scientific commitment to rigorously read literature as autonomous linguistic objects, this group subtly reworked the work of the "Yale theorists" by questioning two New Critical claims embedded in the bedrock of literary-critical practice: (1) the literary work wed dualisms into an organic unity that simultaneously provided worldly and metaphysical wholeness and transcendence; and (2) sound criticism mirrored this onto-theological harmony. Hardly a revolt or shady conspiracy launched from abroad, vanguard critics' challenge to Brooks and company in a secluded, safe domestic harbor at Yale, far away from the sixties limelight, pushed New Critical formalist assumptions to their logical limit. Half a decade before Lit X and the lit major helped open space for the

FIGURE 2.1 A hand-drawn map, most likely by J. Hillis Miller, of the "Colloquium on Literary Criticism" at Yale in 1965 (Courtesy of J. Hillis Miller)

teaching of deconstruction to undergraduates at Yale, the vanguard critics used their rigorous approaches to literature to help institute varieties of protodeconstruction in the American academy.

The chief organizer of the Yale gathering was Jacques Ehrmann, who hoped that the colloquium might "bridge the gap between different cultures, different disciplines, between past and future."[16] Born in 1931 in France, Ehrmann attended the prestigious Collège de Sorbonne, and he earned his PhD in French literature from the University of California at Los Angeles in 1961. He then joined Yale's French Department; soon, through him, "theory was coming from France, and being channeled into the French Department."[17] Ehrmann was in fact the first professor in the United States to offer an introductory course on structuralism; while existentialism was *en vogue* in certain American philosophical circles during the 1950s and early 1960s, structuralism basically remained associated with the Parisian intellectual scene.[18] Despite Ehrmann's ambitious aims for the 1965 Yale colloquium, however, the meeting, which failed to receive any major foundation's support, led mostly to a domestic exchange of ideas. Likewise, Ehrmann's goal for participants to use techniques for reading texts to bridge disciplinary boundaries did not pan out—except, that is, for Ehrmann's and a second attendee's papers on French philosopher Gaston Bachelard. A lack of attendees from disciplines other than literary studies likely hampered such cross-disciplinary efforts.

Ehrmann's grand plans for the colloquium nonetheless reflected the transformed intellectual ambitions of—and growing professional demands placed on—professors of literature. With three exceptions—Ralph Cohen, Oreste Pucciani, and Dante Della Terza—the sixteen critics at the colloquium had earned their PhDs from American universities and entered the profession during the late 1950s and early 1960s, during the golden age of higher education when New Critics' formalism dominated the undergraduate teaching of literature, and academic jobs, resources, and support were plentiful. Shaped by their training and new professional expectations, this cohort of advanced critics understood that harnessing cutting-edge theoretical perspectives in their teaching and writing was necessary for living a successful academic life. A sizable opportunity for career advancement was taken at the small 1965 meeting at Yale; there, attendees would incorporate and develop novel techniques of reading, and not simply those of structuralists but of phenomenologists and of Marxists as well. As for the vanguard critics: though but a subset of the sixteen academics at the Yale gathering, they prominently contributed to this groundswell, and their penetrating reworkings of New Critical intuitions about poetic language were part of the intellectual reward bequeathed by the American postwar university.

Paul de Man: A Man out of Time, a Man of Letters

Perhaps no individual at Ehrmann's "Colloquium on Literary Criticism" was better poised to adopt and adapt new interpretive perspectives to challenge New Critical formalism than forty-six-year-old Paul de Man, then professor of French and comparative literature at Cornell University. A native speaker of French, Flemish, and German who learned English in his native Belgium from an American GI in the aftermath of the Second World War, de Man was versed in continental philosophical and literary traditions; to colleagues, he was the consummate European intellectual émigré. He became known during the early 1960s in literary-critical circles as an extraordinarily charismatic teacher, whom a former student remembered as resembling "a magician" pulling "spells from some old *grimoire*," and for his incisive evaluations of papers at disciplinary gatherings.[19] Most significant to garnering his confreres' respect, however, were de Man's essays, published in leading journals on both sides of the Atlantic. With these pieces, de Man practiced an idiosyncratic formalism indeed. Like the New Critics, he abstained from using sociohistorical reference to interpret texts; and like his precursors, he argued that the forms literature assumed were what made a poem or prose "literary." But, deviating from New Critics, de Man read literary forms, while necessarily wrought during the author's pursuit of meaning and truth, as unavoidably placing conceptual blocks in the path of any interpretation of a text. For de Man, these conceptual impasses often took the shape of ironies and contradictions—precisely the linguistic devices that New Critics believed maneuvered in the text to impart wholeness and harmony. Various literary humanist or New Critical appeals to a privileged cognitive or aesthetic realm—truth, beauty, genius, and the like—could not, according to de Man, resolve these disruptive impasses. For him, literature was simply, though profoundly, perpetually in conflict with itself, its poetic form locked in battle with its poetic content, undermining transcendence and claims of self-presence.

De Man's first close encounter with the close reading of the New Critical kind came two decades before the 1965 Yale colloquium, when he was a graduate student in comparative literature at Harvard during the early 1950s. Then known as a backwater for criticism, the university's literature departments, especially English, were largely staffed with literary biographers and historical scholars studying Elizabethan drama or Christian humanism. De Man's interest in appropriating interpretive tactics from European philosophers, who his advisers felt were obscurantists, was sorely out of place. His fellow graduate students, though, thought he was not; for them, he was a charming, if sometimes prickly, fount of knowledge. As an assistant to Reuben Brower, known as the only representative of the New Criticism at Harvard, de Man saw students employ what Brower called "slow-motion" reading to fruitfully examine "the structure of language prior to the meaning it produces."[20] In addition to helping steer students' attention to texts' complex linguistic forms, Browerian slow-motion reading, for de Man, as William H. Pritchard once summarized, subverted "other practices," such as those that "moved too quickly to paraphrasable meanings" and those that "treated literature as a substitute for disciplines such as theology or ethics or psychology or the history of ideas."[21] Slow-motion formalist reading, de Man realized, not only undermined the persuasiveness of other approaches to or methods of reading poetry and poetic drama, but also elevated the literary critic's intellectual stature.

Though thereafter working within many of the accepted literary-critical parameters set by the New Critics, de Man's essays of the 1950s were strikingly different from those of his contemporaries, for he not only bent formalist orthodoxy in unorthodox directions but indefatigably pointed readers' attention away from the New Critically celebrated modernists and their Eliotic boosters toward the European Romantics of the last quarter of the eighteenth century.[22] Being so out of step almost meant being out of a job. It was fortunate for de Man that as his graduation from Harvard approached in the fall of 1959, Geoffrey Hartman, then a junior professor in English at Yale, suggested to M. H. Abrams, master of literary studies at Cornell, that he offer de Man a position; de Man had impressed Hartman in 1957 with a paper on English Romantic John Keats. Abrams was more than sympathetic to the full-scale critical and historical reevaluation of the eighteenth- and nineteenth-century Romantics. In his *The Mirror and the Lamp* (1953), he wove a grand narrative, arguing that before the Romantics, literature was seen as a mirror reflecting reality, imitating aspects of the external world; for and after the Romantics, literature was the means by which the light of the writer's inner soul poured out to illumine and explain the world.[23] Not a "mirror," then, but a "lamp" was the operative metaphor to understand the form and function of Romantics' writings as well as the intellectual traditions inspired by those who followed in their poetic footsteps.

Part of what persuaded the methodologically pluralist Abrams to hire the increasingly methodologically monist de Man was the latter's 1960 article "Structure intentionnelle de l'image romantique," a pithy piece that offered a postformalist approach to and a reading of three Romantic poets markedly different from Abrams's.[24] As he was to claim in the mid-1960s, Abrams saw the Romantics as employing a hieroglyphic view of nature, explaining that "the best Romantic meditations on a land-scape, following Samuel Taylor Coleridge's example, all manifest a transaction between subject and object in which the thought incorporates and makes explicit what was already implicit in the outer scene."[25] Whereas Abrams saw the Romantics as employing what Coleridge called the concrete universal and the self-authorizing power of the imagination to interpolate inner and outer worlds, de Man saw the Romantics as masters of conceptual paradox, as using their writings to flag contradictions that blocked the dialectic between subject and object, thereby preventing any and all transcendence. In his 1960 article, de Man read Jean-Jacques Rousseau's *La nouvelle Heloise* (1761), lines from book 6 of William Wordsworth's *The Prelude* (1805), and Friedrich Hölderlin's "Heimkunft" (1802) as only seeming to describe secular revelations grounded in aesthetic experiences of the beautiful, natural world. Using language in a way that questioned the ontological primacy of the sensory object, "the[ir] passages [actually] describe the ascent of a consciousness trapped within the contradictions of a half-earthly, half-heavenly nature."[26] The conceptual consequences proliferated: "radical contradictions abound in each of the passages. Rousseau deliberately mixes and blurs the order of the season and the laws of geography. . . . Wordsworth transposes similar contradictions into the complexity of a language that unites irreconcilable opposites. . . . Hölderlin's text also is particularly rich in oxymorons; every word-combination, every motion expresses a contradiction."[27] Rather than producing moments of onto-theological presence by portraying transactions between the self and nature that unveil the sublime beauty of a landscape, de Man's Romantics described the conceptual roadblocks that frustrated transcendence. To avoid cogitating on how Romantics' texts portrayed these contradictions was, for de Man, to remain willfully blind to the post-Romantic predicament that informed poetic creativity as much as literary-critical practice.

De Man's paper at Ehrmann's 1965 Yale colloquium sketched the basic contours of his rigorous reworking of New Critical sensitivities to how poetic language was ironic. His subject was Hungarian Marxist historian and critic György Lukács's *Theory of the Novel* (1920).[28] "Compared," de Man stated, "to a formalistic work such as . . . Wayne Booth's *Rhetoric of Fiction* [1961]," which explored the linguistic, stylistic, symbolic rhetorical devices in narrative, "or to a work grounded in a more traditional view of history such as [Erich] Auerbach's *Mimesis* [1946]," a magisterial story of the representations of everyday life of writers from ancient Greece to the twentieth century, Lukács's "*The Theory of the Novel* makes much more radical claims."[29] There, Lukács argued that, because modern existence had become problematic, the *form* of the novel became problematic. While ancient Greek culture subsisted in a state of magnificent organic harmony, early twentieth-century society lived in fragmented, nonorganic existence, forsaken by God and any transcendent authority or ultimate reality. Lukács's modern novel lucidly illustrated this "transcendental homelessness," as the modern novel's protagonist was often lost in an inorganic world that lacked coherence or the plenitude provided by assurances of metaphysical meaning, causality, and direction. De Man concluded that Lukács's model of the modern novel "emerge[d] in a cogent and coherent way out of the dialectic between the urge for totality and man's alienated situation," between an existential longing for a "homogenous and organic stability" and the reality of experiencing a "heterogeneous and contingent discontinuity."[30] And, de Man proposed, it was precisely by foregrounding "this thematic duality" in our modern age that Lukács was able to determine not only that "structural discontinuities" organized "the form of the novel" but also that irony was "the truth of the paradoxical predicament that the novel represents."[31]

Yet, de Man maintained, though Lukács discerningly identified irony as the truth of the contradictory dilemma that structured the novel's form, Lukács's notion of irony, in a cruel twist, subverted Lukács's novel theory of the modern novel. This was so because Lukács retained in his 1961 preface to *The Theory of the Novel* the "decadent and belated romantic" view of time as "the inward action of the novel" that he had criticized decades earlier.[32] Preserving a linear conception of time, Lukács narrated the development of the novel as continuous and organic, beginning with the archetypal ancient Greek epic and ending with modernists such as Flaubert and Proust. This meant not simply that Lukács's literary history had a beginning and an end and led toward the present form of the novel; for de Man, it meant that the mode of temporality Lukács used to elaborate his supposedly nonorganic theory of the modern and discontinuous novel reinstated an organic conception of time. Lukács ironically succumbed to the very organicity that he had once abolished from his definition of the form of the novel; he only momentarily displaced the concept, and this led to the conceptual contradiction that structured his readings. According to de Man, then, the truth of Lukács's insight that irony was the paradoxical predicament of the novel led to a blindness to the truth that harmony, not even fleetingly achieved by irony, was undone by literature's form, whether that of ancient Greek poetry, the modern novel, or even his own criticism.[33] Lukács's "radical claims" about the novel's form, in other words, unintentionally made irony constitute his writing. Far different than New Critic Cleanth Brooks's notion that irony was a principle of order and unity of great poetry and prose, a midwife and medium to a half-known metaphysical truth, Lukács's poetic irony was unsettlingly uncontrollable, a worldly surprise that, though detectable by the most perceptive and precise of readers, ensnared the most self-aware of writers. If there was a postmodern politics decipherable in de Man's reading of Lukács, it was a politics of poetic difference.

J. Hillis Miller: A Consummate Professional

De Man's self-subversive—nay, protodeconstructive—take on Lukács piqued the interest of thirty-seven-year-old J. Hillis Miller, who would jump at the chance to grasp and develop the postformalist possibilities that de Man espoused. Born in 1928 in Virginia, Miller received his undergraduate degree just before the great postwar expansion of American higher education. His graduate degree, earned from Harvard's English literature PhD program in 1952, was well timed. For, like his father, who as president of the University of Florida from 1948 to 1953 oversaw the school's expansion from three thousand to twenty thousand students, Miller's professional career benefited from the opportunities provided by the academic golden age. After his Harvard graduation and a one-year stint at Williams College, Miller had a quite informal job interview at the annual meeting of the Modern Language Association for a position at Johns Hopkins University; Hopkins was desperate for teachers to handle

FIGURE 2.2 A young J. Hillis Miller at Johns Hopkins University (Courtesy of J. Hillis Miller)

mushrooming enrollment.[34] Miller accepted and in Baltimore fell under the spell cast, not by New Critics, but by one Georges Poulet, chair of Romance Languages and Literatures from 1952 to 1957, who was associated with the Geneva school of literary criticism. The methodological touchstone for Poulet was the work of German philosopher Edmund Husserl, the father of phenomenology. For Husserl, the phenomenological observer could execute scientific judgment by abstaining from judgment about nonevident matters in order to concentrate on extracting the fundamental structures and substance from the subjective experience of phenomena. Following Husserl's philosophical example, Poulet encouraged readers to open their minds so as to interpret literature as expressions of the hidden patterns or structures of an author's consciousness.[35]

Poulet's "criticism of consciousness" captivated Miller, perhaps in part because of its comportment with Miller's religious background. His father had been in the ministry prior to entering the academy, and Miller later reflected that his early exposure to rural Protestant culture shaped his interest in the power of literature to conjure imaginary worlds.[36] In a way semireligious, Poulet's phenomenological literary criticism offered Miller ways to commune with an author's consciousness; Poulet's "criticism of consciousness" aimed to transcend a text's particularities to make total or complete sense of an author's oeuvre. Miller's first major book, *Charles Dickens* (1958), developed out of his 1952 Harvard dissertation and partly funded by a Ford Foundation grant, was not simply dedicated to Poulet.[37] In his book Miller employed Poulet's method "to assess the specific quality of Dickens' imagination in the totality of his work, to identify what persists throughout all the swarming multiplicity of his novels as a view of the world which is unique and the same, and to trace the development of this vision of things from one novel to another throughout the chronological span of his career."[38] Miller's subsequent studies transferred Poulet's "criticism of consciousness" to examine English, principally Victorian, literature. Such a focus situated Miller outside the New Critical mainstream, for Cleanth Brooks influentially classed Victorian authors as undeclared and weak-minded Romantics, whose impressionistic methods made them victims of subjectivism. Miller's phenomenological method also unfashionably teased out the *themes* (content), not the linguistic forms, of prose and poetry. Though the established narrative of English literary history and New Critical formalism dominated his chosen profession's conventions, Miller's adoption of Poulet's approach nevertheless helped him to not only leave his imprint on his field but also position him for the fruitful braiding together of other reading techniques emerging from Europe.

That de Man's protodeconstructive interpretation of Lukács perked up Miller's ears on the floor of Yale's Graduate Hall thus only initially appears unusual. They certainly had different fields and different methods. But Miller and de Man both worked against the New Critical norms of academic criticism and were keen to learn from novel accounts of signification, particularly readings of texts inspired by phenomenological hermeneutics, a theory, of which Poulet's work was a variant, of understanding that texts were a means for sharing the consciousness of the author and representations of an author's consciousness that reveal aspects of the sociohistorical setting in which these texts were composed. The conversation following de Man's Lukács paper staged the two vanguard critics' mutual expectations about literary-critical practice and their interests in phenomenological approaches. After Harvard professor of romance languages and literature Dante Della Terza commented that Lukács's "strength seems to be that of a classical critic seeking out a totalizing view of the world," Miller mused: "I think I understand DeMan's [*sic*] distinction between polyrhythmic and linear time—a hermeneutical time as opposed to an organic time." "But," a curious Miller continued, "how does discontinuous p[o]lyr[y]thmic time escape from the failure of linear in L[ukács]?"[39] Miller appears to have been referring to de Man's suggestion during his Lukács paper that, despite pinpointing the conflict between discontinuous (or polyrythmic) and linear (or organic) modes of time that produced the irony of the novel, Lukács, by employing a narrative of the development of the novel's form, from ancient Greek epic to modern masterpiece, involuntarily reestablished an organic mode of temporality.[40] To explain how he had come to be able to discern different modes of time and their precise effects in the texts that he read, de Man responded that he "tr[ies] to distinguish between an organic view of totality founded on Nature and a dialectical view of totality, founded on human consciousness itself—as described in Heidegger."[41] For de Man, Heidegger's hermeneutic phenomenology provided key conceptual machinery serviceable for homing in on the forms of literature.

Martin Heidegger: his is a name (in)famous among professional philosophers the world over. He was Edmund Husserl's most successful student, and his crimes, which his most famous reader once suggested cast him into "the philosophers' hell," were intellectual-professional as well as political.[42] Heidegger's infamy began after he was appointed *rector magnificus* of Freiburg University on April 21, 1933, a post he enthusiastically held for eleven months. During that period, Heidegger ideologically assented to the Third Reich, efficiently implementing the regime's Aryanization laws, denouncing or demoting those he believed insufficiently committed to the Nazi cause.[43] Heidegger's secured fame in the annals of the Western philosophical tradition, though, was due to *Being and Time*, published in 1927 and originally dedicated to Husserl.[44] In this work, Heidegger, revising his teacher's phenomenology, rejected epistemological inquiry, investigation into what characterizes justified belief from mere opinion, to pursue ontological inquiry, investigation into the meaning of Being, the collective form of existence or presence before differentiation into each specific being. This was hardly empty rumination for Heidegger; he would claim in his inaugural speech as rector that the student body and faculty must serve the Nazi regime because they could help in the communal effort to overcome epistemology—what he called Western metaphysics—leading the *Volk* toward presence, the meaning of Being prior to "ideas" or intellection. After he resigned as rector, Heidegger remained a dues-paying member of the Nazi party for the rest of the war and continued to defend what he called "the inner truth and greatness of National Socialism" in a 1953 publication.[45] Heidegger's actions and statements stained his reputation in West Germany and beyond.

Professional philosophers in postwar America may have steered clear of what they saw as political and obfuscating continental influences in the

1950s like those of Heidegger, but a number of up-and-coming literary critics and scholars during the 1960s—partly motivated by the promise of career advancement, partly because they operated within a New Critical armature that forewarned them about the ironies, paradoxes, and ambiguities of literature—began to orient themselves to the newly available interpretive sensibilities emerging in Europe.[46] De Man, in particular, made exceptional contributions to this American literary-critical repositioning, often while turning to Heidegger's thought in both his teaching and his research. As soon as *Being and Time* was translated into English in 1962, he assigned sections to his Cornell undergraduate students (they were as much overwhelmed as enthralled).[47] De Man also continued to mine *Being and Time* for conceptual devices, frequently professing accord with Heidegger's idea that two modes of temporality organized the hermeneutical understanding of existence: a "vulgar" concept of time (linear and organic time, where a subject conducted epistemological inquiry) and an "authentic" temporality (a discontinuous, polyrhythmic time of Being happened before intellection). Heidegger's notion of the dual tracks of time—"not," de Man clarified to Miller at the Yale colloquium, "Heidegger's actual practice in discussing poets"—became central for de Man's distinctive protodeconstructive reading techniques, as de Man believed it was the conflict between "vulgar" and "authentic" time that structured poetic language (and its implied politics of poetic difference), whether philosophical, literary, or critical. "I think," de Man explained to Miller, "you find such notions of time at work in Lukács, in Hegel's *Phenomenology* [*of Spirit* (1807)] and in much of the best formalist criticism written here in America."[48]

De Man's 1955 essay on Heidegger's reading of Hölderlin's poetry shows how Heidegger's insights into the clashing temporal modes of existence informed de Man's subversive extensions of the New Critics' close attention to poetic language.[49] According to de Man, Heidegger selected Hölderlin as a witness whom Heidegger could say voiced the meaning of Being; Heidegger hence valorized Hölderlin as an authoritative precursor to his philosophical hermeneutics. "For Heidegger," de Man glossed, "Hölderlin is the greatest of poets ('the poet of poets') because he states the essence (*Wesen*) of poetry. The essence of poetry consists in stating the parousia, the absolute presence of Being."[50] However, de Man continued, "*Hölderlin says exactly the opposite of what Heidegger makes him say.*"[51] Repeatedly, de Man underscored, Hölderlin stressed that his poetry articulated the "absolute presence of Being" in the mode of unmediated truth.[52] "As soon as the word is uttered," though, Hölderlin's poetry "destroys the immediate and discovers that instead of stating Being, it can only state mediation."[53] Heidegger's commentary thus reversed Hölderlin's poetic statements, which, while they expressed Hölderlin's *desire* for, did not in fact achieve, unity between word and Being. Like a witness before the jury of his readers, Hölderlin's poetry only *attested* to his yearning for presence; what he actually *articulated* was the paradoxical way that poetic language unconcealed presence only through concealment of exactly the presence it hoped to unconceal. Contrary to Heidegger's reading, Hölderlin's poetry testified to the very impossibility of testifying to witnessing prereflective Being, to experiencing wholeness by transcending the material (ontological) and spiritual (metaphysical) divide.

Heidegger's reversal of the meaning of Hölderlin's poetry, according to de Man, stemmed from Heidegger's very goal to uncover an unmediated substance; pursuing such an aim required shoehorning Hölderlin into a linear representation, thereby obscuring the conflict between orders of temporality that Hölderlin's poetry paradoxically expressed. What's more, for de Man, Heidegger's readings of Hölderlin were *errors*, not *mistakes*. A "mistake" was attributable to incompetence or carelessness, but an "error" was produced by a structural necessity: the conflict between "vulgar" and "authentic" temporality *compelled* Heidegger to misread Hölderlin's poetry. De Man's rigorous reading of how Heidegger inadvertently demonstrated the necessary interpretive error incurred when trying to thematize poetic language subversively evolved New Critics' concentration on the text's ironies and paradoxes. De Man's reading also conferred upon poetry an analytical self-awareness about its unavoidable "internal" difference that philosophical thought, de Man implied, uncritically avoided and even papered over.

The attention Miller gave to de Man at the 1965 Yale colloquium ought not obscure that de Man's interpretive procedures were at variance with the Pouletian phenomenological method that Miller was known for using and developing. Before talking to de Man at the meeting, Miller had in *The Disappearance of God* (1963) and *Poets of Reality* (1965) employed Heidegger's historical hypothesis, derived from his readings of Hölderlin that God's departure from the world left people grieving in a "dürfiger Zeit," to help extract the themes that saturated a writer's work and unified it.[54] In *Poets*, for example, Miller proposed that God's reappearance might have materialized in twentieth-century modernist poetry via the theme of dispersed presence. "The poets of reality"—W. B. Yeats, T. S. Eliot, Wallace Stevens, and others—used their writings as a new romanticism that reunited the fragments (subjects, objects, words, other minds, the supernatural) left after the withdrawal of God. "If there is to be a God in the new world," the poets of reality felt "it must be a presence within things and not beyond them."[55] Miller's two books set research agendas for Victorianists and restored the status of a poetic lineage denigrated by T. S. Eliot and the New Critics. But if Miller had taken de Man's reading of Heidegger's reading of Hölderlin seriously, and he eventually did, Miller would have considered the thematic phenomenological approach he had used as insufficiently attentive to, even repressing, the temporality of literature's linguistic forms. And yet Miller eagerly continued his conversation with de Man at the 1965 colloquium during a lunchtime walk down New Haven's Wall Street, telling his new friend that he was "deeply interested in 'later Heidegger.' 'Oh no,' said de Man with great urgency, 'later Heidegger [the more historical Heidegger] is very dangerous. If you must read Heidegger, read *Sein und Zeit* [Being and Time].'"[56] That Miller would spend "some time early every morning over the next year" heeding de Man's advice signals not only his respect of de Man's intellectual acumen but also Miller's astute professionalism, his sense that new interpretive perspectives must in part evolve from accepted literary-critical practice—that is, from the New Criticism that de Man was transmogrifying.[57]

Geoffrey Hartman: An "Unremarkable" Refugee, a Remarkable Émigré

Hardly the only vanguard critic at Yale who found de Man's Lukács paper pregnant with possibilities, thirty-six-year-old Geoffrey H. Hartman used both his own contribution to Ehrmann's colloquium and the conversations that followed its presentation to raise the question if it were even possible to move beyond formalism. Like de Man and Miller, Hartman, by 1965, enjoyed an advantageous professional position from which to appropriate innovative literary-critical approaches. His childhood, however, was one of sorrow and catastrophe, marked by loss and upheaval. Born in 1929 into an educated Ashkenazi Jewish family in Germany, Hartman, shortly after *Kristallnacht* in November 1939, was evacuated from Frankfurt on a Kindertransport to England, where he resettled for the remainder of the war in Europe. In August 1945, Hartman was reunited with his mother in New York City, just as reports about the atomic bombs dropped on Hiroshima and Nagasaki reached the East Coast. While his mother worked for subsistence wages in sweatshops, Hartman enrolled in courses at Hunter College, previously a women's college that opened its doors to returning GIs; Hartman then transferred to Queens College (tuition free, courtesy of the government), where he earned his BA in comparative literature in 1949. Barely twenty, having studied Spanish, Greek, and Italian at Queens, and with his native German and sufficient English, Hartman entered Yale's prestigious (and René Wellek–run) comp lit PhD program, the first of its kind in America.

Surely owing to Wellek's disposition and pedagogical biases, Yale

Comp Lit put students through an intellectual formation transmitted by émigré European literary scholars, many of whom were veterans or refugees from the continent. This program, Hartman would recall, instilled graduate students with the firm belief in the harmony of European humanist culture and in the need to "affirm the wealth and worth of a literary inheritance that had brought such a wonderful harvest of modernist works, even though these did not prevent political disaster."[58] Unlike the "Yale theorists" over in English, then, Yale Comp Lit was not oriented to a particular procedure of reading that shunned sociohistorical reference. While the eclecticism in Yale Comp Lit likely helped inoculate the temperamentally pluralist Hartman, he felt that it left him on his own, methodologically speaking. Eventually, Hartman encountered the work and person of Erich Auerbach, a German Jewish literary scholar who was forced by the Nazis to relinquish his position at the University of Marburg in 1935 and then resided in Istanbul. Auerbach arrived at Yale in 1950 and made his scholarly reputation with *Mimesis*, where, drawing from the tradition of Romance stylistics, he closely read literary sources as linguistic objects, revealing—in Hartman's words—"exotic grammatical or rhetorical schemes, like parataxis and hypotaxis" that served as departures for insights into the author's social and cultural situation.[59] Hartman's first book, *The Unmediated Vision* (1954), a revision of his dissertation, mirrored Auerbach's approach in spirit if not precisely in method. Carefully interpreting passages from the works of four European poets—William Wordsworth, Gerard Manley Hopkins, Rainer Maria Rilke, and Paul Valéry—Hartman showed that a "common striving for pure representation," for a poetry that mediated between its readers and direct experience (or presence), which "we have sometimes called the imageless vision," was a modern development in literary history that the New Critics, by ignoring the achievements of many Romantic and nineteenth-century poets, had placed in the early seventeenth century.[60]

During his Yale graduate education, Hartman's equal interest in linguistic forms and the sociohistorical contexts from which they sprang led him to become what he later characterized as an "amateur phenomenologist—observing, letting impressions [or themes] resonate, attentive to the perceptibility of things and the act of becoming conscious of consciousness itself."[61] Hartman thus did not reject biography or history for understanding prose and poetry, but he later reflected that his 1954 book was still in a fashion Husserlian, "an example of 'criticism without approach,'" "an exercise in [a] kind of presumptuousness" that believed "one's thought free of assumptions" might practice a "method of complete interpretation."[62] Nevertheless, Hartman explained, his book was also "in pursuit" of a reading method "which could reaffirm the radical unity of human knowledge." While such a goal expressed a kind of supreme faith in the epistemic oneness of human culture and understanding as well as an individual's ability to confirm this oneness, Hartman's still-developing manner of reading was highly ambitious—and unusual—on the American literary-critical scene. When his dissertation adviser Wellek asked Hartman to justify his approach, Hartman innocently explained that he aimed "to present an inductive model for studying *any* literary work."[63] Such an offer of a universally valid technique of reading that concentrated on both the text's leitmotifs and its linguistic forms to conduct sorties into the author's social and cultural setting via the poetry of Wordsworth, Hopkins, Rilke, and Valéry was striking to not only Hartman's Yale teachers; J. Hillis Miller remembered his "intellectual excitement" as a graduate student at Harvard upon happening on *The Unmediated Vision* in Widener Library. "I had never read anything like it."[64]

Hartman's stimulating book exuded originality, but his career in the first half of the 1960s assumed a conventional shape. While he continued his personal defense of European literary humanist heritage after graduation from Yale in 1953, he was turned down for tenure at the university in 1961; this, despite a trailblazing 1962 essay that showed that, contrary to the New Critically induced anxiety afflicting so many in the profession that a Hegelian rise in self-consciousness constrained artistic vision, the Romantics' self-consciousness and their desire to surpass it *enhanced* their imaginative creativity.[65] After Yale's denial of tenure, Hartman bounced around a bit, serving as a visiting lecturer at Hebrew University and the University of Chicago, which he was especially interested in permanently joining. "[W]e don't believe in young geniuses here," a Chicago professor condescendingly told Hartman, who, crestfallen, was let go after one year.[66]

Things were looking up for Hartman and his ambitious scholarship following his assumption of a tenure-track position in English literature at the University of Iowa, which housed a new and promising Comp Lit Department. After the publication of *Wordsworth's Poetry, 1787–1814* (1964), an award-winning book that made the "apocalyptic" Wordsworth the center of critical discussion for decades, Hartman moved to Cornell, joining not only M. H. Abrams in English but also de Man in French. And it was in Ithaca where the two vanguard critics first truly worked together, sharing, Hartman recalled, a "love for literature that welcomed rather than resisted the cultivation of metalanguages drawn from linguistics, rhetoric, philosophy, semiotics."[67] The two also shared that nectar of postwar academic life, funds provided by the National Defense Education Act—passed in 1958 in response to Sputnik—to build Cornell's Comp Lit Department, one of only a handful of such programs

FIGURE 2.3 Comparative Literature faculty, University of Iowa, circa 1965. *Left to right*: Ralph Freedman (seated); Geoffrey Hartman, Curt Zimansky, Rosalie Colie, and Frederic Will (standing). (Courtesy of University of Iowa)

in existence. In addition to establishing permanent faculty lines, like de Man's, NDEA monies helped attract graduate students with generous stipends. By providing such professional opportunities and institutional support, the "military-educational establishment," a student of de Man once quipped, did not realize "what witch's brew it was preparing": an American institution of deconstruction.[68]

Outside Ithaca, too, de Man and Hartman worked alongside one another to modify the formalist armature of literary-critical practice. Consider de Man's paper, presented as part of Hartman's panel, "Romanticism and Religion," at the annual meeting of the Modern Language Association in December 1965.[69] "It is," de Man provocatively declared, "the avowedly somewhat sinister purpose of this paper to put into question" the very premises of Hartman's *Wordsworth's Poetry*.[70] In his book, Hartman read Wordsworth—whose writings he wanted to "fall into" after first encountering them as a child refugee in England—not as a decorous, affirmative poet of nature but as a penetrating, dark poet of imagination whose blank verse emerged from intimations of death.[71] Wordsworth's poetry, Hartman argued, performed a "drama of consciousness" between nature and imagination, the latter a "*consciousness of self raised to apocalyptic pitch.*"[72] Wordsworth's self-aware drama could well have guided him toward metaphysical solutions, toward a spiritual escape hatch; he instead humanized his egotistical "imagination," using poetic metaphors to transmute his apocalyptic impulse into a poetry of earth that—though never wholly effective—mediated between nature and imagination.

In his MLA paper, de Man roguishly pursued his "sinister purpose" by subverting Hartman's foregrounding of the theme of nature as the reconciling entity of Wordsworth's "drama of consciousness." A focus of de Man's: the "connection" Hartman saw Wordsworth's imagination as hopefully renewing in book 6 of *The Prelude* between "'the waters above and waters below, between heaven and earth' in the guise of a 'marriage of heaven and earth [toward which—PdM] the poet proceeds despite apocalypse.'"[73] De Man wondered if this "connection" could "be called a 'marriage' and whether the mediating entity is indeed nature."[74] "The marriage metaphor," de Man argued, "does not express" the exchange "between heaven and earth" but "an act of consciousness" that was not a "natural sensation."[75] Wordsworth's "marriage" led not to mediation—to the transformation of self-consciousness into secular revelation—but toward "the mind" and "its priority over nature while at the same time asserting its unbreachable separation from Being."[76] Inhabiting neither earth nor heaven, nor undertaking a movement from one to the other, Wordsworth's poetic metaphor of "marriage" performed de Man's postmodern politics of poetic difference. It exceeded phenomenological critics' thematizations and formalist critics' formalizations, at one go dramatizing a strange and self-conscious mind abandoned by "nature," "eternity," and "transcendental vision."[77]

Though their approaches to and readings of Wordsworth's poetry sharply differed, de Man and Hartman both helped place his writings at the center of contemporary literary-critical confrontations with the existential dilemmas of alienation and apocalypse. Nine months before the MLA conference, the two had graciously rehearsed their differences at the 1965 Yale colloquium. On the gathering's second day, Hartman's paper, "Beyond Formalism"—a question mark barely implied—boldly reconsidered formalism as *consciousness* of the link between literary form and mind. With flair, Hartman commenced thus: "Five years ago, on this campus, [English literary scholar] F. W. Bateson attacked what he called 'Yale Formalism.' His main targets seem to have been Cleanth Brooks, René Wellek and W. K. Wimsatt, and he has recently added Yale's 'pseudo-gothic Harkness Tower' to this distinguished list."[78] For Bateson, "Yale formalism" isolated "aesthetic fact from its human content"—that is, it detached an artwork's poetic meaning, its beauty, from social explanations and from cultural truths. While sympathetic to Bateson's complaints, Hartman stressed that wholly ending the attention that formalists shower on the text was likely not possible. "To go beyond formalism is as yet too hard for us; and may even be, unless we are Hegelians believing in absolute spirit, against the nature of understanding."[79] Save believing to have leapt into divine presence, Hartman held, the critic would inevitably have to confront that "which has procedural significance, and which engages him mediately and dialectically": "the formal properties of the work of art."[80] In fact, Hartman did "not know whether the mind can ever free itself genuinely of these procedural restraints—whether it can get beyond formalism without going through the study of forms."[81] That limits dictated by an artwork's forms invariably constrained critics' readings of literature did not devastate formalism, however. Rather, Hartman argued, these checks on interpretation elicited a refurbished formalism, one that could even reveal what Bateson saw as art's "human content."

The rest of Hartman's paper determined the ways in which critics, whether avowed formalists or not, overlooked how poetic form was in fact linked to mind (consciousness) and vital to historical existence. Hartman, for example, observed that Cleanth Brooks's formalist readings of Wordsworth's famous Lucy failed to account for the place of Wordsworth's poetry in the record of English literary history, specifically how Wordsworth's lyric was liberated from the "pointed" formal style of the metaphysical poets that heralded it.[82] "Avowed anti-formalist" Geneva critic of consciousness Georges Poulet committed a similar mistake, which led him to overlook the connection between form, mind, and history in his 1964 essay on Henry James.[83] "More formalistic than he thinks," Hartman stated, Poulet read James as searching for his organizing principle, his "point de depart," in all his writings.[84] But Poulet's self-imposed requirement of limiting James's perspectives to a sole consciousness, Hartman stressed, compelled Poulet, so as to avoid the embarrassing problem that there are "as many consciousnesses or cogitos as there are individuals," to also "postulate a period consciousness."[85] While Poulet read James's "consciousness" and writings as evidence of James's cultural "age," Poulet's "need to periodize," Hartman underscored, left "a residual formalism" in Poulet's reading.[86] Poulet's failure to appreciate the "differential relation of form to consciousness" resulted in his failure to understand that the "difficulty of *representation*" he passed over was "a difficulty of [historical] *being*."[87] By using Poulet's reading of James to rethink the gap between a work's form and representation into an existential struggle, Hartman was able to advocate for a reformed formalism, one that recognized the formal constraints placed on reading and, at the same time, connected literary form with the life of the mind and forms of historical existence—that is, with art's "human content."

The commentary elicited from vanguard critics by Hartman's generous extension of the interpretive precepts of "Yale Formalism" revolved around Hartman's critique of Poulet. "I couldn't agree more with the general trend of your paper," de Man declared.[88] But, while he concurred with Hartman that the critic unavoidably employed a formalism, de Man also defended Poulet, whom he oddly suggested *openly* adopted a formalist approach, as in his readings of Blaise Pascal and Saint Augustine. "It was not," Hartman responded, "an unrepresentative essay (Poulet's on James) but something of a relevant Achilles Heel. I admit there are times when he does recognize the shadow side, the anguish, but I do feel he has a general optimism about the progress of consciousness."[89] Thus, for Hartman, Poulet possessed too much confidence not only in the critic's ability to thematize the connection between an author's consciousness and the poetic form he or she used, but also that the author's consciousness, as Hegel claimed, was a spiritual pilgrim that progressively historically rose, via dialectical reversals, to achieve onto-theological presence, accord with itself and the world. But Poulet's certainty was self-deceptive, Hartman was saying: the supposed formal harmony between James's consciousness and his "cultural age" ignored the "shadow-side," the absence that was exterior to consciousness and that escaped any thematized poetic form. Assuming "too optimistic a view of the Progress of Consciousness," Hartman stated in his Yale paper, Poulet prematurely promoted James's literary feat as "a stage in the history of consciousness," ironically ensuring he was unable to grasp the precariousness and historical conditionality of James's achievement.[90]

De Man and Hartman's friendly, if intense, back and forth touched the conceptual crux of Miller's entire research and writing agenda—Miller didn't miss a beat. He agreed with Hartman that in Poulet's essay on James, Poulet retained a faith in a kind of Hegelian ladder—an "angelism," Miller stated. For Miller, though, Poulet's "angelism" manifested itself in the trust that the *critic* could climb the Hegelian ladder to reach, to commune with, the consciousness or presence of an author and the author's "age."[91] Despite what Hartman saw as Poulet's methodological weakness, Miller stressed, Poulet offered great insight into James's writing style, a style both private *and* total, operating on all levels and in all areas of his life and work. "Do you really think," Miller asked Hartman, "Poulet is [a self-avowed] anti-formalist? Isn't it rather that he is going beyond a particular poem to establish the form of a writer's whole oeuvre, or even a whole period."[92] For Miller, as he had argued in a 1963 essay, "Material objects, other people, God in his various models, all are present in Poulet's [phenomenological] criticism, but only as they have been turned into words, that is, into a form of consciousness."[93] Miller's Poulet was a self-declared formalist, explicitly searching for the contour and character of consciousness that organized an author's diverse works and which reflected and was produced by a specific epoch. For Miller, actually, Poulet even moved beyond conventional literary formalism because he extracted a form from an author's oeuvre rather than an isolated text in the manner of a Cleanth Brooks. From Hartman's perspective, Miller, like Poulet, did not account for the historical development of the connection between poetic form and mind. Notwithstanding Miller's methodological differences with Hartman (and with de Man), these vanguard critics' readings of literature together pressed against the strictures and constraints of established literary-critical practice in America.

Evaluating the Yale Colloquium and the Protodeconstructive Project It Instituted

Throughout the Yale colloquium, vanguard critics made significant interventions, but it was on the final day of the intimate event—March 27, 1965—when contributors most directly dealt with how they might answer the question that Hartman implicitly asked in his paper and that he now explicitly put to his colleagues: "What would it mean really to go beyond formalism?"[94] Eugenio Donato, professor of French and Italian, and René Girard, professor of French, both from Johns Hopkins, jointly tendered a tentative answer. For them, moving past formalism required drawing on French phenomenologist Maurice Merleau-Ponty's concept of history, which Girard stated "introduce[d] two terms—reification [when an abstraction is treated as concrete] and totality." "We can start," Girard continued, "with a formalism which is not total but is reified, then we can have a formalism which is reified *and* total." From there, "we can go beyond, to a point at which form will *not* be reified by dialectizing form, such that it will include both the object [literature] and your response to the object [criticism], and can never be broken down into either of those two components. Then we can get a notion of form or structure which is non-reified, and which always destroys itself to include itself in a larger structure, which is a historical dialectic, and which is a dynamic totality."[95] For Girard, it was Merleau-Ponty's idea of history that would help solve the formalist impasse because he cared for history as a complete whole, a single drama in which literature and literary criticism, as Merleau-Ponty wrote in a text published in 1946, "mov[ed] toward a completion and conclusion."[96] That is, for Merleau-Ponty, the historical dialectic progressed toward presence, the unity between the form and content of both literature and criticism; "There is," he would write in a 1947 text, "in the present and in the flow of events a totality moving toward a privileged state which gives the whole its meaning."[97] When this "privileged state" is reached, there will be a genuine "reconciliation of men" in fully universal terms.[98] Merleau-Ponty's formalism was thus also the substance of his Marxism; his Marxism, the substance of his formalism. And such was the promise of critical possibilities, Girard suggested, that Merleau-Ponty's idea of history offered.

But one attendee prominently resisted entertaining the opportunity: Paul de Man. His objections amounted to a defense of his protodeconstruction and its postmodern politics of poetic difference. "It is," the emerging authority on critical fashions stated, "precisely a temporalization of the concept of form" and not the exploitation of concepts of history that required critics' attention.[99] "We shouldn't try to get beyond formalism" to consider form's temporalization, de Man suggested. "There are all sorts of structuralist assumptions within formalism."[100] In fact, for de Man, sound criticism necessitated the detailed examination of those assumptions, structuralist or not. "The confrontation of European and American criticism at this point in History is worthless," de Man curiously stated, considering the provenance of central features of his own evolving postformalist approach. "The next step must be a re-interpretation of the concept of form. In this direction"—and here de Man courteously nodded to Merleau-Ponty's phenomenology—"we have much to learn from Neo-Marxist criticism. That we can again talk about the problem of art and society is a considerable progress. But we should learn to talk about it in the proper way, with the proper terminology."[101] Careful not to outright reject sociohistorical approaches to the literary work—a metaphysician he was not—de Man implored his colleagues to rethink and reapply—to temporalize—the concept of literary form above all other considerations. Doing so, de Man suggested, would forge a rigorous criticism that traced how the conflicting modes of temporality, the necessary divergence between disjointed (or polyrhythmic) and linear (or organic) registers of time, produced poetic language—that is, literary products that fold back into themselves like a topological paradox. Concurring with de Man and hesitating to endorse the feasibility of using Merleau-Ponty's idea of history, Miller reflected that the assembled group had learned from and supposedly advanced beyond *New Critical* formalism; for him, the homologue between New Criticism and formalism was broken: "I was struck by how little attention we paid to the New Criticism. It seems to me be a dead issue. We have gone beyond it and absorbed it."[102] De Man, though, had wanted more, stating earlier: "We haven't yet defined our relation to the previous generation of critics."[103] New Criticism still nettled the critics gathered at Yale.

Vanguard critics' evolution of literary formalism received a professionally sanctioned textual form with the publication of the Yale colloquium's papers in the December 1965 issue of *Modern Language Notes*.[104] In his introductory essay, Miller portrayed the gathering as a testament "to an important shift of focus in American literary criticism."[105] While a "few years ago one would have expected an American colloquium on literary criticism to be a dialogue between our native formalism and other approaches, . . . American scholars may come to develop new forms of criticism growing out of American culture as well as out of the encounter with European thought."[106] For Miller the meeting inaugurated a conversation about how to develop innovative perspectives and methodologies that equally exploited domestic and continental influences and traditions. The Yale colloquium, Miller wrote, "brought a number of the most important . . . [t]ens[i]ons between antithetical approaches"—"the nominalization of literature versus its periodization; . . . temporal form versus spatial form; hermeneutic, polyrhythmic, dialectical, or discontinuous time versus linear, organic, 'natural,' or continuous time; structure versus form"—of the "critical enterprise . . . out into the open."[107] However, Miller stressed, this novel stew of conflicting reading techniques drawn from American and European contexts would not and could not devise a way "to proceed from [the] opposition [of these antitheses] to some grand synthesis transcending the problems of criticism in a comprehensive system—with all the critics clasping hands and singing a final chorus."[108] No, the colloquium participants remained very much in the sublunary sphere. "Ours is a fallen world," Miller wrote, "and literary critics, like everyone else, must endure the *malconfort* of a pull between opposing tendencies of the spirit."[109] Hartman and de Man saw the literary critic as unable to go "beyond formalism," while Miller viewed the critic as an interrogation point, a question mark, fated to inhabit the interpretive conflicts generated by opposing techniques of reading texts. It is nonetheless fitting that all three vanguard critics, de Man, Miller, and Hartman, used the occasion of the colloquium to institute postformalist subversions of approved literary-critical practice, not least because Yale was their future institutional home, where they would assume the mantle of the New Critics and launch their deconstructive project—and, some would say, topple literary humanism altogether.[110]

More Academic Bounty: The Johns Hopkins Symposium and Its Aftermaths

The cloistered Yale colloquium was undoubtedly critical to vanguard critics' research and writing agendas, but the 1966 Johns Hopkins University symposium "The Languages of Criticism and the Sciences of Man" was as big and as important as it got for American humanists. Scratching beneath the glossy surface of popular representations of the Baltimore event—portrayed as "epochal," "a watershed," the "birthplace of 'deconstruction'" and "French theory" in America—reveals the domestic intellectual-institutional networks that fostered the diverse theoretical projects undertaken at and connected to the Hopkins symposium. For not simply the initial episode in Baltimore but associated seminars, symposia, and colloquia during the half decade that followed provided American humanists with ample opportunities to cultivate novel interpretive sensibilities. Offered by private and public agencies, foundations, and institutions, many fruits grown on the academic revolutionary tree were consumed by leading humanists to fuel their cutting-edge research and groundbreaking articles. De Man, Hartman, Miller, and other vanguard critics, for instance, would further develop their postformalist reading techniques from the husk of the New Critical presence. Thus, as influential as the papers presented at the Hopkins symposium were, other communities and settings, fashioned from local and national forces and factors, and outside the glare of publicity, arguably did much more to institutionalize deconstruction in America. By the second half of the 1960s, humanists' endeavors had also contributed to the broader and rather anxious defense about the analytical "rigor" of the "soft" humanities at a time when the "hard" sciences were receiving increased support. Now integral to academic humanists' sense of self and professional advancement, many of these "hard" undertakings were early sources of what became known as "postmodern theory" in the 1970s.

Unlike the 1965 Yale colloquium, the Hopkins symposium received outside funding: a Ford Foundation grant to the tune of $34,000.[111] Hopkins placed a $4.5 million request, but the foundation—and "other private" organizations as well as "the newly established National Endowment for the Humanities"—turned the application down.[112] While Hopkins overestimated philanthropic support for its proposal, the relatively generous foundation grant financed not just a four-day event but more than thirty hours of audiotapes, a series of follow-up colloquia and seminars eventually attended by almost one thousand humanists and social scientists, and a case-bound edition of the conference's proceedings.[113] This support, some contemporaries charged, made the event but an occasion for fostering the policies and practices of the so-called Cold War University. In 1968, the editors of the newly founded *Telos*—a self-described "journal of radical thought"—suggested that, because the Ford Foundation disseminated favorable views of Western powers and promoted the Vietnam War, the Hopkins symposium was an arm of multinational capitalism and American imperialism.[114] It is difficult to deny that foundation support was, by the early 1950s, interlaced with the US government's objective to promote a liberal vision of America's role in the world. "The Ford Foundation's mission," Greg Barnhisel has written, "was . . . to 'strengthen democratic values, reduce poverty and injustice, promote international cooperation, and advance human achievement.'"[115] The foundation's philanthropic mission was also increasingly—and covertly—adjusted to a policy that aimed to help halt Communism's spread. In fact, occasionally, organizations like the Ford Foundation secretly provided support for cultural endeavors that aimed to orient the non-Communist left, say, in France or Italy, toward American interests. Such positioning, it was hoped, would strengthen the Atlantic alliance. Winning hearts and minds required more than altering the reputation of "America" abroad, though; it also meant support for the arts and humanities on the home front.

Seen in this light, the Ford Foundation's grant was conceivably influenced by Washington's policy to promote the American left in order to counter negative images of "America" overseas. Washington's aim to reinforce the Atlantic alliance, for example, mirrored a core objective of the symposium. The event's organizers, Richard Macksey, a polymath literature professor hired at Hopkins in 1958 who had cultivated interest among colleagues for contemporary French thought, and René Girard and Eugenio Donato, both contributors to the Yale colloquium, hoped to build intellectual links between France and America. The second half of the symposium's title, "the Sciences of Man," signaled: bring the good news of structuralism to humanities departments, designated on the continent as the "sciences of man." (Such a gendered title was ripe for later dissection by those wielding interpretive techniques connected to what happened at Hopkins.) In the October 1965 Ford Foundation request, drafted by Macksey, foundation program officers read how a grant would help construct "a vital bridge between European and American humanists."[116] The Yale colloquium provided a limited point of intellectual entry for structuralism into the American academy; the Hopkins symposium was by design far more ambitious in scope.

Yet a "Cold War" rendering of the Hopkins event obscures key elements that informed organizers' postformalist goals. The first half of the symposium's title, "The Languages of Criticism," indicated not only the high status and substantial support then given to humanities as well as the condition of literary education in the United States. That phrase, Macksey later reflected, "distantly reference[d] Ronald Crane's American pluralism."[117] In a 1935 essay, Crane introduced his hypothesis that criticism was "a collection of distinct and more or less incommensurable 'frameworks' or 'languages'" that conflicted in "matters of assumed principle, definition and method."[118] Because these "languages" possessed their own inclinations and limitations, each mode of criticism was but a tool—useful for one or more purposes, useless for others.[119] During the 1940s and 1950s, Crane ran with his thesis, challenging the New Critics' dogmatism and advocating for a pluralist enlargement of the critic's theoretical capabilities.[120] For the Hopkins symposium's organizers, Crane's "American pluralism" was a lodestar, as they intended the event, by multiplying the theoretical resources and vocabularies of criticism available stateside, to assist domestic critics in revising, perhaps moving beyond, literary formalism.[121] Unfortunately, the significance of Crane's pluralism in this context has been forgotten, partly due to publishers' choice to reverse the title and subtitle in the symposium's published proceedings, resulting in *The Structuralist Controversy: The Languages of Criticism and the Sciences of Man* (1970). The quarrel over structuralism was thereafter marked as central to the event.

Primus inter Pares: Hopkins, the Structuralist Event, and American Literary Criticism

Since its founding in 1876, Johns Hopkins enjoyed a privileged intellectual-institutional position from which to launch a major international discussion on an interdisciplinary mélange of humanist methodologies, particularly those debated in literary studies. First, Hopkins was the center of modern philology, the historical investigation of language. Though philology was long past the peak of its prestige by 1966, the Hopkins Philological Association maintained the "lively tradition of textual studies and their relation to more recent critical approaches."[122] Second, Hopkins was once the center for the "history of ideas," an interdisciplinary interpretive strategy developed during the 1940s that focused on the "unit idea," "*assumptions*, or . . . *unconscious mental habits*, operating in the thought of an individual or a generation" that disperse and recombine over time.[123] A. O. Lovejoy was magister of the school, and he gathered scholars from Hopkins's Humanities Group to form the famous History of Ideas Club.[124] Third, Hopkins had been the home of Georges Poulet, who initiated his "criticism of consciousness" there in the mid-1950s, inspiring critics in the university's English Department, notably Earl R. Wasserman and J. Hillis Miller. Fourth, the university, by the mid-1960s, was instituting a scene for a semiunified transatlantic approach to literary studies. Under René Girard's editorship, *Modern Language Notes*, for example, published discussions on structuralist methods by European critics Lucien Goldmann and Roland Barthes; Goldmann's "genetic structuralism" integrated Lukács's Marxism and Jean Piaget's genetic epistemology to consider cultural phenomena, such as the novel, as mental structures in which an object's component parts were dependent on the whole, while Barthes's structuralist analyses of literature challenged traditional French views of the critic's role. Equally key at *MLN* were the Americans who extended their methods in its pages. All these Hopkins-supported achievements in literary studies, many of them interdisciplinary in coloration, reinforced the university's most-favored status in higher education.

Both Hopkins's research strengths in the humanities and Crane's "American [literary-critical] pluralism" are discernible in the Ford Foundation proposal. "Participants in the symposium and seminar," the application explained, "are to comprise a highly interdisciplinary group."[125] Yet with the exceptions of a professor of history of science and a professor of philosophy, six of eight *sponsoring* faculty members hailed from Hopkins's literature departments. And, though the proposal listed seventeen *participating* academics, with twelve coming from abroad and from a range of disciplines (anthropology, classical studies, comparative literature, linguistics, literary criticism, history, philosophy, psychoanalysis, semiology, and sociology), the remaining five scheduled participants were Americans, four hailing from literature departments and one, who pioneered the study of the relationship between language and social context, housed in anthropology.[126] Organizers manifestly aimed for contributors to identify the basic structural problems and concerns in all humanities disciplines, but literature professors dominated. This may have to do in part with how other disciplines had defaulted on the task of processing new intellectual trends from Europe. It also perhaps reflects organizers' belief, traceable to early drafts of the proposal, that "literature offered a privileged testing ground for any theories of interpretation put forth in disciplines concerned with the human phenomenon."[127] The proposal itself justified the implicit focus of the symposium, foregrounding the fact that "American [literary] practice during the past thirty years has seemed to stall at the formalist extremity."[128] Such hesitation presented opportunities, however. "No one is more aware of the fragmentation and decadence of the New Criticism in the United States than its inheritors"; "the thoughtful critic is acutely aware of the theoretical and practical limitations of native 'New Criticism.'"[129] But, the submitted application continued, though "native" critics were "anxiously alert to new promises of salvation," they lacked "a means to assess" the "methodological and axiological implications of the new prophets," "isolated" as they were "from the maincurrents [*sic*] of contemporary European discussion."[130] Foundation support for the Hopkins symposium might kill two birds with one stone: shuttle advanced continental thought to the East Coast and move "native" critics to discard their "concerted" hesitation and develop rigorous reading techniques beyond "the formalist impasse."[131]

But this is not to say that Hopkins symposium organizers' stress on the "humanitarian" aid the event would deliver to "native" critics failed to intertwine with their overarching interdisciplinary goals. The symposium was not only the first public event sponsored by Hopkins's new Humanities Center; it was the first time structuralism was considered as an interdisciplinary phenomenon in America. The symposium's fourteen speakers were a veritable who's who of French semiotic, structuralist, Marxist, and psychoanalytic critics, many setting their critical sights on some sort of methodological horizon or interpretive gridlock. Their topics covered "the status of the subject, the theory of signs, the use and abuse of models, homologies and transformations, synchronic (vs) diachronic approaches, the question of 'mediations' between objective and subjective approaches and the possible relationships between microcosmic and macrocosmic social and symbolic dimensions."[132] In his presentation, for instance, Charles Morazé reduced his mathematical "model" for "literary invention" to three phases—information, cogitation, and intellectual— while negotiating between the "collective" support and control of the inventor and his or her "neurological" creative act.[133] There were also Roland Barthes's and Tzvetan Todorov's "sign-oriented" papers: Barthes investigated the historical shift of "writing" from transitive to intransitive act, the latter being the situation of the writing subject who disappeared into his or her practice; Todorov argued that not only must poetics, the study of linguistic techniques, exploit the funds of contemporary linguistics but, similarly, that literary categories need to play a formative role in critics' comprehension of language's nature.[134]

The *Kairos* of Jacques Derrida in Baltimore

But it was the subversive presentation of then unknown thirty-six-year-old French philosopher Jacques Derrida that reverberated most powerfully with Hopkins listeners and soon after readers in American literary-critical circles. For Derrida may have been added to the Hopkins program late, but his arrival was nothing short of punctual. Though technically committed to studying European thought, though flaunting a playfully ironic style in sharp contrast to the seriously stern Anglo-American critical sensibilities, Derrida's concentration on the contradictions and ironies of the text intersected with established formalist precepts that vanguard critics were doggedly trying to displace. His work would also lend philosophical justifications, theoretical heft, and an air of sophistication to humanists keen to quell anxieties and defend their projects' rigor and legitimacy. Literary critics in English departments were particularly eager in this regard, as the prominence of literary study in American higher education was beginning to somewhat diminish, and New Left radicals were gearing up to denounce New Critical orthodoxy at the 1968 MLA meeting.

Derrida's intellectual formation had begun far from the snowy New Haven winters that blanketed Yale's Harkness Tower. He was born on July 15, 1930, in a suburb of Algiers into a Sephardic Jewish family. On the first day of school in 1942, the young Derrida and his fellow Jewish students were expelled by French-Algerian administrators complying with Nazi Germany's new racial laws. Rather than attend a new school created by displaced Jewish teachers and their pupils, twelve-year-old Derrida found comfort in soccer—as well as the writings of Jean-Jacques Rousseau, Friedrich Nietzsche, André Gide, Jean-Paul Sartre, and many other philosophical and literary figures. After the Second World War, and following intense study at preparatory schools in Algiers and Paris, Derrida gained admittance to the École Normale Supérieure in Paris, that illustrious institution charged with cultivating France's critical spirit. At the ENS, Derrida felt isolated and unhappy, though he completed a master's degree with a thesis on Edmund Husserl in 1954; in 1956, he passed the *agrégation*, allowing him to teach philosophy in France's universities.[135]

After his appointment at the ENS in October 1964 as a *maître-assistant*, a sort of halfway rank between all-powerful professors and their assistants, Derrida published his first text on a then understudied side of Husserl's work: his investigations into how signs, meaning, and ideality protected objectivity or logic against forms of relativism. Whereas American critics like Miller used Husserl's phenomenological investigations to help extract the themes of an author's consciousness from a literary work, Derrida turned to Husserl's text to discover that language subverted Husserl's stated goal to soothe the fraught relationship between philosophy and history. Derrida was particularly fascinated with the father of phenomenology's argument that the birth of scientific and philosophical consciousness could be determined with a new kind of "historical" investigation into the "original" meaning of geometry.[136] For Husserl, the "inventions" of ancient Greek geometers instituted the ideas of objectivity and abstraction. Metaphysical truth, then, started in a particular time and place. Derrida, though, read Husserl as unintentionally highlighting the unavoidable link between transcendental truth and the event of its material emergence: Husserl stressed that geometrical knowledge was connected to specific thinkers, *and* he acknowledged that the transmission and endurance of objective truth depended on its exteriorization in language. "The Objectivity of this truth," Derrida read Husserl's text as reasoning, "could *not* be constituted *without* the *pure possibility* of an inquiry into a pure language in general."[137]

That objective truth was paradoxically contingent on linguistic events did not mean that Derrida rejected Husserl's phenomenological project; nor did it mean for Derrida that Husserl voided his own "historical" search for philosophical truth. While Husserl's text showed transcendental truth as existing in a constitutive relation to specific (that is, historical) uses of language, the contradiction between the existence of ideal objects and their linguistic incarnations steered Derrida to his innovative view that the transcendental field—truth, objectivity, ideality, and so forth—must be reconsidered as "writing." Language, Derrida observed Husserl observing in his text, "document[ed]" and gave *"spiritual corporeality"* to ideal objects to the extent that language functions by *"stating"* and *"communicating* [these ideal objects] *to others."*[138] In addition to "language" giving exterior form to and verbally embodying a common object, however, Husserl also showed that "language" survived the absence of speakers, because language endured in the manner of a physical object, as a material, graphic language—as "writing," that is to say.[139] Though Husserl tried to describe ideal objects by way of a transcendental consciousness, searching for a transcendental ground on which an absolute present could rest, Derrida read Husserl's text as demonstrating that the mechanism by and through which ideality itself appeared in history was language as inscription; "writing" deformed, twisted, and stretched ideality. To rethink metaphysical truth as "writing" for Derrida thus meant appreciating how repetition and dissemination constituted the first communicated objective truths via a tradition lacking the speaker who invented those truths.[140] "The originary Difference of the absolute Origin," Derrida wrote, "is perhaps what has always been said under the concept of '*transcendental*,' through the enigmatic history of its displacements. Difference would be transcendental." For Derrida, Husserl's text revealed the historical origin of truth as writing, as constituted by self-subverting deferrals and differences, by what was always already absent.[141] Written several years after his work on Husserl, Derrida's statement that "there is nothing outside the text" testifies to the influence that Derrida's early interpretations of Husserl's text exerted on Derrida's intellectual trajectory.[142]

The ENS *maître-assistant*'s highlighting of how texts' postmodern topological paradoxes subverted the stated aims of philosophical systems reached a certain comprehensiveness with his reading of Heidegger's *Being and Time.* In the fall session of his 1964–65 ENS seminar, Derrida instituted his "deconstruction" by engaging the conceptual conflict between the themes of temporality and historicity in Heidegger's text: "Heideggerian destruction [of philosophy] is . . . a destruction—that is, a deconstruction, a de-structuration, the shaking that is necessary to bring out the structures, the strata, the system of deposits."[143] Derrida clearly admired how "Heideggerian *destruction*" intended to overturn Western metaphysics, the all-encompassing European tradition of thinking that Heidegger believed reduced the collective form of Being to a self-present object; by privileging self-present meaning, Heidegger argued, Western metaphysics enforced ahistorical hierarchies of meaning or value-laden oppositions, spiritual/material, male/female, and so on, that bury the historical reality of Being before differentiation into specific objects. However, Derrida stressed, Heidegger's text, against its author's intentions, was itself ironically organized by a metaphysical hierarchy. "This absolute privileging of the Present and the Presence of the Present that Heidegger must destroy or shake up in order to recover the possibility of [the] historicity [of Being] cannot be destroyed by [Heidegger] the way one criticizes a contingent prejudice."[144] Heidegger rigorously identified Western metaphysics' privileging of the self-presence of meaning that hid historical Being but, according to Derrida, he made his questioning of this historicity secondary to his questioning of the temporality of Being. By having "grafted" the "problem of historicity . . . onto that of temporality" in this way, Derrida maintained, Heidegger failed to "concrete[ly]" explain what distinguished the question of temporality from the question of historicity.[145] "Ultimately," Derrida concluded, "it is a metaphysical attitude not to take seriously and not to insist on the rootedness of historicity in temporality," and the rootedness of temporality in historicity.[146] Thus, according to Derrida, Heidegger's treatment of historicity in *Being and Time* as a subordinate mode of the temporality of Being was a function of Western metaphysics' privileging of presence that Heidegger himself aimed to destroy.[147] Heidegger's "solicit[ation]" of metaphysics' "privileging of the Present" in order to uncover the historical reality of Being ironically reinstated metaphysics' elevation of the present and demotion of history.[148]

Derrida modulated the strange loop of Heidegger's *destruction* of metaphysics to enhance his close attention to the linguistic contradictions that subverted an author's goals. He came to consider the hierarchical opposition between temporality and historicity that Heidegger unintentionally upheld in *Being and Time* as an example of the control Western metaphysics exerted on all texts. On March 29, 1965, in his seminar's last session, Derrida proposed that the "destruction," as he retranslated it, *deconstruction*, of metaphysical dualisms will be "accomplished slowly, patiently," "tak[ing] hold" of not only "the *signification* history," but also "the whole of language, of sciences, of the human, of the world."[149] For Derrida, then, any identification of the truth of any text valorized presumed present— central or key—meanings while necessarily marginalizing or outright suppressing others in said text. Such a claim constructed a hierarchy or contradiction in the text. Elaborated in the several years following his

Heidegger seminar, Derrida's deconstructive strategy first highlighted this tension and then proceeded to subvert it by showing that the text's apparently incidental, or absent, meanings were actually constitutive of what were presumed essential features of the text. This summary is deceptively simple, too pat, though, and not only due to the seemingly pointillist manner in which Derrida wrote. Derrida's "deconstruction" *required* texts; his dizzying multiplication of conceptual terms—"différance," "trace," "supplément," "mark," etc.—were teased out of and/or grafted onto vocabularies in the writings that he painstakingly read, and each term signified the text's deconstruction. The interpretive tapestry Derrida wove thus, like the New Critics, hewed closely to words on the page. And like de Man, Derrida stared the logical inconsistencies of the text down, for it was there where the institution of his deconstruction transpired.

A year and a half after his ENS Heidegger seminar, Derrida's deconstructive intervention at Hopkins, written in a feverish ten days and delivered in English, became remembered as the event's "event." It did so for several reasons. The year 1966 had already become the annus mirabilis of structuralism, with important texts of the movement published a mere six months before the symposium, while structuralist slogans—the "death of man," "paradigm shift," and the like—were printed as headlines in major French newspapers and miraculously traced into the sands of the Côte d'Azur. At Hopkins, Derrida shrewdly took the opportunity to make his mark, challenging the structuralist enterprise in toto by pinpointing the metaphysical hierarchies that subverted the truth claims in the texts of Claude Lévi-Strauss. Though barely known in America outside a few anthropologists, Lévi-Strauss, the king of structuralism who chose not to attend because of a grueling travel schedule, was, as stated in the Ford Foundation proposal, "something of a culture hero . . . among European intellectuals."[150] Derrida was more than willing to play the dramatic part of Oedipus. Yet Derrida left such an impression in Baltimore also because his paper aligned with organizers' aim to help "native" critics escape their methodological malaise. Vanguard critics still hoped to subvert the reading parameters made customary by the New Critics, even if their work had become mostly an implicit reference point. Here was a French philosopher offering critics demanding ways to read texts foreign enough to seem wholly new yet familiar enough to incorporate into existing theoretical vocabularies and interpretive procedures.

Derrida's coup de grâce in his Hopkins paper best displays how his exacting isolation of texts' contradictions intersected with vanguard critics', especially de Man's, postformalist preoccupations with poetic language. According to Derrida, Western metaphysics' privileging of the self-presence of meaning constructed the conceptual paradoxes that undermined the foundations of Claude Lévi-Strauss's writings: "The ethnologist [Lévi-Strauss] accepts into his discourse the premises of ethnocentrism [Western metaphysical dualisms] at the very moment when he is employed in denouncing them."[151] Lévi-Strauss himself admitted that the "incest-prohibition," which he maintained in his foundational text *The Elementary Structures of Kinship* (1949) set in motion the elementary relations of kinship, made a "scandal" out of the "nature/culture opposition," because it "seems to require *at one and the same time* the predicates of nature and those of culture."[152] The incest prohibition appeared grounded in nature and in this sense could be called universal. But the incest prohibition was clearly also an intentional ban, an adopted custom, and a "system of norms and interdicts; in this sense one could call it cultural."[153] As in Nietzsche's, Freud's, and Heidegger's texts, which received Derrida's deconstructive treatment in earlier sections of his paper, Lévi-Strauss, acknowledging that the incest prohibition was both natural *and* cultural, "destroy[ed]" the entire system of concepts that he used to center his investigations.[154] Indeed, Lévi-Strauss's self-subversion, for Derrida, was structural, inescapable, and unavoidable, because the scandalous incest prohibition that Lévi-Strauss used to organize his text looped back upon itself, performing the deconstruction of the Western metaphysical nature/culture opposition. This was consequential stuff, Derrida implied, because if the incest prohibition was natural *and* cultural, and if this prohibition organized the elementary relations of kinship, then all the relations of society and culture emerged as forms of the nature/culture paradox. Not to put too fine a point on it: all texts were deconstructive.

While every formal presentation at the Hopkins symposium crackled with raw energy, only Derrida's self-contradictory Lévi-Strauss so spectacularly affirmed and undermined the event's organizers' aims. For a plurality of critical vocabularies was considered in Baltimore, though grand hopes to establish structuralism as a comprehensive methodology for the human sciences were dashed; what was supposed to be structuralism's triumph in America produced a nemesis: Derrida. Still, relationships were established and allegiances were made at the event that, in the coming years, helped disseminate not only Derrida's anti-metaphysical philosophy but other work also known as "post-structuralism" as well. Alan Bass, a leader of the Student Committee at the symposium, became a major translator of Derrida's writings during the 1970s, for instance. More generally, Derrida's deconstructive underscoring of the paradoxes that subverted Lévi-Strauss's text resonated with work already undertaken by vanguard critics. Committed to mobilizing novel vocabularies, these critics' postformalist attention to the ironies and contradictions of the literary work paralleled Derrida's reading strategy. Even Derrida's critique of Husserl exerted a certain pull on American phenomenological literary critics. Nevertheless, foreshadowing the widespread confusion that Derrida's project would generate in America, consider how he responded to a question about his reading strategy during the discussion that followed his Hopkins paper: "I believe . . . that I was quite explicit about the fact that nothing of what I said had a destructive meaning. Here or there I have used the word *déconstruction*, which has nothing to do with destruction. That is to say, it is simply a question of . . . being alert to the implications, to the historical sedimentation of the language that we use—and that is not destruction."[155]

(Relatively) Proximate Repercussions of the Symposium

As far-reaching as the effects of Derrida's Baltimore paper were, his intellectual dynamite also had more immediate repercussions, affecting the intellectual trajectories of two leading vanguard critics. J. Hillis Miller missed Derrida's paper, which was delivered on Friday, October 21, at 10:30 a.m., the second-to-last slot at the four-day event and exactly during Miller's teaching time. He received Derrida's bracing message nonetheless, albeit secondhand and from a surprising source: his old mentor George Poulet, who had moved to the University of Zürich in 1957. Poulet was the first to sing the praises of Derrida's paper to Miller. "With great generosity," Miller recalled, Poulet explained that Derrida's presentation "was without doubt the most important paper in the conference."[156] Such unadulterated praise is rare in the academy, even more so given that, while Poulet and Derrida shared an interest in Husserlian phenomenology, Poulet's uses of Husserl ran counter to Derrida's. From the philosopher's perspective, Poulet's thematizations of an origin that organized an author's oeuvre and that provided access to the author's mental world were metaphysical illusions of presence, hence why Poulet's enthusiasm piqued an interest in Miller. If his former mentor was impressed, then surely Miller, as open as ever to incorporating phenomenological hermeneutics into his literary-critical work, should consider the merit of Derrida's work.

Derrida's Hopkins performance would also affect Paul de Man's professional life. Unlike Miller, de Man had met the philosopher before Baltimore; the medium, however, was *par l'intermédiaire du texte*. In 1963, Derrida had reviewed a book by Geneva critic of consciousness Jean Rousset, *Forme et signification* (1962) in Georges Bataille's journal *Critique*.[157] Rousset's text, which he himself said was indebted to "Russian formalists, Anglo-Saxon criticism, in particular American New Critics," likely engaged de Man because his evolving postformalist response to literature's imperative to be read as literature aligned with Derrida's subversive response to the control Western metaphysics exerted over the interpretation of texts.[158] Rousset, the philosopher argued in his review, used a metaphysical opposition between form and meaning that unintentionally undermined his structuralist aims. Rousset's "notion of structure," which "refer[ed] only to . . . geometric or morphological space," "treated the form as the work . . . as if . . . in the masterpiece—the wellbeing of the work was without history."[159] In other words, the meaning of a text, for Rousset, was reducible to a geometric structure. Such an ultrastructuralism helped Rousset identify a text's form, Derrida generously acknowledged. But Rousset's valorization of "spatial models, mathematical functions, lines, and forms" concealed the force of language, the force responsible for shaping the text's form or structure.[160] "Form," Derrida wrote, "fascinates when one no longer has the force [of language] to understand [the] force [of language] from within itself."[161] To interrupt the spell cast by a frozen form, Derrida encouraged consideration of "an *economy*" that escaped and undermined the "system of metaphysical oppositions" between form and meaning.[162] Such an economy was neither a "pure, shapeless force" nor forceless shape but an organization of linguistic differences, differences of site as much as differences of intensity.[163] Inadvertently bringing into sharp relief the generative excess of language, Rousset, according to Derrida, reawakened "the nonspatiality or original spatiality" in the term structure: "the play going on within it metaphorically," that is, as Rodolphe Gasché summarized years later, "the play of displacement that characterized language in depth."[164]

Derrida's underlining of the form/meaning opposition in Rousset's text caught the eye of de Man, whose postformalist project, by the time of the Hopkins symposium, was well under way.[165] There were nevertheless key differences between their work. Often focusing on the texts of European Romantics in an apodictic fashion and with an austere language that bordered on astringent, de Man focused on how poetic language subverted attempts to impart a wholeness and harmony, a presence, to the text. Writing in mischievously byzantine style and with a panache that enacted a message about the figurative nature of language and meaning, Derrida often concentrated on the "play" of a text, the "event" or linguistic force that undermined metaphysical efforts to (re)present structures (or forms) of meaning. De Man and Derrida, however, shared the aim to identify the onto-theological foundations, the unstable hierarchical oppositions, the, one might say, postmodern paradoxes that organized texts. All this they realized over an early breakfast at the Hopkins symposium while divulging to each other their preoccupation with Jean-Jacques Rousseau's "L'Essai sur l'origine des langues" (1781).[166] After their conversation, de Man found himself "anxious to define" his way of reading vis-à-vis Derrida's.[167] De Man's apprehension sprang from at least two sources: he had reached conclusions similar to Derrida's about the temporality of form over a decade ago, as in his 1955 essay on Heidegger's reading of Hölderlin's poetry; and, for de Man, Rousseau was no less than the Ur-Romantic, the writer who enacted and encapsulated the post-Romantic predicament of existence.

The stakes were thus high, not only for the field of Rousseau studies but for de Man as well. Fortune favors the bold, though, and de Man would embrace the opportunity to establish the parameters of his reading procedures via Derrida's reading of Rousseau's 1781 essay, published in the September–October 1966 issue of *Cahiers pour l'Analyse*. As a model of his deconstructive response to the metaphysics of presence, Derrida's essay was then included in the second half of *De la grammatologie* (1967), the text that made Derrida an academic celebrity in France. While de Man's reading of Derrida's reading of Rousseau was not published until 1970, in French in *Poétique*, it would come to attract an enormous amount of commentary.[168] De Man's interpretation of Derrida also played a starring role in shaping de Man and Derrida's friendship and the terms upon which each man's work was understood in relation to the other's in America. Looking back on the exchange in 1984, Derrida himself noted that "the entire . . . history of de Manian deconstruction passes through Rousseau."[169]

As accurate as that might be, de Man's institution of American deconstruction by way of his 1970 article on Derrida turned partly on how he incorporated central features of the philosopher's project into his post-formalist approach to the text. De Man, for example, praised Derrida for not focusing on Rousseau's "psychological idiosyncras[ies]," like so many readers, such as Geneva critic of consciousness Jean Starobinski, who argued in 1957 that Rousseau's paranoia and preoccupations with political persecution shaped all his writings.[170] Rather than offering the theme of Rousseau as a mad father of mad fantasies, Derrida read Rousseau "without leaving the text."[171] Doing so disclosed to Derrida, according to de Man, "that Rousseau's own texts provide the strongest evidence against his alleged doctrine" of "unmediated presence," a metaphysical creed, a phonocentrism really, that gave "primacy of voice over the written word" and adhered "to the mythology of original innocence."[172] Whereas others persistently read Rousseau as describing and longing for naïve ways of living in an immediate relation to truth, to "unmediated presence," Derrida interpreted Rousseau's text to show that Rousseau's commitment to the avowed moment "of unity that exists at the beginning of things, when desire coincides with enjoyment, the self and other are united in the maternal warmth of their common origin, and consciousness speaks with the voice of truth," always intimated an earlier moment. Rousseau, for instance, asserted that the origin of the voice was in the South and that writing was secondary, its origin in the North.[173] But, Derrida underscored, Rousseau subverted these declared moments of self-presence in the text because he described gestures as "a re-course to a more natural, more expressive, more immediate sign."[174] Insofar as a gesture was a form of writing (text), and since Rousseau described "writing" as anterior to speech and, in a manner, basic to it, Rousseau implicitly overturned the priority he explicitly gave to speech over writing. For Derrida, Rousseau's statements in solidarity with metaphysical origins and states of nature therefore "possess . . . all the elements of distance and negation that prevent written language from ever achieving a condition of unmediated presence."[175] In other words, the hierarchical opposition Rousseau erected between speech and writing (or the text) Rousseau himself subverted with and in his text.

Yet, for de Man to truly institute his deconstruction he needed to make a major methodological contribution to the understanding of literature's irreducibility to other discourses. To achieve this goal, he demonstrated the superior rigor of his fidelity to the text, reading Rousseau purely as a self-aware *linguistic object*. Derrida, de Man noted, contended that Rousseau *unintentionally* undermined his professed ontology of presence. For de Man, such a reference to Rousseau's consciousness led Derrida to exclude de Man's insight that Rousseau was "not deluded and said what he meant to say."[176] "The key," de Man wrote, "to the status of Rousseau's language is not to be found . . . in his greater or lesser awareness or control over the cognitive value of his language" but "only in the knowledge that this language, as language, conveys about itself, thereby asserting the priority of the category of language over that of presence—which is precisely Derrida's thesis."[177] Cleverly integrating Derrida's thesis about Rousseau's self-subversion into his own strict attention to the text as a Möbius-strip-like linguistic object additionally presented de Man with the chance to answer the question that critics since the early twentieth century had posed: What was the object of literary science? For de Man, it was the knowledge that a text communicated about itself. And the knowledge that Rousseau's language (text) communicated about itself was "'literary,' in the full sense of the term," de Man argued.[178] The literariness of Rousseau's text, the reflexive understanding it conveyed, was the form that Rousseau's text assumed to flag its own rhetorical mode: Rousseau declared the superiority of voice over the written word but the practice, the figural or linguistic devices, of his text exercised a sort of metacognition of his subversion of the priority he gave to speech. "Rousseau's text," de Man wrote, "has no blind spots: it accounts at all moments for its own rhetorical mode." "There is no need to deconstruct Rousseau," de Man concluded.[179]

De Man's 1970 article not only prominently displayed his meticulous attention to the text but also expanded the analytical scope of his post-formalism. According to de Man, Derrida's blindness to his initial insight about Rousseau's text was "the *necessary* correlative of the rhetorical nature of literary language."[180] And such blindness, for de Man, could occur at *any* site in the round-robin-like circuit among "text-reader-critic."[181] He argued, for example, that Derrida's "historical scheme" about a period of logocentrism, of Western metaphysics' privileging of the apparent truth of self-presence of the spoken word over that of the deferred and different meaning of writing, to which Rousseau belonged, was ironically derived from Rousseau's diachronic fiction of the origins of language. For de Man, the literariness of Rousseau's text inescapably molded Derrida's textual imitation, rendering Derrida's "vocabulary of substance and presence . . . no longer" as vocabulary "used declaratively but rhetorically, for the very reasons that are being (metaphorically) stated."[182] Derrida's "historical scheme" became a rhetorical maneuver, a narrative ultimately about figurative language mistaken as literal language.

While it would be a few more years before de Man refined his proto-deconstruction into the approach he used in his 1970 article, de Man's meeting with Derrida at the 1966 Hopkins symposium motivated him to stake his deconstructive flag. Not only did the postformalist de Man avoid sociohistorical reference to read texts—Rousseau's and Derrida's—as linguistic objects that uncannily folded in on themselves. As de Man's followers would later suggest, his response to and formulations about literary language also bestowed—or, rather, recognized—literature's authority over other forms of discourse. Even a philosopher of Derrida's caliber, it was pointed out, found literature's rigorous reflexivity unmasterable. Demonstrating such comprehensive claims for the critical and uncontrollable power of figurative language would become the mission of the Yale School in the 1970s.

A Vanguard Critic Abroad: Hartman and a Potential Postformalist Overcoming of Structuralism

Testifying to both the intellectual attention that the "structuralist controversy" received in Europe and the growing dominance of American universities in higher education, notices of the Hopkins symposium appeared in major French, German, Russian, and Swiss publications. Structuralism was certainly, though fleetingly, on academic humanists' minds across the North Atlantic world, and Geoffrey Hartman was no exception. But while

Derrida was impishly deconstructing structuralism in Baltimore, Hartman, an alternate presenter at the Hopkins event, was a visiting professor at the University of Zürich (UZH).[183] He was substituting for de Man, who, in 1963, persuaded deans at Cornell and UZH to each pay him full salary and reduce his teaching loads; both schools could enjoy de Man's presence. When de Man invited Hartman to join him at Cornell in 1965, Hartman had agreed to spell de Man at UZH when needed.[184] And before returning to Ithaca in the fall of 1966, Hartman gave the inaugural lecture of the General and Comparative Literature Seminar at the Freie Universität Berlin. Hungarian-Jewish critic Péter Szondi had invited Hartman, with whom he shared an interest in new reading techniques, to the Freie Universität Berlin, a university, like those in America, shaped by the Cold War; the institution's very name signaled its position as part of the "free western world," and its founding, in 1948, was supported by funds from the Allies, including the United States.

Published in a 1966 special issue of *Yale French Studies* (edited by Jacques Ehrmann) on structural theory and practice, Hartman's Berlin talk revealed his historicizing instincts still in tension with his acute awareness of poetic forms. He proposed a new solution to the problem of formalism while exploring how criticism, literary anthropology, and poetic form converged in Lévi-Strauss's structuralism. He began by linking the search for a myth of unity that shielded art against social fragmentation to literary studies' shifting position in the academy. Literary education, he mused, was in "crisis" because "the classics have lost their power to be models for communal behavior."[185] For Hartman, nonliterary forms of media were displacing the formative role that "the classics" played in cultivating students' character and the inculcation of shared values. Hartman was here amplifying concerns, widely voiced by his colleagues in the mid-1960s, about the extent to which technologies of the electronic age contributed to the displacement of the centrality of literary studies in university life. In 1964, Marshall McLuhan famously argued that electronic media had refashioned the ways people exercised their senses. The content of these new media mattered little as the "medium is the message."[186] Or, as an archformalist might say, "The form is the content." That these changes seemed threatening to literary education was a bit ironic, because it was the same wealth that supported both forms of electronic media and the academic revolution, the latter of which helped make the literary critic central to humanities departments' economy of prestige.

Nevertheless, Hartman stressed, the decline in the cachet of "the classics" had its upside: it motivated literary critics and scholars to find and develop critical methodologies that, by aiming to decipher and categorize poetic forms, resulted in "a deepening insight into the nature of model-making" as in the "myth-criticism from Jane Harrison to Northrop Frye, and of the anthropology from Durkheim to Lévi-Strauss."[187] However, Hartman emphasized, somewhat reprising arguments he made in his 1965 Yale paper, critics have too quickly rushed to move beyond formalism, notably by fitting the self-enclosed forms of individual works of art into a totalizing conception of the world of art, like in Frye's myth criticism, the only major approach to literature considered a serious alternative to the New Criticism in the 1950s.[188] With their hierarchical ordering, starting at the level of the letter and rising to the all-inclusive revelations of a divine poet or transcendental truth seeker, myth critics constructed a closed and complete system, what Frye labeled "the verbal universe."[189] Literary structuralists should resist this temptation of presence, Hartman implored, for it courted the violent response of an uncritical mind to what was an uncontrollable universe. Not rejecting structuralism per se, Hartman held instead that the critic required a criticism mindful of the link between poetic form and history: "What we need is a theory of recurrence (repetition) [of poetic form] that includes a theory of discontinuity."[190] Only such a theory that exerted "a genuine historical consciousness vis-à-vis itself" could help the critic avoid reducing distinct literary forms to a deadening sameness and confront the specificity of "the classics."[191] This and no more could "save 'the common nature' of man."[192]

To illuminate how such a postformalist theory could fully understand and appreciate the repetitions and discontinuities of its literary material, Hartman riffed on a parable by modernist Franz Kafka. "Leopards," Kafka wrote, "break into the temple and drink the sacrificial chalices dry; this occurs repeatedly, again and again: finally it can be reckoned on beforehand and becomes part of the ceremony."[193] Once sacrilegious, the raids of the prowling, rapacious leopards become central. Hartman's lesson was clear: "Every society, every relationship, every system [has] its necessary and permitted profanations" that, by way of recurrences, are incorporated into routine.[194] Read as a parable for literary studies, Kafka's tale illustrated what was, in established disciplinary terms, prohibited: the mediation between repetition and the incongruity of poetic forms, social structures, and mental life. By examining this complex dialectic between the "temple," the "chalice," and the "ceremony," literary critics might respect the differences that a structure or form assumed in a specific literary work as well as speaking to communal values and models of behavior. Crucially, though, Hartman himself hesitated at the formalist impasse, neither claiming, with Frye, to move beyond formalism by challenging notions of the self-contained harmony of artworks, nor, like Lévi-Strauss, moving beyond formalism toward shared anthropological truths. In Berlin, structuralism provided Hartman with a platform to theorize postformalist manners of reading, yet these paths he had yet to tread in any specific manner.

From Protodeconstruction to Deconstruction
(on the East and West Coasts)

During a deluge of exchanges with one another and their newfound confederate Derrida in the second half of the 1960s, vanguard critics would bring their postformalist endeavors into tighter focus. While continuing to constructively subvert New Critical interpretive strictures, these critics often enhanced their protodeconstructive reading methods with a renewed devotion to the text's verbal forms. This focus on language was more than vanguard critics' pet project; it was a sign of the postmodern academic times. In his April 1968 memorandum for the University of California San Diego colloquium, organizer Morton W. Bloomfield asked attendees to consider how "the methods of the humanities are 'languages' insofar as they are systems of rules with their vocabularies which unite man with himself, with society and with the world just as the linguistic system united meaning and sound."[195] Placing the "linguistic system" at the center of humanistic inquiry, the UCSD colloquium helped promulgate the idea among humanists that language, rather than being an instrument for knowing something prior to or as a means of self-expression, defined human beings. In part because the New Critical substructure of their entire discipline oriented them toward the text as a linguistic object, vanguard critics enjoyed a privileged position from which to assess and appreciate the precise power of language. These critics were also adept at tapping and then navigating available resources for the humanities—resources that included monies awarded by the Ford Foundation, the Rockefeller Foundation, and *Daedalus* (the journal of the American Academy of Arts and Sciences). This meant the vanguard critics had more than the average academic's chance to pursue robust research programs. At decade's end, their work had built the foundation for the institution of deconstruction in the American academy.

Consider how the innovative research pursued at the Ford Foundation Continuing Seminars and colloquia at Hopkins's Humanities Center sustained the momentum of the earlier symposium. A group of younger Hopkins faculty that included J. Hillis Miller took the center's reins; they decided that the intellectual architecture of the university offered a chance to reorganize seminars, hitherto unadventurously organized by period and discipline. Miller and his colleagues made the center a place for undertaking theoretical reflection on the humanities and the forging of methodological connections among humanistic disciplines and the study of texts.[196] In the 1967–68 academic year, for instance, the center held seminars ambitiously and unorthodoxly dedicated to "Interpretation: Theory and Practice."[197] Derrida, then a visiting professor in Hopkins's Department of Romance Languages, contributed to the conversation with his colloquium, "Literature and Truth: The Concept of *Mimesis*."[198] In his first sessions, Derrida reworked an ENS lecture, "Plato's Pharmacy," that remained within the scope of conventional philosophical concerns. In later sessions, though, he mixed genres, fields of inquiry, even disciplines, outlining parts of two elaborate lectures he would eventually give in 1969 to the Groupe d'études théoriques, organized by the Parisian avant-garde literary journal *Tel Quel*, that juxtaposed excerpts from Plato's *Phaedrus* with Stéphane Mallarmé's prose poem "Mimique" (1886).[199]

Not just the form but the content of Derrida's 1968 Hopkins lectures deconstructively dug deep into "interpretation." "The whole history of the interpretation of the arts and letters," Derrida wrote in the 1972 essay based on his lectures in Baltimore and Paris, was determined by the issue of *mimêsis*, Greek for "imitation" or "representation."[200] According to Derrida, Western metaphysics of presence's control over the interpretation of texts resulted in the denouncement or outright exclusion of mimesis from the more important contemplation of "ideas," nonphysical but substantial concepts that—ostensibly—represented transcendental reality. Derrida turned to an ancient textual source of this opposition, the *Republic*, where Plato condemned poets for producing dangerously seductive imitations of life. Yet Plato's metaphysically induced denunciation of mimesis served a more important purpose for Derrida; it was a "pre-text" for his deconstructive reading of Mallarmé's "Mimique," which Derrida viewed as raising the question "What is literature?"[201] Instead of directly and philosophically answering literature's imperative to be interpreted as literature, however, Derrida suggested that "Mimique" *performed* a notion of mimesis whereby it was no longer possible to consider literature in opposition to (either present or postponed) original reality, as Plato had. For instance, the mime discussed in "Mimique" was Paul Marguerite's Pierrot, whose pantomime booklet mimed (pictured) the murder of his wife. But the mime did not perform a reality that occurred, that was occurring, or that he projected would occur. Mallarmé's discussion of Pierrot's mime was thus neither the empty signifier of fiction nor the full signified of some reality or history but somewhere between these two. The mime in "Mimique" as well as "Mimique" itself enacted a "play" of mimesis; this was a "play" that had no original, no outside referent, no outside text, and demonstrated, for Derrida, that life, like literature, was derivative, an order of mirroring instead of the hierarchic logic of truth and illusion. Like Pierrot's mime, literature, Derrida citing "Mimique" wrote, was "confined to a perpetual allusion without breaking . . . the mirror," pointing toward, without ever becoming, reality.[202]

The rigor, range, and radicalness of Derrida's anti-metaphysical response to the claim of literature at the Humanities Center impressed his twenty auditors. He had in fact intended his lectures to undermine the assumptions of the kind of thematic criticism practiced by members of the Geneva school of criticism, several of whom were former members of the Hopkins faculty. While Geneva critic of consciousness Jean-Pierre Richard, in *L'univers imaginaire de Mallarmé* (1961) extracted the "'blank' and the 'fold'" from Mallarmé's text as "themes or as meanings" to be "mastered," Derrida read the linguistic devices and figurative language of Mallarmé's text as "undecidables," a term he used to describe how Mallarmé's "allusion[s] or 'suggestion[s]'" of reality were a self-subverting consequence of the systemization of meaning, when a predicate that authorized the rules of proof in a system (or form) could neither be proven nor disproven within this system.[203] Derrida's foregroundings of the "undecidability" of Mallarmé's "allusions" intersected with vanguard critics' pushing of the New Critics' devotion to the text's verbal forms to its logical limits.[204] Derrida's seminar likely resonated with listeners at Hopkins due to the manner of his presentation as well. For his self-conscious, intricate, and highly theatrical efforts in Paris mimicked Mallarmé, whose unfinished work known as *Le livre* was poetic, liturgical, dramatic. Derrida's blackboard confirmed his aim to perform his reading of Mallarmé as a simulation or metafiguration of the Mallarméan text; he designated his lectures a "double session."[205] Though he taught his seminars in French, Derrida's auditors at Hopkins were "bowled over" by his engagement with the literariness of the text. "I was straightaway fascinated by the power of Derrida's discourse," Miller recalled. "I'd never heard anything like it. Very quickly, we became friends, and got into the habit of having lunch together once a week."[206]

Much like the way de Man persuaded Miller to refocus some of his scholarly interests during a discussion in 1965 on New Haven's Wall Street, Derrida now prominently stamped Miller's intellectual formation at Hopkins; Miller would use aspects of Derrida's project to transmute his attachment to Pouletian phenomenological-thematic criticism into a postmodern deconstructive approach to literary texts. In his memorandum for the *Daedalus*-funded UCSD colloquium, for example, Miller pondered whether "perhaps Jacques Derrida [was] right" in his Baltimore paper "to see as one characteristic of the current situation in the humanities the rejection of older models of structure."[207] Such a refusal of metaphysical models by American humanists, Miller continued, was part of what Derrida identified as a "turning in the tradition of interpretation," a shift that underlined that "consciousness is language" and that "language (and therefore literature) is fundamentally temporal rather than spatial."[208] Miller's new emphasis on (literary) language not only had much to do with fulfilling the colloquium organizers' request; his "linguistic turn" also had to do with how he, while employing some Pouletian talk of "consciousness," was already habituated to view literature as a linguistic object because of the New Critical parameters that constrained his profession.

Yet another way Miller underwent his Derridean conversion in the context of literary studies in America was Miller's suggestion that adopting Derrida's perspective may result in a deconstructive notion of the scientificity of the humanities. Derrida's ideas, Miller argued, would not simply result in the subversion of the hierarchical opposition between seeing interpretation as an objective *or* subjective act, a deconstruction that might fruitfully respond to colloquium organizers' contradictory command "to make interpretation an objective discipline, a 'science of man'" *and* an acknowledgment that "this may be incompatible with the fact that the quality of subjective life is a main subject matter of the arts."[209] Such a deconstructively rigorous science of interpretation, Miller concluded, might even help humanists respond to "the unprecedented crisis within American society today."[210] "I am," he wrote, "writing this memorandum on the morning after the first serious episode of civil disorder [inserted by Miller: in Baltimore] during the fifteen years I have lived here, with riot, murder, arson, looting on a large scale and the city at this moment under a kind of martial law."[211]

This convergence of sixties events and Miller's "linguistic turn" prove wrong those who would accuse the American institution of deconstruction of antihistoricism and antihumanism. For it was amid the Baltimore unrest of 1968, which, along with a wave of civil disturbances in 125 cities across America, began after Martin Luther King Jr.'s murder on April 4, that Miller came to believe that flagging the self-subversions of hierarchical oppositions in literary masterpieces could help colleagues face and understand humanity's viciousness and absurdity. By "confronting . . . the violence and irrationality within human nature, . . . literature . . . has given man the power to see that the violence is within us and not outside. . . . One thinks today . . . of [W. B.] Yeats's brilliant dramatization, in 'Nineteen Hundred and Nineteen,' of the gradual internalization of violence until: We who seven years ago / Talked of honour and of truth, / Shriek with pleasure if we show / The weasel's twist, the weasel's tooth."[212] Contemplating the failure of public life during the Irish Civil War, Yeats's 1921 modernist poem vividly expressed how violence was embedded in civilized beliefs, attitudes, and values. For Miller, if humanists, like Derrida, highlighted how texts' nonsymmetrical oppositions led to the internalization of violence by privileging certain vocabularies as rational or civilized while marginalizing or excluding a second, "different" set of vocabularies as irrational or uncivilized, then their work would again be relevant to Americans' contemporary experience of chaos and confusion. "The relevance of the humanities," Miller wrote, "will be discovered only by ways of interpretation which get us back inside . . . the great works."[213] And, for Miller, the map that these "great works" provided for finding the cultural importance of each humanities discipline was legible after recognizing and rigorously performing the transformation of interpretation undertaken by Derrida's deconstructions.

Recalled from the wilderness of Cornell in 1967 to assume a coveted joint professorship of English and comparative literature at Yale, Hartman used his UCSD memorandum to further reflect on the theoretical and methodological issues he had raised in Berlin. But in his 1968 paper an even greater attentiveness to American humanists' anxiety about adopting the language of scientific professionals now enjoined his subdued call for fellow critics to develop postformalist ways of reading. The UCSD organizers' appeal to consider a comprehensive theory of the humanities, Hartman observed, was "the main question of recent years," and this request "raised [the issue] again . . . [about] to what extent humanistic studies can consider themselves . . . a social science or a 'science humaine.'"[214] Hartman addressed this issue about the degree to which humanistic inquiry could be scientific by pivoting to a consideration of the practice of "close reading," as standardized by the New Critics, which, he argued, his colleagues were beginning to see as having more "moral rather than true intellectual virtue."[215] Despite all the advanced work done since the end of World War II to move literary studies past imprecise interpretive humanist procedures, Hartman argued, Anglo-American critics believed that a sufficiently rigorous method of reading applicable to all literature seemed improbable. "Many of us feel that the limits of practical criticism have been reached."[216] Yet such a belief was but a loss of imagination as much as nerve, Hartman thought; it existed only because critics overlooked the "one 'science' that binds together not just the humanities but all intellectual activity: the science of interpretation."[217] Thus, for Hartman, a "science of interpretation" was possibly, even justifiably, applicable not only to the reading of literature but to the humanities in general.[218] Precisely what this "science of interpretation" was and how it would extend from poetry to the prose of history, society, and culture Hartman left for future consideration. Still, he was working on it, with his proposal of this topic itself indicative of how much his historicizing disposition strained against his self-aware consciousness of poetic forms and the universal implications he saw in a postformalist response to literature.

Deconstructive Programming: From Hopkins
to the American Literary-Critical Stage

Without doubt, the Hopkins Humanities Center became the most prominent incubator for and distributor of structuralist and poststructuralist
studies in the United States during the late 1960s. The center was also
at the heart of the "short-lived Hopkins School," composed of de Man,
Miller, and Derrida.[219] De Man had left Cornell in 1967 for the position
of professor of humanities at Hopkins; the prospect of a two-year leave
of absence as well as access to the innovative research conducted and
taught at the center lured him. During this period, de Man continued to
challenge New Critical reading strictures, and he did so in ways that pre-
figured his postmodern arguments in his 1970 reading of Derrida reading
Rousseau about the supremacy of literary language. "Whether American
or European," de Man explained in a paper presented at Hopkins's History of Ideas Club, "the main critical approaches of the last decades were
all founded on the implicit assumption that literature is . . . a distinctive
way of being in the world to be understood in terms of its own purposes
and intentions."[220] De Man found this assumption persuasive; literature's
difference from nonliterature was, for him, ontological, a question of
its form or shape, its material existence. What did vex de Man, though,
was New Critics' unexamined faith in the interpretive abilities of critics,
wholesale rejection of intentionality, and concentration on "the surface
dimensions of language."[221] According to de Man, these three intellectual habits prohibited the New Critics from sufficiently and scrupulously
defending the very idea of literary autonomy upon which their formalist
practice was based.

In his paper, de Man aimed to challenge New Critics' views about the
relationship between intention and language to protect the formalist view
of literature's independence from other discourses. For de Man, New Critics' naïve empiricism, which equated the literary object with a natural
object free from the influence of an author's intention, ensured that they
ignored the deeper dimensions of the text's language. De Man, with his
politics of poetic difference, saw the literary text as an intentional entity,
though its forms and meanings never coincide to produce a plenitude of
presence. Such a view subverted New Critical orthodoxy about the self-
enclosed, organic, and whole artwork. It also paved the way for a necessarily rigorous and anti-metaphysical definition of the "literary." "Literary
'form,'" de Man stressed, "is the result of the dialectic interplay between
the prefigurative structure of the foreknowledge and the intent at totality of the interpretative process. This . . . completed form never exists
as a concrete aspect of the work that could coincide with a sensorial or

semantic dimension of the language. It is constituted in the mind of the interpreter as the work discloses itself in response to his questioning. But this dialogue between work and interpreter is endless."[222] According to de Man, then, the interchange between a text's poetic form and meaning and the reader of said text established the "literary 'form,'" though this process always remained incomplete, never reaching a stable presence, as the "literary 'form'" never accorded with the language used to describe it. Such a "historical" view of literary form preserved a text's autonomy while also undercutting attempts, occasionally inspired by American ego psychologists, to extend the belief in an artwork's supposed organic unity to an author's life, with this life seen to express a distinctive "identity theme" in the author's actions and texts. In a way, for de Man, the author's intention was buried within a text's language, but attempts to trace this intention in the text to its author was a metaphysical distraction from the labor of truly precise and scientific reading.

Now at Hopkins, de Man was endeavoring to forge a postformalist alliance; at the end of the fall of 1967, Derrida, at de Man's request, offered a seminar in Paris on "the philosophical foundations of literary criticism" for a dozen graduate students from Cornell and Hopkins.[223] In Baltimore, de Man used money from the Humanities Center—part of the 1965 Ford Foundation grant—to organize a colloquium in Zürich that aimed to inject ideas about the problems of literary interpretation deliberated at the Baltimore conference into European conversations.[224] Held from January 25 to January 27, 1968, the colloquium assembled eleven academics, bringing leading European structuralists, representatives of the Geneva school, and Heideggerian critics into dialogue. Participants in the Baltimore symposium on structuralism—such as Derrida—as well as visitors to the Ford Foundation Continuing Seminars joined the discussions.[225] The Zürich colloquium also introduced European critics unable to attend the Baltimore event, including Geneva school members Jean Starobinski, Jean-Pierre Richard, and Jean Rousset, and included papers by American critics, such as Miller, who addressed the topic of "first person form." Afterward, de Man summarized the Zürich papers as revolving around the issue of "the truth-value of the literary statement," which many had viewed as "rooted in the potential identity of sign and meaning," or form and content.[226] By event's end, participants, having grappled with the challenge radiating from semiology, the study of language as systems instead of as stemming from sociohistorical factors, mistrusted the presumed accord between signifier and signified. Rather than seeing words and things converge, participants underscored their separation, "put[ting]," de Man observed, "the categorical stability of time, self, and form, as the constitutive elements of the literary texts, into question."[227]

In this regard, de Man's postmodern response to the literary imperative was *just* ahead of not only American but European critics as well.

Almost concurrent with de Man's Zürich colloquium were his innovative presentations—which Miller eagerly attended—at Hopkins's Humanities Center as part of a 1968–69 lecture cycle devoted to "*Interpretation*, not the theory, alone, but also the practice, exegesis as well as hermeneutics in three fields—history, art, literature."[228] Published in 1969, de Man's lectures summarized his evolving postformalist views and, as he would note in 1983, "augur[ed] . . . a change not only in terminology and in tone, but in substance," away from "the thematic vocabulary of consciousness and of temporality" toward a "deliberate emphasis on rhetorical terminology."[229] Key to driving de Man in this deconstructive direction were his readings of the figures of "symbol" and "allegory." Much earlier criticism was rooted in an interpretation of the European Romantic aesthetic as opposing the figures of symbol and allegory. The former, as in the writings of Coleridge, Hegel, and generations of German philosophers and the speculations of New Critic W. K. Wimsatt, even fellow Romanticist M. H. Abrams, was often cast as organic and motivated (constrained by the signified); this concept of the "symbol," as Jonathan Freedman has written, was bound to presence, to the onto-theological view of language, to "literally the logocentric," to Christ, the "symbol of symbols" that promised "order and coherence," the metaphysical word made flesh.[230] The figure of allegory, in contrast, was frequently portrayed as mechanical, as arbitrary, as bound to absence. By highlighting how Romantics' poetry in fact subverted the well-established view of their texts as privileging the symbolist over allegorical aesthetic, de Man delivered two knockout blows: he unraveled the conventional reading that Romantic poetry "organically" reconciled mind and nature via the symbol, and he undermined accepted literary-critical traditions that presupposed that the symbolist aesthetic constituted prose and poetry.

De Man's meticulous reclamation of Romantics' prioritization of allegory was but one of a cascade of ramifying readings by the vanguard critics that operationalized deconstruction in America as a rejoinder to the literariness of the text. In the second of his lecture's two sections, de Man offered the unusual pairing of allegory and irony. Extending German philosopher Walter Benjamin's work of the late 1920s, he first examined the late eighteenth-century conflict between allegorical and symbolist aesthetics, retrieving from the early Romantics a lost rhetorical mode of allegory concealed by "a defensive strategy" of the symbol. "Whereas," de Man wrote in the published text based on his lecture, "the symbol postulates the possibility of an identity or identification, allegory designates primarily a distance in relation to its own origin, and renouncing the nostalgia and the desire to coincide, it establishes its language in the void of this temporal difference."[231] Found in lucid passages of Romantics' poetry—Rousseau always a favorite—this abyssal language that rejected the rejection of identity or origin was the figure of irony. Irony, for de Man, was therefore the rhetorical form of consciousness that split the subject, separating, dividing, and distinguishing the self from the self. Irony performed a "doublement," allowing the self to observe the self as an other. "Allegory and irony," de Man concluded, "are thus linked in their common discovery of a truly temporal predicament. . . . Both are determined by an authentic experience of temporality, which, seen from the point of the self engaged in the world, is a negative one."[232] Not the spatialization performed by the symbol, not the onto-theological reconciliation of subject and object, mind and matter, but the antihumanist negative division, due to the temporal dilemma as performed by the rhetorical figures of irony and allegory, articulated "the true voice" of Romanticism—according to de Man. And, because Romantics' poetry undermined the symbol/allegory opposition that informed literary humanist judgment, the reading techniques of "normal" academic criticism such as the New Criticism that see the symbol as offering a whole vision of "man," and even the canonical themes of literary histories—these all required revision along the lines that the Romantics themselves outlined almost two hundred years prior. When de Man's Hopkins lectures became articles, an even greater number of literary critics and their graduate students would wrestle with the revisions his new perspective and vocabulary merited.

Around the same time that de Man delivered his Hopkins lectures on allegory and irony, Derrida commenced his first "publicity tour" of the United States, adding his own "antihumanist" voice to the American institution of deconstruction. Embarking in mid-October 1968 on a lecture series at prestigious East Coast universities, Derrida came to appreciate the American style of education and, what was for him, its comfortable, peaceful environment, which he felt was far removed from the recent sixties turmoil at the ENS. In one paper, supported by the Ford Continuing Seminars series and given at an international colloquium in New York, Derrida, drawing on passages from Hegel, Kojève, Sartre, Nietzsche, and Heidegger, deconstructively answered the question "Where does France stand with regard to man?"[233] But Derrida's very question and his answers reflected how his interests diverged from those of many American literary critics, who were more prepared to consider the literary imperative than new ways to subversively respond to the metaphysical opposition between temporality and historicity that structured texts. In his paper, for instance, Derrida focused on selections from Heidegger's "Letter on 'Humanism'" (1947). Though Heidegger explicitly eschewed anthropocentrism, Derrida stressed, a Western metaphysical humanism remained implicit in his letter because Heidegger placed utmost significance on the closeness or immediacy of *Dasein* (human being) to Being for determining the formal structure of the question of Being: "The value of proximity . . . therefore decides the essential orientation of this analytic of Dasein."[234] Noting the metaphysical dualism that Heidegger erected in the text between the proximity/immediacy of *Dasein* to Being and historical humanism's distance and difference from Being, Derrida then showed the former terms as relying on the latter terms for establishing the form of the question of Being and how this reliance generated the deconstruction, not the destruction, of man: "It is within the enigma of a certain proximity, a proximity to itself and a proximity to being that we shall see constituting itself against humanism and against metaphysical anthropologism, another instance and another insistence of man, relaying, 'relevant,' replacing that which it destroys according to the channels . . . from which we will no doubt emerge."[235] What's more, for Derrida, this deconstruction of the metaphysical oppositions of a text like Heidegger's foregrounded an important decision: one could, as Heidegger unintentionally did, reveal the play between proximity and distance "without change of ground," running the risk of reaffirming or reiterating Western metaphysical dichotomies, or one could "decide to change ground, in a discontinuous and eruptive fashion, by stepping abruptly outside and by affirming absolute rupture and difference."[236] In accordance with his destabilizing engagement with the temporality/historicity binary, Derrida advocated employing both reading procedures, for the weaving and interlacing of interpretations that stood within and outside of metaphysics formed a "new style" of reading, a deconstructive one. For American critics still operating within New Critical interpretive armature, such philosophical questions were novel indeed.

Rounding Out a Half Decade of (Re)Visionary Endeavors

The Ford Foundation grant that underwrote so much advanced research and teaching at Hopkins ended in 1968, and vanguard critics were left to exploit other circuits for honing and promoting their reformist endeavors. Miller hoped to keep Derrida close, believing the French philosopher had much more to offer the critic's fellow Americans. In a June 2, 1969, letter, he thanked Derrida for "agree[ing] to come to the *Daedalus* conference," to be held in Bellagio, Italy, in September 1969. The conference was planned to extend the discussions begun at the May 1968 UCSD colloquium. "Your presence," Miller wrote to Derrida, "will make it more likely to be valuable, but the chance to talk to you and Paul, and to give others there a chance to meet you will be a thing of great personal value to me."[237] In a second letter that day, to de Man, Miller explained that he was "most anxious to see [Derrida] again and to have a chance to introduce him to some others who will be there (our friend Geoffrey, for example!)." That de Man would join Miller and Hartman in Bellagio was enough of an attraction for Derrida to consider attending. Miller wanted de Man, then still a colleague at Hopkins, to know this: "One of the things that I held out as a temptation to Jacques was the fact that you would be at the conference." Miller even fretted that, if de Man did not attend the conference, Derrida might get the wrong idea: "I'd be much disappointed if after all you will miss the conference, or at any rate should be let to know so he [Derrida] won't think I've got him there on false pretenses. (He mentions in his letter how he looks forward to seeing you there.)"[238]

All this strategizing achieved the desired result: Miller, de Man, Hartman, and (very likely) Derrida in the same room together, attending the *Daedalus*-sponsored meeting "The Role of Theory in the Humanistic Studies." Held September 4–7, 1969, at the Grand Hotel Villa Serbelloni, one of the oldest and most elegant hotels in Bellagio, poised on a peninsula that overlooks the luxurious blue waters of Lake Como, the gathering proved personally and intellectually rewarding for the twenty attending humanists. More than anything, though, the meeting crowned vanguard critics' half decade of conversations over how to overcome the interpretive roadblocks posed by formalist principles and set forth their reading strategies to members of top humanities departments in America. Bellagio organizers provided an ideal platform. They wanted participants to think big and consider "the theoretical bases of their studies and work toward some kind of critical philosophy of those disciplines that presently comprise the humanities."[239] Stephen R. Graubard, editor of the 1970 *Daedalus* volume that published the attendees' papers, reflected that participants explored "the boundaries *and* the possibilities of study in the humanities," sometimes by addressing "the intellectual fissures that have become apparent in our time."[240] Copious signs there were: the Soviet invasion of Czechoslovakia in 1968 and, one year later, armed clashes along the border between Russia and China; in America: anti-Vietnam marches, draft-card burnings, self-exilings, and other forms of protest. However obliquely, vanguard critics acknowledged these fissures, and as proof of the group's potent presence, the collected articles "concentrate[d] on one kind of document—the literary text."[241]

In Hartman's paper, which capped his late sixties postformalist efforts to square his historicizing instincts with his awareness of poetic forms, he launched a defense of art's uniqueness that he hoped could function

FIGURE 2.4 Attendees of "The Role of Theory in the Humanistic Studies," held in 1969 at the Grand Hotel Villa Serbelloni. *Standing, left to right*: M. H. Abrams, Paul de Man, Geoffrey H. Hartman, Eugene D. Genovese, Northrop Frye, E. D. Hirsch, Clifford Geertz, Richard Hoggart, Asa Briggs, Walter J. Ong, J. Hillis Miller, and Nils Enkvist. *Seated, left to right*: Frank Manuel, Eric Weil, Stephen Graubard, Roy Harvey Pearce, Morton W. Bloomfield, Talcott Parsons, Geno A. Ballotti, and Henry Nash Smith. (Courtesy of Victoria University Library)

as a literary history. Hartman's paper further formulated his anticipated "science of interpretation," a "theory" of reading that would connect "the form of the medium to the form of the artist's historical consciousness."[242] The relationship between literary form and history had recently stirred debate in West German literary-critical circles, partly due to Hans Robert Jauss's argument that audiences' horizons of interpretive expectations change the meaning of a literary work. First, Hartman cleared the ground of what he saw as the positivistic notion of literary history espoused by René Wellek and New Critic Robert Penn Warren, which "claim[ed] to sing of the whole, but load every rift with glue."[243] This notion considered literature as a reservoir of thought, art as the response to a sociohistorical scene. Such an explanation of the relation between history and text, Hartman argued, failed to account for poetic forms' unruly complexities and their *imaginaire*, their alternate realities that often included a vision of history or cleverly invented a fissure between words and things. Hartman granted that capacious ideas of poetic form, notably Northrop Frye's notion of archetypes and Lévi-Strauss's structuralism, had emerged, but for him these theories avoided how to link novel conceptions of literary form to history. Hartman's solution was phenomenologically and Freudian inspired. The critic should highlight "the artist's struggle . . . with past masters and the 'pastness' of art in modern society"; this struggle organized the relationship between the form of the medium and the form of the artist's historical consciousness.[244] Moreover, artists' battles with earlier forms were but a mode of the common struggle of any cultural practice: "[This] seems to be a version of a universal human struggle: of genius with Genius, and of genius with *genius loci* (spirit of place)."[245] With formal constraints like the genius loci—a fantasy that, Hartman admitted, could inspire the revival of vernacular poetry or, at worst, literary nationalisms—critics could combine cultural and literary history to escape the formalist impasse.

In his Bellagio paper, de Man, too, grappled with the problematic link between literary form and literary history. While Hartman gestured to the history amid the text, however, de Man employed a thematic terminology of consciousness to argue that the writer's penetrating focus on their temporal dilemma generated literary forms.[246] Historians, de Man maintained, could describe the past because their "language and the events that the language denotes are clearly distinct entities," but for writers of literature, "modernity turn[ed] out to be . . . a source of torment," as the writer's acts of originality tucked the past back into the text, involuntarily preserving history in the text.[247] Examples of this textual contradiction, this strange looping, included the avant-garde writings of French modernist Antonin Artaud, which showed that "the more radical the rejection of anything that came before, the greater the dependence on the past."[248] Precisely because they performed acts of textual originality the modern writer depended on their denial that their literary innovations were derivative. A consequence of bearing the weight of the past *and* serving as an instrument of change was that "the distinctive character of literature thus becomes manifest as an ability to escape from a condition that is felt to be unbearable."[249] The modern writer hopelessly struggled to cast off the past only to discover his or her efforts produced the forms that their literary works assumed. De Man then startlingly concluded that "good literary historians" should focus on the contradiction between modernity and history because "the bases for historical knowledge are not empirical facts but written texts, even if these texts masquerade in the guise of wars or revolution."[250] To listeners, after Prague and Paris and only a year after the height of the Vietnam War, de Man must have seemed purposefully out of time, as he reduced literary history, with all its glory and guts, to a verbal object. For de Man, though, flagging the history/modernity opposition at Bellagio, a methodological step toward his later full turn to rhetorical vocabulary, was central for any truly rigorous rejoinder to literature's distinctiveness—to him the temporal paradox of form constituted the literary itself.

But if de Man seemed aloof with his postmodern politics of poetic difference, then Miller was obviously engaged. He used his Bellagio paper to directly challenge his colleagues to recognize how a deconstructive response to the literary imperative was necessary for understanding the state of humanistic study. Many American humanists in the late 1960s had come to believe that applications of scientific methods and discourses to beloved texts would either redeem or obliterate humanistic study. Responding to the deconstruction of literary texts, Miller proposed, provided an exciting third way. "To follow . . . clues out of the labyrinth of . . . our habits of thought . . . until we find ourselves face to face with a paradoxical conclusion in obvious contradiction with the facts" of there being progress *and* decline in the humanities, Miller turned to modernist poet William Carlos Williams's *Spring and All* (1923).[251] Whereas in a 1965 book Miller explored Williams's and five other poets' belief in the progress of poetry and culture, Miller now read Williams's poetry as indicating "both progress and stasis."[252] "*Spring and All* is based on an affirmation of the supreme value of presence . . . , and on repudiation of all that is derived, repetitive, and copied. . . . Authentic life [in Williams' volume] exists only in the present moment of immediate experience."[253] But, Miller stressed, Williams's modernist rejection of symbolism, subjectivism, and supernaturalism as suppressions of the immediate manifestations of divinity in fact failed. Williams's progressive hope to uncover an essential substance beyond representation became a dead imitation of spurned habits of outdated thinking. "Like the tradition lying behind it, [Williams's] theory of art is unable to free itself from the theories it rejects."[254] Because his dream to capture a new and immediate experience free of the past repeated this tradition, Williams's poetic project was a "version of the 'deconstruction of metaphysics.'"[255]

Miller argued to colleagues at Bellagio that Williams responded to his literary predicament in the way that Miller believed his fellow humanists should respond to their interpretive one: the endless subversion of the binary oppositions that were a recurrent theme in metaphysical thought; such deconstruction never halted: "Williams' [poetic] imagination is . . . immediate and mediatorial—imitation, revelation, and creation at once. Like the long tradition he echoes, Williams remains caught in the inextricable web of connection among these concepts."[256] Like Williams, Miller himself, he even underscored, did not escape the deconstruction of the metaphysical dualisms: "My interpretation . . . both destroys the text it interprets and . . . revivifies it. Such a 'deconstruction' puts in question the received ideas of our tradition . . . [and] repeats it . . . in a version of that transit through the texts of our heritage called for by Jacques Derrida."[257] In a manner similar to the poetry he read, Miller's reflexive reading of *Spring and All* deconstructed itself. For Miller, this self-deconstruction, performed "from the Stoics to Nietzsche and the radical philosophers of our own day," revealed that "there is no progress in human history, no unfolding or gradual perfection of the spirit. There are only endlessly varied ways to experience the human situation."[258] That is to say: the deconstruction of metaphysics' value-laden oppositions was the humanities' history and its current and future truth.

At the Forefront of Research in the American Humanities

The Grand Hotel in Bellagio had hosted the first moments of what would become a lifelong camaraderie between de Man, Hartman, and Miller. While these vanguard critics had begun to pursue intersecting research agendas in earnest during the early 1960s, it was not until the 1965 Yale colloquium, the 1966 Hopkins symposium, and a series of late 1960s seminars, colloquia, and conferences that their protodeconstructive subversions of literary formalisms crystallized into deconstruction, which was becoming a legitimate interpretive school. This school could be seen in relation to cultural developments outside the academy: already in the mid-1950s, pop artists like Andy Warhol, Roy Lichtenstein, and James Rosenquist used commonplace advertising, comic books, and mundane mass-produced cultural objects to subvert traditional high art themes of morality, mythology, and classical history; in the late 1960s, the "postwar liberal consensus" of anti-communism, free markets, and interventionist domestic policies shattered, due to the breaking apart of the assumed proper contours of American society. This is not to suggest a causal relationship; neither a symptom nor a cause of either cultural or political changes, deconstruction is better understood as having taken root in a particular academic climate and atmosphere.

By 1970, de Man's, Hartman's, and Miller's elite training and healthy appetite for appropriating and adapting interpretive approaches to literature helped these friends successfully challenge the work of their literary-critical forefathers. But vanguard critics' feats would not have been possible without the needs driven and sustenance given by the academic revolution and the golden age of higher education. For a time, there were still ample funding opportunities, including those provided by private and public agencies and foundations, and research-oriented professorships at supportive institutions. Not to mention theory journals, about twenty of which were founded in the 1970s, that prospered into the 1980s on university and federal funds and that "carried out the aims of advanced research and flourished under the terms of the academic revolution."[259] There had also been a high demand for a massified literary education, which the New Critics had readily supplied, their formalist methods coming to be accepted as equivalent to the very institution of criticism itself and the model for the undergraduate teaching of (English) prose and poetry. Without the golden age of higher education and its academic revolution, then, the vanguard critics would have been without an established literary-critical practice into which they could launch their (funded) interventions. It's not so much that vanguard critics' postformalist work would have fallen on deaf ears but that without those specific conventions to challenge, their intellectual movement could not have developed the particular voice that it did.

Indeed, the rapid decline of the persuasiveness and overt presence of the New Criticism in the first half of the 1960s aligned with institutional expansion to present professional and intellectual openings that the vanguard critics willingly filled. By not only occupying the space relinquished by the New Critics but also capturing spots at the top of the academic pyramid, heading prestigious graduate programs, and publishing influential articles, de Man, Hartman, and Miller were able to develop and supply advanced research that effectively *evolved*—rather than destructively revolted against—formalist parameters. Because much of this work centered on the European Romantic poets, it also prominently called for the rewriting of the historicopoetic narrative that organized research agendas and shaped classroom experiences. The rigor once attributed to the metaphysical poets of seventeenth-century England by the New Critics now was to be displaced to the Romantics. The considerable textual and pedagogical wake left by the work of vanguard critics in turn solicited the navigational efforts of colleagues across the country.

But as de Man, Hartman, and Miller traveled into the professional stratosphere, the postacademic revolution disconnect between humanists' identities as researchers and teachers grew. Perhaps the most noticeable example of this growing disconnect could be seen in the literary critic. And the most visible attempt in literary studies to suture the divide between research and teaching in the early 1970s was undertaken by de Man, Hartman, and Miller at Yale University, once a celebrated center of the New Criticism. By the mid-1970s, this Yale School's pedagogical-intellectual project nearly concealed the reformist labors from which it had evolved during the 1960s. The New Critics had helped to academicize criticism, and de Man and company's texts and teachings, which often questioned the structure of critical reflection itself, were to be received by some as examples of the postmodern excesses that such professionalization wrought.

3

DECONSTRUCTION AS A PEDAGOGICAL-INTELLECTUAL PROJECT AND THE BURDENS OF ACADEMIC CRITICISM

By the end of the 1960s, the wheel of fortune had clearly and dramatically turned for the literary-critical avant-garde. In a 1972 review of Cleanth Brooks's and John Ransom Crowe's recent volumes, Edward Said commented: "The New Critics present today's reader with the muddle of intense amateurism hooked to semiprofessionalism. . . . The unfamiliarity, to me at least, of the audience being addressed and the issues being debated gives the central polemic in [their] essays its frequent air of energetic lostness."[1] At middecade, a reputedly new and perhaps major literary-critical movement would creep into this professional breach. William H. Pritchard reported some of this group's first public stirrings in the winter of 1975. Judging from the titles of several recently published books, he suggested, "very big game is being stalked" in New Haven, "nothing less than the fate of reading, literature, the agonizingly problematical nature of poetry and its interpretation."[2] Indeed, a group of leading critics, theorists, and philosophers of literature—whom Pritchard, tongue firmly in cheek, labeled "The Hermeneutical Mafia"—had made Yale University their hunting ground. Mass media would come to portray this "Yale School"—Harold Bloom, Paul de Man, Geoffrey Hartman, J. Hillis Miller, and Jacques Derrida—as not simply hunting textual game. With pathos-ridden, ostensibly nihilistic readings of texts of the Western literary and philosophical tradition, the group seemingly corrupted vulnerable undergraduates and served raw meat to careerist colleagues, all while undermining the tried and true principles that organized and gave purpose to humanist education—not only at Yale but potentially at colleges and universities across America.

Pritchard was onto something.[3] For, beginning in the early 1970s, the Yale School was united in interpreting and teaching the literary imperative: literature's demand to be read as a language irreducible to but of vital consequence for any discourse, whether ethical, philosophical, political, or historical. To fathom the nature of this supreme textual command, the Yale group disregarded advice as ancient as Aristotle and drew from classical rhetoric, German philosophy, and contemporary French thought to strengthen their commitment to interpreting literary works as linguistic objects. The result was a resuscitation/creation of a discipline of rhetorical reading that established "rhetoric" as the general science of interpretation.[4] Known by the mid-1970s as deconstruction, the Yale School's postformalist discipline of rhetorical reading techniques highlighted a text's figurative language and linguistic devices, often to show how a Möbius-strip-like paradox or contradiction subverted said text's hierarchies of meaning. While a distinct textual and pedagogical project in its own right, the Yale group's demanding response to the literary imperative reinforced postwar academic humanists' habit of adopting features of the discourses of the "hard" sciences to defend humanistic inquiry from accusations of methodological and logical feebleness. Because the Yale group's discipline of rhetorical reading foregrounded the unexpected ways a text undermined itself, however, their work also partook in humanists' practice during the 1970s of embracing "ironic" modes of interpretation. Less a part of the "antirigorist movement of the 1970s and 1980s," the Yale group's meticulous textual responses to literature were an ironic *and* rigorous instantiation of the broader linguistic turn.[5]

The deconstructive rejoinder to the literary imperative played out in seminars in Yale's renowned French, English, and Comparative Literature Departments, where Paul de Man and company taught la crème de la crème and engaged in friendly rivalries, workshopping publications and presentations that, when released into more public settings, deeply shaped the Yale School's reputation. De Man, above all, affected the trajectories of his colleagues and graduate students, the latter disseminating the essentials of his particularly demanding mode of rhetorical reading. Equally—and perhaps surprisingly—key to the Yale School were undergraduate classrooms, in which de Man, Hartman, and Miller coalesced their pedagogical agendas and intellectual programs. These undergraduate courses prominently included those of the literature major. Yale resisted untenured professors' efforts at institutionalizing experimental curricula, but the school bowed to more established faculty; by the late 1970s, the lit major's sequence comprised not just rhetorically revamped versions of Literatures X and Y but de Man and Hartman's new Literature Z as well. As it trained both undergraduates and the graduate students who taught them how to use the science of deconstructive reading, Lit Z closed the circle of the Yale School's pedagogical-intellectual project.

The local powers and peculiarities of Yale throughout the 1970s and early 1980s contributed to the effectiveness (and explosiveness) of the Hermeneutical Mafia's institution of American deconstruction. By offering colleagues and students a more rigorous and self-aware brand of criticism along with an even more technical definition of "literature" that reworked formalist ideas about literary autonomy and revised assumptions about the nature of "proper" criticism, the Yale group bestowed a sense of besieged purpose on literary studies in New Haven. For their science not only presented rhetoric as the general law for reading but also thrillingly undermined views at Yale, including those of the New Critics, that literature was an ersatz religion—a simulated ontological and theological system of meaning—that performed what religion used to do for humanity.[6] Also, from their professional perches at Yale, Bloom, de Man, and Hartman powerfully responded to the literary imperative by reading once-denigrated Romantic poets as deconstructive writers whose subversions of the text's metaphysical dichotomies preternaturally prefigured the science of rhetorical interpretation. Rising to senior ranks in Yale English, Hartman and Bloom, both Jewish, ousted the onto-theological preferences of "high Yale formalism at its high Anglican best," notably the view, critical to the New Critics, that literature was a secularly sacred object.[7] Meanwhile, Derrida's high-profile visiting appointment in comparative literature, which began in 1975, aligned his anti-metaphysical response to the literary imperative with the Yale group's diverse foregroundings of the figurative dimensions of texts; by doing so, Derrida's deconstructive work contributed to his friends' desacralizations of the foundations and parameters of literary education. Altogether, the texts and teachings of this Hermeneutical Mafia helped inject deconstruction into the American literary-critical scene, with Miller and Bloom expressly promoting the notion of a "Yale School."

Despite all these achievements in New Haven, however, deconstruction never became a classroom practice for undergraduates nationwide. The Yale School attracted the attention and devotion of a professorial elite looking for a new and rigorous way to meet literature's demand while also defending its profession's value from skeptics. But the group's work courted critical observers' notice as well. The deconstructive science of reading texts implicitly challenged the "American ideology," a commonsense understanding of authorial intention and history, as well as explicitly debunking the metaphysical strictures that organized literary study. The old guard of the general literary humanist variety came to see deconstruction as a foreign-born assault on its discipline's commitments. Attacks against the Yale group, also fueled by fears of hyperspecialization and the wanton application of alien (read: French) obscurantist and antihumanist vocabularies, signaled a general post-sixties anxiety about the changing status of literary study. Though it may well have raised the prestige of literary culture among some, the very claim of being an arduous science of reading was viewed as antithetical to literary humanism itself. The New Critics had promised the profession, in accordance with traditions dating from the late nineteenth century, general cultivation through literature; they also promised a practice requiring formal training that met the postwar university's needs. The Yale School seemed to promise only a postmodern and puffed-up, linguistically focused version of the latter. In the end, however, de Man, Hartman, and Miller did put a coherent pedagogical-intellectual project into force that locally coordinated teaching and research and generated exciting and compelling responses to literature.

De Man's Commitment to a Text Divided

Of the professors who instituted the ironic science of rhetorical reading at Yale in the 1970s, none contributed more than Paul de Man. "Like that of the fabulous Godot," Yale professor of English Howard Felperin, protégé of Geoffrey Hartman, recalled, "de Man's advent" in the spring of 1970 "had been anticipated" by the university's "*savant garde* with an air of heightened expectation." Vladimir and Estragon interminably and dejectedly waited, but de Man "did not disappoint," arriving with his lecture, "unusually attended by almost everyone," and "greeted with . . . admiration and bafflement."[8] Felperin, right there, switched critical allegiances. He understood: rigorous rejoinders to literature required tackling de Man's meticulous attention to the linguistic divisions and figural dimensions of the text. Yale, too, was eager to bring the Belgian American on board, and job negotiations commenced, with Hartman helping his friend navigate the layers of formalities. De Man, Hartman reported, must first resign from his tenured posts at Hopkins and Zürich. But there was a more serious sticking point: de Man lacked a "big book."[9] Without it, Hartman explained, Yale would never commit. De Man relented and collected nine published articles: four on general literary topics, the rest devoted to Ludwig Binswanger, George Lukács, Maurice Blanchot, Georges Poulet, and Jacques Derrida.[10] The promised book, with chapters that promoted de Man's postmodern views about the rhetorical nature of literary language, produced the hoped-for effect; de Man was offered a tenured joint professorship in Yale's French and Comp Lit Departments in 1970. Aware of Hopkins's new financial difficulties and that outside funding for its prestigious Humanities Center was soon to end, de Man assumed the position; a core member of the Hopkins School was now at Yale.

FIGURE 3.1 Paul de Man on Gott's Island, the place of his summer home and where he was buried (Courtesy of Patricia de Man)

Part of the offer was a three-year DeVane lectureship. Established in 1969 to combat overspecialization, the post was "an opportunity for a scholar . . . to transmit the excitement of [his or her work] to colleagues and students in other fields."[11] Administrators were surprised when de Man turned the seat down; he wanted in exchange a year's sabbatical; he said, "the classroom"—not the grand lecture hall—"most interested him."[12] De Man, it seemed, preferred a more intimate environment to cultivate the next generation of rhetorical readers, and this aim informed his course, Comp Lit 130a, "Nietzsche's Theory of Rhetoric." In this fall 1971 seminar, de Man (figuratively) placed his graduate students among a Parisian intellectual vanguard. That group, inspired by the 1971 publication of a German/French edition of Nietzsche's early writings on rhetoric, enlisted Nietzsche's texts to consider a world after the metaphysical grounds of history and meaning. De Man's class also workshopped what became a 1972 essay in *Diacritics*, where he highlighted the rhetorical form of Nietzsche's *The Birth of Tragedy* (1872), often interpreted as narrating how a dichotomy between a Dionysian (disordered and undifferentiated) reality and an Apollonian (ordered and differentiated) reality birthed ancient Greek tragic theater.[13] Instead of the view, eloquently espoused by M. H. Abrams in *Natural Supernaturalism* (1971), that the Romantics dialectically secularized Judeo-Christian concepts into a new poetic art that performed the spiritual functions of religion, "Romanticism," de Man wrote, "puts the genetic pattern of history in question."[14] And it was Nietzsche, masked Romantic that he was, whose rhetorical dimensions of *The Birth of Tragedy*, de Man argued, executed an "exercise in genetic 'deconstruction'" that revealed that narrative's metaphysically "diachronic, successive structure" was "in fact an illusion."[15] Nietzsche's text deconstructed faith like Abrams's in the artwork as a secular sanctuary that progressively united spiritual and material worlds, producing a state of onto-theological presence.

To rigorously engage the desacralizing spirit of Romantic matters, de Man had graduate students pinpoint the "genetic pattern" found "narratively" (Nietzsche's story of Greek tragedy), "epistemologically" (Nietzsche's theory of knowledge), and "metacritically" (Nietzsche's criticism of the principles, methods, and terms of criticism) in Nietzsche's *Birth of Tragedy*.[16] Between these conflicting textual levels, de Man stressed not Nietzsche's human error, as he had in his 1955 reading of Heidegger's Hölderlin, but the linguistic contradictions that Nietzsche's text itself painstakingly flagged and that undermined its stated claims. As de Man wrote in 1972, Nietzsche's "metalinguistic statements about the rhetorical nature of language" were in tension with "a rhetorical practice that puts these statements into question."[17] For example, while Nietzsche performed a "negative valorization" of Apollonian over Dionysian spirit, he claimed to use Apollonian "representational, graphic language" in order to re-present Dionysian "musical, non-representational language," even though this latter's primal power and wisdom, Nietzsche also suggested, outstripped Apollonian vision.[18] Nietzsche's explicit statements on Apollonian discourse thus undermined his actual rhetorical practice. Constructed out of an aporia that subverted the Apollo/Dionysus hierarchical opposition, Nietzsche's text undermined itself.

This postmodern deconstructive performance in de Man's *Diacritics* article also unfolded in his classroom. De Man, for instance, exhorted his students to perform "reading exercises" with Nietzsche's oeuvre that underscored the rhetorical artifice of the mad philosopher's story of Greek tragedy's origins: "[Nietzsche's] narrative now point[s] to its own purely rhetorical status ... to consecutive works [that] *have to* (?) split in 3 ways: (1) aphoristic (*Philosophenbuch*) Discontinuous Discourse Repetitive + impersonal...; (2) pure allegory (or allegoreme) pure fable; (3) Diegesis, historically narrative texts whose statement is the deconstruction of their genetic pattern."[19] De Man's graduate students were learning the hard art of rhetorical reading techniques to interpret how *The Birth of Tragedy* was a topological paradox, using references to itself and Nietzsche's other texts—his aphorisms, such as his famous description of man as a "meta-phorical animal," his allegoremes, the literal aspect of an implied or allegorical meaning, such as *The Birth of Tragedy*, and his other deconstructive narratives—to disrupt Nietzsche's own genetic account of ancient Greek tragic theater.

Yet the scope of de Man's teaching extended beyond the rhetorical booby traps of the Nietzschean text. Students in Comp Lit 130a received training in the scientific skill of deconstructive reading. "Nietzsche was certainly right when he referred to the nature of the Dionysus/Apollo relationship as '*the* capital question,'" de Man wrote in his *Diacritics* article.[20] Evolving from his postmodern politics of poetic difference, de Man's reflexive interpretive science could ostensibly trace how the rhetorical nature of literary language ensured any text, due to its inbuilt and thus *certain* conflicts, folded back on itself, undoing its premises. His students learned that a text's rhetorical practice subverted faith in presence, both the formalist belief that contradictions unified great prose and poetry and the humanist belief, like Abrams's, in the possibility of restoring a text's meaning. Such faith in the return of a text's past meaning, whether the thought of a period, the views or the development of an author, or the thematic harmony of a work, formed the unexamined onto-theological ground of established interpretive practices in the humanities. In his essay, for instance, de Man examined the argument made by Derrida's allies Philippe Lacoue-Labarthe and Sarah Kofman in 1971 that Nietzsche took a "détour" through rhetoric in his early writings on the way to a full-blown deconstruction of Western metaphysics. Even sophisticated readers like Lacoue-Labarthe and Kofman could ignore how the "rhetoric" of *The Birth of Tragedy* twisted in on itself, unexpectedly and ironically undermining such faith in the presence that gave texts coherence and genetic continuity.

Harold Bloom: An Indomitable Critical Voice

A stab at supplying a postmodern desacralization of literary education, de Man's Comp Lit 130a served as a hinge for his (self-)conscious turn to the rhetoric of the text and use of rhetorical vocabulary. But the class was also, Barbara Johnson recounted, where "the 'Yale School' officially began," where the future colleagues presented their developing deconstructive approaches to literature.[21] At the time, it was still customary to attend colleagues' seminars, and many literature professors "audited [de Man's seminar], including [Professor of English Harold] Bloom, and Hartman."[22] Johnson recalled a particularly stimulating debate on the import of Nietzsche's "On Truth and Lie in an Extra-Moral Sense"

(1873). This essay is a conceptual goldmine for the eager deconstructionist; it speculates on the origin of language and the "drive for truth" and is chock-full of literary and linguistic analysis to boot. Bloom had "a lot to say" about Nietzsche's mocking commentary on "man," that "calamitous curiosity" who "might peer just once through a crack in the chamber of consciousness and look down" to discover "that [he] is 'hanging in dreams, as it were, upon the back of a tiger.'"[23] It can be surmised that de Man, ever more distant from psychoanalytic language and concepts, advocated that Nietzsche's grand tiger performed in a rhetorical mode. For Harold Bloom, though, Nietzsche's tiger embodied the agonizing opposition between the Freudian pleasure principle, by which one avoided pain and pursued pleasure to satisfy biological and psychological needs, and the Freudian reality principle, by which one deferred gratification and satisfied one's desires in socially appropriate ways. Interpreting how this psychological conflict manifested itself in the language of the poet was Bloom's current project.

In fact, de Man's Nietzsche course was held during a period of dramatic transformation for Bloom; he had just begun his formulations of how and why a young and aspiring poet performed various "tropings" or rhetorical modifications upon the lines of an inimitable precursor. Yet de Man's class was not the first time the two met. While interviewing for a junior fellowship at Harvard in the mid-1950s, Bloom chanced upon de Man, who had been awarded such a fellowship from 1954 to 1957; Bloom reported to Hartman, his untenured friend at Yale: "I met a blond Apollo named Paul de Man. He's read your book—*and understood it.*"[24] Besides a shared interest in Hartman's work, though, Bloom and de Man both resisted the New Critics' anti-Romantic historicopoetic narrative and questioned central aspects of their formalist approach.

Still, de Man's and Bloom's intellectual formations really could not have been more different. Born on July 11, 1930, in the Bronx, Bloom was the son of a garment worker and raised in an Orthodox Jewish household; in his telling, he taught himself English at the age of six and made New York City public libraries his second home. Scholarships enabled Bloom to attend Cornell, where he studied under M. H. Abrams, then spearheading a Romantic revival in literary studies. After Bloom earned his degree in 1951, Abrams sent his precocious student to Yale's English PhD program. There, Bloom could only be true to himself, flaunting his Jewishness, actively opposing the New Criticism, and boldly praising his adored Romantics. He searched for his own critical voice as well, and Bloom took lessons from an essay by Nietzsche on the uses of history for life to heart, as he, too, believed only weak readers "echo[ed]" the "most astonishing works" in the "form of 'criticism.'"[25] After he earned his doctorate in 1955, Bloom's vitality, knowledge of letters, and astonishing poetic recall made it basi-cally impossible for the New Critics in New Haven to release him. Some sherry-sipping professors in Yale English thought of Jews as interlopers in Anglo-Saxon heritage and culture, but the Yiddish-speaking proletarian and self-avowed street fighter was offered a tenure-track position none-theless. A decade later, Bloom would be appointed to full professor, one of the youngest in Yale history.

Master competitor and consummate careerist from the get-go, Bloom clearly designed his scholarly interventions of the late 1950s and early 1960s to defy reigning New Critical orthodoxy. For Bloom insisted that imaginative genius, not tight Cleanth Brooksian verbal forms, determined the meaning of great literature. For instance, with *Shelley's Mythmaking* (1959), a rewriting of his dissertation, Bloom provocatively used Jewish philosopher Martin Buber's "I-Thou" concept of relationship to trace the mythopoeic power of Percy Bysshe Shelley's poems.[26] Bloom argued that Shelley, who mistrusted any form of established religious truth, hoped to found a mythic "relation" to an object at the limits of desire. Laboring by sheer force of vision and burning resolve, Shelley made his poems primi-tive and heroic acts that transcended the narrowness of "subhuman self-absorption." Shelley sometimes extended his mythic poetry to the worldly sphere, as in "The Masque of Anarchy" (1819), a call for freedom in the face of the English government's slaughter of a crowd who demanded parlia-mentary representation: "Rise like lions after slumber / In unvanquishable NUMBER! / Shake your chains to each, like dew / Which in sleep had fall'n on you: / YE ARE MANY—THEY ARE FEW."[27] Ultimately, though, Bloom found Shelley's "apocalyptic humanism" tragic, as the walls of the heroic self were transient. The self plunged into the sublunary world, the barriers of petty selfhood raised, and the task of re-creation and renewal com-menced once more. Because Bloom read Shelley's poetry as performing a godlike denial of time and matter, one that offered a visionary imagination antithetical to nature, his zealously rebellious interpretation challenged the often espoused view that the essence of Romantic art was reunion of the alienated subject with nature.

Bloom had started to sketch the content and the form of his anti–New Critical response to literature's demand: the canonic quality of a work emerged from and against the logic of a poet's singular imagination. With *The Visionary Company* (1961), a synoptic revision of the Romantic canon, Bloom hoped to inject Romantic creative principles into the center of literary value by thematizing the meaning of Romantic poems in terms of a dialectical logic between nature and imagination that nevertheless privileged the latter.[28] Bloom also continued to heed Nietzsche's warn-ings about "weak readers," and, taking additional advice from William

Blake ("I must Create a System, or be enslav'd by another Mans," Blake proclaimed in 1804),[29] he began to fashion his own critical style, immersing himself in not only the Romantic poets but American and European philosophers, as well as Freud. These influences shaped a 1969 essay in which Bloom's argument about Romantics' internalization of the machinery of epic poetry set parameters for his career: "The poet takes the patterns of quest-romance and transposes them into his own imaginative life, so that the entire rhythm of the quest is heard again in the movement of the poet himself from poem to poem."[30] For Bloom, all post-Romantic poetry resulted not from a struggle with an external figure; nor was it a self-enclosed formal harmony; nor, as in humanistic, thematic criticism, should it be shoehorned into patterns of cultural history. No, for Bloom, great poetry arose from the mental blocks that obstructed entrance into the poet's personal vision.

Bloom was questing to counter a range of onto-theological norms that structured literary education. Such defiance, coupled with his eruditeness and exaggerated mannerisms, made sympathetic colleagues in English fear (metaphorically) for his life.[31] But as early as 1959, Yale undergraduates recognized Bloom as a "brilliant young English instructor, [who] delivered a spirited attack... on the choice of poets and method of teaching English at Yale, ... stir[ring] some hope for a revival of romantic poetry."[32] By 1966, the context in which Bloom began his teaching career had shifted, thanks in part to his postformalist efforts, permitting the doors of perception to open wider and more easily for his pupils: "Mr. Bloom lectures to his class... as if he were a brother of his romantic forebears.... Hearing Mr. Bloom in person is an unparalleled experience, he 'makes book-learning come alive.'"[33] A year later: "Mr. Bloom... is so passionately involved in the poetry that his viewpoint tends to become monolithic.... But things may change. Another professor Mr. Hartmann [sic], will be teaching the course next year."[34] Bloom's visionary inculcation of undergraduates with how to grapple with the literary commands of the Romantic imagination would, after 1967, dovetail with Hartman's; by 1971, Bloom and Hartman were "twin stars of Yale Romanticism."[35] "'It is,' students wrote, 'Professor Hartman's brilliant insights into the historical context and psychological motives of the poets that add relevance and perspective to the study of the Romantic Movement.'"[36] Friends since first-year instructor Hartman was given an "adjoining" office "in a basement of Yale's Old Campus," Bloom and Hartman, despite using different modes of reading and favoring different Romantic poets, now both imparted a view to students that a sense of universal meanings disclosed by way of careful consideration of poetic form and provenance, including authors' backgrounds and mental states, controlled literature's worth and importance.[37]

The End of the Hopkins School

Following his assumption of a joint professorship at Yale in 1970, de Man began to work closely with Hartman to embed the discipline of deconstructive reading in the university's Comp Lit Department. It was good timing on these old friends' part, because the department was in the midst of a changing of the guard. René Wellek went emeritus in 1972, and along with Wellek went outspoken defenses of orthodox pedagogy in literary humanist education, including what de Man saw as insufficiently rigorous arguments for art's autonomy, use of periods or epochs for determining an artwork's significance, and faith in the reader's ability to aesthetically judge the literary work. This is not to say that de Man rejected Wellek's positions wholesale; de Man, building off of Wellek's diagnosis, argued in 1966 that a crisis of identity and mission was the locomotive that drove criticism.[38] De Man's rhetorical renovation of Yale Comp Lit was also abetted by a personnel shift in French, his other departmental affiliation. Jacques Ehrmann died of cancer in June 1972, never completing his project, which he explicitly aligned with Derrida's "philosophical" enterprise, to subvert "the dichotomy which separates ordinary language from poetic language" by showing that "language was founded on poetry."[39] "If one accepts this thesis," literature became no longer an "aristocracy of discourses" but *"a particular manner of reading and deciphering signs."*[40] De Man would fill the intellectual vacuum at Yale left by Ehrmann, leading Comp Lit to assume a central avenue in America for the proliferation of exacting rhetorical reading techniques.

To aid in his endeavor to displace Wellekian views of the purpose of comp lit, de Man worked to convince Jacques Derrida to guest lecture in the department. Still at the ENS, and with the funds for his visiting professorship at the Hopkins Humanities Center almost depleted, Derrida must have understood that, if he accepted, it would mean adjusting his philosophical project more to the task of responding to the literary imperative. The professional opportunities likely seemed promising, though. For, in the early 1970s, Derrida's popularity in France was waning and his writings received praise from only a handful of American philosophers; phenomenologists at Northwestern University employed Derrida's texts to reformulate hermeneutic questions, while Newton Garver's preface to David Allison's 1973 translation of Derrida's *Speech and Phenomena* (1967), a collection of essays on Husserl's theory of signs, helpfully positioned

Derrida's work in relation to Anglo-American philosophies of language.[41] Nevertheless, Derrida's work was often seen in the profession as "fuzzy," unscientific, irrational, the latest example of a long line of solipsistic French products.[42] Derrida had to find paths other than philosophical to make headway stateside.

It helped that there were a number of early American mediators who marshaled Derrida's philosophy in terms of the debate between literary history and literary formalism. In the winter 1972 issue of *Diacritics*, for example, the applicability of Derrida's deconstruction to literary studies took hold via a kind of textual bonding between de Man and Derrida; that de Man's aforementioned Nietzsche essay, where he suggested that Derrida "attempts to see the conceptual crisis of language," was included in the issue shaped this reception.[43] There were also those who discerned that Derrida was a strange species of historian; the author of a spring 1972 *Diacritics* review of *De la grammatologie* (1967) noted how Derrida's deconstructive endeavors modulated Heidegger's destruction of metaphysics and its history.[44] Though Derrida's earlier published texts focused a great deal on the issue of "history," this was later obscured once Derrida's work was ushered onto the American literary-critical scene. Even Derrida's own textual practice and readings contributed to the concealment of the central part that the mid-1960s deconstruction of the temporality/ historicity opposition, upheld in Heidegger's *Being and Time*, played in the shaping of his subsequent texts. Within a few years, questions concerning a text's rhetoric, established in part by de Man, almost wholly buried Derrida's "history."[45] De Man did not sabotage his friend's treatment in America; he did, however, tend to valorize the linguistic aspects of Derrida's work. A colleague would reflect that de Man "was fond of" using the word "*thematization*" to "characterize the misreading of Derrida as a 'philosopher' whose 'philosophical system' was somehow 'about' writing."[46] Teasing out an overarching understanding of Derrida's deconstruction, in other words, masks its rhetorical character. What de Man really wanted, though, was to enlist Derrida into his efforts to rhetoricize the metaphysical underpinnings of literary education.

Another motivating factor behind de Man and Hartman's decision to invite Derrida to guest lecture was the hope to rekindle the productive disagreements between Derrida and French psychoanalyst Jacques Lacan, and this time to do so around the issue of how they each engaged literature qua literature. Derrida obliged.[47] In the published text partly based on his 1972 lecture at Yale, Derrida used Lacan's reading of Edgar Allan Poe's "The Purloined Letter" (1844) to deflate the onto-theological assumptions, the philosophical pretensions, of Lacan's psychoanalytic project.[48] Drawing from the Saussurean distinction between signifier and signified,

Lacan read the queen, the detective Dupin, and other characters in Poe's narrative as positioned in relation to a circulating signifier—the purloined letter—that never could become a signified, because the letter's content never could be disclosed. Operating free of the signified, the letter as signifier repeated a triangular structure consisting of the unaware and unseeing subject, the concealing and seeing subject, and the knowing and seeing subject. But, though the letter as signifier affected each subject's alignment with the others, Lacan insisted that the absent signified (the letter as content) remained indivisible: "The materiality of the signifier" does not "admit partition. Cut a letter in small pieces, and it remains the letter it is."[49] This letter as signifier was also unrepresentable; it was not the "symbol only of an absence. . . . [The purloined letter] will be *and* not be where it is, wherever it goes."[50] "This is why," Lacan concluded, "what the 'purloined letter' . . . means is that a letter always arrives at its destination."[51] In this way, Lacan interpreted Poe's "indivisible" purloined letter, a signifier of the absent letter as signified, as performing Freud's repetition compulsion.

For Derrida, however, Lacan's structuralist reading of Poe pivoted on a purloined letter that in fact deconstructively disrupted these ontotheological attempts to fully present a text's form and meaning. Derrida read Poe's "The Purloined Letter" as narrating a chain of unanticipated mistakes to highlight how the hierarchical oppositions that organized Lacan's interpretation of Poe undermined themselves.[52] Derrida argued that Lacan's division of the purloined letter into a circulating "signifier" and never disclosed "signified" amounted to a castrating dichotomy. To circulate, Derrida underscored, Lacan's "indivisible" letter as signified had to be divisible—it was actually this risk of *not* returning to an origin that rendered possible the "itinerary of the signifier" through which each subject was structurally aligned in Poe's story. Lacan's presumed absent substance or content—the letter as signified—was therefore a divided and deferred chain of signifiers. Yet it was not simply the *content* but the *form* of Lacan's Poe that subverted Lacan's metaphysical privileging of the purloined letter's absent substance. Though structured by the Oedipal law of the father, which promised the return of the letter, the fragmentability of the letter as signifier permitted different narrative frames.[53] Because he constructed an intersubjective triangle that erased the difference between narration and narrated narrator, Lacan forsook this possibility; instead he tried to force Poe's story into a narratorless triangle, a metaphysical form that eliminated gaps or divisions between author, story, and reader. According to Derrida, though, the purloined letter—that is, both Poe's fiction and its signs, its signifiers and signifieds—was always split and postponed, thereby already escaping while also structuring attempts to pin it down.

FIGURE 3.2 *Left to right*: Paul de Man, Shoshana Felman, Jacques Lacan, Alice Kaplan, and Geoffrey Hartman at Yale in 1975 (Courtesy of Patricia de Man)

Derrida's 1972 lecture presented a rigorous engagement with how the disruptive figural power of literature and literary language punctured the metaphysics of psychoanalytic discourse to his comp lit audience, who were then intensely searching for interpretive procedures and theoretical perspectives applicable and transferable to texts regardless of their genre, geographical origin, or national tradition. The linguistic terms of French structuralism and Derrida's counteroffensives trickled more into Hartman's postformalist work, for example. More generally, though, Derrida's subversion of Lacan's project by way of an exacting reading of Poe captivated his audience, which must have pleased Derrida, who in a 1971 interview explained his belief that "certain texts classed as 'literary' . . . [seem] to mark and to organize a structure of resistance to the philosophical conceptuality [metaphysical dualisms] that allegedly dominated or comprehended them."[54] The attention Derrida devoted to "literature" thus had a tactical quality, in that, for him, a "literary" text announced and performed a logic, a materiality suppressed by metaphysics, that challenged its own aporia. While not part of the long-standing effort to identify *what* literature was or to sustain its authority over other discourses—that was de Man's primary aim—Derrida's underscoring of the text's "'literary' practice," by seeming to make national, linguistic, and temporal borders more or less irrelevant, did deflect complaints that dated to the very founding of comp lit departments in America about comparative research—namely, that the discipline lacked comparative interpretive standards. Literature professors who sought a rigorous defense of their profession against accusations of analytical weakness could have done far worse than take up Derrida's deconstructive response to literature's demand, which turned all texts into self-deconstructive ones. Derrida's work also seemed to promise the exciting subversion of the boundaries that framed most humanist scholarship, which was customarily organized, as in comp lit, temporally and nationally.

While Derrida's reading of Lacan's reading of Poe's detective story fueled the institution of American deconstruction, the Hopkins School, such as it was, reached its end. Forty-four-year-old J. Hillis Miller, after two decades in Baltimore, defected in 1972, accepting a tenured professorship in Yale's English Department. Hopkins's administrators, facing financial shortfalls and the loss of yet another prominent faculty member, recognized "the Yale attempt at having what we have had these several years."[55] Part of what Hopkins had had was de Man, whose legacy at the university's Humanities Center included "a small doctoral program" in comp lit "modeled on the one de Man ran so successfully at Cornell."[56] But Miller's trajectory was by that point clear. He had already begun to underscore how the patterns of literary history—period, genre, and so on—integral to literary humanism concealed the topological paradoxes that undermined literary texts' meanings. In a review of M. H. Abrams's 1971 book, Miller released Nietzsche's demystifying theory of rhetoric on Abrams's assumptions concerning imitation, reading, language, and secularization, recommending de Man (and Derrida) as models of how to perform a "reinterpretation which is also a deconstruction" of the Neoplatonic and Christian narratives that structured Abrams's thematic readings and their onto-theological suppressions of Romantics' texts' subversive figural contradictions.[57] It surely made sense for Miller to want to join Yale's galaxy of critics, many postformalist. "I was," Miller recollected, "attracted by once again having de Man as a colleague, not to speak of [Maynard] Mack, Brooks, Warren, Hartman, Bloom, etc."[58] Yet what also sealed the deal was that at Yale, Miller believed, he would be able to impart his pedagogical-intellectual project to "superb students," for Yale attracted what Miller and his colleagues nationwide considered the best undergraduate English majors.[59]

Miller in fact was likely the first teacher to show Yale undergraduates in English how to use the de-idealizing scientific art of rhetorical reading to engage literature's claim to be self-aware language too complex to be incorporated into other types of discourses. In a fall 1973 course, one undergraduate proposed that his final paper might "consider language, maybe along the lines of de Man; or Derrida, or perhaps Poulet—and then consider the *religion* in [Gerard Manley] Hopkins's poems—along with his use of language . . . (following the rhetoric + development of some poem or two)." Another student suggested that he or she offer "some close readings of Wordsworth with special attention to the concept of Artistic tension as it is established through various linguistic (or semantic) devices." The student continued: "Wordsworth, aware of the symbolic consciousness' [*sic*] of a critical reader, uses those symbols . . . [of] the old man's staff, or, for that matter the old man [in] 'Resolution and Independence' (1807), . . . ambiguously, so that the reader is unable to fix in his mind exactly what the significance of a potentially symbolic object is." This junior would also use Wordsworth's "opening and last stanzas" of "Lucy Gray" (1799) to investigate the strain of this "ambiguous temporality." For Wordsworth, the junior observed, had the "tendency to obscure the temporal duration and/or position of his (or his narrator's) actions by juggling his [or his narrator's] tenses." In addition, Miller's student would use "the wooden bridge in 'Lucy Gray'" to grasp "the 'meaning' of a word or image as it is altered by its *position* in a poem." Lastly, the junior proposed to employ "Wordsworth's concept and use of metaphors, taking 'metaphor' as a general term applicable to anything from word to an entire poem" so as to ask "what [Lucy] has . . . come to 'mean' to (1) the reader, (2) Wordsworth."[60] While not strictly reflexively flagging the Möbius-strip-like paradoxes of a literary text's metaphysical hierarchies, Miller's students had evidently been familiarized with the desacralizing ways to rhetorically rejoin the literary imperative then being bandied about in Yale's halls and lecture rooms.

Miller's rhetoricized inroads into established literary-critical practice with English undergraduates overlapped with his friend de Man's acquisition of control in the French and Comp Lit Departments, both of which he came to chair, the former from 1974 to 1977. With his "infighter" talents, de Man further instituted deconstruction at Yale by rhetorically grappling with literature's distinctiveness. This was a much-needed methodological advance, he wrote in a seminal autumn 1973 *Diacritics* article, because "from a technical point of view, very little has happened in American criticism since the innovative works of New Criticism."[61] In his *Diacritics* piece, de Man diagnosed and prognosed, concentrating on three terms— "semiology," "grammar," and "rhetoric"—that, taken together, might help "dislodge the age-old model," employed by René Wellek among others and often protected "under the aegis of the inside/outside metaphor," of opposing intrinsic to extrinsic criticism.[62] By "semiology" de Man meant recent attempts in France to apply the Saussurean scientific study of signs, how an arbitrary system of linguistic differences provided the value of a sign, the difference between signifier (form) and signified (content), to all discourses. The second term de Man examined was "grammar." French literary structuralists, de Man reported, combined the scientific study of grammatical forms and rhetorical figures to explore the ways a text was structured by a metonymical axis of language (at the level of the sentence) and a metaphorical axis of language (at the level of the word). Importantly, de Man stressed, when a reader attempted to finalize a reading of a text, he or she moved from the metonymical to the metaphorical axis, from combined to substituted words. De Man cited four lines of W. B. Yeats's celebrated "Among School Children" (1928) to demonstrate the consequences of this interpretive decision:

> O chestnut tree, great rooted blossomer,
> Are you the leaf, the blossom or the bole?
> O body swayed to music, O brightening glance,
> How can we know the dancer from the dance?[63]

If Yeats's last line is read grammatically, de Man held, then the poem appeared to achieve presence, an onto-theological wholeness or resolution of the division between being-in-the-world and transcendent idea, in that the dancer and the dance realized a formal and fundamental unity. But Yeats's last line could also read as ending in a state of uncertainty or irresolution, and the text genuinely wanted to know: What is the difference between the dancer and the dance? This indecision led to the final term that de Man examined: "rhetoric," which he saw as performing that pervasively contradictory condition of language, whereby grammatical (logical/formal) analysis could not finalize a text's meaning: "Two entirely coherent but entirely incompatible readings [of Yeats's poem] can be made to hinge on one line, whose grammatical structure is devoid of ambiguity, but whose rhetorical mode turns the mood as well as the mode of the entire poem upside down."[64] Ensuring indecision between the text's literal and figurative aims, the "rhetorization of grammar" subverted not only the scientific efforts of literary structuralists to isolate a univocal meaning of any text, but also historians' attempts to fit texts into representations of a period, an author's views and evolution, or the unity of an oeuvre.[65] De Man's scientific skills in deconstructive reading promised to show how the inherent logic of the text, always already disrupted by the nature of the text itself, subverted logical analysis, undermining all efforts to silence the siren song of literature's rhetorical demand.

With a meticulous "de-constructive reading" of a six-page passage from Marcel Proust's *Swann's Way* (1913), de Man then validated the power of rhetoric to subvert the use of the inside/outside metaphor to differentiate intrinsic from extrinsic criticism and master the meaning of a text. Proust's text "describes the young Marcel . . . hiding in the closed space of his room in order to read."[66] At first glance, de Man stressed, this passage "contrasts two ways of evoking the natural experience of summer and unambiguously states its preference for one of these ways over the other: the 'necessary link' that unites the buzzing of the flies to the summer makes it a much more effective symbol than the tune heard 'perchance' during the summer."[67] Proust's text thus valorized the sameness between the buzzing of the flies and the summer. This identity was achieved through a "perfect synthesis," a substitution by way of the metaphorical axis of language, between the "properties of coolness, darkness, repose, silence, imagination and totality" that governed Marcel's chamber and "the heat, the light, the activity, the sounds, the senses and the fragmentation that govern the outside."[68] The text's fusion of metaphysical oppositions through metaphor "render[ed] the presence of Summer in the room more complete than the actual experience of Summer in the outside world."[69]

However, de Man emphasized, Proust's privileging of the metaphor of "the flies" obscured the text's own rhetorical practice; the metaphorical substitution that produced the presence of summer was in fact a relational and contingent metonymic contact between the inside and outside of Marcel's room. For young Marcel's cool repose in his room, de Man quoted from Proust, "supported, like the quiet of a motionless hand in the middle of a running brook the shock and the motion of a *torrent of activity*."[70] The metaphor "torrent of activity," de Man underlined in an expanded version of his article, was metonymic because (1) "the coupling of two terms . . . is not governed by the 'necessary link' of resemblance . . . but dictated by the mere habit of proximity" *and* (2) "the reanimation of the numbed figure takes place by means of a statement ('running brook') which happens to be close to it, without however this proximity being determined by a necessity that would exist on the level of transcendental meaning."[71] By relying on figures of exchange incompatible with the text's own thematizations, Proust merely *appeared* to close "the ring of antithetical properties" between the coolness of Marcel's inner sanctuary and the heat of the summer outside and allow "for exchange and substitution" but actually undermined his own metaphor of "the flies."[72] In 1949, Cleanth Brooks saw metaphoric language as poetry's secularly sacred device that indirectly appealed to universal ideas; for him, this circuitous demand demonstrated literature's uniqueness.[73] A quarter of a century later, de Man grappled with how a literary text (Proust's) valorized but at the same time desacralized metaphorical exchange by way of metonymical language. And for de Man, the way literature deconstructed itself ensured its very distinction as literature, with its "internal" poetic difference, its twisting back on itself, undoing efforts to employ the inside/outside metaphor to either protect the literary text from or subsume it into other types of discourses. As demonstrated by Proust's text, literature's self-deconstruction came before and was constitutive of all texts.[74]

By the autumn of 1973, de Man, Miller, and to an extent Hartman, were all practicing deconstruction at Yale and orienting students to the rhetorical facets of literature. Miller was thrilled to have joined in the building of this deconstructive institution. In an August 10 letter to Bloom, he excitedly wrote: "You particularly came to mind when in the Phillips Bookstore here I found *The Anxiety of Influence* [1973] shelved in a section consisting entirely of poetry."[75] As much a personal as professional manifesto, Bloom's *Anxiety* used a Nietzscheanized Freud to argue that a great poet refracted a revered precursor's verse. For Bloom, the younger poet, an "ephebe" or "weak poet," overcome by his or her celebrated predecessors' literary triumphs, languished, only able to feebly copy the patriarch. Anglophile T. S. Eliot's theory that great poets achieved access to the literary tradition by piously honoring their antecedents via "a continual self-sacrifice, a continual extinction of personality," long inspired English literary histories, but Bloom's "strong poets," who, like their "weak" brethren, acutely felt their "belatedness," freed their own artistic voices by creatively misreading and concealing their debts to their ancestors: "The history of fruitful poetic influence . . . is a history of anxiety and self-saving caricature of distortion, of perverse, willful revisionism without which modern poetry as such could not exist."[76] Bloom postulated that strong poets' (mis)readings of their forefathers followed six major categories or ratios derived from the practices of philosophy, religion, physics, and, yes, rhetoric—clinamen, tessera, kenosis, daemonization, askesis, and apophrades. Using the last relation, Bloom, for example, noted that Alfred Tennyson's "Maud" (1855) seemed to echo Eliot's "The Waste Land" (1922), while Shelley's poems bore a resemblance to passages in Yeats. In this fashion, Bloom revealed the uncanny contradictions of the poetic tradition that overturned assumed hierarchies of priority. With all his revisionary ratios, though, Bloom declared to have systematized a "theory of poetry," as de Man praised in an influential review, that demystified "the humanistic view of literary influence," adding to "a more rigorous practical criticism" and enriching the "patterns on which academic literary history is based."[77] The theory also flew in the face of the genteel culture of English departments everywhere; in Bloom's psycho-poetic universe, literary history as a sequence of courteous and open revision was but a naïve fantasy.

Bloom's equal care for texts' psychological and rhetorical sources is legible in *Anxiety*, yet the manifesto should also be read as a response to the literary-critical fathers he apprehensively felt threatened his own imaginative project. Bloom laid this out explicitly, as *Anxiety* was dedicated to W. K. Wimsatt, Bloom's beloved Yale teacher, and implicitly, as Bloom's notion that literary tradition was a body of rhetorically distorted readings of (precursors') poems broke with Wimsatt and other New Critics; Bloom's theory of poetic influence countered the idea that the autonomous literary work was the fount of civilizing doctrine or humane values. Hartman recognized this all in his review of *Anxiety*: "[As] Blake contended with Angels and Swedenborgians, Bloom engages the sky-gods of Modern Criticism and Romantic Scholarship."[78] But, Hartman continued, "since the deviousness of the critic matches that of the poets he admires, there is little direct polemics."[79] With *Anxiety*, Hartman witnessed, Bloom, obliquely wrestling with his teacher M. H. Abrams's tracing of the cheerful debt that the Romantics owed to Judeo-Christian tradition, argued that "the dynamic of [literary] history is governed by a necessary demon rather than a necessary angel."[80] Bloom worked as well to free himself of Northrop Frye, whose *Fearful Symmetry* (1947) inspired Bloom's first book. Frye used ahistorical, metaphysical, Christian-inspired categories of comedic and tragic archetypes to respond to literature's demand, but Bloom, in Hartman's words, "re-introduce[d] the 'sour myth' of Time into criticism," showing that the "continuity of literary history . . . reposes on a 'lie against time,'" a lie against (the influence of) past masters.[81] Though Bloom's theory of influence suggested that even strong poets failed to achieve a pure originality and complete autonomy—poetry *was*, he argued, a kind of repression, and not a negation, of admired predecessors' works—Bloom's aim to best his strong teachers was a literary success, of sorts. For what better way to antithetically overcome his esteemed professional forefathers than by fulfilling his poetic vision of Romantic self-fashioning and having his writing on poetic influence become like the very poetry he so revered?

In the early years of the 1970s, as English, French, and comp lit departments around the country welcomed advanced thought from Europe, Bloom, de Man, Hartman, and Miller's dense web of references to and commentaries about one another's work began to make clear to those in the profession that a new circle of critics was rising at Yale. The group's high and hard techniques of rhetorical reading, becoming known as deconstruction and done in the name of literature itself, promised to give readers a comprehensive understanding of literature qua literature, frequently of the way literature's paradoxes circle back to undermine their foundations, that desacralized the tenets of literary humanism. In constant conversation with one another, the men also developed meaningful friendships, routinely attending professional meetings and often traveling together. In his August 10, 1973, letter, Miller wrote to Bloom of his summer plans, concluding: "I'd much enjoy having your company (and Paul's) on the drive back" to New Haven from Cambridge, Massachusetts.[82] De Man similarly wrote to Miller that he hoped to "see you in Cambridge" and that "Geoffrey . . . may also be coming [from Zürich] . . . , though it isn't certain. But Harold . . . is bound to be there."[83] The friends would absorb interpretive insights from one another's lectures and writings, the multiplying effects of which eventually grew into a pedagogical-intellectual project around deconstruction at Yale. Hartman's and Bloom's contributions to this rhetoricized institution drew particular nourishment from the shifting faculty roster in Yale English; the onto-theological tendencies of the department's leading lights beckoned them.

The Neo–New Critics' De-Christianization of Yale English

"There is a shared sense of impending doom," Howard Felperin mordantly observed in late 1974.[84] An entire generation of grayed critics had departed Yale's English Department in a period of three or four years, most notably New Critics Robert Penn Warren (retired, 1973), Cleanth Brooks (retired, 1975), and William Wimsatt (died, 1975).[85] This famous block of formalist critics had provided a certain unity to not only the undergraduate teaching of English literature in New Haven—English 25 was their major pedagogical contribution—but also the image of Yale as a protector of orthodoxy. For, within the culturally strategic core of the university, a High Church Episcopalianism fraternized with New Critical formalist precepts, above all the belief that great poetry was an "organic unity" that, because it gripped a "concrete universal," many viewed as Christian. Wimsatt, "whose graduate seminar on the history of poetics was legendary," Hartman fondly recollected, had climaxed in *The Verbal Icon* (1954) with an attempt to lead Christian critics to the New Critical light of symbolic language.[86] In *Modern Poetry and the Tradition* (1939), Brooks stressed that a quest to liberate a Christian faith from the barrenness to which it has been committed in the modern world was what most shaped T. S. Eliot's poetry.[87] On the heels of the rapid demographic diversification of the Yale student population during the 1960s, which started with recruitment from "public schools," these sensibilities endured until approximately the mid-1970s, after Jewish American Bloom, who once characterized the department as "an Anglo-Catholic nightmare," and German Jewish Hartman, who judged it as possessing a "severe evangelical atmosphere," rose to senior positions.[88] Extending the work of first-wave agents, who challenged the public stature of Christianity in America from the 1930s through the 1960s, Hartman's and Bloom's teachings and texts developed and employed styles of rhetorical reading that all but openly cleaved the conflation of criticism and Christian metaphysics.[89] This helped desacralize and democratize literary studies.[90]

Assuming responsibility in English after their elders' departures, though, required "Neo–New Critics" (Hartman's coinage) to overcome new constraints.[91] Across the country, retrenchment following the 1973–75 recession forced universities and colleges to adjust their education to the labor market.[92] These policies stunned humanists, whose careers had been spent in cocoons of funded and expanding programs. The "new vocationalism" in English departments merged with post-sixties questioning of literary education's worth, placing more pressure on the link between the teaching and research arms of the profession; the latter had swelled in importance after the academic revolution, while the former now suffered from the job crisis for newly minted PhDs, increased class sizes, and heavier course loads. In Yale English, faculty positions were left unfilled, requirements for tenure raised, and competition for leave, research, and travel funds intensified. "Continued cutbacks in federal funding and the almost non-existent job market," undergraduates mused, "have conspired to make life for the student who intends to pursue graduate study in English . . . as grueling and as worrisome as that of the pre-med."[93]

These unexpected burdens affected the Neo–New Critics, in part encouraging them to eventually play out their projects in other departments and programs. Some in the small faction believed replacing Yale's literary-critical luminaries was nigh impossible. "Part of the problem now," Miller was quoted as saying in a 1974 *Yale Daily News* piece, "is there are no more Geoffrey Hartmans around."[94] Other English members simply felt their community in tatters. "In the last year almost everyone has given up the pretense that there is a community," medievalist Dewey Faulkner lamented.[95] A response to this grim situation from Yale humanists had come, and in the form of a council in 1973, which Hartman chaired, that addressed the "fragmentation" of "community" in "the graduate school and the faculty."[96] Yet hope springs eternal in Yale English, and discerning onlookers saw a critical group emerge. The *Daily News* author opined: "Hartman is the new Wimsatt."[97] The author expanded the analogy: "Bloom, Hartman, and Miller all live in close quarters, and they will . . . make political decisions about hiring and tenure. . . . Their philosophies

FIGURE 3.3 Illustration by William Blake, revised by undergraduate student Laurie Kerr in 1974. Handwritten text reads: "With thundrous noise and dreadful shakings, Wimsatt, Brooks, Warren & Mack—Still groaning with their Labours— part from the mighty Culler, & linking arms, Rise to the heavens of Beulah, Left alone, Culler laments in pain, divides three-fold, & hurls his emanations, Hartman & Bloom, aloft through the dark Reaches of Time & Space. In Misery supreme, the Sons & Daughters of Eli, The Junior Faculty, gaze upon the dark futurity, knowing they are forgotten." (Courtesy of *Yale Daily News*)

will always be individual, but they . . . will all fit perfectly together . . . like the pieces of a puzzle." "[They] will learn to accommodate . . . the writings of Wimsatt's generation, until someone builds . . . a new Yale tradition."[98]

Hartman began to exuberantly contribute to this budding Yale establishment by using his rhetorical skills to challenge core New Critical beliefs, showing how critic and artist both deconstructively grappled with literature's demand to be read as literature. His desacralizing subversion would radically democratize the critic's task. In a 1973 article, for instance, Hartman formulated parts of his new interpretive science while accounting for texts' figurative language by questioning the onto-theological hierarchy between transcendent artwork and degraded textual commentary.[99] This probing, he confessed, developed from both his desire to fulfill a "superiority complex vis-à-vis other critics" and overcome an "inferiority complex vis-à-vis art"—standard New Critical fare was to see criticism as a fallen, worldly depiction of a numinous poetic object.[100] But Hartman, always with an eye to literary history, also stressed that contemporary circumstances stimulated his longing to subvert the text/commentary dichotomy. "We have entered an era . . . [in which] Longinus is studied as seriously as the sublime texts he comments on; Jacques Derrida on Rousseau almost as interestingly as Rousseau."[101] In Hartman's new "era of writing," the poet-critic reveled in their poetic powers while the poet-artist enjoyed analytical-critical power. Such a radical reversal of established priority meant that extreme formalists' extreme objectification of the artwork did not closely re-present but mirrored this work's reflexive accounting of its own status as a linguistic object. Cleanth Brooks's notion of a poetic work as a "well-wrought urn" contained "mortal ashes," Hartman later reflected.[102] Because he enhanced the cultural worth of critical commentary—in fact literature—and amplified the cognitive value of literature—really a critical commentary on itself—Hartman raised the status of both to the plane of rhetoric. Yet his postmodern undermining of the metaphysical dualism between critical commentary and poetic text most conspicuously elevated the prestige and expanded the purview of the critic, who was no longer beholden to venerating the secular sacred object but partook in the poetic endeavor by writing intricate commentaries, themselves artworks.

Hartman's anti-metaphysical transgression against the three-centuries-old orthodox critical prose tradition in English intersected with his community-building efforts, backing of the study of Romanticism, comparativism, interest in appropriating the vocabularies of the heresies against French structuralism, ambition to acquire a "greater measure of philosophical dignity," and admiration of de Man's "analytic acumen."[103] And these all led him to *Glas* (1974).[104] An opus that emerged from Derrida's 1971–72 seminar at the École Normale Supérieure in Paris, *Glas*, Hartman believed, persuasively addressed the relationship between art and community by cultivating a reflexive discourse that rhetorically wrestled with the literary imperative. "I recognized in *Glas*," Hartman explained, that "the Romantic dream of *Symphilosophieren* . . . which pointed to a symbiosis of philosophy and art, had finally come to fruition."[105] Experimental, nonlinear in argument and citation standards—wordplay, aural resonances, interruptions, and supplements abounded—*Glas* spanned two parallel columns. The left: a sustained reading of the sober philosophical discourse of Hegel, his interest in relations, the family, and the proper, and whose dialectic aimed to reach and describe "savoir absolu," that metaphysical form of a completely self-sovereign subject who incorporated alterity and made it useful for society.[106] The right: a series of selections from the fiction and plays of Jean Genet, an avowedly marginal author, a self-confessed "traitor, thief, informer, coward and queer" whose writings undermined the incorporation and resolution of binary oppositions, ultimately leading to self-presence, the final and ultimate synthesis of meaning: the marrying of being-in-the-world and transcendent reality—the very goal that Hegel intended to realize.[107]

Offering an interpretation of Derrida as a close ally in the rhetoricized reformation of literary education, Hartman's two essays on *Glas*—the first published in winter 1975, the second in spring 1976—became the most important writings in English on Derrida since de Man's 1970 rhetorical reading of Derrida's deconstructive reading of Rousseau.[108] By rendering the "magical" and/or "polemical" "instrument" of Derrida's deconstruction into a "critical" tool for engaging literature's exceptionality, Hartman used *Glas* to elevate the status of literary-critical discourse.[109] Derrida's "juxtaposing [of] Hegel and Genet is itself a subversion of historical or genre criticism," Hartman wrote.[110] And for Hartman, Derrida's instrument of this deconstruction was an attention to language's slipperiness, to what he called "freeplay," the indecisive movement of language that undermined the "positivity" of philosophy, of metaphysical dualisms. Awareness of "freeplay" steered critics to the task of creative reading, an interminable process that protected the text's autonomy, as any knowledge of the text submitted to linguistic freeplay "leads always to other texts and further writing."[111] Hartman's casting of Derrida's "freeplay" as a Nietzschean element that functions like art, however, ironically did risk aestheticizing—even ontologizing—Derrida's project.[112] Hartman wrote: "The wit of art, he [Derrida's Nietzsche] implies, is a will to power over the will to power. Art represents as something on the way to art what is subversive of it. It makes the truth—that is, untruth, error, the endlessness of desire or will or wit itself—bearable."[113] Whether or not he rendered Derrida's deconstruction into a transcendental law of interpretation or not, Hartman saw the disruptive power enacted by language's "freeplay" as a textual will to power that consoled the restless will to power and knowledge. Hartman's affirmation of Derrida's linguistic will to power made texts, the genre did not matter, into a boundless reflexive art form, thus desacralizing veneration of the literary object.[114]

Hartman's endorsement of Derrida's philosophical response to the literary imperative also suggested Hartman's essays were themselves a "magical" tool to help him supersede his departed colleagues in Yale English. For, by "*mitsingen*" with Derrida, Hartman honed his own rhetorical powers.[115] Like Derrida, whose text spiritedly opened by "'joycing' the name Hegel into *aigle*," deleting an *H* that is silent in French, Hartman used his "writing," as he subsequently put it, to "disclose an echo rather than an image, so that the sounding word has reverberations that transcend the economy of clarity and form"—a thriftiness habitual in English departments and endorsed by the likes of Lionel Trilling—to produce "contradictions" that shake the "temples of wisdom and science."[116] Hartman's critical essays were self-referentially multidirectional, using oblique, figural interconnections that traced each of *Glas*'s columns, showing the "delimited verbal and semantic space" as "barely encompass[ing] (if not all) such border crossing."[117] Hartman, for example, read Derrida's use of *Sa* (his acronym for "savoir absolu") at the beginning of *Glas* as an intentional wordplay with its homophones *Sa* ("signifiant") and *ça* (French for "id"). "*Sa*" operated as a "knot," Hartman argued, that brought together homophones in a way that allowed Derrida's use of *ça* in a discussion of Genet later in the text to subvert "so-called absolute knowledge," initiating "a Thousand and One Nights of interpretive pizzazz."[118] Of such energetic evenings Hartman's essays were but a couple. And yet, Hartman recollected, "*Glas* . . . confirmed that the ideal of totality . . . was not only impossible . . . but also dangerous . . . because it denied something was always left over or out, treated as dirt, excess, irrelevant texture."[119] Undermining his own Romantic ideal of *Symphilosophieren*, Hartman's rhetorical readings of *Glas* helped him better understand the claim of having shut off and shut down the disruptive figural dimensions of the text. Hartman saw this claim as an extratextual fantasy of reaching Being, the transcendental signified, a fantasy he implied was harbored by the Nazis.

The crisis in Yale English encouraged Hartman to expand his rhetorical kingdom—his spirited punning with Derrida's *Glas* moved critic Denis Donoghue to muse whether his graduate students wrote "dithyrambs" or "dissertations"—and deepen his Romantic-inspired destabilizations of the Christian-inflected onto-theological opposition between "objective" critical writing and "subjective" creative writing.[120] In contrast, Bloom hoped to found a school of criticism centered on his theory of poetic influence that avenged himself on his gentile New Critical parents, those zealots of literature who willfully ignored what Bloom saw as the anxiety, the belatedness, and the oppressiveness of exile that spurred great poets to refract their esteemed predecessors' verse. While younger colleagues understood that Bloom's "absolute individuality, autochthonic originality, transcendental selfhood" was at stake in his quixotic undertaking, senior members in Yale English, like A. Dwight Culler, were simply skeptical: "Having gone out of fashion [influence studies] will now come back into fashion. I don't quite see the school growing up that he thinks will rise."[121]

Attendees of his DeVane lectures—he was appointed to the prestigious post in 1974—overheard speculation about Bloom's not-so-secret aim: "Student gossip holds that the series represents Professor Bloom's attempt to 'defy' the New Critics at Yale. . . . If this rumor be true, how shameful."[122] In an excited display of technical virtuosity that reworked his DeVane lectures, Bloom extended his Nietzscheanized Freudian model of literary history in three new books, transforming himself, a colleague observed, "from a critic of high standing into a cult-figure of sizable proportions."[123] New Critics feared that politics had replaced religion and believed that poetry could serve as an edifying substitute, but Bloom's tracings of poets' rhetoricized lies against time, against their intellectual debts, depleted poetry of its sacredness, treating these texts as radical democratic acts. Bloom had started an intradepartmental guerrilla war against the philosophical-spiritual politics of poetry that shaped literary humanism and permeated classrooms at Yale.

Advancing his six revisionary ratios by modulating his linguistic sensitivity to poets' struggles against the twilight of art, Bloom's *A Map of Misreading* (1975) aligned rhetorical terms like metaphor, metonymy, and synecdoche with Freudian psychoanalytic terms. With this baroque "map of misreading," Bloom commandingly proclaimed, one could chart the flow of tropes and stances, echoes and resistances, across poems; he for example, coaxed from Shelley's "Ode to the West Wind" (1820) lines and images that rhetorically deflected the presence of Wordsworth's "Intimations of Immortality" (1807).[124] But Bloom's highlighting of strong poets' rhetorical detours also, like Hartman, challenged the sacred critic/poet dualism. "A poet is strong," he declared in *Kabbalah and Criticism* (1975), "because poets after him must work to evade him. A critic is strong if his readings similarly provoke other readings."[125] Colleagues protested Bloom's conspicuous self-promotion; he insisted, though, that "strong" criticism was a kind of "strong" poetry, and vice versa. No longer poets and their poems, then, but a chain of rhetorical readings, a sequence of repressed texts and more repressed texts, and every repressed text— including Bloom's—was a "crisis-poem," decodable, no less, with Bloom's map of misreading. This subversion of Eliot's view of literary tradition was nothing if not thorough.

The act of broadcasting his theories outside Yale English seems to have heightened Bloom's considerable chutzpah. While second-generation (academic) Jews cautiously spoke about their origins in the 1960s and 1970s, here was the first critic in the English tradition—the street fighter from the Bronx—not simply asserting his Jewish identity but placing a mystical tradition within Judaism at the heart of "Western" culture. He, for instance, provocatively argued in *Kabbalah and Criticism* that the late medieval systems of Kabbalist Moses Cordovero, the "first structuralist," he declared, and Kabbalist Isaac Luria, "archetype of all Revisionists," he proclaimed, showed that all great post-Miltonic poems were determined by "the anxiety of influence" and followed patterns laid down by the "thaumaturgical rabbis."[126] Bloom thus revealed that the promise of the authentically Christian society Eliot hoped for in 1933 had been an authoritarian cultural power play. And in his slim text's final pages, Bloom outright attacked the New Critical deference to poetry. Wimsatt, famously indifferent to poets' or readers' intentions, equated the work's inner formal unity with a Christian moral and aesthetic worth; Bloom, though, decreed that poems obtained the *illusions* of metaphysical presence, of unity, form, or even meaning from other poems.[127] Snatching away the ontological primacy accorded to the so-called original artwork by continually reversing the hierarchy between text and commentary, Bloom scandalously suggested that rhetorical readers (strong critics *and* strong poets) were "children of the dawn," whose writing created fantasies of presence, casting their creations as having more coherence, form, and meaning than poems "written . . . in the evening-land" of yesterday.[128] Bloom's intimidating expectation that others master the taxonomy (tikkun, zimzum, etc.) he drew from several language systems and then *Kabbalah* to detect texts' rhetorical refractions made even J. Hillis Miller ask: "Can [the reader] really be expected to make practical use of such terms?"[129]

But Bloom's extravagant psychoanalytically informed attention to the figural dimensions of the text was, as before, also a resistance. For Bloom feared how his admiration of his fellow Yale colleagues might threaten his unique visionary struggle with literature's demand. In August 1974, Bloom wrote to Miller: "I also look forward to returning from Boston hopefully on Tuesday afternoon, perhaps with both of us accompanied by the Notable Deconstructor Paul de Montevideo (true, natural son of the superb Mrs. Alfred Uruguay)."[130] Bloom's sobriquet linked de Man to modernist poet Wallace Stevens's Mrs. Alfred Uruguay, who pursued her identity by approaching a mountain of meditation—Uruguay's capital Montevideo, etymologically, is a mountain of vision—the wrong way round. Like Mrs. Alfred Uruguay, Bloom believed, de Man formulated an incomplete path toward the text: he rejected the poet's hidden struggle with the crushing weight of literary history and reversed the priority between poetic vision and poetic text by limiting poetic meaning to its unruly figural elements; de Man, Bloom wrote in 1973, ignored "the power of the mind *over* language and the universe of sense."[131] In a second August 1974 letter, Bloom further divulged his anxiety, telling Miller that he "spent the summer reading + brooding on De Man, Miller, [and] Derrida. . . . But in the end I cheerfully reject you all, because you ride the great Beast *Concept!*, the Beast from the Sea!"[132] Joyfully spurning (and rhetorically responding to) his collegial, continental-influenced shadows, Bloom not only accused them of being metaphysicians because they exclusively focused on language but also oriented his writing more to American writers—Emerson, Whitman, and Stevens—whom Bloom praised as true prophets of a self unearthing its lost meaning via singular combat with poetic tradition.[133] Bloom, nevertheless, admitted kinship with his foils: "I too believe that texts can only be interpreted as other texts . . . , but whatever the poets who matter . . . may *mean*, we had better learn to *restore* their meanings as well as *de-mystify* them." Bloom felt that his colleagues' rhetorical reading techniques only responded to poetry's "internal" deconstruction. And yet, Bloom still ended his letter with a deep display of anti-metaphysical respect: "I prefer Paul to all reconcilers, even Geoffrey, but I wish Paul would forget *all* the philosophers he has ever read!"[134]

Though looming ever larger in the American literary-critical avant-garde imagination, the Neo–New Critics were but a small group in Yale's large English department. But they had Jewish allies at the university helping to pull apart the Christian metaphysics of literary humanism: a generation behind Hartman and Bloom, Leslie Brisman, revising Bloom's theory of poetic influence, argued in his first book (1973) "that the Romantic fascination with [John] Milton is a matter of choice rather than [as Bloom had it] anxious obligation," while the previously mentioned Howard Felperin extended post–New Criticism deconstructionist approaches to the study of Shakespeare (1972).[135] But by middecade Bloom, Hartman, and Miller began to move their deconstructive endeavors elsewhere at the university. Miller grew more attached to the expanded notion of textuality explored in Comp Lit. Hartman, embracing "the age of writing" so as to subvert "gentlemanly" criticism, also turned to Comp Lit. And Bloom? He escaped the department altogether. In his August 1974 letter to Miller, Bloom wrote: "I *don't* look forward to Eng. Institute or to this yr. at Yale, as I am dead weary + sad. I have seen [A. Dwight] Culler + given him the glad news that I am now Bloom Professor of Bloom, never again to attend Eng. Dept. professors' meetings, committee meetings etc."[136] With the help of Bartlett Giamatti, Yale president and former English faculty member, Bloom became an extradepartmental professor of humanities, free to pursue his post-Miltonic truth, his discipline of rhetorically reading poets' lies against time to reveal the paradoxes of literary history that reverse hierarchies of poetic innovation. It is, of course, hardly unexpected that Bloom would declare independence, and for reasons other than professional: his was on some level a personal intellectual crusade against the anti-Semitic edifice of Anglo-American "culture" and vision of "man" that Yale English helped erect.[137] By contrast, Hartman, dedicated to the

German Jewish assimilative ideal of cosmopolitan *Bildung*, never sought such complete autonomy but worked, alone and with others, against the not exactly subtle anti-Semitism propounded in the department. Nevertheless, it became clear that, while the Neo–New Critics weathered the storms within and subverted the norms of English, their desacralizing engagements with texts' rhetorical dimensions were more welcome in the more cosmopolitan Department of Comp Lit.

A "Yale Group" Rallies around Rhetoric in Comp Lit

As soon as Miller moved to Yale in 1972, he set the machinery in motion. De Man, too, greased the wheels, reporting to Derrida at the end of April 1974: "Enthusiasm for your presence . . . at Yale will not fail to triumph over the administrative obstacles."[138] In January 1975, de Man could finally inform Derrida of Yale's offer of a three-year visiting professorship in Comp Lit. Accepting this offer, though it did not require him to resign from his position at the ENS, obligated him to end his contract with Hopkins, where he had stayed for two stretches in 1968 and 1971; Derrida had already canceled his future stay at Hopkins, set for 1974, for reasons that might have had to do with missing de Man's presence there. Derrida accepted the Yale appointment, and, in the next few years, his deconstruction, which took shape at the margins of university life in France, would be welcomed in prestigious literature departments across America. Derrida's increasingly overt focus on texts' "'literary' practice" as he assumed his Yale post also smoothed the incorporation of his deconstructive project into—or, if nothing else, facilitated its association with—the discipline of rhetorical reading that de Man was instituting in Comp Lit. Derrida, de Man believed, was not simply a much-needed ally to aid in shifting the department's attention to the reflexive interpretive science that grappled with the disruptive figural elements that tied the text in knots. For de Man, Derrida's philosophy could help demonstrate that literary language was prior though essential to all discourse. De Man, a former student explained, "was ambitious in the noblest sense of the term," and "guessed that [Derrida] would be able to shift the lines of force in the American academic world."[139] The calculation proved prescient; Derrida became a European ambassador of advanced thought that questioned established ideas not only about the unity of the artwork but about the metaphysical dualisms that constituted Western culture itself. And with Derrida's work assimilated into the mission of Comp Lit and the help of Miller's and Bloom's publicity efforts, news spread of a "Yale School" that, for those sympathetic, exemplified how to rigorously engage the claim of literature.[140] For critics, however, those very same deconstructive interpretive strategies developed and discussed in Comp Lit's "secret library" on Charles W. Bingham Hall's secluded eighth floor would come to be seen as a traitorous endeavor that destroyed literature and the coherence of the humanities.

Beginning in 1975 and for the next three years, every September, before the new academic year at the ENS, Derrida offered a three-week seminar in Comp Lit's library that contributed to the institution of rhetorical reading at Yale. His seminar, which ran for approximately twenty sessions, with one-third at Yale and the rest in Paris, was really two parallel courses: one always on Heidegger, the other moving from Francis Ponge in 1975 to Maurice Blanchot in 1976 and then to Freud in 1977.[141] Closely following an all-day lecture from the previous summer, Derrida's Ponge seminar pushed all the right desacralizing buttons; the audience was eager to hear how Derrida's "genuinely new 'science' of reading" might help address the enduring crisis of comp lit, a crisis stemming from a lack of focus and unified practice.[142] The seminar constituted a sustained consideration of lines from Ponge's short poem "Fable," which Derrida, taking immediate inspiration from the rhetorical studies of Gérard Genette, read as deconstructive Heideggerian "thing" that subverted the onto-theological subject/object binary: "With the word *with*, then, begins this text / Of which the first line states the truth."[143] Ponge's poem, Derrida argued, was an interminable reflexive performance, a topological paradox, an endless rhetorical reading of itself: a mise en abyme, or "placement in abyss," that identified, in advance of any interpretation, operations of reading and writing already signified in Ponge's poetry.[144] Implementing what it said that it said while also highlighting what it did, Ponge's poetry foregrounded its own poetic structure, its difference from itself. And while doing so, Ponge's abyssal deconstructive readings provoked the reader to question sociohistorical (humanist) approaches to "a corpus," such as the view that an author's proper name (Ponge) served as a stable link between a text, an author, and the author's style. For instance: Ponge's oeuvre, Derrida suggested, sprang from "the chance of his name": "ponge" in French can mean sponge, as clean and/or soak up; "signsponge/signéponge" means both "sign" sponge and signed ponge.[145] By infinitely and creatively redoubling themselves, then, Ponge's poems rhetorically read themselves, making hierarchic boundaries vacillate until commentary entered the text, thereby challenging the idea that a reader outside the text could produce new deconstructive readings of Ponge's poetry; this was poetry that punned to dizzyingly invent itself as a fable or allegory for how and why a text named and constituted itself.[146] Derrida's Ponge (the text) was always already a step ahead of any rhetorical reading or rhetorical reading technique, its uncannily inventive contents and forms ensuring the interminability of comp lit's crisis; readers, whether willing or not, must learn, as bricoleurs, to resourcefully dwell within the discipline's deconstructive remains.[147]

Whereas Derrida devoted his recent ENS seminars to more or less explicitly philosophical topics—his 1975 seminar *La vie la mort* investigated how "the scriptural [or deconstructive] model imported from cybernetics and adopted in biology" could "account for the genesis and structure of the living"—Derrida's engagement with the literary imperative in his Heidegger/Ponge seminar at Yale typified how his "deconstruction" (a word he barely used, instead fashioning many other terms to signify the text's Möbius-strip-like self-subversion) was to be viewed in the American academy for quite some time: he practiced a sophisticated "poststructuralist" criticism that centered on figural language, an ironic linguistic turn turned into deconstruction.[148] Take Jonathan Culler's *Structuralist Poetics* (1975), which presented Derrida's work in relation to literary semiology, underlining Derrida's undermining of the language-based paradigms of structuralism.[149] There was also the fact of Derrida's academic fame. Jeffrey Mehlman, a Yale graduate student during the late 1960s and early 1970s, reflected in 2010: "Word was beginning to spread through Yale that Europe's 'greatest philosopher' happened to be not only in New Haven but . . . in the Yale French Department [*sic*]."[150] It was reasonable to assume that Derrida's work belonged to and in literary studies. De Man considered Derrida's local influence on the American institution of deconstruction clear. "I can't tell you," he wrote to Derrida, "how much good your stay did all of us, your friends here, all those who listened to you with passion, and myself in particular. The results of your teaching are starting to appear. . . . It is literally the first time for very many years that a group from varied backgrounds has gathered together in Yale to pursue an intellectual goal."[151]

This goal's precise dimensions were under serious consideration by Miller, who, in 1975, assumed Cleanth Brooks's post in English as Gray Professor of Rhetoric and joined the institution of deconstruction in Yale Comp Lit. Miller proposed that he and his friends were jointly inventing/discovering a science of rhetorical reading to tackle the enduring crisis about literature's being-in-the-world that drove criticism and comparative literature. The "Yale Group," Miller wrote in an October 1975 journal entry, "is riven by fissures but sharing a problematic or set of questions or putting into question."[152] A week later: "Ahha, I think I see a way to speak of the Yale Group. . . . The Yale Group is Dionysiac in . . . the sense that might be symbolized by the marriage of Dionysus to Ariadne: the labyrinthine explanation of the labyrinth criticism as the uncanny."[153] Miller was using the myth of Ariadne's thread in the Minotaur's labyrinth as an analogy for the Yale group's responses to texts' rhetorical elements.[154] In a 1976 article, Miller would explain that whereas "Socratic, theoretical, or canny" critics (like Jonathan Culler et al.) were "lulled by the promise of a rational ordering of literary study on the basis of solid advances in scientific knowledge about language," "uncanny" critics (the Yale group) showed how "encounter[s] with an 'aporia' or impasse" undermined such a metaphysical quest / scientific program.[155] "This is why," Miller journaled, "they have been assaulted by the reviewers: [the] moment (in different [ways] for Bloom, Hartman, De Man, Derrida) when it no longer makes rational sense, when the bottom drops out, or when there is an abyssming."[156] While structuralists employed innovative scientific methods to logically organize literary study—that is, to iron out the paradoxes of literary texts—the Yale group developed a counterlogic. This science/discipline of rhetorical reading rigorously grappled with literature's mise en abyme, with how strange textual loops subverted the rational ordering of literary study.

Miller's frequently battered "Yale Group" found public hearing in a November 1975 omnibus review in the *New Republic*. There, Miller subtly engaged the literary imperative by deconstructing the hierarchical opposition between his "Yale Group" and Wallace Stevens's *The Rock*. He proposed that he, de Man, Derrida, Hartman, and Bloom were "members . . . of a new group of critics" for whom "the fundamental issue at stake . . . is the question whether the 'cure of the ground' which [Wallace] Stevens demands of poetry and of discourse about poetry is to be a 'grounding,' a making solid of the foundation, as one 'cures' a fiberglass hull, or whether the ground is to be cured by being effaced, made to vanish, as medicine cures a man of disease by taking it away."[157] Though by "no means unified in their methodological commitments," Miller stressed, the Yale circle's members each pondered how "the cure of the ground"—the preservation *and/or* removal of a foundation—organized poetry and criticism of it.[158] Both the Yale group's work and the literature they wrote about, for Miller, circled back on themselves to question their very premises.

The word that spread about this "Yale Group" and their mise en abyme suggested awareness, if not a complete understanding, of their reflexive interpretive science. In his *New York Times* review of Hartman's *The Fate of Reading* (1975), Richard Poirier noted that the way Hartman presented his newer work asked for "his accomplishments" to "be taken as part of a community enterprise."[159] William H. Pritchard, in the winter 1975–76 issue of the *Hudson Review*, mentioned the adventures of "The Hermeneutical Mafia" at "meetings of the M.L.A., the English Institute, and other professional organizations."[160] But he also charged "members of this community [with] seem[ing] to" write and speak "above all to each other."[161] Aware of this accusation and the anxiety it signaled about the growing rift between his profession's teaching and research arms, Hartman summarized in 1976: "This higher criticism [i.e., deconstruction] bursts upon a scene of mass education where English teachers are trying to instill a minimum of literacy and objectivity and are now made to feel defensive by more than their students. They are being asked to consider interpretations very self-conscious in style, that move swiftly from useful commentary to hermeneutic highjinks, and expand literary history to include the hinterland of rhetorical and theological terms."[162] To the newly ordained critical clerisy, the Yale group's institution of deconstruction could make criticism "relevant" to social needs, solve comp lit's existential crisis, even provide humanists with a tactic to reassert cultural prestige. As with the New Criticism, access and ability were seen as the only barriers to the potentially democratizing effects of a universally applicable way of reading. As a criticism of science, however, the American institution of deconstruction appeared to produce yet more crisis. For those teaching in the massified English departments across America had fewer and fewer resources for such complex and reflexive modes of criticism. As departments were increasingly called upon to justify their existence due to the newly adopted policies in tertiary institutions that aimed to improve training and education so as to meet the requirements of the labor market and industry, the new economic necessities created an ever more aggressive professional environment, especially in language and literature departments, intensifying professional protocols and expectations for career advancement. And though their postformalist work evolved from their earlier subversions of literary-critical traditions, the Yale circle quickly garnered a reputation as outrageous postmodern anarchists. During an unprecedented and precarious moment for their profession, the group promulgated an imported, elitist, inward-looking criticism that encouraged the most damaging of pedagogical and interpretive extravagances.

De Man's fall 1975 Comp Lit graduate seminar, "Rhetorical Readings," epitomized how the institution of deconstruction could provoke such conflicting views. In his course, de Man made his bid that the discipline of rhetorical reading operated as and disclosed the primary science of interpretation, showing how rhetoric was prior to but fundamental to philosophical and psychoanalytic discourses.[163] In his seminar, de Man circulated Derrida's 1971 essay "La mythologie blanche," which at the time was Derrida's second major publication translated into English.[164] In it, Derrida deconstructively read the metaphysical opposition between metaphoric and proper meaning in texts from Aristotle to Hegel, Nietzsche to Heidegger. Derrida argued that any philosophical effort to decipher the proper meaning of metaphors subverted itself, as a metaphorical system always structured discussions of metaphor; thus, metaphor did not simply block a concept's content and could be exposed but produced metaphors of metaphors. For example: Derrida foregrounded how the Platonic proper meaning/metaphor opposition failed to account for how the root "sense" was articulated in both sense (the signified) and the senses (the sensory signifier). Since "sense" indicated what was both integral and alien to "senses," "sense" undermined Plato's philosophical division between signified and signifier, sense and the senses.

In his seminar, de Man dexterously enlisted Derrida's deconstructive project to reinforce his claim about the universal applicability of rhetorical reading. Derrida, de Man lectured, said the "same thing [about metaphor] that he ... said in *De la grammatologie*," "La mythologie blanche," and his 1967 article on Freud. In the third piece, Derrida read Freud as giving an account of the tropological mechanisms of the psyche that bent back on itself, undermining his own conclusions about memory.[165] Freud, Derrida maintained, metaphysically relegated writing as secondary to the processes of memory, but he also conjectured that memory functioned metaphorically. Memory, Freud wrote, was a "forest of script," a "landscape of writing."[166] Freud's metaphors for memory performed a metaphorical totalization, in that Freud used them as a basis of resemblance to name or convey the essence of memory. But by using metaphors of writing, Freud, ironically, made the substitutions and repressions of (his) "writing" primary for psychological processes of memory. Freud's writing metaphors deconstructed the metaphysical opposition that he erected between writing and memory.

De Man bent Derrida's reading of Freud's "psyche (memory)" into terms consonant with his rhetorical project. Responding to Derrida's 1967 observation that Freud "opens up a new kind of question about metaphor, writing, spacing in general," de Man instructed his graduate students "to induce a further understanding of writing from the writings of Freud." Like Derrida—"In the frame," de Man lectured, "around [Freud's] text, D. took his difference"—de Man took his difference. "I am only going to formulate into crude language what [Derrida] said with refinement." "By saying that ... memory is a scene of writing," de Man explained, "we are saying that it is ... unreadable, but has to be read."[167] By "unreadable," de Man meant how, due to the operations of literary language, a text not only did not correspond to its own presentation of itself but showed how this was the case as well. In a 1976 article, de Man would call such reflexive readings "allegories of unreadability," the rhetorical reading "of a figure (for example, metaphor) which relapses into the figure it deconstructs."[168] For example, the unreadable metaphors of (Freud's deconstructive model of) memory, de Man lectured, guaranteed that the "deciphering of a dream is *another* dream[;] the unconsciousness of an unconsciousness is *another* unconsciousness."[169] He never wrote on Freud, but de Man, here, seemed to impart a lesson about literary studies' legitimate scope similar in spirit to the view he was once credited to have given in response to disapproval of his maximalist textualism: "If you want to talk about men, you are in the wrong field. . . . We can only talk about letters."[170]

Those interested in using sociohistorical approaches to rejoin the literary imperative, then, were in the wrong seminar, the wrong comp lit department, indeed the wrong institution. For nonrhetorical readers, de Man's focus on "letters" simply avoided the outside of the text. Despite their allied approaches, even de Man's friend and colleague Hartman never did share what he referred to in 1988 as de Man's "purity of deconstructive thought," a purity that did "not reveal . . . its situatedness, its personal or ideological context."[171] For de Man, however, "letters" were disruptive and fundamental to all discourse. Had an undergraduate teacher of English, from, say, a state school in the Midwest, peeked in on de Man's class, he or she could be forgiven for believing that the arduous struggle of academic specialists had reached a destructive apotheosis. But in fact, de Man claimed in 1979 that a "rhetoric of reading reaching beyond the canonical principles of literary history . . . remains dependent on the initial position of these very principles."[172] To be sure, de Man's students *were* taken down rigorous interpretive paths with strange vocabularies to discover prose and poetry as much stranger than thought. Yet this constructively *subverted*—did not *replace*—the literary humanist's undertaking. And, certainly, de Man did in the early 1970s abandon his historical study of Romanticism due to what he saw as literature and its rhetoric undermining the summarizing of texts and the synthesizing of narrative threads. He made the rhetorical reading of texts' unreadability paramount and he positioned graduate students in a subversive relation to the Eliotic notion of literary tradition as passed down via appropriation of linguistic devices, New Critical detections of Coleridgean symbols in literature, and the Wellekian study of prose and poetry as an education of values—perhaps *this* was de Man's deconstructive historicism.[173]

XYZ; or, the ABCs of Deconstruction

It was the spring term of 1977, in Linsley-Chittenden Hall, a Romanesque building on the High Street edge of the Old Campus, and Hartman was finishing a lecture in Literature Z. Hartman's lecture was based on a paradox introduced in the famous final lines of John Keats's poem "Ode on a Grecian Urn" (1820): "Beauty is truth, truth beauty,—that is all / Ye know on earth, and all ye need to know." In the first half of the century, many commentators parroted T. S. Eliot's assessment that Keats's lines were "meaningless," "a serious blemish on a beautiful poem" that rendered it defective.[174] Not Cleanth Brooks. In a 1944 essay that became an icon of New Critical analysis, he suggested that Keats's final lines be understood in the "total context of the poem," as Keats's paradox was related to how each of the poem's five stanzas resolved the conflict between the bustling life depicted on the urn and its images of a pastoral frozen for eternity, resulting in a well-wrought urn.[175] In Lit Z, Hartman wrought a "Grecian urn" rhetorically self-aware. The urn's speaker, Hartman wrote in an article, was an "explainer-ravisher" whose addresses "tease and evade our meditation," for "each frame in the turned object [the urn] repeats a questionable shape . . . until its mystery is in danger of being dissolved, its form broken for the sake of a message."[176] Rather than solace, the Grecian urn offered, in Keats's words, "a heart high-sorrowful and cloy'd, / A burning forehead, and a parching tongue." Coming to the podium to deliver his lecture on Locke, Kant, and Marx, de Man handled the transition with his ironic aplomb: "Professor Hartman has given you beauty, now you will get de trut" (de Man's Flemish-inflected pronunciation of "the truth"). A gasp escaped from the audience. A teaching assistant afterward visited Hartman's office to ensure that his feelings were unhurt.[177]

This amusing anecdote hints at the serious role undergraduate courses in the once controversial literature major played in imparting the ABCs of deconstruction. In a manner reminiscent of the New Critics, de Man, Hartman, and Miller closed the gap between their research and teaching by aligning the lit major's mission with their rigorous discipline of rhetorical reading. Their pedagogical-intellectual success hung mostly on local factors, above all de Man's, Hartman's, and Miller's exploitation of the favorable conditions already established for the American institution of deconstruction in the lit major. While, in French and Comp Lit, de Man had gained a good deal of control, in Yale English, Miller and Hartman were two members of a large, storied, and conservative department. The relatively new and comparatively small lit major lacked history and precedent, and its experimental spirit lingered. This provided the three friends the opportunity to teach deconstruction to undergraduates, to show students how literature and the literary language of any discourse reflexively dissented against being treated as a secular chapel where worldly worship yielded presence, metaphysical unity, and harmony. In this way, the Yale School's desacralization of literary education in New Haven contributed to a similar process occurring across the American humanities.

Miller's involvement in the lit major began when he was appointed its director for the 1973–74 year, but it was not until he succeeded Peter

Brooks as director in 1980–83 that he decisively exerted his deconstructive teaching agenda there. In the fall 1981 iteration of the course known successively as Lit X, Man and His Fictions, Narrative Forms, and Literature 120, Miller encouraged students to be skeptical of using interpretive principles to grapple with the literary imperative. As a consequence, sophomore Judy Wurtzel found herself lost in an abyss of reading. In response to a question Miller posed—"How does one know if one's interpretation of a text is correct?"—Wurtzel confessed: "I have discovered no absolute standard by which I can judge analysis & say 'Yes, this is correct.' . . . There seems to be a limit—determined more by moderation & good sense than by rule or formula. . . . But where that limit lies is still questionable."[178] But staring into such an interpretive void accelerated undergraduates' habituation to quasi-deconstructive styles of reading. Junior Juliet Guichon was this class of student by early fall 1980. In her answer to Miller's question, she stressed the deconstructive requirement of self-effacement when engaging the text: "The validity of one's reading of a work is determined by the text itself. The text stands alone and must be interpreted in relation to the unwritten rules the author implies throughout the work."[179] Students not all that invested in the literary texts favored by de Man and company even internalized the ascetic ethos taught in Narrative Forms. In the fall 1979 version of Lit 120, sophomore Ashley Curtis, who majored in Chinese and biblical literature, supplied an exemplary response to Miller's question: "A valid interpretation of a literary work can be supported by references to the text. It cannot be destroyed by other references to the text, unless this potential destruction is an essential part of the interpretation."[180] De Man's postmodern politics of poetic difference seems to have filtered into the consciousness of Yale undergraduates by the early 1980s.

Lit X also inspired Miller's undergraduates to produce essays of a labyrinthine complexity and quality that undermined the onto-theological grounds of literary study and the metaphysical response to literature's demand to be read as complex language irreducible to other types of texts. Consider a final assignment in 1979, which required pupils to parody a school of critics that Jorge Luis Borges described in his short story "Tlön, Uqbar, Orbis Tertius" (1940). Students were to "attribute two works . . . to the same author and discuss how one revises and elaborates the plot model of the other." In his paper, sophomore Bill Jewett, imitating Borges's style and stance, deconstructively wove a mise en abyme with Miller's rhetorical readings of Freud's "Wolfman" (1918) and Joseph Conrad's *Heart of Darkness* (1899), explaining how both works "developed two examples of enigma with complementary yet diametrically opposed

methods: in . . . 'Wolfman' the reader sees the unknown illuminated by
clues, whereas in . . . *Heart of Darkness* the reader sees clues illuminated by
the unknown."[181] In addition, Jewett used Miller's readings to argue that
Freud's and Conrad's stories "progress through a process of revelation in
opposite directions yet end up in the same place."[182] Exchanging clue for
enigma, enigma for clue, and reversing beginning and end, Jewett's (or
was it Miller's?) Freud and Conrad turned out to be deconstructive detec-
tives who meticulously subverted (one another's) narrative form, not just
temporally but structurally as well.

Jewett's paper surely provided pedagogical pleasure to Miller because
of its remarkable ironic internal mirroring that highlighted and interrogated how Jewett's text rhetorically read itself. In fact, from the start of his
reflexive textual work, Jewett alerted readers that it was he and Miller—not
simply Freud and Conrad—who were guilty of the essay's strange loops. It
was a "T.A." named "Miller," Jewett suggested, who distributed (the real)
Miller's deconstructive interpretations of Freud's and Conrad's stories for
Jewett's (fictional) professor's assignment in "Elementary Hermeneutics
(conducted in English)." "This T.A.," Jewett continued, "sat down at one
of the Library's terminals, accessed his account, and [after typing] in 'Eng.
Enigma.19326.random, Eng.Enigma/inv.19327.random; TEXT'" received
copies of "*Freud's Wolfman*, Author: General Library, Writer: Miller" and
"*Conrad's Heart of Darkness*, Author: General Library, Writer: Miller." The
TA then delivered "Miller's two texts" to the (fictional) University of Tlön
professor; this professor, in turn, delivered Miller's rhetorical readings "to
his class with instructions to write a paper on the writer's treatment of
enigma, a paper revolving around the most spectacular connections possible without strict regard to their truth." Beyond this playful fictionalizing
of Miller and his texts, Jewett even deconstructively began his paper on
Miller's rhetorical readings of Freud and Conrad by placing scare quotes
around it all. Jewett's inverted commas self-knowingly advanced the deconstructive claim that texts referred in a frame-in-frame way to other
texts; they consigned his paper to another layer in his carefully staged mise
en abyme. The real Miller was likely impressed with Jewett's ironic use of
intertextuality. But Jewett's fictional University of Tlön professor, following a series of arch remarks—"It seems by explicating the given texts you
have unwittingly ascribed to them a closure. By the very nature of your
diagrammatic approach, you have concretized what you meant to leave
vague or 'enigmatic'"—awarded his student a C, concluding: "Your paper
has some merit for what it is; also, grade inflation compels me not to fail
you. For your next paper, I expect to receive a more apt fiction."[183] More
rhetoricization, more deconstruction of presence, was required if Jewett

wanted a truly fantastic grade. Here indeed was an undergraduate whose reflexive rigor disputed the centuries-old prejudice that a heightened self-consciousness like that of the Romantics depleted creative powers.

After Lit X, the next letter floating in the lit major's desacralizing alphabet soup: Y. The spring 1982 iteration of Literature Y—or, per Yale administration, Literature 300b: "Introduction to Literary Theory"—sometimes taught students the discipline of rhetorical reading during its usual sequence of theoretical perspectives of American and European philosophers, critics, and thinkers; in the final weeks, the course shifted focus to feminist criticism and Afro-American studies. Lit Y instructors used many local resources to achieve their pedagogical goals, including prominent deconstructionists. De Man began a visiting lecture thus: "Our question will be how and why there is a point, for literary theory, to read Derrida." De Man proceeded to orient his reading of Derrida and Lit Y students toward one another: "[For Derrida] the question of the possibility of theoretical discourse is found with special acuity *in relation to literature*. . . . Considerable merit, in my opinion, of D. is his scope et [*sic*] not as application but as problematization." De Man's Derrida, Lit Y students learned, was vital for any rigorous engagement with the literary imperative, above all, because of the staggering range of Derrida's responses to the complications of reading prose and poetry. To support his contention, de Man proceeded "historically, traditionally," providing a chronology of Derrida's "philosophical concerns" as a "young man in the mid 1950s," before turning to Derrida's use of Saussure, which revealed "the originality of D."[184]

In Lit Y, de Man therefore promoted his rhetoricized Derrida, a philosopher in line with de Man's commitment to showing that rhetorical reading was the foundational interpretive science. For example, de Man highlighted how Derrida's use of Saussure's theory of language helped Derrida "think the doubleness of the text"—that the text was "unavoidable, structurally + hermeneutically, phonocentric/graphocentric"; that the text uncontrollably oscillated between presence and absence. Because this rhetorical (or literary) duplicity shaped *all* texts, de Man lectured to undergraduates, there could "*not, never*, [be] a rejection or even an Aufhebung ["sublation" or "incorporation"] of Saussure, of Hegel, of Freud, etc. or of metaphysics, voice, . . . phenomenology, hermeneutics, etc," but only the "displac[ement of] the discourse of science, of phil[osophy], of theory." For de Man as much as for Derrida, it seemed, the text's doubleness—its rhetorical performance or self-deconstruction—always already threw a wrench into the dialectical engine of rejection or integration, ensuring that the careful reader must confront the figural disruption of metaphysical attempts to resolve the text's divisions, a confrontation that subverts the assimilation of texts into an interpretive synthesis, such as into the themes of biography. What's more, in de Man's lecture, the ever-mushrooming number of networked terms that Derrida used to indicate his deconstruction became integrated into de Man's reflexive interpretive science. Derrida's thorough focus on the doubleness of the text led him to devise, de Man stated, "terminological designation[s]," such as "trace (signifier/signified)," "archi-trace (origin/linear development)," "*espacement* (spacing)" and "supplement (more/less)," that implemented the "non reflexive doubling necessary but *not conceptually* stable" way to foreground the text's treachery. This emphasis on the text's doubleness, de Man predicated to students, "will be the task of literary criticism in the coming years."[185]

While Lit X and Lit Y were important lit major courses, it was in Literature Z where de Man, with Hartman and then Miller, most effectively imparted deconstruction to undergraduates. In Lit Z, "Reading and Rhetorical Structures," students learned how a sufficiently rigorous rejoinder to the literary imperative required close grappling with the text's ironic contradictions. The class would make its inaugural run in the late 1970s, though its design dated from the first half of the decade. At a May 6, 1974, meeting of the governing board of the lit major, Miller unreservedly backed his friends' development of Lit Z; it would, he explained, "fill out the curriculum."[186] Reasons for the sophomore-level course's eventual success are traceable to a 1975 proposal written with de Man's flair and full of his vocabulary. Conventional approaches to literary education, faculty read, lag behind cutting-edge pedagogies that "moved toward literature as a language about language, or a metalinguistic discipline best understood as a response to the specific complexities and resources of language."[187] Lit Z offered to train students to deal with literature's references to and comments on its own irresolvable figural conflicts. Though this way of approaching the text might be viewed as "new-fangled," the Lit Z proposal continued, it "represents in fact a return to an age-long [marginalized] tradition which rooted the study of literature in philology, poetics, rhetoric, and grammar."[188] Part of this suppressed tradition that questioned onto-theological efforts to grammatize and logico-historicize language, Lit Z would teach students how to carefully identify the rhetorical dimensions of the text that were prior to though constitutive of any text's meaning. To a degree extending New Critical Browerian slow-motion reading, de Man's and Hartman's deconstructive teaching strategy appealed to faculty hoping to preserve accepted pedagogical methods; for them, Lit Z's strict and consistent approach turned back Lit X's sixties-inspired breathless expansion of the text. For those eager to move beyond established boundaries, however, the course rigorously refined Lit X's free-for-all. De Man's and Hartman's dual appeal, in the end, conceivably accounted for Lit Z's successful adoption in the lit major.[189]

The debut of Lit Z in spring 1977 saw de Man building his deconstructive discipline with canonical European philosophical texts. He, for example, showed students how the literary language of René Descartes's *Meditations on First Philosophy* (1647) unsettled the text's attempt to stabilize the self's existence. There was a "much more radical mood" in *Meditations*, de Man lectured, than usually acknowledged. Instead of Descartes's affirmation "I think, therefore I am," de Man proposed "I doubt that I am therefore I am" as the interpretive principle rhetorically inscribed in Descartes's text, specifically in his "critique of [the] epistemological unreliability of self as a trope." De Man continued: "The cogito (I am, I exist), the certitude of existence is a trope, i.e. grounded in a . . . field of language (and not in the nature of things as they are, that is to say, as ontologically grounded) that discovers its own displacement." "Thus," de Man concluded, Descartes's cogito was in fact a "linguistic fashioning of the I."[190] With de Man's rhetorical reading of *Meditations*, Lit Z students meditated on a doubting cogito, produced by reflexive language, who learned of his or her separation from the empirical world.

But the epistemological-textual consequences of de Man's rhetoricized Descartes extended beyond mere ironic detachment. Students considered the "temporal discrepancy" in *Meditations* between Descartes's cogito and his "delusions," by which de Man meant Descartes's hypothesis in his first meditation that an evil demon might be misleading Descartes into believing in the illusion of an external world. "The act of judg[ing whether there is an external world] does not come from seeing," de Man lectured, "but from *meditating* i.e. positing of I as catachresis." By identifying how Descartes used the trope of catachresis—customarily meaning semantic misuse but for de Man referring to the arbitrary link between signifier and signified, language and thing—students were not simply inculcated with the view that the cogito, the "I" or self, was randomly imposed upon existence but learned how Descartes's philosophical text rhetorically responded to literature's demand. "I" was a "linguistic catachresis" in *Meditations*, de Man explained, and Descartes's "I" existed in the text "precisely [at] the point where the *temporal* correspondence between the act of thought and its performance takes place [and] breaks down." The import of this textual collapse was that the metaphysical dichotomy between "I" and external world buckled as well. Rather than perceiving an *outside* world, then, Descartes's "I" conjured itself via contemplation of itself—though this reflexive "I" was also an other, alien to itself. Descartes's rhetorical positing of an "I" and an external world set in motion textual oppositions that questioned the stable identity, the presence, of each antithetical concept.

The result, de Man concluded to Lit Zers: "The polarities [of Descartes's thought experiments that tested whether "I" was awake or asleep, sane or crazy] are not just reversed, but the possibilities of a clear choice between them has been blurred so that I am a state of fundamental indecision/undecidability about the essential modalities of existence."[191] By contemplating de Man's rhetoricized Cartesian cogito, students were introduced to de Man's deconstructive argument that the power of literary language unsettled the dualisms that institute philosophical discourses, whether attempting to stabilize the presence of the self or not.

During the second month of Lit Z's inaugural run, de Man and Hartman required students to sit at the feet of a demanding master of philosophical suspicion aligned with the pair's deconstructive teaching aims: Friedrich Nietzsche. "Descartes can be said to be poetic," de Man lectured, "precisely because even his most extreme form of mental vigilance cannot master the rhetorical power of language and inscribes this power in his text." But while Descartes implicitly marked the deconstructive claim of literature, "the Nietzsche text . . . makes this [literariness or self-subversiveness] explicit." To demonstrate, de Man and Hartman distributed an exercise that solicited students to poetically dance with the ur-deconstructor of metaphysical dichotomies: "In the second part of the essay *Truth and Falsity* [1873] (pp. 512–15), Nietzsche sets up what appears to be a contrast, a polarity, between the man of 'science' and the man of 'art.'"[192] Lit Zers were to rhetorically respond to this ahistorical juxtaposition in and with Nietzsche's text. "By a close reading of this section [of *Truth and Falsity*], you are invited (1) to discuss the structure of this opposition and (2) to examine its implications with regard to the relative *value* of both activities, in themselves as well as with regard to history."[193] With four "suggestions to assist . . . in organizing [their] thoughts" about Nietzsche's text, students combined de Man's strict attention to (literary) language with Hartman's mindfulness of poetic form in relation to genre and period to engage with how Nietzsche's rhetoric shaped and subverted his polarity between "the man of 'science' and man of 'art.'" The Lit Z teachers went on to invite students to deconstructively read selections from Aristotle's *Poetics* and Plato's *Republic* that tried to differentiate between prose and poetry. But, de Man lectured, "behind all these distinctions" in the ancient Greeks' texts, "stands a wavering problematic of prose/poetry."[194] Students rhetorically read sections of *Poetics* and *Republic* to contemplate this undecidable interpretive knot. They studied how the figurative language of these texts subverted the philosophers' value-laden distinctions.

In the third iteration of Lit Z, renamed Lit 130b and offered in spring 1979, de Man, with Miller as coteacher, taught his science of rhetorical

Literature Z

Exercise II

"Science" and "Art" in Nietzsche's Truth and Falsity
in an Ultramoral Sense

In the second part of the essay Truth and Falsity (pp. 512-515), Nietzsche sets up what appears to be a contrast, a polarity, between the man of "science" and the man of "art". By a close reading of this section, you are invited (1) to discuss the structure of this opposition and (2) to examine its implications with regard to the relative value of both activies, in themselves as well as with regard to history.

Preparation

The following guidelines are given as suggestions to assist you in organizing your thoughts. If you find them cumbersome or obscure feel entirely free to ignore them and to follow your own inclinations.

(1) How does the opposition between "science" and "art" relate to the theory of language as figuration developed in part I of the essay in answer to such questions as "What is a word?" (p. 506) or "What is therefore truth?" (p. 508).

(2) In section II, Nietzsche seems to be using a valorized language, as if he were advocating a preference for certain mental activities over others. Note also that many of the metaphors and polarities used in section I recur in section II (consider, for instance, such figures as wake/sleep (dream); master/slave; falling/rising; building/destroying; play/seriousness; truth/delusion, etc.) How are the value judgments that appear in section II influenced by the use of these figures? Is the influence of the figures on the value-statements consistent with the theory of figuration that is propounded in the essay?

(3) Section II also contains sequential and explicitly historical language (such as, for example, the reference to Greece on p. 515). How does this historical language in part II relate to the theory of figuration in part I?

(4) Does Nietzsche's own writing, in this essay, classify his text under "art" or under "science?" Does this have consequences for Nietzsche's own historical situation?

Writing

Write a 5 page essay on "Science" and "Art" in Nietzsche's Truth and Falsity incorporating answers to some of the questions suggested above, or similar ones that may occur to you.

Due in section on Thursday, February 24th.

FIGURE 3.4 An exercise from Literature Z in which undergraduate students were asked to write an essay on Nietzsche's *Truth and Falsity in an Ultramoral Sense* (Courtesy of J. Hillis Miller)

reading with canonic modern and Romantic poetic texts. He began with what would become a locus classicus of the Yale School's deconstructive enterprise: Yeats's "Among School Children" (1928). Upon a first reading, de Man told students, Yeats's poem asked four questions, each straightforwardly answered by a different stanza. These stanzas formed a "ring," a "(give+take, show+tell)," around the poem; one naturally read the poem's last question—"How can we know the dancer from the dance?"—to conclude the poem's formal questioning: "One cannot know the difference between the dancer and the dance," de Man explained. But, he lectured, the grammaticality of that last sentence continually solicited answers. "Please tell me," the final line pleaded, "how can I know the difference?" Evidence in the poem could not conclusively determine which of the incompatible interpretations—the rhetorical or the grammatical—was correct, students learned. Yeats's last question prevented the reader from definitively resolving whether one can know the difference between dancer and dance. "*Unable* to decide," de Man stressed, "you *have* to decide." He pressed Lit 130ers to continually reassess the seeming transparency of Yeats's final question and thereby subvert the onto-theological reading that the four questions fashioned a hallowed ring, or closed a circle, around the poem. De Man impressed his reflexive interpretive science on his own "schoolchildren" by directing them to rhetorically read the unresolvable contradiction between literal and figurative meanings. "For, don't forget," he wryly noted, "you are inscribed *in* the poem."[195]

Other Lit 130b lectures explored how the rhetorical elements and figurative language of Romantics' texts served as the self-deconstructive building blocks of all discourse. As he had argued in a recent article, de Man lectured that Percy Bysshe Shelley's death poem, the ironically titled *The Triumph of Life* (1822), "peels, like an onion"; it articulated "questions" that commented on the poem's unfolding action and generated sets of contradictory, "undecidable," figurative meanings. To ease his students into how to foreground these metafigures, these rhetorical dimensions of the text, de Man would focus, he explained, on "the most difficult passage of [*Triumph*], the passage always *erased* in favor of historical + political opinion [and] facts": "[T]he structure of forgetting" performed by Shelley's lines "Of the young year, I found myself asleep . . . / Like this harsh world in which I wake to weep, / I know not."[196] Shelley's lines, which declared states of both sleep and wakefulness, suspended the reader between two equally possible interpretations. Was Shelley asleep, as Shelley wrote, "Under a mountain, which from unknown time, / Had yawned into a cavern, high and deep"? Was Shelley awake? "I know not." Elsewhere, de Man elaborated that Shelley's indecision was a site of forgetting "not just because it indicates (*représente*) a compulsive undecidability . . . so unbearable it was to be repressed, but because the situation itself . . . arises . . . as a fluctuation between knowing and not-knowing [whether "we are awake or asleep, dead or alive"], like the symptom of a disease that one remembers and that recurs only at the very instant that one remembers its absence." "Forgetting," de Man concluded, "escapes here the polarity of absence and presence that is the constitutive principle of any binary system. It is, in fact, the deformation, the asymmetrization, the disfiguration of these systems."[197] In de Man's comprehensive science of rhetorical reading, the forgetting or disfigurement elaborated on and performed by Shelley's lines, and more generally his *Triumph*, established and undermined the philosophical dualisms that structured every text. *Also sprach* Professeur de Man.

Further awakening his Lit 130ers' state of forgetting to the rhetoric of all discourse, de Man asked students to ponder how stanza 5 of William Wordsworth's "Ode: Intimations of Immortality" (1807) performed a chiasmus, a rhetorical figure in which two related words, grammatical forms, or concepts were reiterated in reverse order, executing a repetition often with a cruel twist. "Our birth," Wordsworth poesied, "is but a sleep and a forgetting; / ... Not in entire forgetfulness, / And not in utter nakedness, / But trailing clouds of glory do we come." With these lines, de Man lectured, Wordsworth offered a profoundly undecidable puzzle: "You remember limbo and you forget life. [Wordsworth] valorize[s] limbo as Heaven. [He] has denunciation of *birth* as forgetting. . . . [If] to *know* is to go back to before birth" "is *not to know* to forget what one knew?" "I don't know," de Man cheekily reflected, "if not to know is to *forget* that I know." With dizzying Möbius-strip-like journeys of chiasmic reversals offered by Wordsworth's poetry, de Man led Lit 130ers to rhetorically recognize the "forgetting"—the figural deformations or asymmetrizations or the self-deconstruction—at work in any text.

Following his discussion of Wordsworth, de Man returned to Shelley's *Triumph* to explore how its web of extended metaphors, which de Man argued were often and inaccurately considered unintelligible, generated *Triumph*'s deconstructive narrative and historical movement. By rhetorically reading the accord and discord between "gliding," "threading," "treading," and "trampling" motions of light, Shelley's luminous metaphor in *Triumph*, de Man lectured, fashioned an undecidable. For de Man, the imposition of the metaphor of the sun at the start of Shelley's poem— "Swift as a spirit hastening to his task ... the Sun sprang forth ... and the mask / Of darkness fell from the awakened Earth" (lines 1–4)—was a catachresis, a linguistic event, not a transcendental signified (outside the text) that ordered the narrative. Rather, the sun in *Triumph* performed the "positing power of language," turning events in Shelley's poem into acts of "inscription" that imposed upon and erased one another. For de Man, the transformation from "glide" to "tread" and then to "trample" fragmented the luminous metaphor of the "sun," which set the events of the Earth in motion in *Triumph*. Though Shelley portrayed light's gliding as remaining upon a reflective exterior and permitting a mirrorlike image to come into existence—the "light" was "Amid the gliding waves and shadows dun"—he also made light's treading motion burst through the surface and terminate its hovering existence on the specular surface: the classical goddess of the rainbow, "Iris," Shelley wrote, who initially "bore a chrystal glass" with "palms so tender" that were able to "tread" among the drifting surfs, eventually "trampled its fires into the dust of death." Because Shelley's luminous metaphor of "light" drifted on top of and forcefully penetrated the watery surface, the only certainty Shelley offered was an undecidable between gliding and crushing movements. But as the sun treaded and trampled, it also "threaded all the forest maze." "Th[is] motion" in Shelley's poem, de Man lectured, "from thread to tread to trample . . . *wears down* the metaphor of the sun as cognition (thought)." "I draw attention," de Man stressed, to "thread-tread" because "I am no longer paraphrasing a meaning—the erasure of the sun *is* the wear and tear, the erosion of figuration by the play of the signifier."[198] Tracking Shelley's uses of "light" directed Lit 130ers not only to Shelley's increasing linguistic violence against forms of understanding but also to de Man's notion that even the most continuous and natural event, the rising of the sun, was a metaphor for the arbitrary power of language.[199] At the end of de Man's explication, right before spring break, he himself left his students atop an aporia, an undecidable: "I leave you suspended. . . . 3 weeks from now, after vacation, . . . Prof. Miller will put an end to your gliding suspense."[200]

Lit Z was undoubtedly the most pedagogically powerful course in the lit major, but classes outside the lit major at Yale in the late 1970s also advanced de Man, Hartman, and Miller's group effort to teach the discipline of rhetorical reading to undergraduates. In one of Miller's 1978 English poetry courses, delivered when Miller served as chair of the department, junior Carl Goldfarb highlighted the self-deconstructions of Yeats's "The Wild Swans at Coole" (1917), in which Yeats pondered the changes since he had counted the swans on the estate of his friend Lady Gregory at dusk nineteen years earlier. Initially, Goldfarb's Yeats appeared to offer readers a stable foothold on his poem's meaning: "Yeats shapes an emblem as he transforms the natural swans of the second stanza—mounting, wheeling, and clamoring—to the meaning laden emblems of the fourth and fifth stanzas—unwearied, unaging, mysterious, and beautiful."[201] However, Goldfarb stressed, readers' hopes for a straightforward narrative about the swans' voyage from change to permanence, from transformation to presence, from nature to spiritual emblem, were dashed, as Yeats "contradicts himself"; he "claims 'All's changed . . .'" since he first counted the swans but also that "the swans have not changed," "are 'unwearied still,'" "Their hearts have not grown old."[202] "In formal terms," Goldfarb wrote, "the poem deconstructs itself, laying bare the change that Yeats had tried to cover."[203] Thanks to Yeats's rhetorical dexterity, his swans paradoxically did *and* did not transition from the sublunary to the celestial world.

Like the Yale School members, Goldfarb deconstructively grappled with literature, reading Yeats rhetorically instead of as a representation of nature and/or some transcendental truth. In the final two lines of the poem's third stanza, Goldfarb maintained, Yeats seemed to suggest that the reader should trust the onto-theological independence of his swan emblem. He "explains both the power of the emblem, it's 'so lovely that is set to right / What knowledge or its lack had awry' and its illusory appearance, it's 'so arrogantly pure, a child might think / It can be murdered with a spot of ink.'"[204] (In the margins, one of Miller's teaching assistants exclaimed: "That is, by being written about, [the swans] turned into writing!").[205] Goldfarb rhetorically read these lines, arguing that Yeats's swan emblem could in fact be killed with a spot of ink, not because of its sublime wholeness and independence from nature, but because the emblem itself was actually the real swan. While Yeats gave the impression of sketching a strict opposition between emblem and swan, he actually subverted it. "The child is indeed right," Goldfarb wrote, though "his reasoning is mistaken," as "the swan can be murdered by a spot of ink, not because the swan is so pure, but because the swan is itself only a spot of ink."[206] ("Yes, good!" was scribbled in the margins.)[207] An apposite illustration of the extraordinary ways undergraduates contributed to the Yale School's project, Goldfarb's deconstructive reading revealed how Yeats's couplet undermined the metaphysical dichotomy between Yeats's swan emblem and his real swan.

To the degree that they became hermeneuts of suspicion, self-aware debunkers of dualisms, and scientific slayers of foundational truths, XYZ-ers synchronized de Man's, Hartman's, and Miller's deconstructive teaching and research agendas that put literary language as the center of humanistic inquiry. By teaching undergraduates how to rhetorically engage with a text's figural language, this pedagogical-intellectual endeavor contributed to the linguistic turn writhing within humanities departments and desacralized a swath of approaches to literary education. Because these accepted approaches buttressed Yale's self-conception as a champion of cultural order, de Man, Hartman, and Miller's project also undermined the very hierarchy Yale charged itself with defending. That such a subversive achievement was not easily replicated elsewhere was partly a function of Yale's peculiarities, notably the precedent established by the lit major, the sheer contingency of de Man, Hartman, and Miller working alongside one another, Yale College faculty's commitment to combine the fruits of research and teaching, and faith in undergraduates to meticulously underscore chiasmic reversals, aporia, undecidables, mise en abymes, and catachreses in already demanding texts. No matter the comprehensiveness or rigor of de Man and company's rhetorical readings of "the text," persuading unprepared students or harried teachers of the salutary effects of deconstructing the onto-theological views about poetry and prose that supported literary humanism would prove difficult at other institutions.

At Yale, though, XYZers were primed to receive the ABCs of the friends' nearly two-decades-long attempts to rethink literary education. Lit 130 (Lit Z) proved this effort's linchpin. By leading sections of undergraduates, the course's teaching assistants not only honed their own ability to convey a text's postmodern complexities in a limited time; they also generated drafts of what became some of the first published "de Manian" readings: Timothy Bahti on Walter Benjamin, Andrzej Warminski on Hegel, and others' deconstructions of canonical texts.[208] And Claudia Brodsky, Cathy Caruth, Tom Cohen, Deborah Esch, David Ferris, Tom Keenan, and Kevin Newmark went on to "deconstruct" major literary or philosophical works after having been TA lecturers in Lit 130. De Man himself believed the course quite effective and saw it as a part of his rhetoricization of literary study at Yale. "It was in part on the basis of his experience in The Literature Major that de Man," Peter Brooks recalled, "once proposed replacing the graduate Department of Comparative Literature with a Department of Poetics, Rhetoric, and the History of Literature."[209] While this never came to pass, in 1979, an arduous new track in the lit major allowed undergraduates to do work in comp lit for the first time. Such a path, which Wellek had earlier forbidden, could perhaps have only been forged while de Man was chair of Comp Lit and during the period of the Yale group's greatest authority.

The Consolidation of the Yale School and the Distribution of Lessons (Un)Heard

The heydays lasted from 1977 to 1982, about a half decade. During these years, the Yale School "arrived" on the American literary-critical stage, with expositions of deconstruction, English translations of six of Derrida's books, as well as Miller's and Bloom's publicity efforts, attracting allies as much as conjuring enemies. From old guard literary humanist to old-fashioned New Critical formalist, from dignified cultural conservative to scrappy Marxist firebrand, from American ego psychologist to Lacanian or Foucauldian Left, from conventional literary historian to biographer of the poets and littérateurs, the destabilizing drama of the Yale School's deconstruction became a popular target indeed. Accusations against the group and its work ratcheted up in frequency and intensity just as the 1979 oil shock and then the Reaganite restoration led to further cuts to tertiary schools and literary studies' reputation (and reality) as a profession riven by rancorous debates and bitter rivalries grew. "Deconstruction," Denis Donoghue stated to the *New York Review of Books* in 1980, "appeals to the clerisy of graduate students, who like to feel themselves superior to the laity of common readers."[210] "At Johns Hopkins, the debate over deconstruction wrenched apart the French department," *Newsweek* reported in 1981.[211] "By developing an arcane technical terminology and by demanding an exhausting apprenticeship in the reading of their own criticism (as well as in the works of selected European critics and philosophers)," critic Donald Reiman wrote to the *Times Literary Supplement* in 1983, "the entire Yale school . . . close[s] off from careers in teaching literature students of working-class background."[212] Still, for a vocal minority, deconstruction looked like it might be the longed-for glue to reconstruct the pieces of literary education; shards of postformalist methods and schools of interpretation resulting from the fragmentation of New Critical substructure could be reassembled. For many engagé academics housed in humanities departments, however, the implied ideological analysis and explicit theoretical complexity in the Yale group's work would never solve the post-sixties impasse of the oppositional, yet toothless, ivory tower intellectual chained to carrels and classrooms. Radical academics saw de Man and company, whether unable or unwilling to act as political agents, as exemplifying the newer criticism's conservatism, its cliquishness and sclerosis of professional rank. To these radicals, lacking any positive agenda, the Yale School's "rhetorical turns" were just more forms of depoliticized close reading and thus just as reductive and idealist as any formalist theory, contributing to comp lit's, criticism's, and the humanities' continuing crises and the unraveling of literary studies' teaching and research arms.

The starkly conflicting responses to the American institution of deconstruction ironically stemmed in part from the Yale group's self-promotion. By failing to clearly explain why they believed deconstruction was the sine qua non of not only literary studies but humanistic inquiry as well, by occasionally stressing its seemingly exclusive focus on language, and by in some cases deemphasizing its pedagogical effects, the Yale School unintentionally obscured their texts' and teachings' focus on meeting literature on its own subversive and contradictory terms. This all added to the miasma surrounding their work, feeding into confusion and hysteria about deconstruction.

As the group solidified their base at Yale, Miller was the first of the friends to proselytize the science of rhetorical reading, seeking collegial converts at the panel on "The Limits of Pluralism," held on December 28, 1976, at the first ever session of the Modern Language Association's Division on Philosophical Approaches to Literature. This MLA panel occurred in the wake of heated and heady deliberations about the merits of methodologies part of the linguistic turn. In 1973, Hayden White, subverting the difference between literary and nonliterary language, maintained that any of four poetic tropes—metaphor, synecdoche, metonymy, or irony—"pre-figured" a historical text; Edward Said, in 1975, argued that literary history should be "beyond deconstruction."[213] Such discussions primed participants and audience for the ensuing fireworks at the MLA panel, contributing to an emerging critical consensus that deconstruction was solely a set of arguments about language and its interpretation. In his paper, University of Chicago professor of English and committed pluralist Wayne Booth suggested that his colleagues should avoid dogmatism and "reconstruct a critical commonwealth," a republic in which the critic, loyal to how he or she personally marked off the "limits of meaning," would be open to other approaches.[214] Booth struck a congenially pluralist pose, but M. H. Abrams saw Miller's (and Derrida's) deconstruction as setting quite a devastating standard for literary studies.[215] For Abrams, Miller's assertion that each stanza, paragraph, and even word performed a mise en abyme guaranteed that the critic, "suspended by the labyrinthine lines of a textual web over the blank abyss that those black lines demarcate," produced "only . . . writing . . . equally vulnerable to deconstruction."[216] By insisting on the indeterminate meanings of the words on the page, which prohibited the humanistic belief that the text was the product of and controlled by an intentional agent or presence, Miller not only depersonalized and destroyed the meaning of artworks but prevented literary historians from identifying harmonies between text and context; Miller withheld the edification so many readers sought.[217] For Abrams, Miller's deconstruction thus hardly unified but rather attacked the humanities at its most vulnerable and venerable spot: the literary text.

An important moment had arrived, for the methodological disagreements and deliberations at the MLA would color the reception and legacy of the American institution of deconstruction. In his paper, Miller, unexpectedly and perhaps confusedly to many in the audience, assimilated literary history into his deconstructive approach. After an etymological exploration of the word "parasite" that undermined the parasite/host metaphysical hierarchy, Miller rhetorically read Shelley's unfinished *The Triumph of Life* to affirm and embrace Booth's 1976 endorsement, with caveats, of a deconstructive history as a historicist practice that was "plainly and simply parasitical" on traditional literary-historical discourse. *Triumph*, Miller suggested, rhetorically responded to literature's demand, as it contained "affirmed, negated, sublimated, twisted" texts that became "the ground of [*Triumph*] and something [*Triumph*] must annihilate by incorporating it, turning it into ghostly insubstantiality."²¹⁸ Because *Triumph* vampirically sustained itself on this spectral sustenance—the "parasite"—that it rejected, Miller's Shelley wrote a deconstructive history, a text that rhetorically read its own and other texts' "possible-impossible task of becoming its own ground."²¹⁹ Such a deconstructive undertaking inaugurated innumerable ways to read its narrative. And, for Miller, the accusation that he, Derrida, and de Man, were "parasites" feeding on texts' "host" meanings was in fact praise, for this was how Shelley's *Triumph* grappled with literature, a text that included itself and all the texts that constituted the pageantry of literary history.

With his rhetorical reading of Shelley's last poem, Miller submitted a textual model to his colleagues of how literature's accounting of its linguistic irreducibility was integral not simply to the dynamic that structured historical discourse but to the deconstructive writings of the Yale School as well. After its publication the following year in *Critical Inquiry*, however, "The Limits of Pluralism" MLA debate supported the view, gaining traction in American humanities departments, that deconstruction was mainly a contribution to linguistics, the scientific study of language/writing and its structure. "It is often said," as Abrams claimed, "that Derrida and those who follow his lead subordinate all inquiries to a prior inquiry into language," specifically "*écriture*, the written or printed text."²²⁰ But for those with less attachment to the sacred paradigms of literary studies, the MLA debate conveyed the reformist potential of the postmodern discipline of deconstruction. After the MLA panel, University of Chicago English professor David Bevington wrote an animated letter to Miller: "Your talk on the limits of pluralism ["and . . . the whole program"] . . . sparked several long + productive conversations on the question of determinacy [of meaning], and must have given hundreds of teachers new insights into what they are supposed to be doing."²²¹ Far from the radical linguistic skepticism Abrams saw, Bevington felt Miller's deconstructive Shelley offered an affirmative pedagogical agenda, albeit one that foregrounded only limited features of Miller's and his friends' comprehensive aims. Such enthusiasm would fade in time; it also reinforced the assessment of deconstruction as primarily a linguistic endeavor.

Fatefully, the pedagogical successes of the Yale School's de facto leader helped marginalize the scientific program of rhetorical reading in the reception of deconstruction in the United States. For de Man had begun to coordinate the alienated exigencies of the profession, promoting his deconstruction in a manner that emphasized linguistic analysis. In a summer 1976 seminar at Yale supported by a grant from the National Endowment for the Humanities, de Man taught a group of university and college teachers that rhetorical reading was universally applicable

FIGURE 3.5 A 1982 poster promoting a lecture on deconstruction (Courtesy of J. Hillis Miller)

to all discourse because of the nature of language; language's disruptive power undermined the separation of literary from critical, philosophical, and/or autobiographical texts—these were "facile generic distinctions," he would write.[222] To seminar attendees, de Man announced that they would learn a "way of reading, playing off structure *against* movement . . . De-construction" by way of Enlightenment philosophes' "18th century discussion of language," focusing on book 3 of British philosopher John Locke's *An Essay Concerning Human Understanding* (1689). For de Man, Locke's implicit rhetorical practice in the text ironically subverted his explicit philosophical statements about rhetoric: Locke wrote that "rhetoric as eloquence" was mere "persuasion" but also employed stirring tropes to expound his own philosophy of rhetoric. He wrote of "Language being the great *Conduit* where Men convey their Discoveries, Reasoning's, and Knowledge from one to another"; he warned against the "*legions* of obscure, doubtful, and undefined Words" that are "like the *dens of robbers*, or *holes of foxes*."[223] Sorely overlooked figure in literary histories of the late seventeenth and early eighteenth centuries: philosopher John Locke.

The British philosopher's text also rhetorically read itself, de Man lectured, while developing a philosophy of language that anticipated contemporary semiotics and linguistics. Locke, de Man emphasized, wrote about the "(1) arbitrariness of sign," how there was "(2) no analogy between sign and meaning," "(3) no imitation, representation between sign and meaning," and "(4) no authority in usage." This Lockean deconstructive theory of reading avant la lettre, de Man suggested to seminar attendees, was particularly legible in Locke's account of attempts to define the "word gold," a "signification," Locke wrote, that was "hard . . . to determine": children for instance "have annexed" the word to "the shining yellow part of a peacock's tail," while others joined the word to "certain parcels of matter." For Locke, however, the crucial issue was that no power made fusibility "part of the essence signified by the word gold, and solubility but a property of it."[224] Locke's "gold" was thus first a metonym (how the children used it), then a metaphor (for the precious metal), and finally a catachresis, an arbitrary and reversible link between signifier and signified.[225] Focusing on how Locke's philosophical text answered literature's imperative by undermining its stated aims while expounding a proto-Saussurean philosophy of language, de Man taught teachers the scientific skills of rhetorical reading, showing how one seemingly dry empiricist's essay holds the theoretical resources needed to alert students to the figural elements of texts that undid the onto-theological dualisms that structured formalisms, periodization, and thematic restorations of a text's meaning.

Six years later, in the summer of 1981, de Man offered "Rhetorical Reading," a seven-week NEH seminar that again foregrounded his painstaking attention to the desacralizing potential of figural language. This time, de Man coached twelve teachers (more than sixty applied) in how "an awareness of the rhetorical properties of language influence[d] the modalities and expectations of our reading and, consequently, of the way in which the reading of literary works is taught to undergraduates." Owing to what de Man described as its "pragmatic approach," the course's only prerequisite was the ability to intensely focus on the *letter*—not the *spirit*—of the text; "no specialized knowledge of philosophy or of any of the authors selected for discussion" was required. The nothing if not cultured de Man nonetheless proposed an impressive sequence of challenging works that ranged across genres, disciplines, and the North Atlantic: "Keats, Baudelaire, Yeats, Pascal, Kleist, Henry James, Hegel, possibly Melville or Goethe or Proust, Derrida, and [Paul] Ricœur."[226] To realize his teaching goals, de Man enlisted Yale colleagues, each of whom had his or her twist on the hard art of rhetorical reading. Professors David Marshall (English) and Andrzej Warminski (a former de Man student), Bloom, Fredric Jameson (French and Comp Lit), Barbara Johnson (also a former de Man student), Moshe Ron (English and Comp Lit at the Hebrew University), and "other passers-by on the Yale Campus" gave visiting lectures. It was, de Man reflected, a resounding success: "These seminars are beginning to have a positive and far-reaching effect"; "participants return to their institutions and . . . can exercise some influence on curricula, methodology, and recruitment policies."[227] Such were some of the effects, from de Man's perspective, that an increased attentiveness to the rhetorical resources of language inculcated by de Man's teachings had beyond the Old Campus's neo-Gothic halls.

Yet, notwithstanding de Man's and Miller's best efforts to spread the universally subversive good news, the American institution of deconstruction became known in the profession as the province of one department at Yale: Comp Lit. And this department became known for one person's pedagogical enterprise: de Man's, both his personal canon—Rousseau, Hölderlin, Hegel, Schlegel, Nietzsche, Wordsworth, Benjamin, and so on—and his mentorship of graduate students, a relationship that he found "much more satisfactory than in Europe," because the teacher "has a very direct professional relationship" to students, who were "future colleagues."[228] De Man's intellectual clout—his slim output of essays belied its magnitude—added to the sense of mission his students and colleagues felt; for devotees, de Man's reflexive interpretive science exorcised the New Critical, Wellekian, and Eliotic ghosts that haunted literature departments still. The educative process in de Man's seminars often went like this: de Man—a "diamond-cutter"—cleaved a passage from a text; "it was possible to spend a week on a sentence";[229] he did not explain why, though his selection was often a postmodern moment where the text commented on itself or its own activity of composition;[230] he would then dedicate class sessions to framing and reframing this textual knot; his students took a shot at considering the text "on the level of language."[231] Finally, he presented his "rhetorical reading," which his cadre of students would pore over after hours, extracting what interpretive techniques they could to begin to formulate their own challenges to accepted literary-critical practice.

There was no better textual illustration of the intellectual formation that de Man's graduate students underwent in Yale Comp Lit than the 1979 issue of *Studies in Romanticism*, which included his students' reworked papers from his 1977–78 yearlong, NEH-sponsored seminar.[232] "Close reading and rhetorical analysis are eminently teachable," de Man observed in the issue's introduction.[233] And this could be substantiated with how "techniques of rhetorical, as opposed to thematic, analysis are used [in the essays] with remarkable ease. . . . Tropes are taken apart with such casual elegance that the exegeses can traverse the entire field of tropological reversals and displacements with a virtuosity that borders on parody."[234] Timothy Bahti, for example, shifted "the perspective" on Wordsworth by showing the link "between mind or imagination and nature" in the poet's writings as "always mediated by rhetorical, textual constructs and situations."[235] The volume's contributions by Barbara Johnson (on Melville), E. S. Burt (on Rousseau), and Cynthia Chase (on Wordsworth) performed similar rhetorical engagements with the text, contributing to the view that the deconstructive project as a whole was the scientific study of language, which in some essential way sprang from de Man. No less than Bloom would affectionately protest to de Man: "You clone, my dear: I dislike what you do as a teacher, because your students are as alike as two peas in a pod."[236] And since, for Bloom, de Man erroneously overlooked how literature *is* the author's anxious rhetorical refraction of an esteemed predecessor's poetry, de Man's clones replicated his mistake.

However, once every fall it was not de Man but Derrida, "trailing yards of white scarf and draped in soft, elegant suits," whom Yale Comp Lit graduate students emulated.[237] While the philosopher began his visiting professorship in the second half of the decade, he continued to promote his philosophical rejoinder to literature's appeal in the late 1970s. Derrida's attention turned to the United States after the French minister of education denied him a chair at the University of Nanterre and then eliminated the position altogether. Meanwhile, his Yale visits increased demand for him and his work, and he made himself available after his comp lit lectures (delivered in French), which began at 7:00 p.m. and lasted late into the night. Derrida's brief stays became so vital to the goings-on of Yale Comp Lit that when his duties in France kept him from delivering his seminar in fall 1981, Hartman wrote to him: "I'm afraid we've all become addicted to your presence, and September seems very empty without you."[238] Others, though, saw Derrida as a threat. "Your influence in the United States is growing," de Man observed in a May 1977 letter to Derrida, "with all the aberrations and hardenings of position that this implies."[239] Some, indeed, helped make common the view that Derrida's friends at Yale and their students had tamed Derrida's radical philosophical force. In a widely read 1980 book on literary criticism since midcentury, Frank Lentricchia cast deconstructionist criticism in America as a fall into an ahistoricality that contradicted its Derridean origins; de Man's notion of "the undecid-able," the socially committed critic maintained, was "the formalist's final response to a repressed and alienated social existence."[240] For Lentricchia, de Man's work was merely aesthetic daydreaming, a vestige of Arnoldian idealism fixated on divorcing culture from everyday life. Meanwhile, American philosophers, by and large, ignored or derided Derrida.[241] At Yale, Ruth Marcus, whose contributions to symbolic logic revolutionized her field, repeatedly failed to stop his visits. And in the pages of *Glyph* in 1977, John Searle, responding to Derrida's 1971 reading of J. L. Austin, mocked Derrida's alleged claim that "writing is language's privileged mode of operation."[242] According to Searle, such statements confirmed the French philosopher's irrationality. Many humanists would come to see Searle as a heroic defender against Derrida's trespasses on the territories of linguistics and the philosophy of language.

For those either unaware or unappreciative of de Man's comprehensive view that the science of rhetorical reading was required to sufficiently grapple with the literariness of the text, de Man's attempts to bring Derrida's work more in line with his ambitions for comp lit might have seemed unwarranted and part of his unjustified concentration on language. For de Man, however, this all was necessary for the American institution of deconstruction. In November 1979, de Man lobbied Yale University Press to publish a book by Derrida that grew, he wrote, "out of the seminar [Derrida was] conducting at Yale." Derrida's work was "of major interest to students of philosophy, literature, linguistic and psychoanalysis," de Man argued. "The book will . . . be less esoteric than the earlier ones, and less clearly bound to the idiosyncrasies of the Parisian literary scene" and "will be particularly rewarding . . . [because] it will be written with an American audience specifically in mind and will address issues and authors . . . familiar to an American audience."[243] The press turned down de Man's offer, but in Derrida's six 1979–80 lectures he modulated his deconstruction to engage a key text that influenced comp lit's institutional-intellectual history. Though it was only one aspect of Derrida's project, his lectures in Yale Comp Lit could give the impression that he was on board with de Man's goals and that, like de Man, he was most interested in the complications of literary language.

For instance, Derrida organized his first lecture around a "conceptual opposition": comp lit's declaration of "its right to existence" due to having "its origin . . . in historical acts of foundation" *and* comp lit's affirmation of "the day when no one feels the necessity of the possibility of referring to the foundation of the law. . . . Then the institution dies."[244] For Derrida, three nouns, "Institution," "Literature," and "Translation," "resist[ed]" or "defeat[ed]" this "facile" metaphysical dualism.[245] For an example of the deconstructive potential of "Literature," Derrida pivoted to a 1963 essay by René Étiemble, professor of comp lit at the Sorbonne. There, Étiemble, according to Derrida, formulated and used a "concept of general literature" that shaped the "original foundation" of "every department of 'comp lit.'"[246] Étiemble extended the idea of literature "to all culture," but left unasked: "What is literature and what is not literature in all of this?"[247] That Étiemble left this question unasked was not a marginal issue for Derrida. Either what Étiemble viewed as all of culture belonged to comp lit in a kind of general literature, rendering unclear why Étiemble saw literature as governing all culture, *or* Étiemble upheld literature's distinctiveness, raising the problem of defining the "'literariness' of literature" and undermining Étiemble's "encyclopedic field."[248] With his "concept of 'general literature,'" Étiemble performed not only "a fundamental indetermination . . . at the center of the concept of literature," Derrida lectured to his Yale audience, but a "paradox" that organized comp lit, for without "a precomprehension of what literature means," it remained undecided what was compared in comp lit.[249] With this deconstructive reading of Étiemble's "Literature," which also briefly explored Étiemble's claim that his ideas were in agreement with René Wellek's about the crisis of comp lit and call "for the comparativist" to distinguish "good" and "bad" literature, Derrida adjusted his project to the rhetoricized endeavors in de Man's Comp Lit.[250]

Derrida thus tuned his anti-metaphysical philosophical instrument to deconstructive chords at Yale, adding to American academics' appraisal of deconstruction as a language game. This assessment was partially justified. De Man, for example, *did* frequently foreground texts' rhetorical and figural dimensions in his Comp Lit classes. In their fall 1980 seminar 816A, de Man and Hartman, while correcting what they deemed pedagogic malpractice, emphasized the post-Romantic inattentiveness to linguistic functions. During "the 18th c," de Man lectured, there was a "proximity of P[hilosophy] and poetry due to a +/- explicit stress on language," but a "neglect + forgetting of [this] language element" had "recent[ly]" occurred "due to the bad *teaching* of l[iterature]."[251] To counter this poor schooling, de Man rhetorically read the literary imperative in Hegel's philosophy. He underscored paragraph 20 of Hegel's discussion of the deictic nature of the first-person singular pronoun in the *Enzyklopädie* (1817).[252] "*The* central question in Hegel was now, here and especially I," de Man lectured, because it was in the present that subject and object ostensibly interpenetrated, undertaking the metaphysical journey toward self-realization, joining material and spiritual reality. But, for de Man, Hegel's paragraph in fact offered a reflexive theory of literary language that subverted this reflective philosophical tradition. "*I* cannot say I," de Man emphasized about Hegel's text, because each articulation of "I" separated the particular "I" from general validity; when the word "I" was uttered, exteriorized, the word assumed a universalization and could be shifted to any I, any *here, now,* and/or *this*.[253] "Our reading of paragraph 20," de Man wrote in 1982, "threatens the stability of the predicate sentence 'I am I,'" ensuring the "very enterprise of thought . . . paralyzed from the start."[254] This rhetorical "I" made Hegel's metaphysical system into an allegory of the dislocations between philosophy and history, literature and aesthetics, theory and experience.

To increase Comp Lit 816A students' scientific sensitivity to the "language element" that always undid the metaphysical separation between philosophical and poetic texts, de Man used his rhetoricized Hegel to interpret Wordsworth's and the English Romantics' texts. "Are these questions [about Hegel] relevant for the reading of English Romanticism?" de Man asked, before answering with evidence teased from "Wordsworth['s] moment of textual inadequacy of metaphor of interiorization in 'Essay on Immortality Ode.'"[255] M. H. Abrams and Bloom had read Wordsworth's poems as metaphors about internal dwelling places, mansions, habitats, and the like that expressed the genesis of subjective identity, the presence of the "I" to itself. With Hegel's allegory of the disarticulation of "I," de Man highlighted how the rhetorical dimensions of Romantic poets' texts subverted their own recollection of the personal memories of external landscapes that produced such self-presence. And to aid in imparting the universality of Hegel's deconstructive allegory, de Man referenced his coteacher, demonstrating how "Hartman on Wordsworth . . . center[ed] on the matters of the *now*"; it was Hartman who underscored Romantic poetry's failures of interiorization. Indeed, in a 1975 text, Hartman championed "stay[ing] . . . with forms so abstract or contrary that no one could plead, [as Goethe's Faust,] 'Verweile doch, du bist so schön'" (Linger a while, you are so beautiful).[256] Tarrying with the disfigured forms of poetry helped the reader pinpoint the figural language that undermined the recollection of memories and interiorization of meaning that served as the origin and presence of the self. Or, as de Man pithily told 816A students: "Disjunction of aesthetic + linguistic."[257] Such lessons illustrated not only how de Man's science of rhetorical reading undermined genre distinctions between philosophical, literary, and critical texts. His emphasis on the "language element" also contributed to the particular spin that was being put on the Yale School's endeavor.

Deconstruction and Criticism (1979) did much as well, with the volume obscuring the import of teaching to the group's project of rhetorical reading. The Seabury Press' initial plan for the collection seems humble. "Harold Bloom," Justus Lawler, the editor in chief at the Press, wrote in an August 1977 letter to Miller, "has told you of our conversations concerning a book to be written by yourself, Paul De Man, Jacques Derrida, Geoffrey Hartman, along with Professor Bloom. . . . We see this book as primarily directed to course use, both on the undergraduate and graduate levels."[258] This targeted readership would have likely surprised contemporaries; difficult it was to imagine undergraduates making their way through and then applying de Man and company's thicket of counterintuitive vocabulary. That the volume was initially conceived as a practical guide for learning the discipline of rhetorical reading, however, was indirectly verified by Bloom. He, in the summer of 1977, "thought [*Deconstruction and Criticism*] up, got the publisher, brought everybody together and gave the book its title."[259] He also phoned his friends, asking each for an essay on Shelley's *The Triumph of Life*. Only de Man and Miller truly wrote on the poem, but Bloom's choice of Shelley, Cleanth Brooks's and Robert Penn Warren's go-to example of how not to write poetry, suggests how much he envisioned the volume as an act of pedagogical parricide of the New Critics, whose formalist constraints the Yale School struggled against.

When published, however, *Deconstruction and Criticism*'s contributors' outsized ambitions merged with the volume's projection of a group focused on specific *research* questions to bury the Yale School's teaching interests. In his 1977 letter to Miller, Lawler had modestly requested: "What we above all want to avoid is the appearance that this is a collection of separate pieces by five scholars who happen to share an institutional affiliation."[260] Hartman insisted: "There should not be a blurb saying [the volume] is a manifesto." "But you can't fight the advertising industry," he would humorously reflect.[261] Hartman's introduction suggests he worked to allay Lawler's fear nonetheless: "A shared set of problems" oriented contributors' texts: (1) "What kind of maturer function . . . may [criticism] claim . . . beyond the obviously academic or pedagogical"? (2) What is "the importance—or *force*—of literature . . . [and] what does that force consist in"? "The priority of language to meaning," he continued, "expresses what we [contributors] all feel about figurative language, . . . the strength of the signifier vis-à-vis a signified . . . that tries to enclose it."[262] The most basic outline of the Yale School's pedagogical mission was downplayed here; the circle instead practiced "a new rigor," a "relentless focus" on how texts' rhetorical elements subverted onto-theological dichotomies, including text/commentary and meaning/language.[263] And yet: "*Caveat lector,"* Hartman wrote. "For [Bloom and Hartman] the ethos of literature is not dissociable from its pathos, whereas for deconstructionist criticism literature is precisely that use of language which can . . . show that [pathos] too is figurative, ironic, or aesthetic."[264] By distancing himself and Bloom from "boa-deconstructors" de Man, Derrida, and Miller, Hartman sidelined how the Yale School saw rhetorical reading as essential for the needed overhaul of literary humanist education.[265] And his casting of deconstructionist criticism as dedicated to ironic language was another portrayal that reinforced views about deconstruction.

The volume's essays themselves also masked the constitutive link between de Man and company's research and teaching programs. In his piece, Derrida enacted the deconstructive "logic of the undecidable" so as to consider the problem of translation, splitting his piece into two forms of unequal size: the lower—famously a one-hundred-page footnote governed by a principle of economy—aimed at the highest possible translatability; the upper—with its allusions, puns, textual loops, and speculations—very nearly rendered the lower fold's straightforward diction untranslatable.[266] While Derrida mused about the problems of translation in both folds, he discreetly questioned the American institutionalization of deconstruction, pointing readers toward the subversive political effects it still might have. Upper: there was a "'Yale' key" that "locks and unlocks, opens and closes" certain opportunities; lower: this "key" for "decoding" was difficult to determine.[267] Bloom, in his essay, traced the etymology of the word "meaning," finding that it was related to "moaning," and concluded: "A poem's meaning is a poem's complaint."[268] And this complaint was, as he had been arguing since the early 1970s, lodged by a strong poet who, after the psychological shock of a distinct vision, violated the literary forms of poetic fathers: "[This] breaking of form . . . depends upon the operation of certain instances of language, revisionary ratios, and on certain tropological displacements in language."[269] Bloom only indirectly touched on pedagogical issues; his strong poets "make themselves free, by their stances toward earlier poets, and make others free only by *teaching* them those stances or positions of freedom."[270] In his contribution, de Man performed an exacting rhetorical reading of Shelley's relationship to Romanticism as "dramatized in" *Triumph*, focusing on "the encounter between the narrator and the figure designated by the proper name Rousseau."[271] For Shelley, de Man deconstructively read, Rousseau was a recognized legislator of the highest importance, a writer whose "words have acquired the power of actions."[272] Rousseau was the premier pedagogue. In Shelley's poem, Rousseau appears as a guide and adviser to the poem's narrator (Shelley), yet as Rousseau comments on historical figures and his own origin to the narrator's question "what is Life?" he cannot offer a definitive answer, asking the same question back to the narrator, providing what de Man called "the madness of words."[273] De Man referred to this linguistic process as "disfiguration," and this deconstructive activity was *Triumph*'s meaning and its link to Romanticism.[274] For such a charismatic teacher, de Man wrote an essay that, though parts can be read as allegory for his own relationship to students, did not explicitly make the connection to his own "real life" pedagogy. What would the reception of deconstruction in the United States have been if *Deconstruction and Criticism* presented the Yale School, for all of the group members' differences, as a pedagogical endeavor, wagering to unearth and employ a science of rhetorical reading that subverted the onto-theological presuppositions of literary education and could serve as the primary discipline for all interpretive endeavors throughout the humanities?

Winners and Losers in a Ring of Deconstructive Criticism

In her presidential address at the 1980 MLA convention, Helen Vendler called on the professional body to contemplate its elemental experience of literature, to recall its prelapsarian innocence.[275] The very articulation of such a request bespoke the profession's great insecurities about the value of literary education and the status of literature, insecurities that left a palpable longing for that golden age when literary studies was not just safe from economizing administrators, skeptical students, and the bitter rivalries of interpretive groups but flourishing, flush with financial and cultural capital. A year before Vendler's appeal, Josué Harari had likened the present-day "critical struggles" of special interest groups as "a ring of criticism," a "game" in which "everyone is eventually a loser."[276] Certainly, many in the profession and increasingly in every humanities department felt that the post-sixties theoretical mayhem had made their ivory tower into a postmodern Tower of Babel, with the Yale School speaking quite a seductive tongue. That de Man maintained "literary studies should be severely restricted in terms of numbers," that he modeled behavior in which a reader should take whatever amount of time needed to identify and meditate on a text's linguistic dilemma or topological paradox, that his students ranked departments with unforgiving eyes—it all seemed like a parlor game of a hyperprofessionalized elite.[277]

The old Yale hegemony appeared to have mutated into an oppressive new one. Maximizing the prestige and power afforded by their posts, Bloom, de Man, Hartman, and Miller willingly played the part of rhetorically aware hierophants whose responses to literature's imperative undercut the secular faith in the power of prose and poetry to serve as a replacement for the weakening position of established religion. The Yale

School's discipline of rhetorical reading was a postformalist genus of "the new rigorism": an intensified and ironized attention to the verbal art of literature that bestowed analytical heft to the teacher-critic, elevating the worth and position of literary study in the academic humanities and the university in general. Unlike the success of the New Criticism in the nation's undergraduate classrooms, however, the Yale group's undertaking remained to an extent confined to their university's literature departments, even as it attracted a following of specialists by way of publications and conference appearances.

Those who focused on the supposed coterie criticism practiced by the Yale School in some ways contributed to the perception that the group's work necessarily sought to destroy literary humanism. De Man's use of images of mutilation, violence, death, and muteness during the half decade of the "arrival" of the Yale School to describe the rhetorical operations of texts surely gave the impression that deconstructive criticism had killed the "man of letters."[278] "The threat posed" by deconstruction was "real and substantial," as Michael P. Clark has noted, in that its "challenge" to "the formal coherence of the poem and its discursive autonomy" was a challenge to "the philosophical foundation [the metaphysical dualisms] of Western humanism," since "the poem was the aesthetic embodiment . . . of [this] philosophical foundation."[279] If poetry was the expression of a philosophical truth, then its subversion was real. The deconstruction of texts seemed both a mirror and an engine that drove the "weightlessness" of the cultural realm of postindustrial American society.

Deconstruction did challenge any claim of presence, coherence, or foundation. But the Yale group sought not to annihilate but rather to revise literary humanism and therefore stood in a productive relationship to it. This productive relationship is evidenced not only by the scholarship that they engaged with but their claims that literature's demand was a universal demand made by all discourse (texts). The true scope of de Man and company's pedagogical-intellectual endeavor is also more fully appreciated by understanding the classroom experiences and academic politics at Yale. Unfortunately, the Yale School never made any direct summary statement about its overarching mission. Doing so would have been antithetical to the very science of rhetorical reading to which they were committed. And when leftist opponents accused the Yale group of conservatism by sheltering "the text" from social contexts, arguments given by deconstructionists like Barbara Johnson that the "political attitude" of deconstruction was the implied call to "examine authority in language" was unsatisfying.[280]

Admittedly, the critiques and criticisms of the Yale School's institution of American deconstruction did respond to the challenges that the group's teachings and texts posed, and were not entirely unfounded. But as the notoriety of the group peaked, Hartman and Bloom had already begun to pursue projects that unfolded outside the critical circle. Having a different relationship to Yale and its self-ordained humanism partly explains the two's deviation, but, really, Hartman and Bloom were never wholly committed to the cause. With his open weave of mind, Hartman extended his work in the pulling apart of the amalgamation of criticism and Christian metaphysics by cultivating different communities and modes of discourse. Welcoming Lacan's and Derrida's twin attentiveness to Freudian psychoanalysis and language since the early 1970s, he organized the important group "Psychoanalysis in Humanities" and pushed for a Humanities Center at Yale.[281] On the heels of the 1970s resurgence in the study of the history of Judaism in American universities, Hartman also became invested in religious discourse and radicalized practices of Judaism.[282] In early 1981, he was appointed cochairman of Yale's new Judaic studies program; Hartman considered Jewish Studies as "a variant of 'opening the canon'" and wanted "intellectual equity for a learning-tradition . . . as old as Rome and

FIGURE 3.6 The founders of the Fortunoff Video Archive for Holocaust Testimonies. *Left to right*: Dori Laub, William Rosenberg, Geoffrey Hartman, and Laurel Vlock. (Courtesy of Yale University)

Athens."[283] That same year, he helped establish Yale's Fortunoff Video Archive for Holocaust Testimonies, after which he wrote about the archive project and the Holocaust and further considered a distinct "psycholinguistics" that addressed the link between words and psychic wounds.[284]

Separating and institutionalizing Jewish exegesis, which Hartman believed literary criticism had, to its detriment, abandoned, was a proposition that "Bloom Professor of Bloom" had little truck with. He even jokingly called Hartman "Ayatollah Hartmeini."[285] For Bloom, literature qua literature contained the imaginative drama of humankind's deepest desires; it alone encompassed the spirit's heroic struggle for originality via rhetorical deflections of past masters. Bloom's own fight to become as singular as the literature he championed meant that he, no longer required to perform official duties in Yale English, would naturally see his overt influence decrease in the department. Bloom's texts were assigned to the university's Comp Lit graduate students, but his six revisionary categories never achieved a robust presence in the broader literary-critical lexicon. In fact, neither his *Agon* (1982) nor his *The Breaking of the Vessels* (1982) evoked the excitement elicited by his earlier antithetical criticism.[286] This mattered less than ever for Bloom, especially as his engagement with Gnosticism and the American philosophical tradition of pragmatism began to foreground a strong poet's rhetorical detours of his or her personal spiritual experience. To conduct his "Bloomology," however, the Bronx street fighter had had to vanquish his literary-critical and literary-historical challengers. Intent on subverting Yale English's and the academy's onto-theological inclinations from the start of his career, Bloom may have thought he'd delivered the knockout punch. But streets would become full once again. For out of public view was a full-scale Yale countertradition within a Yale countertradition, suppressed and marginalized in most popular and academic representations of the Yale School. It would reveal what was perhaps most at stake in the deconstructive acts that undermined the metaphysics of literary-critical practice in New Haven during the 1970s.

4

FEMINIST CULTURAL POLITICS

The Brides of Deconstruction and Criticism

"Like others of its type, the Yale School has always been a Male School."[1] So Barbara Johnson wittily observed in her talk "Gender Theory and the Yale School," an ironic twist on the title of the Contemporary Genre Theory and the Yale School conference held in Norman, Oklahoma, from May 31 to June 1, 1984. ("Gender" in French is "Genre.") Indeed, the Yale School was often portrayed as a male province. For example, the author of that 1981 *Newsweek* article on the "all-out war" in literature departments between traditional humanists and "deconstructionists" praised the Yale School as a group of "formidable *men* of letters."[2] Academic representations, including a number aligned with de Man and company, also placed feminist deconstructionists at the margins. In *On Deconstruction* (1982), a broadly diffused manual of the interpretive art, Jonathan Culler did extensively explore Derrida's male feminism from *De la grammatologie* (1967) onward—Derrida, in 1975, in fact coined the neologism "phallogocentrism," the metaphysical privileging of the masculine (the phallus) in the construction of meaning. And Culler directed readers to the *écriture féminine* (gendered women's writing) of Hélène Cixous and Luce Irigaray. But he also described Shoshana Felman's *La folie et la chose littéraire* (1978)—where Felman highlighted "literature's constitutive relation to what culture has excluded [the "feminine"] under the label 'madness'"—as "a wide-ranging collection of essays by a member of the '*école de Yale*.'"[3] Culler seemed to interpret Felman more as a Yale daughter, or maybe, as Johnson remarked in her 1984 talk, a "member of the Yale School, but only in French." To Johnson, Culler, while an ally, subtly upheld the metaphysical hierarchy that cast intellectual circles as masculine, sidelining Felman for "no reason other than gender."[4]

The reality hidden by Culler's and others' value-laden portrayals was that a group of feminists at Yale with distinct though overlapping responses to literature prominently contributed to the American institution of de-construction. The "Brides of Deconstruction and Criticism"—the title of the informal cadre's proposed feminist countermanifesto—comprised not only Johnson and Felman but Margaret Ferguson, Margaret Homans, Mary Poovey, Eve Sedgwick, Gayatri Spivak, Jack Winkler, Judith Butler, and others. Rather than marginal to the "Male School," this group argu-ably *was* the Yale School. For beginning in earnest during the late 1970s, these feminist deconstructionists achieved astonishing pedagogical and intellectual successes, partially by redirecting the Male School's science of deconstructive reading away from an emphasis on rhetoric, rhetorical terminology, and the self-subversion of hierarchical oppositions in (often Romantic) prose and poetry toward the troping of gender, sexual differ-ence, race, and psychoanalysis in a wide range of texts. The Yale School's excessive focus on the formal qualities rather than the specific content of texts possessed much untapped potential that this second generation of deconstructionists identified and adroitly exploited, and while they fol-lowed through on the Male School's promise that a science of rhetorical reading was before yet vital to any discourse (text), the Brides promoted a feminist linguistic turn.

In fact, the Brides' rigorous foregrounding of how texts' figural di-mensions undermined onto-theological dualities of sex, gender, and race helped revise literary humanist traditions and canons; transformed ar-eas of study, such as Mary Shelley studies, Romantic studies, Lacanian studies, and Subaltern studies; and established others, such as trauma studies, queer theory, and gender studies. Yet it was the Brides' achieve-ments in classrooms, in addition to their trailblazing publications, that truly put a deconstructive screw to the Male School's desacralizations of humanist education, creating a place for feminist-deconstructive inter-pretive procedures and the readings they generated. While some Brides intervened in undergraduate classes, perhaps most notably Johnson in her 1980 revision of the lit major's core course "Man and His Fictions," other feminists' curricula in Yale French, English, and Classics contributed to the mainstreaming of feminist deconstruction in humanities departments and, eventually, academia more broadly. This work was part of the emerg-ing academic left, whose scholarship and teaching advanced a cultural politics that helped "victims of socially acceptable forms of sadism"—such as women, gays, and people of color—"by making such sadism no longer acceptable."[5]

Circumstances at Yale greatly influenced its feminist-deconstructive moment, the institutional history of which aids in the understanding of how the category of "gender" surfaced and was disseminated, altering late twentieth-century American political culture.[6] Not only local reverberations of the paroxysms of the sixties but also the post-sixties goal of expanding the demographic and cognitive boundaries of the humanities aided feminists' commitments to broaden the conceptions of personal identity on campus.[7] After "Male Yale" opened its doors in 1969 to women undergraduates, professors, administrators, and students, stimulated by second-wave feminist teachings, agendas, and writings as well as the politics of the gay liberation movement, lodged feminist protest and affirmation in diverse settings. As much top-down as bottom-up, feminists' efforts triumphed over much internal opposition from fellow humanists, like those in Yale English, and helped to establish Yale's Women's Studies Program in 1979. Also offering critiques of and alternatives to second-wave approaches to feminism, Yale's feminist literary-critical luminaries deconstructed the sexed hierarchies that ordered texts, curricula, and schools, eventually breaking apart sex and gender in a manner that would come to be poststructuralist third-wave feminism.

Opportunities for the Brides to pursue their postmodern research and teaching programs came primarily from the decline in disciplinary authority in literary studies in the late 1970s. During these years, the rigor of deconstruction, many hoped, would halt this decline; it did not, though, partly due to the increased professional requirements of a bureaucratized university culture and the questioning of accepted standards for literary education that followed the post-sixties proliferation of theoretical perspectives and discourses in the humanities. While caught between the pincers of a weakened disciplinary authority and retrenchment after the golden age of higher education, the Brides' feminist engagements with the rhetorical dimensions of texts undermined gendered, sexed, and raced dichotomies, providing paths out of the überformalist blind alleys and textual halls of mirrors produced by the middle-aged and male Yale School members' deconstructive reading techniques, which for many represented a methodological impasse for literary studies. Because the Brides' work—here dramatically, there subtly—was engendered at a school that saw itself as defending cultural orthodoxies, a duty that involved mobilizing conceptual and institutional hierarchies that privileged white men and the masculine, their feminist deconstructions were infused with subversive power. No one avoided political reference more painstakingly than de Man, and no one problematized it more compulsively than Derrida, but feminist deconstructionists' teachings and texts were vehicles for a postmodern feminist cultural program that cleared corridors in the American academy during the 1980s, even coming, by the twenty-first century, to influence nonacademic life on both sides of the North Atlantic.[8] The masculine metaphysics of (literary) humanism would never be the same.

The Struggle for a Women's Studies
Program at Yale University

Colleges and universities in the United States dramatically expanded after the Second World War, but women's slice of the academic pie—full-time positions in the humanities and sciences as well as the undergraduate population—shrank. Reversing a trend during the first quarter of the twentieth century, this decline was partially the result of the Servicemen's Readjustment Act of 1944: since less than 2 percent of returning soldiers were women, the principal recipients of the GI Bill's funding were men, and it was these men, with their preferences and proclivities, that largely shaped colleges and universities during the 1950s. Other reasons for the decrease included the postwar celebration of domesticity, which placed family obligations, especially childcare, on women. This culturally assigned burden of caregiving, combined with the challenges of a career that increasingly stressed the pursuit of robust research, made it onerous for women to secure permanent faculty positions. The confluence of professional pressures and cultural obstacles facilitated an across-the-board decline in women's academic professional prospects, just as there emerged an even "more scientific, more mathematical, more male-centered approach to scholarship."[9]

Under the guise of objectivity, this approach marginalized, and in some cases expunged, the traces women left on the humanities—and higher education generally—during earlier decades. For instance, whereas John Dewey's philosophy of pragmatism, which abjured otherworldly abstractions so as to attend to social practice and reform, attracted a substantial number of women to philosophy departments during the 1920s and 1930s, this significantly changed in the years before and during the Second World War as pragmatists were charged with harboring a moral softness associated with femininity. This accusation coupled with the postwar rise of the analytic philosophical tradition, supposedly apolitical, logical, and rigorous, to seemingly sweep "feminine" pragmatism, and women pragmatists, into the dustbin of history. Such sidelining of women and "feminine" approaches to philosophical practice and theory in the 1950s and early 1960s was hardly unique; it was repeated in many other disciplines. In literary studies and art history, the intersecting ideologies of modernism and the New Criticism—meant to orient the reader toward the formal and ostensibly genderless aspects of a literary text or artwork—left little opportunity for incorporating women's perspectives.

There were nevertheless reasons for progressive women and their allies to believe that equality in American higher education might yet arrive in the foreseeable future. The professional and intellectual situation for women in academe, for example, improved slightly after the passage, in 1958, of the National Defense Education Act, which made federal funds available for training in languages, a traditionally "feminine" field. Another ray of hope issued in the early to mid-1960s with predictions that the current supply of faculty would soon be unable to meet student demand generated by the postwar demographic bubble. Such demand would offer women with PhDs the opportunity to join the professoriate and participate in the academic revolution.[10] Such optimism was sorely misplaced, however. By 1969, the massive resources previously funneled into higher education were being redirected elsewhere. Colleges and universities suddenly encountered financial constraints and were unable to continue their fantastic rate of expansion. Faculty hiring ground to a halt, and, by 1973, PhDs, above all those in English literature and European or American history, found themselves without job prospects—a situation vastly different than just a half decade before.

Women activist scholars nonetheless redoubled their efforts to increase the presence of women and women's perspectives on campuses. Inspired by second-wave feminists' efforts to alter laws and policies limiting women's sexual, familial, work, and reproductive rights, these activists reshaped the research and pedagogical programs of women scholars in the humanities in the late 1960s and throughout the 1970s. In addition to establishing committees at annual disciplinary meetings—such as the Modern Language Association (1968), American Historical Association (1969), and American Philosophical Association (1970)—and petitioning the Department of Education to suspend federal contracts with universities that could not produce an affirmative action plan for women and minorities, feminist activist scholars, in 1972, helped push Title IX of the Education Amendments through Congress.[11] This national law advanced the goal of equality for women in colleges and universities by requiring public and private schools that received federal funding to offer equal opportunities, such as financial support, to both sexes.

Second-wave feminists' political efforts outside university walls also formed an important part of the push for women's studies courses. There was little consensus about these classes' topics or even aims, but feminist curricula—which challenged androcentric conceptual structures, scholarly canons, and disciplinary and institutional hierarchies—sought to promote individual autonomy and equality between the sexes.[12] Feminist courses expanded the humanities' demographic and cognitive boundaries. While a September 1970 anthology of women's courses at the tertiary level contained only seventeen syllabi, by 1974 a marked transformation had occurred, with 4,658 women's courses at 885 colleges and universities.[13] Women's studies programs followed a similarly explosive trajectory, the first two founded at San Diego State College and Cornell University in 1970; five years later, there were 270 programs; in 1981, 350.[14]

The establishment of these courses and programs overlapped with the sixties-stimulated political unrest and social transformation that threatened Yale's self-image as a custodian of cultural—read: sexual—orthodoxy. In 1969, Yale's governing body, at the urging of President Kingman Brewster, decided to admit 588 women—"the female versions of Nietzsche's *Uebermensch*," according to the April 1969 issue of the *New York Times Magazine*—to the college's undergraduate ranks of over four thousand men.[15] Many alumni resisted this challenge to the established sexual order.[16] A fair share of undergraduates resisted as well; some even organized a "Keep Yale Male" campaign. In the pamphlet *The Rape of Yale*, circulated during the August 1969 matriculation ceremony and endorsed by William F. Buckley Jr., Julien Dedman (class of '49) sardonically bemoaned

FIGURE 4.1 The cover of Julien Dedman's 1969 pamphlet, *The Rape of Yale*

how Brewster, "intellectually ravished by the sirens of 'Change,'" had "emasculated Yale's most time-honored tradition."[17] In another pamphlet, Lux et Veritas, Inc., founded in August 1970, attacked Yale's administration for implementing coeducation without consulting alumni and without raising the necessary funds. But most scandalous was the dispersal of female students among the twelve residential colleges.

Working against this resistance, Dr. Elga Wasserman, chair of the Planning Committee on Coeducation, and her colleagues believed Yale must patiently and resolutely increase the number of women faculty, administrators, and undergraduates.[18] Faculty started to plan a women's studies program, drawing vision and vigor from the noticeable work of second-wave feminist activists on campus. In the fall of 1970, Yale offered its first women's studies course, "Women in Male Society," while undergraduates, that December, founded a Women's Center, albeit without university backing.[19] Still, the center encouraged both public and private discussions of "women's issues," including sexual harassment, anorexia, and abortion. The center also hosted a chapter of the National Organization for Women, which aimed to "bring women into full participation in the mainstream of American society." By the mid-1970s, the Women's Center at Yale hosted panel discussions ("Sexism at Yale," fall 1976), consciousness-raising groups, self-help groups, a women's studies discussion table, and a faculty women's lunch table. Additionally, the center published a feminist course critique, the *Freshwomen's Booklet*, in the fall of 1975, and *Women's Words*, a feminist journal, in spring 1976.[20]

These efforts, in concert, aimed to upset the hierarchy that marginalized women and "the feminine" on campus and underwrote the university's conservative culture. However, the founding of a women's studies program proved to be neither smooth nor quick. A 1972 "Report on Coeducation" advocated rapidly moving the school toward sex-blind admissions—Yale had achieved a ratio of forty women to sixty men in the undergraduate college of forty-eight hundred—but a 1971 internal report explained that, in "a school dominated by men of the Old Blue tradition where women are tolerated only," professional pressures and obstacles— which included serving on more committees than male colleagues and an imprecise policy for maternity leave—were compounded by open and persistent harassment.[21] According to an Undergraduate Women's Caucus report, in the fall of 1976, a professor commenced English 29—"a survey course, spanning the whole European literary tradition," from Homer to Beckett, that is—with "a slide portraying a man about to be raped by the Sphinx for his attempt to enter Thebes." "After a brief discussion of the slide, [the English professor] turned to the class and remarked: 'All men face the same threat of a hungry, gaping vagina.'"[22] In a similar case that same term, a literature professor quoted from Machiavelli's *The Prince* (1532): "I am absolutely convinced that it is better to be impetuous than circumspect, because Fortune is a woman and you must, if you want to subjugate her, beat and strike her." "After finishing the quotation," the Women's Caucus report stated, the "professor made some laughing remarks about it and changed the words slightly to say, 'like a woman, Fortune must be raped and beaten.'" The professor repeated this altered quotation three times. "How do you do it?" a student asked. He replied: "I'll tell you guys after class," drawing guffaws.[23] It was precisely such hostile and threatening discursive and physical acts that fostered the deep-rooted androcentric and misogynist environment at Yale that second-wave feminist scholars and students intended to overturn.

Yale feminists' efforts did result in the expansion of the number and scope of women's studies courses. By 1971, Wasserman's Planning Committee on Coeducation organized eight such courses. In the fall of 1974, visiting instructor Betty Friedan used her course "The Sex-Role Revolution: Stage II" to reconsider her famous critique of the confinements and frustrations of American women in *The Feminine Mystique* (1963), arguing that the first stage of second-wave feminism soon would conclude with the ratification of the Equal Rights Amendment, which aimed to terminate legal differences between men and women. Feminism, Friedan suggested, might then enter a new phase in which women and men worked together to address the double enslavement of women—in the home and in the workplace.[24] Radical feminists considered Friedan's argument reactionary, but those sympathetic likely saw her thesis as pointing to what might lie beyond second-wave feminists' aims to ensure equality for women. Regardless of where Yalies stood, however, Friedan's women's studies class signaled that the move of American feminists away from a second-wave emphasis on political rights and equality toward questions of culture was filtering into seminar rooms and lecture halls.

Yale feminists during the early to mid-1970s were scarcely disconnected from contact with feminists' efforts elsewhere. *Ms.* magazine was founded in 1971; Florence Howe started the Feminist Press in 1970; and the interdisciplinary journal *Signs*—central to the early development of women's studies—followed in 1973.[25] In New Haven, women's organizations and groups—Belladonna Publishing, the Connecticut Feminist Federal Credit Union, and the New Haven Women's Liberation Rock Band, to name a few—promoted feminist goals. Meanwhile, Yale faculty and graduate students developed curricula that furthered second-wave feminists' sexual politics. One of them was Catherine MacKinnon, a graduate student in political science who earned her law degree from Yale in 1977. For MacKinnon and her socialist-feminist allies, truth was defined by questioning the hierarchy between male and female, between masculine and feminine, that organized institutions and knowledge. And for them, the university should decode, assess, and communicate this truth. "A curriculum is a map of reality," MacKinnon wrote in 1978. "It presents a categorical series of unities of life, world and thought divided by time, place and manner of investigation, and united into disciplines according to people's experience of truth. As changes in disciplinary boundaries illustrate, the experience of truth is a social experience."[26]

In her courses MacKinnon sought ways to equalize the male/female value-laden opposition, even as her understanding of the link between the university and women's collective experience changed; her teaching also reflected the reorientation among some radical feminist scholars away from sociostructural approaches toward more cultural issues. For instance, according to some of her students, MacKinnon's fall 1976 seminar "Socialism and/or Feminism," which "focused in part on the experiences of women in China and Vietnam," revolved too much around her interest in Marxist theory and practice.[27] In contrast, MacKinnon's fall 1977 American studies class "Feminism and Humanism: An Introduction to Women's Studies" was, according to a colleague, broadly devoted to political theory, including political equality and individual autonomy in the United States and the world.[28] MacKinnon's emphasis on the diversity of feminisms—"liberal, radical, and left"—in her revamped "Feminism and Humanism" the following year can be attributed to the fact that it was planned to be the central course of the inaugural semester of the Women's Studies Program, but it also signaled many feminist scholars' growing abandonment of sociostructural methods of interpretation.[29]

MacKinnon's sexual-cultural politics were also reflected in her legal advocacy. In 1977, she advised attorneys who represented five female undergraduates at Yale to test her new legal theory, parts of which she published in *Sexual Harassment of Working Women* (1979). MacKinnon theorized that sexual discrimination happened more frequently in subtle than overt ways, that "the unwanted imposition of sexual requirements in the context of a relationship of unequal power" comprised illegal sex discrimination.[30] Specifically, MacKinnon urged students to sue Yale for doing nothing to halt "quid pro quo" sexual harassment (sex for better grades) by male professors; Yale denied women the right, guaranteed under Title IX, to an equal education, MacKinnon argued. Brought by the feminist law firm the New Haven Law Collective, founded by MacKinnon and other lawyers, the 1979 case *Alexander v. Yale* was the first to use Title IX in charges of sexual harassment against an educational institution. Though the federal appeals court dismissed the charges in 1980, Yale eventually introduced a grievance mechanism for the reporting of sexual harassment. Within a decade, MacKinnon and her peers transformed sex discrimination law and contributed to the emerging cultural understanding of what constituted sexual harassment, protecting the gains of feminists at Yale and other colleges and universities.[31]

MacKinnon's legal work roughly coincided with the experimental session for Yale's Women's Studies Program during the 1978 summer term.[32] Professors and graduate students alike—including American historian Nancy Cott, social psychologist Faye Crosby, and sociologist and law professor Hesung Koh—inundated the Women's Studies Task Force with course proposals that aligned with not only second-wave feminists' mission of legal equality. These courses also aligned with feminist teacher-scholars' research into cultural areas and topics, research that aimed to combat intolerance of difference, a goal shared by the greater academic left. Faye Crosby's class "The Psychology of Women" complemented her scholarship on the cognitive and emotional barriers of working women, some of whom, even though they understood that women workers did not receive the respect and remuneration they earned, believed that they, individually, evaded sexual discrimination.[33] Nancy Cott's class "Women in the United States in the Twentieth Century" was related to her pioneering *The Bonds of Womanhood: "Woman's Sphere" in New England, 1780–1835* (1977), where she explored how the private writings of unknown middle-class women during the late eighteenth and early nineteenth centuries became the tools by which these women not only defined their sexual identity but understood the economic and political restrictions that confined them.[34]

The course of assistant professor of classics Jack Winkler provides an especially clear window into the synergy between the developing Women's Studies Program and the feminist cultural aims then pursued by an insurgent flank in Yale's literature departments. Winkler helped produce *Come Out Tonight*, an hour-long gay radio show broadcast every Sunday, organized Yale's first Gay Rights Week in April 1977, and supported the Connecticut Sexual Orientation Bill; he was also the only man and only professor to join the 1980 Title IX lawsuit against the university, though he had left for Stanford in 1979. In his scholarship, he was equally reformist; his research program involved applying feminist approaches to Greek and Latin texts. With a 1981 essay, Winkler used an openly lesbian-feminist thesis that a woman's ability to produce poetry was enhanced by the fact that she wrote within the confines of a language constructed by men. He demonstrated this thesis with the ancient Greek lyric poetry of Sappho, whose familiarity with men's *and* women's separate languages and cultures granted her the ability to reconceptualize sexual categories: "For

FIGURE 4.2 Jack Winkler (*left*) at Yale's first Gay Rights Week in 1977. Here, Winkler participates in the dance in front of Sterling Memorial Library that concluded the event. (Courtesy of the Yale AIDS Memorial Project)

[Sappho] the sexual is always something else. . . . Her sacred landscape of the body is at the same time a statement about a more complete consciousness, whether of myth, poetry, ritual or personal relationships."[35] By prohibiting the partitioning of the sexual from the emotional, Winkler's Sappho employed poetry to birth a world in which women were not mere sex objects but self-determining and autonomous individuals.

Winkler's later research developed in part out of his 1978 summer course, "Sexual Politics in Literature." Drawing from the new field of feminist literary criticism initiated by Mary Ellman's identification of "phallic criticism" in *Thinking about Women* (1968); Elaine Showalter's "gynocriticism" in *A Literature of Their Own* (1971), which aimed to recover the characteristics of language, genre, and authority of "women's writing"; and Kate Millet's exploration of sexual relations in literature in *Sexual Politics*

(1970), Winkler's course placed the question of sexual politics front and center.[36] It challenged the ideological misdirection that portrayed literature as a male domain, revealing women's achievements, perspectives, and writing techniques—usually either excluded from or sidelined in literary canons and traditions—as central to the enterprise of literary creation. Winkler's course showed students that masculine traditions constituted what they once believed was "literature," explored how men and women writers' ideas about the feminine and femininity shaped texts, and investigated male and female visions, sensibilities, and apperceptions of the world. And yet this *was* only one course.[37] The Undergraduate Women's Caucus warily—and tellingly—observed in 1977, "Yale's fulfillment of *her* [*sic*] own potential demands a confrontation with the question posed by the presence of women—which has just begun."[38] Judging from this observation, Yale cultural feminists, too, expressed the patriarchal conceit that Yale was a maternal protector, albeit one that would eventually subvert established conceptual and institutional hierarchical oppositions between male and female, masculine and feminine.

A Feminist Turn of the Deconstructive Screw and the Founding of Yale's Women's Studies Program

It was in and around the literature major that an important feminist challenge to the male biases that informed literary humanism transpired. As early as 1973, the major's inaugural year, female students protested the androcentrism of its core course, "Literature X: Man and His Fictions," and its textbook of the same title, viewing them as ignoring or marginalizing women's literary achievements.[39] Seven years later, Barbara Johnson was launching feminist deconstructions in the lit major, aiding the transformation of the undergraduate teaching of literature occurring there. Johnson had arrived at Yale in 1969 as a graduate student in French literature and in 1977 earned her PhD, with Paul de Man as her adviser. That same year, Yale French hired Johnson as a tenure-track assistant professor. Opening ways out of the methodological dead end promoted by the Yale School's disproportionate concentration on rhetoric, rhetorical vocabulary, and the self-undermining of dichotomies in canonical texts, Johnson became a key figure in the most culturally subversive faction of the American institution of deconstruction: its feminist moment. For the feminist wing of the deconstructive movement expanded the science of rhetorical reading to confront the masculine metaphysics that underpinned Yale's humanist self-image, de Man and company's styles of postformalist criticism, and the assumed genderlessness and sexlessness of literary-critical practice.

But many of the important feminist-deconstructive rejoinders to the literary imperative that Johnson and colleagues on the academic left at Yale articulated in teachings and texts would only appear at the tail end of the 1970s. Actually, Johnson's intellectual formation in graduate school initially involved neither an overt commitment to feminism nor a deep engagement with Derrida's work, which she first encountered in a 1969 class given by Jacques Ehrmann on the French avant-garde literary magazine *Tel Quel*. Though Johnson had been focused on the work of Jacques Lacan, she was tasked with translating one of Derrida's Yale Comp Lit lectures into English, on the basis of which she was asked to translate his book *La dissémination* (1972). Johnson quickly found Derrida's anti-metaphysical response to literature more compelling than Lacan's psychoanalytic approach. While Lacan made interpretive leaps without explanation, Johnson believed, Derrida was explicitly "a reader, and that's what [she] aspire[d] to be."[40] *La dissémination*, for example, comprised an "Outwork" that flagged the deconstruction of the metaphysical hierarchy that privileged origins, beginnings, and, ironically, introductions over derivations and copies; subsequent sections highlighted when and where texts by Plato, Stéphane Mallarmé, and Phillipe Sollers undermined, intentionally or not, the hierarchical difference between origin and copy, reality and representation.

Before fully embracing a deconstructive cultural politics of the literary text, Johnson made her name in the profession with incisive de Manian rhetorical responses to canonical writings and influential readings of them. In her 1977 MLA paper "The Critical Difference," Johnson deconstructively read Roland Barthes's reading of Honoré de Balzac's short story "Sarrasine." Prior to interpreting "Sarrasine," Johnson glossed, Barthes conceptualized a hierarchy between "readerly" and "writerly" texts. For Barthes, "Sarrasine" was a "readerly" text, in that it was "constrained by considerations of representation: it is irreversible, 'natural,' decidable, continuous, totalizable, and unified into a coherent whole based on the signified. The writerly [text, in contrast] is infinitely plural and open to the free play of signifiers and of difference, unconstrained by representative considerations, and transgressive of any desire of decidable, unified, totalized meaning."[41] Not only, Johnson argued, did Barthes's attempt to filter Balzac's "Sarrasine" through his onto-theological readerly/writerly opposition deconstruct itself; Barthes labeled "Sarrasine" as readerly but his "*treatment* of it" by fragmenting and pluralizing the text seemed "to illustrate all the characteristics of the positive, writerly end" of Barthes's metaphysical dichotomy.[42] But Barthes's reading was, in turn, deconstructed by "Sarrasine" itself. For "Sarrasine" undermined the pursued/pursuer dichotomy, which for Johnson was analogous to Barthes's dichotomy of writerly/readerly. Balzac's story about a conceited seducer who unknowingly pursued a castrato provided a "subversive and unsettling formulation of the question of sexual difference."[43] In the story, "the [pursued] castrato is both *outside* the difference between the sexes and at the same time the *literalization* of its illusory symmetry. He is that which subverts the desire for symmetrical, binary difference *by fulfilling it.*"[44] This deconstruction of the pursued/pursuer binary mirrored Barthes's inadvertent deconstruction of the "opposition between unity and fragmentation" in his own text, between readerly and writerly texts, that is. With these deconstructions, Johnson argued, Barthes's reading and Balzac's story unintentionally traced the rhetorical response to literature's demand, revealing the internal critical/poetic differences in their texts that made their writings "literary."

Besides hinting at her forthcoming feminist deconstructions, Johnson's paper provided an opportunity to demarcate the parameters established by her teachers for the careful highlighting of the "de-construction of a text," of the "warring forces of signification within the text itself."[45] "If anything is destroyed in a deconstructive reading, it is not the text," Johnson stated in a de Manian manner, "but the claim to unequivocal domination of one mode of signifying over another. A deconstructive reading is a reading that analyzes the *specificity* of a text's critical difference from itself."[46] Johnson's deconstructive response to literature subverted the notion that a univocal—or transcendental—signified centered the signifiers of the text, whether literary or critical.[47] In this style, Johnson's rhetorical interpretive strategies accorded with de Man's deconstructive grappling with the literary imperative, superseding and subverting New Critical formalist, structuralist, and phenomenological interpretive procedures, because each claimed to isolate the shape or meaning of literature, its form and what it was "about," or indicated. Still, Johnson's deconstructive acts, like those of her teachers, did not destroy disciplinary boundaries. Like earlier formalist approaches, Johnson's focus remained on the text itself—deconstruction, as Johnson practiced it, continued to concentrate on the rhetorical dimensions of literature.

Johnson also traced texts' self-deconstructions in her first book (1979), based on her Yale dissertation on Charles Baudelaire. And Johnson again used a de Manian/Derridean deconstructive response to literature, revising the thesis of a 1959 book by French critic Suzanne Bernard. Bernard explored the "Icarian" property of Baudelaire's *Petits poèmes en prose* (1869): the text's impossible-to-fulfill quality of desiring to exceed or surpass itself while paradoxically aiming to negate "its own conditions of existence."[48] This property, Bernard maintained, made Baudelaire mourn his own poetic endeavors for not having broken free of the meaning or form of his previous poems. Johnson, though, suggested that "the

[Icarian] fall recounted in the *Petits poèmes en prose* is not that of a subject who falls from poetic paradise into the prosaic world, but rather that of the paradise itself, which differentiates itself from itself."[49] For Johnson, *Petits poèmes en prose* rhetorically read itself, always already subverting organic wholeness or metaphysical oneness. This deconstruction of paradise, Johnson argued, was precisely what produced the dialogue in Baudelaire's writings between genres—between prose and poetry—and his texts. Baudelaire's prose poems, for Johnson, were "literature"; they were metapoetry, reflexive texts in conversation with Baudelaire's other texts; his prose poems were inter- and intratextual poetic performances of and about poetry. And this "literary" way of questioning its own linguistic forms generated the uncertainty that undermined the standing of poetry and any classification of genre: "Neither antithesis nor synthesis, the prose poem is the place from where the polarity—and therefore the symmetry—between presence and absence, between prose and poetry, *disfunctions*."[50] Further, for Johnson, not only were prose poems' "*disfunctioning*" constitutive of this genre's shape and meaning, but a strict and rigorous reading of these prose poems would *necessarily* reproduce the poems' undermining of themselves. Though Johnson's focus subverted the New Critical faith in the onto-theological primacy and wholeness of the artwork in that she proposed that her deconstructive reading was a topological paradox, a kind of literature that undermined itself, she also reinforced the recognized disciplinary boundary of literary studies in that the texts she interpreted were customarily classed as literature.

Soon after this book, however, Johnson began to move past the issue of the literariness of literature that so consumed de Man, foregrounding political and social implications of the rhetorical dimensions of texts in ways that he never did and Derrida often made difficult to discern. Johnson's newfound explicit feminist cultural politics was evident in her paper, "Le dernier homme," presented at a July–August 1980 colloquium organized around Derrida's work and held in Cerisy, France. Instead of complaining, like many participants, "especially by Americans, about the mechanical application of Derridean deconstruction, in America, to literary studies," a routinization that ostensibly divested it "of its original radical force," as Jonathan Culler recalled, Johnson modified the Male School's science of rhetorical reading to underscore how Mary Shelley's literary texts subverted the universal and hence metaphysical pretensions of Western humanism and Romanticism.[51] While Derrida's October 1968 paper "The Ends of Man" highlighted the self-undermining ethnocentrism at the heart of all humanisms—by universalizing "Man," Derrida argued, humanists anthropologized European "man," objectifying the human and speaking for others in "Western" vocabularies—Johnson here exposed the humanist project as a self-subversive, destructive male fantasy: "To speak of Mary Shelley's *Frankenstein* [1818] is immediately to approach the question of *man* indirectly through what has always been at once excluded and comprehended by its definition, namely, the *woman* and the *monster*."[52] With his monster, Johnson's Dr. Frankenstein aimed to fulfill Enlightenment philosophes' humanist program—a human Western, rational, and implicitly masculine. However, because his ostensibly universal "Man" was sexed, Dr. Frankenstein—that humanist-creator par excellence—was unable to complete his experiment, which required a female monster that equaled his male. Dr. Frankenstein could conceive, but not birth, his female monster: his frightful vision of a new Eve actually led him to destroy his rough draft. Johnson's deconstructive *Frankenstein* was thus a complex and visionary meditation on the onto-theological opposition between male and female that violently excluded the feminine presence responsible for yet which undermined the identity of Western "Man"—as evinced by the actions and imagination of Dr. Frankenstein himself. In the end, Johnson's "Le dernier homme" helped raise the profile of Shelley, who was receiving long overdue attention in literary studies by the academic left, and facilitated the reorganization of the literary canon of the British Romantics—until then, all men.

Johnson's research agenda and her teaching would become a closely intertwined cultural program that showed how and why a thorough deconstructive reply to literature's demand was inescapably feminist. Her Cerisy paper, for instance, overlapped with the feminist shift in her classroom teaching. While helping teach the fall 1980 iteration of "Man and His Fictions," Johnson rerouted the course's subversion of the onto-theological presuppositions of literary education back on itself, reflexively fashioning a feminist path through this central and implicitly masculine route of the lit major.[53] Likely because of Johnson, who joined the lit major's governing board in 1980, this version of the course was not simply retitled "Narrative Forms" but included a lecture by Johnson on *Frankenstein* and a seminar discussion that compared Shelley's text to Jean-Jacques Rousseau's *Confessions* (1782).[54] What's more, Johnson and her coteachers asked undergraduates to write a four- to five-page essay that investigated, first, how "the narrative" of *Frankenstein*, Rousseau's *Confessions*, and Dickens's *Great Expectations* (1861)—all texts that Johnson rhetorically read as being to a degree autobiographical—were "implicitly or explicitly addressed to a listener/reader" and, second, how this "affects the narration."[55] Put differently: how did Shelley's, Rousseau's, and Dickens's "autobiographical" texts' hidden or open rhetorical techniques (that aimed to speak to readers) shape those texts? By teasing out how these authors' narratives' linguistic devices and figural language oriented the reader, students deconstructed the male/female dichotomy that structured literary humanism: they considered a female presence and feminist affirmation in literature, reading Shelley's *Frankenstein* as a deconstructive critique of "Man." By calling into question what constituted autobiography, Johnson's students also challenged the accepted male conventions of the genre. Narrative Forms thus primed students for future rhetorical acts that undermined the metaphysical hierarchies that ignored or sidelined the "feminine" in other texts, institutional settings, and pedagogical traditions. And, because of the traditional function given to literary education at Yale for the cultivation of character, Narrative Forms students' feminist deconstructions of Lit X's masculinist subversions of literary study further subverted the myth of the school as defender of cultural orthodoxies.

Other literature professors at Yale contributed to the demanding and distinctive feminist institution of deconstruction to constructively disrupt the masculine metaphysics of literary humanism. Margaret Homans, who graduated in 1974 and then earned her PhD in English from the university in 1978, has suggested that she sought an education that examined standards of gender and sexuality in literature and culture. While doing her dissertation partially satisfied that yearning, her hunger reflected the extent to which professors' pedagogy and the culture in Yale English still enforced gendered and sexed dichotomies. In her dissertation—directed by J. Hillis Miller—Homans explored the ways Dorothy Wordsworth, Emily Brontë, and Emily Dickinson "textually conscious of their femininity, responded to a literary tradition that depended on and reinforced the masculine orientation of language of the poet."[56] But for Homans it was, above all, modernist Dickinson, by using her eccentric position outside masculine artistic styles, who "discover[ed] that all language is figurative, and therefore that the traditions of Romantic writing that hinder Wordsworth and Brontë need not be taken as necessary truths."[57] It was not just that a hierarchical opposition erected by the Romantics between male and female valorized masculinized techniques of writing—and, Homans implied, privileged the masculine conventions that shaped all forms of post-Romantic knowledge. It was that the presumed masculine orientation of language obscured the figurative in women's writing. And, while in the masculine modernist tradition figures of speech were often defined as ornaments of language (and writing), in marginalized feminist cultural traditions, such as those to which Dickinson belonged, they were a constitutive part of language, basic to understanding. With this reading, English doctoral candidate Homans demonstrated, against the Male School's elevation of the male Romantic poetic tradition, how the science of rhetorical interpretation could promote a feminist linguistic turn.

In Homans's later book *Bearing the Word* (1986), she complicated this feminist insight about rhetoric as the essential though unsettling ingredient to any discourse while charting a path between an American feminist literary criticism that held there to be "a realm outside language called life or experience" and a French feminist literary criticism that saw "all experience" as occurring "within a system of representation, usually identified as Lacan's symbolic order."[58] Subverting the assumed opposition between American and French feminist literary-critical traditions, Homans believed, permitted the reader to home in on the Western metaphysical myth that women were linked to literal, direct, and unembroidered language (particularly concerning reproduction), whereas men were allied with or maintained a power for figurative or symbolic language that deferred referents. Focusing on "four recurrent literary situations," which she baptized as "bearing the word," Homans underscored this hierarchical opposition in "the thematics of female experience" and "women's special relation to language" in nineteenth-century fictions by women writers.[59] In George Eliot's *Adam Bede* (1851), for instance, Homans foregrounded how Hetty Sorrel's "figurative concealment of a newborn but dead passion" for Arthur Donnithorne was actualized in her literal "concealment of a newborn but dead baby."[60] For Homans, this and other literary situations in which women bore the word exhibited the disruptive powers of figural language on the unvarnished truth.

Homans's late 1970s feminist work stands in stark contrast to the culturally conservative views long expressed by male Yale English professors. A most prominent example: Harold Bloom, whose teachings' and texts' desacralizations initially had such democratizing effects in the department and on the profession. During the 1960s, Bloom was considered a literary-critical visionary, but his views were also a product of repressive and antidemocratic masculinist traditions. He remarked in a 1965 essay, later included in a widely distributed popular edition of *Frankenstein*, that because Shelley's novel "lacks the sophistication and imaginative complexity of such works" as William Blake's *Book of Urizen* (1794) and Lord Byron's *Manfred* (1817), it "affords a unique introduction to the archetypal world of the Romantics."[61] For Bloom, Shelley's work was a supplement—at most an introduction—to that of her husband Percy Bysshe Shelley and other male Romantics. His disdain was also apparent in a 1974 letter to J. Hillis Miller: "I don't believe the level-down process *can* be halted, at Yale or elsewhere. A majority of the voting members in the Yale Eng. Dept., 5–7 years hence, will be made up of a coalition between housekeeping women (younger + already on the scene) and safe professional men (older + to be brought in from outside starting now)."[62] Like other American Jewish men who fought to end the quotas that restricted admission and hiring of Jews in Ivy League schools during the 1950s and 1960s, Bloom may have seen feminists' demands for affirmative action in his department as mirroring the logic underlying quotas for Jews.[63] The academic left's post-sixties enlargement of the boundaries of the humanities sometimes turned avowed proponents of cultural pluralism into ardent traditionalists.[64]

Bloom's resistance hardly halted the coming transformation. Notably, feminists extended the central principles of his theory of poetic influence, as in the seven-hundred-page *The Madwoman in the Attic* (1979).[65] In it, Sandra Gilbert and Susan Gubar rewrote Bloom's post-Miltonic patriarchal model of rhetorical refractions, arguing that nineteenth-century women writers, such as Jane Austen, Emily Dickinson, and Mary Shelley, attempted to use their texts to attain autonomy by confronting the difficulty of seeing themselves as isolated literary voices, voices devoid of poetic foremothers. Whereas Bloom saw male poets' repressed anxiety about the influence of monumental forefathers in their poems' rhetoric, Gilbert and Gubar identified women authors' "anxiety of authorship" about their exclusion from literary tradition in their writings. Not a male anxiety of poetic priority, then, but a female anxiety about being barred from literary tradition generated and structured the paradoxes of literary history. For Gilbert and Gubar, women writers specifically engaged their existential dilemma by making their writings "cover stories," double-voiced texts in which a feminist subtext of self-governance and originality was hidden within a more orthodox story; their female characters, for example, often embodied the dichotomy between "angel" or "monster"/"madwoman."[66] To reclaim these feminist literary role models revealed a "secret sisterhood" within the Western tradition.

Bloom's reactionary fear of the "level[ing]-down process" in Yale English shows clearly his own androcentric prejudice and the masculine metaphysics that shaped his views. Yet still more critics studied at or joined Yale English who gave feminist-deconstructive replies to literature's imperative.[67] Some answered, like Johnson would in her 1980 Cerisy paper, with British Romantic texts. Mary Poovey, for instance, started to work alongside Bloom in 1974, even before earning her PhD from the University of Virginia. Hired to teach, not her dissertation fields of eighteenth- and nineteenth-century English literature, but narrative theory, Poovey never considered herself to be a member of a school of thought, though she believed herself to have learned as much from "the high theoretical textuality" of Miller, de Man, and Hartman as from the "historicism" of Fredric Jameson, who, in Yale French, was increasingly interested in how "language was part of culture as opposed to being all of culture."[68]

Poovey's rhetorical reading of *Frankenstein* (1980) not only helped re-

write Shelley's place in the canon of British Romanticism but signaled the
political ramifications of this interpretation. Instead of a primer for her
more complex male counterparts, Poovey's Shelley "feminizes... Percy's
version of the Romantic aesthetic," interrogating the Romantic dream of
self-sovereignty.[69] For example, though Shelley portrayed Dr. Frankenstein's monster as the symbolic fulfillment of the doctor's imagination—
and in this regard supported Romantics' male metaphysical fantasy of
self-creation—she also rendered the monster mute, incapable of pursuing his own creative endeavors. Poovey's Shelley sympathized with Dr.
Frankenstein's Romantic undertaking but also implicitly chastised his
masculine dream of self-assertion, for it was through the immediacy of
the voice that the subject gained coherence and power. Poovey's Shelley thus obliquely destabilized political projects rooted in the Romantic
aesthetic, an onto-theological vision of an autonomous—and implicitly
male—subject capable of agency, of self-direction. These political projects, which included classical Marxism and liberalism, were grounded in
the paradoxical view that each consciousness possessed unity, and this
unity was achieved by metaphysically either opposing or sometimes removing the links between self and other.

During the 1970s, feminist deconstructionists in Yale French and Comp
Lit too expanded rhetorical reading techniques to show literature's claim
as separate and central to historical discourse. Like Johnson's hiring in
French, Margaret Ferguson's employment by Comp Lit was unusual—she
earned a BA in the history of art and English literature at Cornell University in 1969 and, in 1974, a PhD in de Man's Comp Lit—though fortu-
itous; after serving on the Women's Studies Task Force throughout most
of the 1970s, Ferguson became known as a member of "the Yale School
of Renaissance criticism."[70] In a 1978 article that formed the basis for a
1983 book, Ferguson examined a figural tension in Renaissance literature
between a pull toward antiquity viewed as a whole and singular truth and
an opposition or a resistance to this undivided past. This linguistic tension, Ferguson argued, is traceable in French poet and critic Joachim du
Bellay's defense of the French language in his *La deffense* (1549). In light
of du Bellay's milieu, his use of the word "*defense*" not only had "legal and
military connotations" but "like any good defense... hides an offense" and
performed a tension that undermined itself: "*La Deffense* does not offer a
unified poetic theory at all; rather, it presents a significant pattern of contradictions."[71] This pattern was legible in the paradoxes and conflicts that
du Bellay identified in the relationships between *la langue françoyse* and
antiquity, contemporary Italy, contemporary French writing, and even
du Bellay himself. The result of these different ways by which *La deffense*
rhetorically read its cultural content and form was that du Bellay placed

himself in a state of suspense, exiled between present and past. Ferguson's colleague in English, Thomas M. Greene, summarized this type of broadened de Manian interpretation: "[The] movement back and forth between a nourishing, overshadowing tradition and a groping, miraculous invention is precisely the movement of the *Deffense*, which needs to be read synecdochically as the fissured crystallization of an era."[72] Conventional scholars emphasized the importance of an author's biography and cultural background for understanding a literary text, but the kinds of "unstable vacillations" that Ferguson identified as paradigmatic in Renaissance literature offered a sociohistorical variant of deconstruction.

While Ferguson, Poovey, Homans, and Johnson pursued their feminist responses to literary language's disruptions in a manner that enlarged the scope of the science of rhetorical reading in their home departments, they were also actively involved in the establishment of a women's studies program during the late 1970s. But the retrenchment that followed the 1973–75 recession had already constrained such work; efforts to propagate women's studies courses, by as early as 1975, began to falter, and the hiring of permanent women faculty for the program put on hold. In the second half of the 1970s, women held only five—1.6 percent—of the tenure-track positions in Yale's arts and sciences division. Shoshana Felman, after earning her PhD at the Université Grenoble Alpes, held one of those five positions, joining French in 1970 and, in 1973, with de Man's support and despite some stiff faculty resistance, becoming the department's first tenured woman.[73] Felman's interlocking research and pedagogical projects appropriated Lacan's psychoanalytic theories and aspects of de Man's rhetorical reading strategies to forge a rigorous way to register the power of literary language to describe, signify, and repress "the feminine." Felman, though, initially established her reputation internationally as an interpreter of Lacan, whose work was met by French feminists with much criticism at the time. In his Parisian 1972–73 seminar on "Femininity," Lacan, while criticizing essentialist views of "Woman" as a category of identity, offered his reading of how language and representation symbolically generated the feminine. "There is no such thing as *The* woman," Lacan confrontationally announced, "where the definite article stands for the universal."[74] Only a year after British psychoanalyst and feminist Juliet Mitchell introduced Lacanian ideas to Anglo-American feminist thought, Felman ran a graduate seminar at Yale on Lacan (in French) during the fall of 1975. She also worked with de Man and Hartman to bring the psychoanalyst to campus for a widely attended lecture in late November that year.

Lacan presented the political effects of his work as uncertain—at the reception at Felman's home after his lecture, a student asked: "What are the political implications of your psychoanalytic research?" "It's like a tablecloth. What you gain on one side, you lose on the other," Lacan replied.[75] Felman thought otherwise, and began to incorporate Lacanian theories to elaborate her own feminist-deconstructive cultural politics. In a winter 1975 essay, Felman reviewed recent works influenced by psychoanalytic theories that examined woman's place in American and European critical discourse to explore Western culture's gendered imposition of madness.[76] She rhetorically read American second-wave feminist and psychotherapist Phyllis Chesler's *Women and Madness* (1972), which argued that women were pathologized because society was sexist, and French feminist philosopher and psychoanalyst Luce Irigaray's *Speculum de l'autre femme* (1974), a critique of women's exclusion in philosophy and Lacanian psychoanalytic theory. According to Felman, Chesler's and Irigaray's texts both revealed that if, "in our culture, the woman is by definition associated with madness, her problem is how to break out of this (cultural) imposition of madness *without* taking up the critical and therapeutic positions of [masculine] reason: how to avoid speaking both as *mad* and as *not mad*."[77] For Felman, women's challenge was to develop a deconstructive way of reading that navigated between the onto-theological opposition between madness (woman) and reason (man). To do so, women, speaking "not only against, but outside of the specular phallogocentric structure"—that is, in contradiction with and external to the Western metaphysical subordination of woman and the feminine—could, in turn, establish "a discourse the status of which would no longer be defined by the phallacy of masculine meaning";[78] such a rhetorical response subverted masculine metaphysics and its myths that organized and oriented values and meaning. Felman's "woman" disrupted the kinds of essentialism common in Anglo-American second-wave feminist discourses like Chesler's and extended Irigaray's critique of phallocentrism (the privileging of masculinity) to phallogocentrism (a focus in language on the phallus).

During the second half of the 1970s, Felman's psychoanalytically inflected feminist articulation of deconstructive reading was part of a new focus in American and French criticism that recognized "women's writing" as a distinct activity that transformed masculine categories of understanding and knowledge. Across the Atlantic, explorations of "women's writing" became a field unto itself. Hélène Cixous (friend and ally of Derrida), in her 1975 essay *"Le rire de la méduse,"* the English translation appeared in 1976, advocated that women embrace and employ *écriture feminine*, the psychological inscription of the female body and female difference in language and culture. With *écriture feminine*, women could engage their own felt otherness, a foreignness that resulted from masculinist metaphysics' positioning women as a supplement to an essential man in representational systems, to reassert their understanding of themselves and the world.[79] Elaine Marks and Carolyn Burke, in 1978, are customarily considered to have imported the first comprehensive analyses of contemporary French feminist discourses like those of Cixous to an American readership, yet Felman had already suggested the interpretive scaffold within which such French theoretical texts would be read as they became available in translation.[80] For in her aforementioned winter 1975 review, Felman argued that the distinction between an empirical/pragmatic and a theoretical/linguistic formulation of feminist issues—an opposition she rhetorically read as expressed by the differences between Chesler's and Irigaray's texts—received cultural expression in the opposition of American and French intellectual systems.[81] Automatically constructing such a binary between national-cultural forms, Felman might have proposed, partakes in (the masculine) metaphysics' erasure of "women's writing" that her deconstructive project aimed to disrupt.

An apogee of feminist deconstructionists' engagements with literature qua literature in New Haven was reached with the publication of the 1977 *Yale French Studies* (*YFS*) special issue titled "Literature and Psychoanalysis," which Felman helmed. In the issue's introduction, Felman stressed that the *YFS* essays intervened in the hierarchical opposition between psychoanalysis and literature, with psychoanalytic theories usually viewed as possessing the keys to unlocking the meaning of a literary text. Each of the volume's essays, however, considered "the relationship between psychoanalysis and literature *from the literary point of view.*"[82] "[The] intention is to [rhetorically respond to the literary perspective in order to] disrupt altogether the position of mastery as such, to try and avoid *both* terms of the alternative [for example, either psychoanalysis or literature], to deconstruct the very structure of the *opposition*, mastery/ slavery."[83] According to Felman, rhetorically reading literature subverted the metaphysical mastery/slavery dichotomy, in which the first term is conventionally coded as masculine and the second as feminine, showing that psychoanalysis yielded insights into literary texts as much as literary texts yielded psychoanalytic insights. And though psychoanalytic discourses were literary texts and literary texts were psychoanalytic discourses, it was by grappling with these texts from the *literary perspective* and its inherent figural unruliness that undermined the identity of both.

Felman argued her deconstructive thesis in her *YFS* essay on Henry James's novella *The Turn of the Screw* (1898). She highlighted that when American literary critic Edmund Wilson declared himself exterior to and reporting on the essential meaning of the story in a 1934 essay, he became, in a kind of transference between text and reader, unintentionally trapped by James's story, repeating a role performed in it. Felman pointed to how (male) Wilson aimed to "exclude," "from the place of meaning and of truth," the (female) narrator of James's story "as mad" but "precisely . . . repeat[ed] her very gesture of exclusion, [thereby] *includ*[ing] *oneself*, in other words, within her very gesture of madness."[84] Like James's narrator, Wilson's attempt to adopt a position of objective mastery over the text became an act of personal psychosis or hysteria, involuntarily deconstructing the structure inherent in the interconnecting and co-implicated binaries psychoanalysis/literature, science/fantasy, objective/subjective, and male/female. Felman rhetorically read *The Turn of the Screw* to illustrate its capacity as literature to dislocate these metaphysical oppositions.

The 1977 *YFS* special issue was also a venue for other Yale feminist deconstructionists to underscore deconstructions executed from a literary standpoint that questioned the psychoanalysis/literature hierarchy. In her contribution, Barbara Johnson laid groundwork for her later politically and socially modulated rhetorical reading procedures, deconstructively responding to literature's disruptive potential, its Möbius-strip-like paradoxes, to one-up the "father of deconstructive philosophy." Johnson reversed the established priority in the American institution of deconstruction between Lacan's 1966 psychoanalytic reading of Poe's "The Purloined Letter" (1844) and Derrida's 1975 deconstructive reading of Lacan's reading of Poe (an earlier version of which Derrida presented in de Man and Hartman's comp lit colloquium in 1972). Derrida's deliberately provocative interpretation of Lacan's reading of Poe's story, Johnson maintained, "repeat[ed] precisely the crimes of which [Derrida] accuses [Lacan]."[85] This duplication of the interpretive offenses transferred the repetition compulsion that Lacan identified as organizing Poe's text "to the scene of its reading," to Lacan's interpretation of Poe and to Derrida's reading of Lacan's reading of Poe. Johnson was particularly attentive to two of Derrida's charges: (1) Lacan made the lack of the purloined letter's meaning (the reader never discovers the content of the purloined letter) into "the truth of lack-as-castration-as-truth"; and (2) Lacan neglected "to consider 'The Purloined Letter' in connection with the other two stories of Poe's 'Dupin's Trilogy.'" Johnson stressed, though, that Lacan actually neither "use[d] the word 'castration'" in his reading of Poe nor failed to develop "the relation between symbolic determination and random series" between his other stories.[86] "By filling in what *Lacan* left blank" and "by dismiss[ing] Lacan's 'style' as a mere ornament, veiling, for a time, an unequivocal message," or content, Derrida repeated "precisely the gesture of blank-filling for which he" criticized Lacan.[87] Performing interpretive moves that emphasized Lacan's stress on the absent content in Poe's texts, and discounting Lacan's *manner* of reading Poe, viewing the latter as simply "rhetoric," Johnson's Derrida remained under the control of Western metaphysical dualisms; upholding the valorization of philosophy over literature, Derrida claimed to have identified the content of Lacan's text over its style. But, according to Johnson, the literary nature of Lacan's reading of Poe escaped Derrida's interpretation.

With her essay, Johnson skillfully showed that Poe's story—and literary texts more broadly—already knew, content-wise, and hid more, formally, than *maîtres-penseurs* Derrida and Lacan ever could. Derrida, for his part, "got the most pleasure from [Johnson's] *tour de force*," finding her "overturning" of the import between his text and Lacan's satisfying; he would approvingly quote Johnson's conclusion that "*the positions*" between the two "*seem now to be reversed: Lacan's apparently unequivocal ending*"— that "a letter always arrives at its destination"—"*says only its own dissemination* [deconstruction], *while* [Derrida's] '*dissemination' has* [ironically] *erected itself in a kind of 'last word'* [on Lacan and psychoanalysis]."[88] Yet, by dizzyingly reversing the priorities and positions between texts, turning winners into losers and losers into winners, the Johnson-Derrida-Lacan-Poe whirligig showed readers not only the limitless desacralizing consequences of getting in the rigorous ring of deconstructive criticism. It showed literature's postmodern power to at once be part of yet unsettle discourses, whether philosophical, psychoanalytic, or otherwise.

Johnson's, Homans's, Poovey's, and Ferguson's deconstructive research and teaching agendas were part of a feminist cultural politics that challenged traditions at Yale in the late 1970s. In May 1979, Yale's Core Faculty Committee met with the Course of Study Committee to reach a final decision on the fate of the Women's Studies Program. Recollections vary about the subsequent faculty vote on the proposal, but nearly all recall the distribution of an anonymous memo that satirized the application and Yale's academic bureaucracy for entertaining the institutionalization of an explicitly feminist program. The memo was ostensibly from "the Committee for the Ruination of Academic Programs" and planned a major in "Grossness." Appalled at CRAP's Grossness—a clear projection of the masculinist prejudices at Yale—faculty from across fields and disciplines rallied behind the women's studies proposal, and it passed by a wide margin.

At Yale and elsewhere, the diversification of student and faculty demographics during the 1970s increased the felt need for knowledge and approaches to knowledge that reflected an array of life experiences, experiences that could not so easily be squared with the universalist paradigms developed by the white men who composed the teaching corps during the golden age of higher education. The new undergraduate program, and soon after major, at Yale legitimated women's studies nationally, bringing it "out of the academic ghetto," as a 1983 *Newsweek* article unartfully described it. This triumph of the academic left in New Haven contrasted starkly with the political agenda pursued by new right and family values proponents to neutralize feminists' public policy agendas.[89] In 1982, Yale's Women's Studies Major debuted, just as the ratification deadline of the Equal Rights Amendment expired. While many nonacademic feminists concentrated on social change, antidiscrimination, and a positive role for federal and state governments, the new right and family values proponents were emboldened by recently elected president Reagan, who emphasized conservative traditions, individual initiative, and deregulation—all of which effectively deemphasized the power of the government.[90] And yet, though second-wave feminism's "broadest common plank" buckled in the public-political arena, Yale's academic feminists—the Brides of Deconstruction and Criticism being a cutting-edge subversive guard that put the deconstructive screw to the American institution of deconstruction—had achieved a significant victory.[91]

Feminist Subversions of Masculine Metaphysics beyond New Haven

Though psychologist John Money during the mid-1950s was the first to employ the term "gender role," it was cultural work by literary critics and scholars—especially feminist deconstructionists—during the 1980s that promulgated a number of theoretical perspectives and critical approaches today associated with queer theory and the field of gender studies. This work undid the conflation of sex and gender: sex was metaphysical, signifying a being or transcendental signified, whereas gender referred to the cultural role of an individual or an individual's concept of themselves. Eve Kosofsky Sedgwick's feminist-deconstructive reply to literature's imperative was vital for this undertaking. Sedgwick earned her BA in English literature from Cornell, where Neil Hertz introduced her to a mixture of New Critical, psychoanalytic, and deconstructive reading techniques. In 1971, she entered Yale's PhD program in English. Sedgwick disliked her graduate school experience—not least because she felt there was no "feminism, let alone gay and lesbian studies" at Yale.[92] Nevertheless, Sedgwick must have somehow been nourished during those years, as her 1975 dissertation, directed by J. Hillis Miller, provided a foundation for her later subversive efforts in queer theory and gender studies.[93]

But it was only after assuming a non-tenure-track professorship at Hamilton College in 1978, which she took because permanent positions were ever more difficult to land, that Sedgwick believed she "learned feminism." She not only helped form Faculty for Women's Concerns, a group that sought to improve the situation of women faculty and students, but also immersed herself in feminist theory and literary-critical texts, such as *Madwoman in the Attic* and *Sexual Politics*.[94] In the process, she refined her ways of reading literature, as evidenced by what she now saw as the rhetorical function of Gothic veils, often worn by women in Gothic novels. While American psychoanalytic critics as well as second-wave feminists read the Gothic facade as suppressing a self or aspects of a self, Sedgwick proposed in a major 1981 article in *Publications of the Modern Language Association of America* (*PMLA*) that the Gothic facade—such as the blood-soaked sheets in the bandit's house in Matthew Gregory Lewis's *The Monk* (1796)—did not veil some hidden meaning or form of self, but was "a function of spreading, of extending by contiguity, a particular chain of attributes among the novel's characters."[95] Because the veil hid female characters' true identities, the veil made female characters' bodies exchangeable; on the other hand, the veil made female characters assume one another's fundamental character traits. With her rhetorical figure of the Gothic facade/veil, which publicly, contingently, and constantly negotiated the attributes and moral qualities of individuals, Sedgwick pointed readers to literature's deconstruction of the binary opposition between public and private self, an undermining that encouraged a rethinking of identity's limits.

Sedgwick's 1981 article was but one of a growing textual chorus that inscribed female protest and affirmation, often in a rhetoricized key, into prestigious academic publications, and this work, in turn, helped pivot many academic feminists away from the second wave of political equality toward more cultural concerns in a manner that would be called third wave. Certainly, these feminist textual interventions sometimes occurred simply because of a lack of opposition. The *PMLA* published Sedgwick's paper, she supposed, because of "its newly implemented policy of sending out articles for review without identifying the name or the institution of the author, hindering the functioning of the 'old-boys' club that had dominated its pages."[96] This disruption of the "'old-boys' club" was also abetted by seismic institutional and intellectual changes in higher education. Beyond the increasingly diversified makeup of colleges and universities, these changes placed a number of state universities on par with those of the Ivy League in terms of national ranking, administrators' ambitions, and research agendas of faculty. There nevertheless remained the need for intellectual cohorts to organize and push for change.

One such cultural advance came with Felman's, Homans's, and Ferguson's combined assistance when *Yale French Studies* published "a collaborative intellectual project" in a 1981 special issue undertaken by "a seven-headed monster from Dartmouth" whose "gender is feminine," "training . . . academic," and "orientation . . . feminist."[97] This "unusual issue," guest editors wrote, emerged from a tradition of cooperation that began at Dartmouth in 1972, after the institution first admitted women undergraduates and recruited women faculty, and that "culminated in 1978 in the creation of an interdisciplinary Women Studies program, the first among the previously all-male Ivy League schools."[98] In the special issue, the editors (as Shoshana Felman had in 1975) implored readers to correct the "mistake" of overemphasizing "the distance separating French feminists from their more pragmatic American counterparts."[99] Such an excessive emphasis, they stressed, in fact masked "a developing connection between French and American feminists," as discernible "not only in our volume" but in publications such as *The Future of Difference* (1980), *New French Feminisms* (1980), and recent "issues of *Signs, Feminist Studies* and *Critical Inquiry*."[100] The editors might have added: in the texts and teachings of feminist critics ensconced in Yale English, French, and Comp Lit whose deconstructive responses to the claim of literature undermined the culture-wide control that Western metaphysics' privileging of men and the masculine exerted.

Indeed, the essays of *Critical Inquiry*'s 1981 special issue "Writing and Sexual Difference"—edited by Elizabeth Abel, the only woman of the journal's six coeditors—were prompted by none other than Barbara Johnson's deconstructive argument, made in her 1981 essay, that "literature . . . inhabits the very heart of what makes sexuality problematic for us speaking animals."[101] "Literature," Johnson continued, "is not only a thwarted investigator but also an incorrigible perpetrator of the problem of sexuality."[102] This special issue's contributions underlined how sexual difference—both the hierarchic differences between the sexes and the differences within sex—was not marginal but inescapably engrained in culture. Jane Gallop observed that the publication was exceptional, because, in it, "an American woman"—Johnson—was portrayed as exemplifying deconstruction, then habitually "seen as French male thought." "Such a choice," Gallop explained, "avoids the usual gendering and nationalizing of the encounter between feminism and deconstruction, transposing what is usually represented as a difference between nationalities or between the sexes into a difference within American women critics."[103] The special issue's highlighting of the variance in interpretive styles and contents among American feminist critics therefore deconstructed popular as much as academic depictions of deconstruction as a Gallic male domain.

By underscoring the social and political consequences of deconstruction, Johnson and her colleagues further expanded the range of their rigorous rhetorical engagement with the text. The journal *Diacritics*, in 1982, published a special issue on feminism that, again, included an article by Johnson, in this case one where she rhetorically read *Frankenstein* to coax answers to questions about motherhood, the woman writer, and autobiography from Nancy Friday's *My Mother / My Self: The Daughter's Search for Identity* (1977) and Dorothy Dinnerstein's *The Mermaid and the Minotaur: Sexual Arrangements and Human Malaise* (1976).[104] Johnson read Friday as using her life events to "demonstrate her thesis" that, though inhibited by the dominant parenting model, there was a possibility for "woman" to love if she accepted her identity as distinct from her mother's.[105] Like Friday's work, Dinnerstein's text also employed an autobiographical perspective—"The book was written partially in mourning for her husband," Johnson noted—to investigate the question of motherhood.[106] Women could lead fulfilling lives, Dinnerstein maintained, if men strove for equality, by, for example, contributing to child-rearing, which, when left entirely to women, produced resentment and infantilization.

However, despite Friday's and Dinnerstein's uses of autobiography to explore the cultural institution of parenthood, Johnson stressed, their texts repeated and reinforced the masculine metaphysics that shaped motherhood and thus ironically supported the very positions against which they wrote. Friday's and Dinnerstein's texts were self-deconstructive. For instance, though Friday aimed to liberate the mother and daughter from "a heritage of self-rejection, anger, and duplicity" created by "the myth of maternal love" that "both mother and daughter continue to punish themselves for never having been able to achieve," Friday still longed for her mother's "love and approval," as evinced by her "huge book."[107] And, while Dinnerstein wrote in a style that clearly rejected "more traditional forms of scholarship" so as to overturn "the types of imbalance and injustice the prevailing asymmetry in gender relations produces," she "plead[ed] not for the validity but for the urgency of her message."[108] Johnson argued that because Dinnerstein relied on pathos—on "the urgency of her message"—she reproduced the hierarchy that elevated the rational male over the irrational or hysterical women, thus reducing the disruptive potential of her text's cultural intervention.

For Johnson, the ways Friday's and Dinnerstein's texts reinscribed sexual relations stood in contrast to Shelley's *Frankenstein*, the literariness of which subverted the masculine dichotomies that controlled the institution of motherhood and the question of the woman writer via Shelley's approach to the genre of autobiography, a genre that was part of "a humanistic tradition in which the man is the measure of all things."[109] Shelley's feminist deconstruction was signaled, Johnson suggested, by Shelley's rejection of the chance in 1831 to write an autobiographical narrative for the first "popular" edition of *Frankenstein* that would explain the link between her life and her novel. Rather than consider *Frankenstein* a reflection of herself, Shelley proposed that readers view Shelley the author as a supplement to *Frankenstein*.[110] Yet, Johnson pondered, "How does an appendage" who rejected autobiography, and implicitly did so due to the humanist tradition that rendered the genre masculine, "go about telling the story of *her* life" and thus answer the question of the "specifically feminine autobiography"?[111] Shelley's resolution, according to Johnson, was to write *Frankenstein* with an aim and in a fashion wholly different from those undertaken in conventional autobiographies. Turning to Lacan for his formulations on how the "distortions" and "transpositions" of language shaped readings of and dealings with social censure, Johnson rhetorically read Shelley as *unintentionally* writing her "true" feelings and desires with and in her text by *intentionally* placing *Frankenstein* outside the genre of autobiography.[112] Shelley's 1831 introduction, Johnson argued, should thus be interpreted as hinting at how *Frankenstein* overturned the (male) genre of autobiography, making woman into the measure of all things and subverting dominant traditions of motherhood. Johnson's Shelley achieved what Friday and Dinnerstein did not because these writers failed to rhetorically respond to the masculine tradition of autobiography, as *Frankenstein* not only birthed Shelley—*Frankenstein* was Shelley's "hideous" textual progeny, her "Frankenstein Monster," her exposed and monstrous appendage—but Dr. Frankenstein, though raised by loving parents, abandoned his child and attempted to steal the role of women by producing a being, a monster, while both "reach[ed] an equal degree of alienation and self-torture."[113] Ultimately, Johnson's rhetorical response to Shelley's text subverted the masculine metaphysics that prejudiced literary-critical practices, revising the canon of British Romanticism and the interpretive focus of the "Yale School."

During the early 1980s, feminist literary critics tangentially linked to Yale also took positions at the deconstructive movement's front line. In a 1980 article, Gayatri Chakravorty Spivak, professor of English and comp lit at the University of Texas at Austin, chastised the Yale School for establishing a new old-boys' club by recanonizing the male-dominated literary canon as self-deconstructive texts. This recanonization, Spivak suggested, constricted Derrida's anti-metaphysical project, which included underscoring how a text's phallocentrism and phallogocentrism undermined the text's stated positions.[114] In another essay, Spivak emphasized the untapped feminist perspective of Derrida's work. While sympathetic contemporaries, such as Christopher Norris, thought Derrida's "equation" linking women, sexuality, and writing was suspicious, Spivak

Dr. Gayatri Spivak

Steve Pumphrey, TSP Staff

FIGURE 4.3 A newspaper photo of Gayatri Spivak in 1980 (Photo by Steve Pumphrey, *The Daily Texan*, 10/17/1980, di_11627, The Dolph Briscoe Center for American History, The University of Texas at Austin)

foregrounded how Derrida's "critique of phallogocentrism and radical questioning of all discourse" implemented a "'feminization' of the practice of philosophy"—that is, deconstructively engaged the sexed dichotomies that constituted the texts of the philosophical tradition.[115] This led to an "ultimately political practice," Spivak claimed. "I learn from [Derrida], but I must then go somewhere else with it."[116]

Where Spivak went was to develop an influential discourse that combined features of deconstructive, feminist, and Marxist reading techniques to flag a text's phallo(go)centricism. Take her contribution to the 1981 *Critical Inquiry* special issue devoted to feminism, a translation of and introduction to a short story by Indian writer Mahasweta Deva. Spivak rhetorically read the relationship between the story's villain Senanayak, an educated male army officer, and the tribal woman Draupadi, whom Senanayak captured and degraded, as a deconstructive allegory of the relationship between the "First-World scholar" and the "Third World." For Spivak, Senanayak approximated a "Western-trained" scholar-informant because he, while "identify[ing] with the enemy," the "Third World," "in *practice* . . . must destroy the enemy, the menacing other."[117] Senanayak's inability to understand Draupadi's tribal song hammered home to readers the "place of that other that can be neither excluded nor recuperated," with Draupadi's identity, undecidable, assembling and disassembling Senanayak, and vice versa.[118] Then, in her influential essay "Can the Subaltern Speak?," initially presented in the summer of 1983, Spivak deconstructively signposted the philosophical dichotomies that organized Western postcolonial critics' readings of texts. Such studies, Spivak argued, often reinscribed neocolonial political, cultural, and economic domination by performing "epistemic violence" on the "remotely orchestrated, far-flung, and heterogeneous project to constitute the colonial subject as Other."[119] Rather than attempt to pinpoint what many postcolonial critics celebrated as a (Romanticized and) static "Other" who existed outside of colonizers' military power and regimes of knowledge—a metaphysical approach to the text that raised, indeed reinforced, an onto-theological opposition between the colonized and the colonizers—Spivak advocated identifying a deconstructive concept of identity that operated in the text beyond binaries through a system of shifting differences. Unlike First World Marxists or liberals who considered the colonial powers as straightforwardly repressive, Spivak's rhetorical reading foregrounded how identity—specifically gender—was not derivative of a suppressed presence, and thus a function of repressive philosophical dualisms, but deconstructively constructed by deferred differences and distinctions.

Spivak's growing prominence in the 1980s among the *savant garde* often obscured her intellectual formation alongside and in conversation with members of the Yale School. After graduating in 1959 from the University of Calcutta, she earned her PhD in comp lit at Cornell in 1967 under de Man. In Ithaca, many exoticized Spivak, but de Man treated her as an equal. Relatedly, Spivak raised the question of when and in what ways power was exerted on the "Other," personal or otherwise, in her first publications. Though at first glance a conventional description of Yeats's life, poetry, and his reinvention of Celtic mythology, Spivak's 1974 book— developed from her doctoral thesis—positioned Yeats's poetic achievements in relation to British colonialism in Ireland.[120] Spivak's implicit critical stance toward the imposition of foreign values upon indigenous cultures was also found—in coded form—in her epic eighty-page 1976 introduction to Derrida's *De la grammatologie* (1967).[121] There she alluded to having conducted her translation of Derrida's text from 1970 to 1975 in "*Iowa City, (New Delhi—Dacca [sic]—Calcutta), Boston, Nice, Providence, Iowa City.*"[122] In January 1973, Spivak had traveled to Dhaka, the capital of Bangladesh, where she photographed some of the hundreds of thousands of Bangladeshi women raped by members of the Pakistani military during the 1971 Bangladesh Liberation War. Spivak's experience in Dhaka was, she has recalled, a "secret starting point" of her *De la grammatologie* translation.[123] It also shaped her later feminist deconstructions of subaltern studies; the violence against women during the Bangladesh Liberation War was partly a legacy of the British Raj and 1947 Partition of India, in that members of the colonized (Pakistani military) adopted the colonizers' (British) tools and dehumanizing perspectives against fellow colonized (Bengalis). Spivak's Dhaka experience informed her view that feminist protest was at stake in Derrida's deconstructive project. Overturning and reinscribing thousands of years of Western metaphysics, in which *logos* (the Greek term for speech, thought, law, or reason) was cast as male, the deconstructive reader-philosopher in her preface to *Of Grammatology* was a "she [who] deconstructs."[124]

Spivak's translation of and introduction to *Of Grammatology* was personally as much as professionally ambitious, and not simply because only a handful of Derrida's texts had been translated into English by the mid-1970s. Until then, Spivak had concentrated on writing literary criticism. In a letter of support for Spivak's application for a Guggenheim Foundation grant to fund her translation, de Man recognized the difficult task ahead. He endorsed "Mrs. Spivak," who "would be very well qualified" to deal with "Derrida's style," which is "often imaginative and poetic as well as technical."[125] Yet, de Man wrote, Spivak must improve her grasp in several fields of knowledge. "The proposed introduction and commentary," de Man continued, "would have to involve a wide area of competence. On this point, I don't have the necessary evidence to vouchsafe for Mrs. Spivak's ability to deal with the problem of locating Derrida in contemporary French thought." "I," de Man warned further, "have not, as yet, seen any writing of hers that shows unusual strength in the area of literary theory or the philosophy of language." "As she points out herself" in her application, Spivak, de Man concluded, must "strengthen her knowledge of linguistics and philosophy."[126] Spivak's introduction to *Of Grammatology* in fact ended up devoting considerable space not to placing Derrida in his French philosophical milieu but to Derrida's deconstructive strategy with respect to influential figures such as Heidegger, Nietzsche, Husserl, Freud, Hegel, and Lacan. She demonstrated that, because Derrida's deconstruction "always . . . produce[d] the counter-reading out of the latter's protective hedging," an interminable deciphering of the concept of precursor resulted.[127] Green-lit by Derrida's own deconstructive engagement with the traditional notion of intellectual predecessors, in which forerunner and follower are endlessly reversed, Spivak appeared to evade grappling with the problem of intellectual influences and institutional contexts to focus on the act of translation and mediation.

Spivak's epic preface that reflexively performed Derrida's deconstruction with the topic of Derrida's forerunners, along with her translation, helped authorize much interpretive freedom around Derrida's work. She, for example, famously translated—and fatefully so—Derrida's statement that "il n'y a pas de hors-texte" as an antirealist sally: "There is nothing outside of the text."[128] The context of Derrida's eminently quotable statement was the ENS in the mid-1960s; part of Derrida's point was that, because the world and its objects—"the text," the construction of meaning—was organized by "differential references," or "traces," the structures to which the Althusserians and Lacanians at the ENS turned were as contingent and unstable as the economic or psychological structures they wished to ground there. Yet Spivak's "there is nothing outside of the text" reinforced the views, first held among literary critics and scholars but then across the American humanities, that Derrida merely played silly language games with written materials and that his followers slyly manipulated the meaning of a text. While Spivak's introduction to and translation of *Of Grammatology* has met with disapproval from the Derridean camp over the years, Derrida himself took a liking to her work precisely because the French language, literary theory, the philosophy of language, and present-day French thought were "foreign" to her. In her telling, this "otherness" made Spivak an ideal translator. Because of her "other" education and background, Spivak's writing embodied and enacted the deconstruction of Western (masculine) metaphysics.

Post-Male Yale and the Literariness of Gender/Genre

Toward the mid-1980s, while non-sociostructural feminist theories of interpretation captivated many academic humanists' attention, the Yale feminist-deconstructive moment seized up, its contributions to the American institution of deconstruction moving elsewhere.[129] Felman, Homans, and Ferguson remained at the university; Felman joined Cathy Caruth (another of de Man's graduate students) and Dori Laub to use deconstructive reading techniques to tease out the relationships between trauma and literature.[130] Johnson, though, left, taking her feminist engagement with the literary imperative to Harvard in what was a watershed moment, since that most prestigious university, including its French and Comp Lit Departments, had been resistant to "theory." At Harvard, Johnson helped establish a women's studies program, and, in the fall of 1983, offered her first course, "Black Women Writers," which was in sync with Johnson's pioneering 1984 feminist-deconstructive response to Zora Neale Hurston's

Their Eyes Were Watching God (1937), a novel that recounted the story of Janie Crawford, an African American woman struggling for her freedom under patriarchal domination.[131] Hurston's text, Johnson foregrounded, implicitly employed a tetrapolar structure that cross-sectioned the hierarchical oppositions male/female and white/black in order to construct Crawford's identity. In Johnson's diagram, Hurston positioned the black female identity along the horizontal hierarchy of gender and then along the vertical hierarchy of race. With this feminist-deconstructive epistemology, Hurston defined the outlook of Crawford's self. Applying Hurston's way of knowing to the role of voice in the novel, for example, showed that there were several ways of speaking that combined and thus subverted the binaries public/private, outer/inner, objective/subjective spaces, as to privilege one term over the other would naturalize and thus metaphysically hierarchize gender and race. For Johnson, Hurston's *Eyes* showed that the "female voice . . . must be recognized as divided in multiple ways."[132] By alerting readers to how Hurston's novel deconstructed gendered and raced hierarchic differences, Johnson's rhetorical reading underscored an embedded epistemology far more capacious than the interpretations characteristic of "high deconstruction." It also dovetailed with other contemporary feminists' groundbreaking efforts in the decade's first years to expand the cognitive limits of the academic humanities by considering race as much as gender in their analyses of culture and society.[133]

In these same years, the chance for feminist deconstructionists at Yale to issue a collective statement that promoted their reflexive interpretive science and the political implications of its response to literature's demand passed. Johnson recalled: "At the time of the publication of *Deconstruction and Criticism* [1979], several of us—Shoshana Felman, Gayatri Spivak, Margaret Ferguson, and I—discussed the possibility of writing a companion volume inscribing female deconstructive protest and affirmation centering not [like Bloom's initial plan] on Shelley's 'The Triumph of Life' . . . but on Mary Shelley's *Frankenstein*."[134] This "*Brides of Deconstruction and Criticism* never quite got off the ground," Johnson explained, though "it is surely no accident that the project was centered around monstrosity."[135] Outrageous, scandalous, obscene in the 1970s, the feminist-deconstructive engagement with literature was, a half decade later, accepted as part of a larger and broader, legitimate and reasonable, feminist undertaking in the academy. After women's studies was approved as a major at Yale in 1981, for instance, the National Endowment for the Humanities awarded the program a multiyear implementation grant to help students and professors in the fledgling major forge collaborations across the disciplines; several prominent professors on campus welcomed this opportunity and incorporated new research on women into their lectures. A second NEH grant supported bringing in guest lecturers and a lunchtime series, which provided a forum to participate in the expanding community of feminist scholars at the university.[136]

Such inroads at "Male Yale," however, hardly meant that the entire literary-critical community enthusiastically embraced Johnson and company's feminist perspectives and critical practices. The degree to which the elders of the Yale deconstructive community did *not* adopt feminist reading tactics was conveyed by Johnson in a January 1984 paper delivered at a conference to "which Geoffrey Hartman, Hillis Miller, and Paul de Man had been asked to speak about genre theory in relation to their own work."[137] Johnson provocatively maintained not only that the question of gender (remember the wordplay here: "genre" is French for "gender") was a question of literature, but also that the question was broached in recent essays by her former teachers and colleagues. Johnson argued that Harold Bloom, "perhaps without knowing it," showed in 1978 that "reading is" a "gendered activity."[138] He interpreted Keats's ballad "La Belle Dame sans Merci" (1819) less as "a love story" between the knight at arms and the Belle Dame than as "a story of failed translation," because the woman's name "can only be expressed in another tongue."[139] Miller, too, opened the problem of gender as a question of texts' rhetoric. In a 1978 essay, Johnson glossed, Miller sexualized an "image of deconstructive criticism as 'parasitical,'" fashioning a "vegetal metaphor" that was "both feminine and parricidal"; for Miller, the deconstructive parasite was a text's peripheral figural elements that, when flagged with rhetorical reading techniques, revealed to readers the chief linguistic issue in a text. Johnson saw such "gender codes of literature, or of criticism" in Miller's engagement with Shelley's *Triumph of Life*, a poem, Johnson stressed, that told "again and again . . . the story of the failure of the attempt to abolish difference" or, rather, the failure to eliminate what masculine metaphysics makes "parasitical"—that is: "cancerous femininity."[140] Even Johnson's beloved teacher de Man, who textually tiptoed around social and political references, had, in a late 1970s essay (and 1976 seminar), implicitly cast deconstruction as a gendered activity. De Man suggested that, though Locke tried to contain the problems that "metaphors, tropes, and figural language" caused for establishing philosophic truth, he "eloquent[ly]" denounced "eloquence," recommending that, "like a woman, which [rhetoric] resembles . . . , it is a fine thing as long as it is kept in its proper place."[141] Like so many in the history of Western culture, de Man's Locke subordinated rhetoric to philosophy, deconstruction to metaphysical dualisms, with the suitable relationship between them being that the former, coded as feminine and seen as mere linguistic or material ornament, was secondary to the more important masculine philosophical essence or spiritual signified.

To fully develop a truly rigorous and reflexive science of reading, however, required wrestling with one's own texts. Johnson was up to this task in her 1984 talk; no deconstructionist's work was safe from her laser-like underscoring of how the question of gender/genre was also a problem of literature. Johnson turned her attention to *The Critical Difference* (1980). Her collection of essays, Johnson suggested, was a "book produced by the Yale School" and "haunt[ed]" by "the question of sexual difference . . . from the beginning."[142] "Johnson," Johnson bravely explained, "concludes her preface with some remarks about ignorance that apply ironically to her book's own demonstration of an ignorance that pervades Western discourse as a whole."[143] According to Johnson, the Johnson of 1980 adopted an Olympian bearing that merely *seemed* to remove texts from gendered language and cultural forms. Phallo(go)centrism so roundly controlled Johnson's essay collection that the onto-theological dichotomy that coded its "genderless" language as masculine was barely legible. And though "[i]t would be no easy task to undertake the effort of reinflection or translation" that not only exposed the "naturalness of female effacement in the subtly male pseudogenderlessness of language" but also retrieved the "existence and knowledge of the female subject" and "answer[ed] . . . the question of gender and sexual difference" in "existing patterns of culture and language," such was the massive responsibility surprisingly suggested by Bloom's, Miller's, de Man's, and, yes, even Johnson's earlier published texts.[144] Johnson's 1984 talk clearly announced the existence and aims of the feminist countertradition within the American institution of deconstruction. It also indexed a historical pattern of postwar criticism in which intellectual heirs intensified the "rigor" or "scientificity" of forerunners' approaches: here was Johnson's feminist-deconstructive criticism subverting deconstructive criticism, which itself emerged in large part via the subversion of New Critical protocols and principles.

The shift toward feminist concerns during the 1980s in literary studies and in research agendas across the humanities that occurred at Yale was seen elsewhere in New England as well. Many of these centers of feminist cultural activity, extensions of intellectual and institutional ecosystems built during the academic revolution, stimulated the development of new interpretive possibilities. Hoping to amplify the impressions being left by "the feminist talks, meetings, films, conferences, and other events" in Boston during the early 1980s, Ruth Perry, founding director of the Women's Studies Program at MIT, started, in 1984, to publish an influential monthly newsletter, *Women's Studies around Boston*.[145] There was also the important Boston Area Colloquium on Feminist Theory, first held in the spring of 1982 at Northeastern University, which showcased advanced feminist thought and work.[146] There, MIT professor of mathematics and humanities Evelyn Fox Keller presented the lecture "Gender Ideology and the Development of Modern Science," derived from her research into the cultural tradition of a gendered dichotomy that, by characterizing "objectivity" and "reason" as masculine and "subjectivity" and "feeling" as feminine, shaped the history of science.[147] The newsletter and the colloquium assisted, by fostering interpersonal and professional opportunities, the continuing diversification and diffusion of feminist (literary) theories in the Boston area.

Eve Sedgwick joined this growing feminist community, moving, in 1980, to Boston University for her first tenure-track position. She had agreed to head BU's recently founded Women's Studies Program and would disseminate her interpretive procedures to help establish the bona fides of the still nascent field of gender studies. At that time, Sedgwick began to read the rhetorical function of "the Gothic" not as restricted to a genre of late eighteenth-century British literature but as fashioning a view of modern gender and modern homophobia. She tentatively stepped toward this thesis in a 1983 article on Charles Dickens's *Our Mutual Friend* (1864–65), a novel seemingly about a sexual triangle, with two men, Eugene Wrayburn and Bradley Headstone, smitten by the same women, Lizzie Hexam. Sedgwick, however, underscored the quasi-homosexual relationship between Wrayburn and Headstone. The anxious rivalry and fierce interactions between them over Hexam, according to Sedgwick, was a network—class-based here, gender-focused there—along which male desire communicated with itself; for Dickens, Sedgwick wrote, "the erotic fate of every female or male is also cast in the terms and propelled by the forces of class and economic accumulation."[148] Sedgwick's article, she later noted, was "met with 'disbelief, interest, disbelief'" among Victorian literature scholars and critics.[149] Still, Sedgwick used the piece as a touchstone for *Between Men* (1984), which deconstructively read the collapse of systems of symbolic-linguistic exchange between men about women in the Gothic novel as "crystalliz[ing] for English audiences the terms of a dialectic between male homosexuality and homophobia."[150] This "unspeakable"—homosexuality—rhetorically operated, according to Sedgwick, as an "electrified barrier" between classes, sexual preferences, and generations, arousing, guiding, or revealing the reader's homophobia.[151] On the other hand, "male traffic in women," Sedgwick concluded, cohered homosocial bonds—male friendship, mentorship, entitlement, rivalry, not to mention hetero- and homosexuality.[152]

Written and published during a difficult period for the gay liberation movement—the HIV retrovirus was identified in 1983—*Between Men* located cultural sources of homophobic attitudes and helped legitimize the field of gender studies as well as the fields of men's studies and gay studies. Sedgwick further unveiled how the covert social codes and submerged stories in canonical authors of English literature advanced a deconstructive politics after moving, in the fall of 1984, to a tenured position at Amherst College. At Amherst, all male until 1976, Sedgwick locally revised literary canons while "teach[ing] the English department's year-long introductory course in reading and writing... successfully advocating... for the first-time inclusion of the town's local poet, Emily Dickinson, previously regarded as too minor to be included with the likes of Robert Frost, the town's other local poet."[153] Sedgwick also was active in establishing, in 1987, Amherst's Department of Women's and Gender Studies. That Amherst agreed to add "gender" to the program surely reflected Sedgwick's hand, yet it reflected a larger change in academic feminists' concerns too. Meanwhile, Sedgwick's star rose higher among the academic left. In 1988, Stanley Fish recruited her to Duke University's English Department, then an exciting epicenter for the development and proliferation of new ways to respond to the literary imperative. The department also became a frequent target of conservative culture warriors' sensationalist exposés of "tenured radicals," for their apparently unethical focus on promotion, publication, and publicity; such tenure-chasing self-absorption ostensibly eroded the once secure power and prestige of literary humanist education. Sure enough, soon after joining Duke, Sedgwick started to receive hostile attention from academics and journalists, conservatives and liberals alike. For example: at the third annual Lesbian and Gay Studies Conference, held at Yale in 1989, audience members were so disruptive during Sedgwick's paper—they repeatedly shouted, "Are you a lesbian?"—that at moments she halted reading.

Then came the deconstructive cultural politics performed by "Jane Austen and the Masturbating Girl," a paper Sedgwick delivered at the 1989 Modern Language Association annual meeting and which—*before it was even delivered*—drew truly hysterical disapproval for its apparently willful warping of the sexual subtext of Jane Austen's *Sense and Sensibility* (1811), a distortion that defiled the secular temple of literature. In her paper, "the QED of phobic narratives about the degeneracy of academic discourse in the humanities," Sedgwick juxtaposed Austen's rendering of protagonist Marianne Dashwood's emotional turmoil when John Willoughby deserted her, British critic Tony Tanner's normalizing treatment of Emma Woodhouse in Austen's *Emma* (1815) as a woman who had to be shown that she was not as important as she thought herself to be, and a nineteenth-

FIGURE 4.4 Eve Sedgwick at Amherst College in the mid-1980s (Courtesy of Amherst College Archives)

century medical report about a so-called therapy administered to a girl who enjoyed masturbation.[154] Reading "emotional self-indulgence" as a cipher for female self-pleasure, Sedgwick contrasted Austen's portrayal of Dashwood's emotional turmoil as analogous to the medical account of the masturbating girl and Tanner's humbling of Woodhouse for her self-pity as analogous to the Victorian doctor's ghastly "cure." For Sedgwick, both Austen's Dashwood and Woodhouse challenged the gendered binaries enforced by cultural traditions of heterosexuality and patriarchy. For nationally syndicated "punditterati," like George Will, Sedgwick was, she herself recounted in 1991, "more dangerous than Saddam Hussein," not simply for her sexually perverse reading of a canonical text in English literary history but for how this reading violated scholarly rules of evidence and objectivity: Austen herself sometimes portrayed her writings as defenses of middle-class women's moral and intellectual uprightness.[155]

As dangerous to the onto-theological underpinnings of humanist education as she was to the culturally conservative, Sedgwick enlarged the applicative range of her feminist rhetorical reading to all of Western culture, an expansion that solidified her position as a major deconstructive voice in gay studies. In her next book, *Epistemology of the Closet* (1990), Sedgwick suggested that the deconstruction at work in Victorian literary classics, including Herman Melville's *Billy Budd* (1891) and Oscar Wilde's *The Picture of Dorian Gray* (1890), illustrated how sexual orientation during the late nineteenth century had become as essential to personal identity as gender had for centuries and that "virtually any aspect of modern Western culture, must be, not merely incomplete, but damaged in its central substance to the degree that it does not incorporate a critical analysis of modern homo/heterosexual definition."[156] Integrating into her approach such a critical exploration, Sedgwick, for example, rhetorically read the relationship in Melville's novel between the characters Billy Budd, Claggert, and Captain Vere, asking, "Is men's desire for other men the great preservative of the masculinist hierarchies of Western culture, or is it the most potent of threats against them?"[157] Sedgwick's deconstructive readings drew from many sources, not least of all Foucault, but her unhappy Yale experience in the first half of the 1970s certainly helped position her professionally and intellectually to vigilantly identify and undermine the masculine metaphysics that obscured how issues of gender and sexual orientation were central to the English literary canon and Western thought and culture.

Relatively concomitant with Sedgwick's rhetorical responses to Victorian literature were Judith Butler's feminist readings of philosophical texts, which, like Sedgwick's work, greatly enlarged the purview of the American institution of deconstruction. As a Yale undergraduate and then Yale graduate student in philosophy during the late 1970s and early 1980s, Butler "attended a seminar by Derrida," "often audited Paul de Man's lectures," and discovered Foucault in a women's studies faculty seminar.[158] Her feminist interests were only indirectly exhibited in her first book, *Subjects of Desire* (1987), a revision of her 1984 dissertation that examined G. W. F. Hegel's influence on twentieth-century French philosophers. In this text, Butler deployed Foucault's ruminations on the discursive processes of subject formation and Derrida's deconstructive strategy to highlight meaning as a nonoriginary citational "event." In the second half of the 1980s, though, Butler's research and writing began to explicitly focus on feminist questions. In a 1986 article, Butler deconstructively read Simone de Beauvoir's *The Second Sex* (1949), vital for second-wave feminists, as challenging the "cultural status quo" with a vision that "to 'choose' a gender" was to interpret the body as "a mode of enacting and reenacting received gender norms which surface as so many styles of flesh."[159] Similarly, in a 1988 article, Butler employed the texts of Freud, Merleau-Ponty, Derrida, and de Beauvoir to argue that gender assumed a performative

FIGURE 4.5 Judith Butler at Wesleyan University in the 1980s (Courtesy of Wesleyan University)

or theatric value in which individuals' acts were "renewed, revised, and consolidated through time."[160] Butler's soon to be famous articulation of the *performance* of gender as *producing* gender had commenced.

She powerfully and persuasively delivered this feminist perspective in *Gender Trouble* (1990), which became a key resource for queer activists and an artifact of third-wave feminism. In her book, Butler deconstructively read cultural texts' dichotomies such as I/other, man/woman, heterosexual/homosexual as contingent, ideological constructions. Perhaps most prominent was Butler's deconstructive interpretation of the drag queen, conventionally viewed as a man in a woman's clothes and therefore a man with only the appearance of a woman. However, Butler stressed, because drag queens reflexively constructed their gender identity via repetitive actions and rhetorical codes, a formation without which the man/woman hierarchic difference possessed no meaning, the drag queen's gender was mimicry. "*In imitating gender, drag implicitly reveals the imitative structure of gender itself—as well as its contingency.*"[161] The drag queen thus subverted the metaphysical notion that gender was stable or possessed a transtemporal substance, for if mimicry was the foundation of gender, then gender was performative, a discursive construction without ground. The political consequences of Butler's deconstructive drag queen were multiple, such as the undermining of second-wave feminists' view that "women" were a group with shared characteristics and interests as well as the assumption that sexual identity was an ontological (biological) or theological (transcendent) reality buried behind expressions of gender. Moreover, Butler showed that even the subject/object binary (man as subject and woman as "other") that was basic for second-wave feminist philosophies and practices deconstructed.

Representative of how the Brides of Deconstruction and Criticism and their fellow academic subversives transformed—and became—the top brass of the theoretical revolution in the humanities was their work at a six-week-long summer program for graduate students and emerging scholars at the University of California, Irvine, hosted by the School of Criticism and Theory. From its inception in 1976, the SCT was haunted by the issue of sexual difference, and in the 1980s feminists applied styles of deconstructive reading to subvert the school's gendered and sexed hierarchies. In 1992, Geoffrey Hartman reported that during his SCT stewardship, from 1981 to 1987, "advanced criticism began to be accepted into the universities," and "new contestations began their vigorous, invigorating! Questioning: Feminism, in particular."[162] "A formidable intellectual energy," Hartman later wrote, "was released, spiked by an unrestrained use of 'patriarchal,' 'hegemonic,' 'phallologocentric,' etc." At the SCT, foregrounding unspoken androcentric hierarchies became a serious interpretive sport, exercised with the physical spaces of the SCT itself. "Nothing was deemed to be accidental: in one of the school's plenary sessions," Hartman wrote, "even the seating arrangement (in a standard auditorium, not a circle but rising from front to back) was challenged as authoritarian. Everything literary and nonliterary came under scrutiny for its possible symbolic or ideological implications."[163] Hartman welcomed the part that the SCT played in cultivating innovative styles of interpretation that questioned metaphysical binaries, but he also felt that academic feminism at the school and elsewhere occasionally resulted in the vilification of men via the pretense of scholarship. Proponents of this view found unlikely allies in conservative commentators, who saw a subterranean base known as "theory" as facilitating a new awareness of gender in classrooms that imposed, George Will wrote in 1991, "collective amnesia and deculturation," disintegrating "the common culture that is the nation's social cement."[164] But such perceived forgetfulness and deculturation—achieved, Will wrote, by "deconstructing"—was really a reculturation. The interpretive theater that feminists performed at the SCT helped colleagues to reorient their research to highlight subversions of the masculine metaphysics that shaped culture.

The feminist reculturation that rattled the old (male) guard at the SCT was best exemplified by Gayatri Spivak's 1982 SCT lecture, which, Hartman remembered, had a shocking effect, inspiring "debates on what an *écriture feminine* would look like."[165] Entering the ironic ring of deconstructive criticism, Spivak disentangled a feminist-deconstructive reply to literature's imperative embedded in a text written by a "philosophical father of deconstruction": Derrida's 1972 reading of the "supreme spasm" in Mallarmé's *Mimique* as a double miming of the orgasm of monsieur Pierrot's unfaithful wife Columbine.[166] "I'm going to tickle my wife to death," the mad clown avowed, after miming various ways of killing his partner.[167] Derrida deconstructively interpreted Pierrot's "spasm"—Pierrot's final answer of how he will murder his wife without leaving evidence—as a "hymen," an undecidable, as an either/and, because it united both virginity and consummation.[168] In fact, when Pierrot finally murdered Columbine, he too, as a mime, succumbed to his own tickling/spasm, which became a "masturbatory suicide."[169] Spivak turned the feminist screw of deconstructive reading on the phallo(go)centrism of *Derrida's* reading, highlighting Derrida's foregrounding of the faked orgasm, an enactment in which a male actor (Pierrot) usurped the language of a woman's desire (Columbine). "The faked orgasm now takes center stage. The Pierrot of the pantomime 'acts' as the woman 'is' ('Pierrot is Columbine') by faking a faked orgasm which is also a faked crime."[170] In this way, Spivak used her SCT lecture to extricate the postmodern gendered politics of both *Mimique* and Derrida's text.[171]

As the dusk of the Reagan era fell, a taking stock of the relationship between feminism and deconstructive literary criticism and theory was under way, despite the fact that feminist deconstructionists were moving in new and different directions. Noting "the apparent . . . decline of deconstruction as an orthodoxy in U.S. literary criticism," the 1988 special issue of *Feminist Studies* explored deconstruction's usefulness for feminist scholarship and politics, how, in Mary Poovey's words, "deconstruction's project of demystification" exposed the texts that composed Western culture as structured by gendered and sexed hierarchical oppositions.[172] In the *Feminist Studies* issue, for example, American historian of France Joan W. Scott—who, in a significant 1986 paper that bore the intellectual traces of Derrida and Foucault, argued that gender was based on perceived differences between the sexes and a way of signifying power differentials—engaged the "equality vs. difference" debate among feminists in America. Scott aimed to split the difference. Adopting the goal of "equality," she argued, forced "one . . . to accept the notion that difference is antithetical to it."[173] On the other hand, "If one opts for difference, one admits that equality is unattainable."[174] What rested beyond the impasse, Scott suggested, was "a 'deconstructive' political strategy."[175] "In the face of powerful tendencies that construct the world in binary terms," the deconstructive approach to politics showed the pursuit of equality as not opposed to the pursuit of difference but as the "ignoring of difference between individuals for a particular purpose or in a particular context."[176] Such a pragmatic political strategy echoed Spivak's 1984 concept "strategic essentialism," through which different minority groups could act on the basis of shared identity during a struggle for equal political rights.[177]

To demonstrate the real-world complexities of the "equality vs. difference" issue and explore how a "'deconstructive' political strategy" might help navigate this debate, Scott turned to a twelve-year-long legal case against Sears.[178] In 1984, the Equal Employment Opportunity Commission charged Sears, the largest American chain of department stores, with sexual discrimination against women in job promotions among commissioned sales staff. The relatively low percentage of women in commissioned jobs, Sears argued, was not the outcome of discrimination but of women's own preferences. Both plaintiff and defense called feminist historians to testify as expert witnesses. On behalf of Sears, Rosalind Rosenberg, according to Scott, "unproblematically linked socialization to individual choice";[179] Rosenberg did not historicize but more or less *described* how women's traditional values explained the gender imbalances in its labor force, thereby unintentionally supporting the metaphysical, essentializing view of gender and sex. Sears's lawyers also deployed a metaphysical argument, albeit a more overt one, suggesting, as summarized by political theorist Zillah R. Eisenstein in 1988, that "women's goals and values, as wives and mothers, led to their preference for lower, non-competitive jobs."[180] Historian Alice Kessler-Harris backed the EEOC, though, Scott observed, she "had trouble finding a simple model [for the court] that would at once acknowledge difference [between the sexes] *and* refuse it as an acceptable explanation for the employment pattern of Sears."[181] The court decided in favor of Sears.

The EEOC's case could have been argued and, hopefully, decided differently. Scott suggested that feminist historians in similar legal situations might use a "'deconstructive' political strategy" to question "fixed gender categories as normative statements that organize cultural understandings of sexual difference."[182] Submitted evidence to the court in the Sears case could have retold the story of women's work "as part of the story of the creation of a gendered workforce," when in "the nineteenth century, for example, certain concepts of male skill rested on a contrast with female labor (by definition unskilled)."[183] Such a narrative would illuminate for judge, jurors, and the record the contingent emergence of a hierarchical opposition often considered natural and how this historically constructed dichotomy persisted, adopted by men and women workers alike in the contemporary world. Granted, feminist-deconstructive cultural histories differed from feminist-deconstructive literary criticism, but both shared a post-sixties intellectual lineage and were affiliated with the long struggle to develop and institutionalize women's studies. And, while, as Eisenstein noted, the new right, neoconservatives, and antipornographers were equating pornography, sex, and violence "to reorient the public discussion of sexual expression away from equality toward sex 'difference' in the context of phallocratic heterosexual sex," scholarly interventions that employed a deconstructive political approach were vigorously undertaken if not inside federal courts of law, then inside classrooms throughout American humanities departments in the last decade of the twentieth century.[184] The Sears battle may have been lost, but this kind of important cultural work by the academic left was triumphant in universities and colleges, decisively shaping the views of students and scholars who passed through the academy's door.

The Ne Plus Ultra of Yale Deconstruction

Dedicated in 1993 on Rose Walk, a brick walkway through Yale's Old Campus, Maya Lin's *Women's Table* is a massive green granite circle with a time line of female enrollment at the university inscribed in an inward spiral that increases toward the center. By graphically representing the number of female students hidden within the school's almost three hundred years of androcentric self-representations, Lin's memorial performed a feminist reading of "Male Yale." *Women's Table* can also be profitably seen as a belated response to Johnson's pressing question in her 1984 talk on genre theory: "Would it have been possible for there to have been a female presence in the Yale School?"[185] An affirmative historical reply is due. To be sure, the illusion, produced by an implicit hierarchical opposition that depicted intellectual circles as masculine, that the Yale School was composed of men remains prevalent. While popular and academic publications outright ignored or sometimes saw them as shadowing the Yale School, however, the Brides of Deconstruction and Criticism and their feminist subversions of the masculine metaphysics that upheld texts' gendered, sexed, and raced hierarchies affected numerous scholars' research and teaching programs. Part of the larger post-sixties democratizing trends in higher education toward inclusion and the valorization of difference, aspects of feminist-deconstructionist reading practices had, by the early 1990s, become normalized in many humanistic fields and disciplines. Even the slightest run-in with American academic culture over the last four decades reveals the lasting effects of the feminist-deconstructive moment.

A fair share of feminist deconstructionists' success was due to their talent for maximizing the opportunities and following the protocols for career advancement firmly established during the academic revolution and resultant bureaucratization of university culture. Entering the profession *just* after feminist activists started in the early 1970s to critique androcentric approaches to teaching and knowledge production, Yale feminist deconstructionists lived, breathed, wrote, and taught in an academic environment where the possibilities of feminism grew, the call for ever more rigorous techniques of reading in the humanities intensified, and the professional rewards—awards, prestige, and disciplinary authority—that compensated scholars' generation of deeper, finer, more ironic readings of texts became greater. Certainly, these feminist projects were constrained and cathected by the economizing of the mid- to late 1970s, though being a professor or graduate student at an elite university like Yale provided a bevy of advantages. Feminist deconstructionists also encountered male resistance; their endeavors were seen by opponents as unworthy, irrational, subjective, even perverse. From the perspective of the Brides and their allies, such reactions were not simply wrong but precisely the kind of masculine metaphysical response that failed to seriously answer the call of literature. Conservatives liked to link feminist deconstructionists with the counterculture activities of the New Left of the sixties, but those earlier nonconformists could never have made it in the competitive world of post–golden age academia.

Though unceremoniously concluding by the late 1980s, the Yale feminist-deconstructionist moment endured long enough and was formidable enough to undermine—or desacralize—the masculine metaphysics, the onto-theological dualisms, at work in the "Male School," Yale's self-image, and established literary-critical practice. While using feminist perspectives to develop rhetorical reading techniques that accounted for the blind spots of de Man and company, the Brides also informally inherited the mantle of theoretical innovation that the Hermeneutical Mafia had earlier inherited from the New Critics. Without the combined factors of the post-sixties rise of feminism at Yale and Yale's conservative culture, especially in its literature departments, where pedagogical imperatives of an Eliotic and Arnoldian nature remained to a degree operative, the Brides' transformations and establishment of fields of study would likely have assumed far different shapes and forms. Hardly aiming to destroy humanist artifacts and traditions, Johnson and company's feminist work subverted the control that Western metaphysics' privileging of men and the masculine exerted on the reading and writing of texts, on teaching and learning, and on the maintenance and creation of culture and the institutions that produced and legitimated it.

Like that of the "Male School," the Brides' work seemed to supporters to protect the prestige of literary studies in the academy even as its power to signal social status in American culture waned. Nevertheless, the Brides' pedagogical-intellectual project, to a degree, indirectly contributed to forces weakening the established coherence and purpose of the discipline. While clearly expanding the scope of legitimate topics in literary studies, the Brides' feminist tracings of the deconstructive figural potential of literature appeared to some to undercut justifications for the profession's existence. The same question that confronted the "Male School," then, also confronted the Brides: If the anti-metaphysical power of literature was prior but essential to all discourse, then what turf belonged to a department of literature? The feared answer was: every department was a literature department. Of course, such drastic changes did not come to pass. But inheriting the overall evolutionist thrust of deconstruction, Johnson and company extended the science of rhetorical reading to give a feminist reply to literature's demand, altering and adjusting the institution of American deconstruction to the task of cultural reform.

The Brides' undertaking included a discernible and democratizing expansion of literary language. And this expansion contributed to the establishment of women's studies programs, of which there were more than six hundred across the country by the end of the twentieth century and that enrolled more students than any other interdisciplinary program. The ways in which these programs developed testifies to the crucial part that feminist deconstructionists and their allies played in advancing feminist research and curricula. During the 1990s, women's studies programs were often either flanked by gay and lesbian studies programs or added "gender" to their titles, as Yale's did; in 2004, Yale's program took its current form as "Women's, Gender, and Sexuality Studies." The difficulty that academic humanists today have in speaking categorically of "women"—except in inverted commas—marks a sea change in thinking and writing about sex and gender. We can see a similar shift in much discourse in the public sphere, where the cultural consequences of feminist-deconstructive literary critics and associates give the lie to the all too frequent accusation that the intellectual work of academic humanists has little resonance outside campus walls.

5

SPEAKING IN TONGUES

The de Man Affair and History with(out) Rhetoric

The Committee on the Research Activities of the Modern Language Association rejected de Man's contribution to its 1981 volume *Introduction to Scholarship in Modern Languages and Literatures*. His provocative thesis on the emergence and possible futures of literary theory was the likely cause: "The main theoretical interest of literary theory," de Man wrote, "consists in the impossibility of its definition," while the potential challenges that literary theory faced were not to be "with its polemical opponents."[1] Literary theory was interesting because it was undefinable, and resistance to this undefinable theory came not from a flesh and blood intentional agent but from "the use of language about language."[2] And such nonreferential "resistance," de Man explained, rested in how the rhetorical dimensions of language produced an excess of indetermination that undermined the grammatical (logical) analysis of a text. "Nothing can overcome the resistance to theory since theory *is* itself this resistance," de Man serenely wrote.[3] The upshot was that the text, whether classed as biographical, critical, historical, prose, or poetry, *is* the unavoidable paradoxes of language that endlessly restage linguistic conflict. Finding publication in a 1982 special issue of *Yale French Studies*, edited by Barbara Johnson, de Man's essay was standard fare for readers already initiated into the deconstructive arts, as it nicely reviewed the challenges that de Man's idiomatic science of rhetorical reading posed to the parameters and procedures of "normal" criticism.

However, while de Man and colleagues were offering deconstruction as a corrective to illusions of immediacy, freedom, and historical knowledge, other academic specialists' reassertions of the ideological coordinates of literature were afoot. In the early 1980s, just as mass media were discovering the deconstructive "revolution" and charging its Yale champions with destroying humanistic judgments of value, discriminations between high and low cultural artifacts, and principles of taste, a number of literature professors set sail for shores of sociohistorical consequence. These scholars sought to expertly navigate between the Scylla of a de Manian focus on texts' linguistic divisions and the Charybdis of a positivist confidence in texts' references to reality. For they had come to consider literary-critical projects—de Man's reflexive response to the literary imperative above all—as ahistorical and apolitical; it was all of a sudden quite chic to adopt historical and political approaches. In 1981, Fredric Jameson, recruited to Yale French by de Man in 1976, influentially advocated a rhetorically aware Marxist criticism, suggesting that his colleagues failed to recognize the subjugated "political unconscious" shaped by the transcending narrative that constituted and enclosed every text.[4] The early 1980s also saw the rise of the New Historicism, a quasi movement that, in a style that resembled historicists' resistance to the New Criticism a half a century earlier, sought to reintroduce the literary text into the larger network of texts in which it was fashioned. More broadly, literary scholars, often under the aegis of Michel Foucault, deemed deconstructionists' attention to texts' contradictions excessive, and moved away from the view of a text as a linguistic object that subverts itself to the view of a text as an intricate site of ideological and historical contests that come from all cultural corners and every intellectual stratum.[5]

This alteration of the landscape of literary studies was hastened by the displacement of the American institution of deconstruction to the University of California, Irvine, in the mid- to late 1980s. Composed of Yale School members Miller, Derrida, and several of de Man's former students, the UC-Irvine deconstructive establishment freed rhetoricized pedagogies and writings from disrupting metaphysical hierarchies at Yale and tailored them even more to graduate training and research; this modification aided the distribution of deconstruction to academic humanists invested in exploring conceptual questions about texts—that is, "theory." The institution of American deconstruction at UC-Irvine was facilitated by motivated administrators and professors who had, since the 1970s, worked to satisfy the growing desire and professional need among academic humanists for theoretical perspectives and advanced interpretive tactics. Providing such homegrown support for specialization in the field of (literary) theory, it was believed, might help solve the "crisis of the humanities" that followed the end of golden age of higher education. More voices joined the conversation but did so as material support plummeted.

De Man's death in 1983 also accelerated the Yale School's move to UC-Irvine and helped the, in part generational, transformation of many American literary critics' and scholars' theoretical commitments. But perhaps nothing marked and sparked a collision of deconstruction and history without rhetoric more than the discovery, in 1987, that de Man had contributed almost two hundred pro-German articles to the Nazi-controlled press during the occupation of his native Belgium at the beginning of World War II.[6] Opponents of deconstruction of all stripes jumped at the chance to declare de Man's collaboration the cause of his "antihistorical" and antihumanist reading techniques and the subtext of his postwar writings. Defenders of literary humanism piled on, assailing the entire literary-critical edifice as academic careerism gone mad; it was morally rotten, unable and unwilling to fulfill the Arnoldian mission to transmit the refinement and spiritual elevation provided by the great works of the Western literary and philosophical tradition. The de Man Affair provided ample ammunition in particular to the cultural right, which was anxious to prevent postmodern "barbarians in tweed" from establishing further beachheads in humanities departments. The revelations about de Man delivered a devastating sucker punch to his friends and colleagues, and Derrida's deconstruction of de Man's wartime articles was viewed as an attempt to excuse de Man's moral culpability, putting the real nail in the rhetorical coffin of the deconstructive empire.

Regrettably obscured by all the accusations and counteraccusations during the de Man Affair were not only the reasons for deconstructionists' readings of de Man and the differences between de Man's and Derrida's interpretive techniques, however. Also obscured were the changing fortunes of academic literary study and the situation of the "intellectual" in American life. Partly because of the postwar growth of higher education and specialization of knowledge in the academy, the "intellectual" could no longer claim authority on politics and aesthetics. And when the de Man Affair brought general humanists outside the academy and specialists within, like deconstructionists, into dialogue, they spoke in different discursive tongues.[7] Campus politics intersected with broader public opinion to become a notorious episode in the culture wars.

The School of Criticism and Theory and the Death of de Man

The dawn of deconstruction on the West Coast might have seemed unlikely. Compared to Yale, the University of California, Irvine, appeared to offer little to specialists seeking the newest and most innovative literary theories. Founded in 1965 as part of the California Master Plan for Higher Education, which funded new campuses to accommodate the surge in college-bound veterans and the baby boom, and erected on the former Irvine Ranch in Orange County, UC-Irvine barely existed at its opening ceremony.[8] In contrast to Yale's neo-Gothic architecture, the university flaunted only new buildings, many with futurist designs—sweeping arches, expressionist forms, and aspects of California architecture, such as red-tiled roofs and clay-tiled walkways. Where Yale partook in the dark sublimities of yesteryear—and all the powerful hierarchies that came with it—UC-Irvine seemed postphilosophical, positioned gracefully in a peaceful Mediterranean clime—breezy, sunny all year round, free of misty and musty metaphysics. But with monies from the state pouring into its higher education system, UC-Irvine started to look like a theorist's promised land.

The institution's fresh face, adventurous vibe, and generous funding did in fact attract faculty who specialized in the nascent field, such as Murray Krieger and Hazard Adams. After earning his PhD from Ohio State University in 1952, Krieger became the M. F. Carpenter Chair in Literary Criticism at the University of Iowa, which he held from 1963 to 1966 (Hartman was a colleague). In the 1950s and early 1960s, Krieger used New Critical formalist approaches to explore existentialist topics. By the late 1970s, he was openly defending his and allies' work against what he perceived as European theoretical perspectives, particularly deconstruction. Krieger had joined UC-Irvine in December 1966, when Adams recruited him. Adams himself had participated in the struggle at the University of Michigan against entrenched opposition to literary theory, and, in 1971, sketched the genealogical roots of literary theory back to Plato.[9] Together, Krieger and Adams would make it a specialty of their department at UC-Irvine, the Department of English and Comparative Literature, courting famous critics and scholars who belonged to the theoretical fold.

Established in 1976 and picking up some of the slack left by the Hopkins Humanities Center earlier in the decade, Krieger and Adams's School of Criticism and Theory, which offered a month-and-a-half summer session and a program during the academic year, secured new space for literary criticism grounded in theory. Funding for the SCT was obtained from both UC-Irvine and the National Endowment for the Humanities; the latter awarded a $244,991 grant, one of the largest one-year awards given by the NEH or private foundations to a university up to that point. From the outset, Krieger and Adams hoped the SCT would cultivate an "American theoretical capability that can challenge the Continental movements that have dominated theory and criticism in the Humanities during the last decade."[10] And, out of this theoretical aptitude developed through the study of diverse schools of literary theory, Krieger believed that specialists might create a discourse that united the disciplines of the fragmented humanities. According to a note in the October 1975 *PMLA*, the lack of "such a [unified] conception . . . in our intellectual communities" was a "major reason for the crisis in the humanities."[11] The SCT was thus designed to facilitate experts' learning and advancement of postformalisms in order to integrate humanistic discourses that then could be used to solve the crisis of the splintered humanities. Such investment in SCT attendees' abilities to cultivate a homegrown theoretical sensibility responded to the increased professional demands that the post-1973 economic crisis placed on the humanities in general and literary critics in particular to deploy and/or develop complex reading techniques. This investment also indicated the position and prestige still accorded by the bureaucratized university to the critic and literary studies.[12]

It turned out that the sixty postdoctoral and graduate students' discussions during the six courses, weekly colloquia, and forums of the first summer session of the SCT—held from June 21 to July 30, 1976—failed to produce a unified concept of humanistic discourse. The discussions during the summer session instead reflected how the post-sixties multiplication of critical schools and methods for use by eager experts subverted the conventions and the content of literary humanist education. For example, topics discussed during the session's "Last Forum" included "the [recent] attention to writing as against or in addition to literature" and "the many and various new understandings of what reading is and why it happens"; this attention to reading and writing undermined established distinctions of genre and the difference between literary and nonliterary texts.[13] Gregory L. Ulmer, professor of English at the University of Florida, asked questions that reflected his colleagues' growing awareness and anxiety about the shaky ground upon which their teaching now rested: "Is there something like a traditional set of classic texts and a lucid writing style that is the *sine qua non* of higher education? Or is it desirable to provide the student with a methodological training uncommitted to any single tradition or mode of thought (if that is possible)?" Other SCT attendees went straight for deconstruction, suggesting that its practitioners' concentration on "rhetoric" unreasonably undermined literary education. "Derrida's devaluation of logic in argument," an attendee observed, "would seem to call into question the teaching of literature as a valid enterprise." "Why," another asked, "is it so disturbing when Harold Bloom crosses the line, blurring the distinction between imaginative writing and criticism?"[14] Barely beginning the work of integrating humanistic discourses, SCT participants parsed literary theories and schools of critical thought with an eye to the classroom and to repairing the fraying link between the teaching and research legs of the profession.

Krieger and Adams's quixotic humanist unification project by way of theory battled strong headwinds. By the school's second year, a virtual hurricane of antihumanistic discourses, greatly aided by English translations of Michel Foucault's works, passed through American humanities departments. Accelerating a broader shift in the 1970s from "objectivist" to "constructivist" models of knowledge, Foucault's work disseminated the notion that knowledge was not simply a contingent construction but a distribution of power, an instrument of domination. Krieger himself directly confronted one arm of this antihumanist hurricane during the 1977 SCT session, warning that that "deconstruction" threatened to "become" hegemonic, its "following among younger scholars" reaching "well beyond the precincts of literary study." Passing over the Yale School's claims that their reflexive science of reading showed how literature's demand was essential to all discourse, Krieger continued his cautionary tale about the literary-critical center of the antihumanist storm: the "power" of deconstruction "rest[ed] on totally new and revolutionary grounds that would destroy the basis of all traditional criticism," for example removing the "distinction between critic and the poem which is its object" and consigning them to a "world . . . reduced utterly to language."[15] Such a reduction, Krieger implied, destroyed the system of humanist values enshrined in and embodied by literature. Krieger struck a chord, but not one that lasted; a year later, students and scholars at the SCT's "The Last Forum" considered the "broad attraction Derrida has been having on recent Anglo-American scholars and critics, specifically . . . the extent to which this popularity is indicative of an anti-humanistic tendency . . . and whether this is why so many of us find deconstruction exciting rather than threatening."[16] Krieger had been arguing that "poetic presence" could serve as a basis for a revitalized literary humanism, but specialists at the SCT distrusted that such a goal could be reached.[17] They also found the Yale School's singular concentration on the disruptive power of figural language and the challenge it presented to humanism quite thrilling.

Such enthusiasm derailed Krieger's ambitious aims for the SCT; economizing did the rest. Financial problems had actually plagued the school almost from the start. Despite the NEH's initial support and the SCT's resounding success, the agency denied Krieger and Adams's renewal application. UC-Irvine provided funds for the 1978 and 1979 sessions, but after the state of California passed Proposition 13, which limited state income from taxation, the university's budget was cut and the SCT's 1980 session canceled altogether. The next year, the school moved to Northwestern University and thereafter was peripatetic.[18] Intersecting with this venue change and oddly resonating with Krieger's postspecialist restoration dream were the first of many sensationalist articles outside the academy on the antihumanist specialists inside university walls who sought to destroy literary humanism; it was these crafty experts who created the "crisis in the humanities." According to the previously mentioned 1981

Newsweek piece, a full-throated battle for the future of literary studies was under way between generalists, "partisans of the humanist tradition who believe that the purpose of criticism" should, "in Matthew Arnold's words, . . . 'propagate the best that is known and thought in the world,'" and "deconstructionists," extreme specialists who "have a decidedly nihilistic philosophy of life."[19] This conflict likely informed SCT organizers' decision to ask attendees of the symposium that celebrated the arrival of the school at Northwestern to consider "how the humanities, and literary critics in particular, can challenge the way people think about social, political, and historical matters."[20] As German literary scholar Wolfgang Iser had posited in a 1979 article, literary theory was becoming "increasingly dependent on the relationship between literature and society—a relationship which stood in urgent need of clarification."[21]

Despite this widely articulated need for some sort of reconciliation between literary theory and history with or without rhetoric, SCT attendees continued to grapple with deconstruction, that most specialized of literary theories. The 1981 summer session again revolved around how the Yale School's rhetorical reading techniques (and other postformalisms) affected the teaching of literature. Krieger circulated questions, gathered from attendees, for discussion at the final colloquium: "What are the consequences for literature in the classroom of recent claims about textual instabilities and undecidables?" "How does recent theory affect the classroom treatment of naïve or out-of-bound student interpretations (if any can still be declared out of bounds)?" "Are we ready to take the pedagogical consequences of recent tendencies in theory to equalize all writing?" "Shall we alter the principles on which we create syllabi of courses in literature?" "Is there no longer to be any privileged roll-call of literary works to be taught?"[22] The apprehension about deconstruction's effects in the classroom palpably grew. But participants at the SCT stopped just short of blaming the Yale School for the "crisis in the humanities."

When the SCT moved to Northwestern, none other than Geoffrey Hartman assumed leadership and turned its mission away from attempting to use literary theory to create a universal humanist language. In the 1982 session, he asked participants to consider "fundamental issues [such] as the nature of human communication and of human creativity in the arts and sciences, the relation between the arts and technology, and the role of the arts in maintaining an open society."[23] Hartman, though, still had one foot in the Yale School's endeavor, and brought in de Man, whose SCT seminar provided what champions of humanism would have seen as a picture-perfect demonstration of the linguistic corrosive that deconstructionists poured on the best that had been thought and known. Extending his cycle of Yale Comp Lit courses on aesthetic theory, de Man's SCT seminar offered "close readings of a series of literary, philosophical, and critical texts from the sixteenth century to the present dealing with the tensions between the linguistic and the aesthetic components of texts as well as with the ideological consequences of these tensions."[24] Though de Man promised to explore texts' political effects, however, he still stressed that the unresolvable struggle between a text's linguistic and aesthetic elements—that is, the text's self-deconstruction of metaphysical dualisms—prevented any easy sociohistorical reference, and, as a result, required thorough examination first. He explained to attendees: "We will stay the longest time within the first stage of this process namely rhetoric/aesthetics," because "accusations of avoidance of ideological concerns are, in fact, rooted in 'theoretico-linguistic' considerations." "Truly political thought," the politically evasive de Man lectured to his SCT students, "is accessible only by way of critical aesthetic theory."[25]

With a battery of texts by Kant, Coleridge, Hegel, Marx, Walter Benjamin, Althusser, Adorno, and others, de Man highlighted how a text's conflict between rhetoric and aesthetics executed a "strategy of [the] recovery of truth by way of its deconstruction" that thwarted any straightforward reference to a signified outside the text, such as those used by literary historians or biographers, to control the text's meaning. De Man first considered the very text that instituted the Yale School, Nietzsche's philosophical fragment "On Truth and Lie in an Extra-Moral Sense" (1873). The rhetorical practice of this text, de Man suggested, subverted its aesthetic (onto-theological) claims about rhetoric; it thereby offered a fertile point of entry into the initial stage of de Man's deconstructive response to aesthetic theories. Consider Nietzsche's oracular answer to his question, "What is therefore truth?": "A mobile army of metaphors, metonyms, and anthropomorphisms—in short, a sum of human relations." To contend "that truth is trope," de Man lectured, "is to say that truth is the possibility of making a definitional proposition." But because truth is a "collection of several tropes"—Nietzsche's "metaphors" and "metonyms"—the "possibility of several different propositions" always remained possible. While Nietzsche's claim that truth was a collection of nonidentical propositions was not "disruptive" of Nietzsche's argument, de Man continued, his use of the word "anthropomorphisms" was, because it aestheticizes, it "freezes [the] chain of transformation into one single entity [being or signified] that excludes all others." "Although trope is not anthropomorphism," de Man lectured, "anthropomorphism is a trope (or structured like a trope)." For example: Nietzsche's employment of the trope of "anthropomorphism" was the cause of his "odd" declaration that "truth" was a "mobile army." "Is truth a general, who has tropes fighting for him, against error[?]" de Man playfully asked. "No"; Nietzsche's "truth is" not "dialectical" and does not even lead "to the negative knowledge of error as truth." Instead, Nietzsche's use of the truth trope "anthropomorphism" undermined his definition of truth. For de Man, Nietzsche's claim about truth was "disruptive" because it subverted the tension between linguistic and aesthetic dimensions, between rhetoric and anthropomorphism.[26]

Unfortunately, de Man's expert examination at the SCT of precisely how rhetorical and aesthetic elements structured the ideological consequences of texts was cut short. "Little over a week into the session," Hartman recalled, "[de Man's] skin took on a yellowish tinge. Since he would do nothing about it, we made a doctor's appointment for him; the doctor immediately sent him back to New Haven for a complete examination. An 'unreferenced' tumor was diagnosed. It was putting pressure on his liver and was too close to be removed." Leaving aside the sad irony that an unreferenced tumor threatened the life of a critic most known for his stringent refusal to employ social and historical references, de Man left the SCT summer session early, though "not without," Hartman remembered, "seeing every student in his seminar until late at night, to discuss their ideas, or simply to chat and so tide them over."[27] Even as he physically weakened, de Man's devotion to his students, to helping them become expert deconstructive readers, was unwavering. In fact, it could indeed be argued that de Man's greatest contribution to the institution of American deconstruction was his work as a teacher.

While get-well cards for de Man poured in, Miller secured his position as a leading authority in literary theory and criticism. His 1982 book would seal his national reputation. In it, Miller deconstructively distinguished between two "intertwining" modes of repetition in seven nineteenth- and twentieth-century English novels: a "Platonic" mode, "grounded in a solid archetypal model" in which an original, transcendent ideal served as the template for later similar examples, and a "Nietzschean" mode, the "subversive ghost of the first" in which "ungrounded doublings" arose "out of the interplay of . . . opaquely similar things."[28] Miller highlighted the ways each novel was organized by the Platonic establishment of a "Figure in the Carpet"—not only images, metaphors, and motifs but also on a larger scale of episodes, characters, and plots—and the Nietzschean unraveling of the Platonic order.[29] This agonistic struggle between these two manners of repetition produced a topological paradox, Miller stressed, that undermined any hope of identifying a univocal meaning or sense in the text: "[T]he indeterminacy [of Conrad's Lord Jim (1900)] lies in the multiplicity of possible incompatible explanations given by the novel and in the lack of evidence justifying a choice of one over the others";[30] Emily Brontë's *Wuthering Heights* (1847) resisted "a single definitive reading" because the "center," "the head referent," the "innermost core" was absent.[31]

Miller's book led to job offers from universities seeking to bring the famous critic and theorist on board and raise the profiles of their literature departments. He declined them all, including one from the rapidly growing University of Florida because he believed Yale continued to offer him ideal conditions for the integration of his deconstructive teaching and research programs. To be sure, administrative and committee responsibilities demanded much of his attention—he had directed dozens of dissertations—and the university's conservative culture could be frustrating. It was Miller's investments in teaching, however, that most encouraged him to remain at Yale. His "main reason for staying," he explained in a letter to Yale's president, was "the privilege of teaching what must be the best students both undergraduate and graduate, to be found anywhere."[32] The caliber of the students allowed Miller to treat his classrooms as workshops where he could experiment with heady concepts and innovative interpretive positions. "The classroom," he reflected, "is for a humanist his laboratory, at least for me, the place where one tries out new ideas and works out the things which are written up and published later."[33] Tellingly and most importantly, though, Miller implied in his letter that the synchronization between research and teaching agendas that he, Hartman, and de Man together executed at Yale was perhaps unique and imparted a deconstructive disposition and way of reading texts to Miller as much as to students. "Though I know I could in time establish a new 'laboratory' at Florida," Miller explained to a dean there, "my own current work is so intimately bound up with the particular teaching situation I have at Yale that I have found myself unwilling to give it up at this time."[34]

Had he accepted the Florida position, Miller would have missed the opportunity to audit de Man's Comp Lit seminars, which remained an exceptional medium through which the hard art of rhetorical reading still passed. De Man's courses also epitomized how only those skilled in taking his arduous linguistic turn (like Miller) could confidently grasp the intricate insights into the relationship between politics and aesthetics that de Man believed a reflexively scientific attention to figural language might provide. The specialized deconstructive knowledge that de Man imparted was virtually unintelligible to the uninitiated, but not for the suitably equipped Miller, who dutifully attended de Man's fall 1982 Comp Lit 817a seminar, the topic of which, de Man explained, was how the "explicit philosophical theme" of the "relation of [the] category of aesthetic to epistemology" was linked to an "implicit question" of "the relation of the category of the aesthetic to the theory of language," principally how "sign, symbol, trope, rhetoric, grammar" operated in Hegel's, Kant's, and Schiller's texts.[35] Investigating this subject with him, de Man suggested, would allow students to supersede the readings of the "American Romanticists": M. H. Abrams and W. K. Wimsatt, whose insufficiently rigorous response to the appeal of literature produced the view of the aesthetic (the artwork) as a sublime experience, "a culminating and procreative marriage between mind and nature."[36] "It's not," de Man opined, "a good sign if the interpretation of Romanticism centers on the Sublime"; "[it] leads to [a] focus on the relation of Romanticism to Theology," which is "not necessarily the central point."[37] For de Man, the uncritical concentration on the sublime—for example, Wimsatt believed poetry incarnated the "translucence of the eternal [Christian truth] into the temporal" through the Coleridgean symbol—signaled a failure of nerve to face how a text's linguistic conflicts made sublime (onto-theological) moments "fall apart," a self-deconstruction that disrupted the wedding of oppositions, such as mind and nature. But, for de Man, rhetorical readers could unearth the "*ungedacht*," the unstated model of language employed in Hegel's, Kant's, and Schiller's texts that undermined these texts' assertions of aesthetically merging mind and nature to produce presence.[38]

Literary critics, according to de Man, were the best prepared to excavate the embedded theory of literary language that "critically" unraveled the "category of the aesthetic" in Hegel's major texts;[39] they had the expert tools with which to burrow under the surface of the text to identify how language ever so subtly unsettled spiritual and ontic claims of presence: "Traditional philosophy departments have been against this kind of oblique reading. . . . That things are not as they seem to be has been more available in literature departments."[40] "Official Hegelian orthodoxy," de Man furnished as a relevant example, obscured Hegel's actual "treatment of the Sublime."[41] Conventionally read, Hegel's *Ästhetik* (1835) narrated the progressive dissolution of art—with art constituted by a "sublime moment" of the aesthetic—since Greek antiquity. "The Sublime [in the *Ästhetik*] is a moment in the 'History' of the aesthetic category in general: a certain moment in the diachronic development of the beautiful."[42]

De Man, however, rhetorically read Hegel as *explicitly* arguing that the sublime historical moment allowed for the appearance of *Geist*, a kind of shared onto-theological consciousness or "mind," but as *implicitly* deploying a theory of literary language that ensured any moment of metaphysical presence, of the aesthetic (as art), did *not* manifest *Geist*. According to de Man, Hegel's deconstructive subversion of his philosophical system hinged on his use of the category of the aesthetic as "the passage from recollection to memory."[43] For Hegel, de Man lectured, "that which is inward is recollection," the "temporal" process through which "perception and representation enter consciousness as interiorization."[44] Such recollection "is inward" because "that which is preserved . . . is in something, a well."[45] In contrast to memory as recollection, Hegel opposed memory as memorization, "as *Gedächtnis*." Memory as memorization was unavailable phenomenally because it was, de Man lectured, "purely exterior and mechanical: to remember a text, you must pay no attention to its contents. To remember a text, forget immediately what is in it. Remembering is purely external."[46] For de Man, then, in Hegel, the aesthetic (art) was expounded as the epistemological passageway from recollection to memory, from *Erinnerung* to *Gedächtnis*. It was a sublime historical moment, for Hegel, when "you forget your recollections and only remember your notations . . . [which] can be called the way that the Idea manifests itself sensorially" as the beautiful artwork.[47]

A key to de Man's rhetorical reading of Hegel's text, though, was de Man's unorthodox argument that Hegel's *Ästhetik* actually suggested that *Gedächtnis* (and thus the manifestation of *Geist* and the aesthetic) could not be captured in the artwork. This was because "language appears in Hegel at the moment of the Sublime."[48] During moments of aesthetic experience, de Man glossed Hegel's text as implying, "there's a purely empty link" between memory as recollection and memory as memorization.[49] And this empty link that de Man expertly extracted from Hegel's text guaranteed that the "aesthetic moment *par excellence* in Hegel" undermined the "correspondence between sign and meaning," signifier and signified, word and thing, subverting the coherence of Hegel's philosophy of art.[50] Put differently: if the epistemological vessel (the linguistic category of the aesthetic) as suggested by Hegel's text always already broke the empty connection between recollection and memory, Hegel's explicit argument that great art externally preserved interiorized perceptions and representations fell apart. Detectable by using de Man's rhetorical reading techniques, Hegel's own model of language ensured Hegel's claimed unification of the two different types of memory could never occur in the work of art. This had far-reaching desacralizing consequences, de Man intimated: interpreting "the *Aesthetics*" as a Möbius-strip-like response to the disruptive claim of literature excavated an implicit theory of language that subverted the sublime experiences that anchored symbolist aesthetics and the artwork as a symbolic presence.

De Man's reading of Hegel, in other words, deeply undermined the humanist belief that art aesthetically embodied, accumulated, and conveyed philosophical truth and ideals. And because symbolist aesthetics organized philosophical systems, "ethics is [revealed as] fundamentally discursive" and "the law, as discourse, is no longer sacred in origin."[51] De Man, it seemed, wanted to unearth theories of figural language in philosophical texts to eventually reckon deconstruction and history, but he, again, side-stepped sociopolitical reference, simply hinting at how "the aesthetic as a *value*" became the dominant way to think about the aesthetic and how this mode of thinking affected "problems of the social and politic[al]" world.[52] "History," Miller logged de Man explaining, "is a pedagogical device—If I say there's an historical line from Hegel to Nietzsche, don't ask me to show you that line—it's only for teaching—*that's* my line."[53] De Man thus used his science of rhetorical reading not only to suggest that philosophical claims about the aesthetic undermined themselves but also to call for the comprehensive rhetoricization of interpretive theories and practices of literary education rooted in the onto-theological concept of the aesthetic—in other words, all of humanism.

De Man's "antihistorical" postmodern politics of literary language never did neatly fit the established right or left spectrum. But though the overt political effects of his reflexive interpretive science remained murky to the unversed, de Man himself seemed to have clarity and purpose. Even as he faced the pain caused by his inoperable tumor, he continued to impart his specialized deconstructive knowledge to students, "historically" soliciting this knowledge from an intellectual tradition sidelined by metaphysics. In the spring of 1983, de Man taught Lit 130b with Andrzej Warminski and, in the fall of 1983, quite ill, held his Comp Lit seminar at his home. There, de Man challenged accepted views that scientific and humanistic work progressively improved, maintaining that theories of rhetoric elaborated by contemporary philosophers and literary critics—Tzvetan Todorov, Gérard Genette, Paul Ricœur, Derrida, and the like—had already been expounded in the texts of eighteenth-century philosophical and literary figures. While the "development of poetics (literary theory), as applied linguistics, implies a 'return' more or less [made] explicit to rhetoric," de Man explained, "this return to rhetoric [was] in fact a return to the 18th century."[54] The "recent" orientation of academic specialists toward rhetoric—a focus for not only the Yale group but others, like American literary critic and theorist Kenneth Burke, who saw rhetoric as "symbolic action"—was for de Man an uncanny homecoming to the deconstructive intellectual traditions of the Age of Enlightenment and the European Romantics. Sadly, de Man's "historical" investigations ended prematurely. On December 21, Comp Lit student Haun Saussy recalled, "Peter Brooks came in and told us that Mr. de Man had died that morning. He was in tears and we all went down the hall with ashen faces. 'Well, that's it,' said one classmate."[55] A chapter had closed, and with it went the hope among de Man's devotees that his discipline of rhetorical reading would not simply

FIGURE 5.1 Paul de Man in 1972 at a location in the Alps near the site of his uncle's presumed suicide (Courtesy of Patricia de Man)

solve the crisis of comp lit, as it provided a theory of interpretation applicable to any text, but also once and for all demonstrate the ways literary language constituted and unsettled discourse. Buried on Gott's Island, in Maine, where he had spent his summers, de Man became a material inscription, a name carved on a cemetery stone, marking the absence of a founder of American deconstruction.

Mourning de Man and the End of the Yale School

Virtually everyone in Yale's literature departments attended the January 18, 1984, memorial service. In reverent tones, de Man's former students and colleagues stirringly spoke of his singular importance in Yale's and the wider literary-critical community; most emphasized his teaching; all grappled with the fact that, now that their leading light was gone, it could never be the same.[56] "It was Paul's intellectual passion that sustained the teaching of literature at Yale," Hartman reflected. "In the space war of the theorists, he became the Yoda figure." "All who heard him, as teacher, friend, or colleague, changed their relation to the written word."[57] A grieving Derrida took the lectern to offer a brief tribute. He recalled first meeting de Man "at a breakfast table in Baltimore"; after that, "nothing has ever come between us, not even a hint of disagreement"; and he recollected his last telephone conversation with de Man, who, seemingly reflecting on his life's work, quoted a poem by Stéphane Mallarmé that emphasized poetic legacy as more about intellectual dissemination than personal authority.[58] Felman believed that the timing of the service was apt: "Wednesday afternoon—this very hour—was throughout the years the time reserved for Paul de Man's class. It is fitting that we should to-day recall him in *his teaching time*, for his teaching now recalls us, and will never cease to summon us."[59] Johnson witnessed: "The last thing he probably would have wanted to be was a moral and pedagogical—rather than merely intellectual—example." But paradoxes of de Man's example abounded: "He never sought followers; people followed him in droves. He was ironic toward discipleship; the country is dotted with his disciples." "In a profession full of fakeness," Johnson concluded, "he was real; in a world full of takers, he let others take; in a crowd of self-seekers, he sought the truth, and distrusted it."[60] Ellen S. Burt, assistant professor of French at Yale, spoke of what she viewed as de Man's "moral trait," his "complete detachment from the claims of subjectivity or individual personality as was possible." And there was an important and ironically socially inflected upshot of de Man's intense focus on the text: "Women," Burt continued, "gained by his detachment" because "he had himself no time to waste being seduced, disquieted, or threatened" and "thus no time to waste vindictively barring [women] from effecting a full entry into the profession." Detached, yet invested, a genuine voice who, Johnson pointed out, mistrusted the words "integrity, honesty, authenticity, generosity, even seductiveness," de Man, whose "gait," "shrug of the shoulders," "set of the head," and "quizzical smile," Burt recalled, captivated students and colleagues, was deeply mourned.[61] "We shall not look upon his like again," a former colleague wrote decades later.[62]

The Yale community was united in remembrance of de Man, and despite the significant differences between his deconstruction and that of others of the Yale group, those distinctions remained nearly indiscernible. But as Derrida paid tribute to de Man in several forums, the differences between his philosophical answer to the metaphysics of presence and de Man's rhetorical reading techniques could be gleaned. In March 1984, Derrida delivered three lectures in Yale's Comp Lit library, "a place," he observed, "we shall never be able to name, use, or recognize . . . without thinking of Paul de Man," that deconstructively engaged the memory of de Man. In the first sentence of his first lecture, titled "Mnemosyne," after the Titaness who personified memory, Derrida obliquely referenced his philosophically modulated deconstruction, declaring that he had "never known how to tell a story";[63] that is, he had never known how to organize a narrative that re-presented the past, a story "oriented toward the past" that simply and straightforwardly brings this past into the present.[64] Instead of telling such a narrative, Derrida wanted to "talk ... about ... that future which ... comes to us from Paul de Man."[65] And in his second lecture, Derrida explained that he would deconstructively speak of "'memories' in memory of Paul de Man," and for personal reasons—"to remain awhile longer near my friend, to keep watch over, take in, slow down, or annul the separation"—as well as scholarly ones—as "'memory' was for Paul de Man a place ... of original, continuing reflection, yet still generally hidden, it seems to me, from his readers."[66] To proclaim that memory was a secret refrain in de Man's texts must have been surprising to Derrida's audience—de Man was known for his stance against psychological discourses. To support his curious thesis, Derrida underscored selections from de Man's writings, including his 1982 essay on Hegel, which explored how "the relation ... between memory and interiorizing recollection, is not 'dialectical,' as Hegelian interpretation and Hegel's interpretation would have it, but one of [deconstructive] rupture, heterogeneity, and disjunction."[67] Then, during his third lecture, Derrida fashioned de Man's writings to accord even more with Derrida's deconstruction (of psychoanalytic texts) by foregrounding a passage in de Man's *Allegories of Reading* (1979) that Derrida read as arguing against the postulation that memory was nostalgic: Memory, for de Man, Derrida said, is "future oriented and prospective"; "there is only [in de Man's text] the promise and memory, memory as promise, without any gathering possible in the form of the present."[68] While de Man's aim in these last texts was to reveal how literary language disrupted the symbolist aesthetics used in literary humanism, Derrida's audience could be excused for supposing there was no daylight between the two pillars of deconstruction in America.[69]

Derrida's elision of de Man's rhetorical project continued in two April 1984 lectures at Cornell on Francis Ponge's metapoetic poem "Fable." It so happens that it was with this poem that Derrida deconstructively responded to the literary imperative in his first Yale Comp Lit seminar in 1975, which de Man had helped to arrange. Ponge's poem, Derrida suggested, pronounced and performed the central elements that characterized de Man's work. Derrida saw the poem as reflexively and vertiginously enacting its purpose and form; its first lines read: "With the word *with* begins then this text / Of which the first line states the truth"; its last lines: "(AFTER seven years of misfortune / She broke her mirror)."[70] Since, Derrida stressed, Ponge's "Fable" was a "myth of impossible origins," a fable that executed "itself ironically as ... [the] truth of allegory and allegory of truth, truth as allegory," "to remember this starting point" in "Fable" was actually "to *mime* a starting over" with de Man.[71] Yet to believe that a wholly new beginning could occur was a metaphysical illusion, as demonstrated by "Fable" itself, the strange looping of which undermined the onto-theological search for origins by both reiterating "with" and reversing its chronology with its closing lines; this was similar to how de Man's writings, particularly his groundbreaking 1969 essay, "The Rhetoric of Temporality," echoed the figural conflict between the diachronic and synchronic forms that structured prose and poetry.[72] With Ponge's "Fable," Derrida therefore parodied starting over with de Man, using the poem as an ironic allegory of de Man's criticisms' contradictory entanglements with texts' performatives and constantives, acts and statements. That Derrida expressed an affiliation with de Man and as they were both deconstructive specialists, the conflation of their approaches by some was understandable.

Yet Derrida's depiction of his friend as a "great thinker and theorist of memory" was a way not only to keep his friend close but also to indirectly respond to the cottage industry devoted to blaming deconstruction and associated theoretical methodologies for the growing "crisis of the humanities."[73] An early supplier was professor of English Walter Jackson Bate, who, in a 1982 *Harvard Magazine* essay, gave a ringing defense of classic literary humanism in order to rescue the humanities from their "worst state of crisis since the modern university was formed."[74] For Bate, the overproduction of PhDs and public disillusionment with higher education were factors that generated this predicament. But the real focus of Bate's complaints was humanities (especially English) professors' hyperspecialization, which he felt produced undesirable courses and fields of study—including women's studies, gay studies, and ethnic studies—and recondite scholarship as a "separate preserve, apart from the common experience of life."[75] Crowning the academization of literary studies and the devouring of the nonspecialized public intellectual by the university, hyperspecialization and the "suicidal movement among 'leaders of the profession'" that it brought about was best represented by "deconstructionism," a reading "procedure gloriously free of any necessary relationship to history, to philosophy, or to human lives" and which endorsed a "nihilistic view of literature, of human communication, and of life itself."[76] The destructive perspective of "deconstructionism" disintegrated a common culture rooted in the "legacy of *litterae humanoires*" and undermined centuries of accumulated "classical" humanistic trust in the "moral and educative effect on human character of knowledge."[77] Deconstructive specialists thus plunged the humanities into oblivion. Bate's counsel: "The whole cultural heritage is too important to leave to . . . the 'experts.'"[78]

Defenders of a general literary humanism and its ability to impart universal wisdom from the cultural politics of deconstructionists materialized with startling frequency in middlebrow publications. In 1982, William Bennett, Reagan-appointed chairman of the NEH, clearly motivated to protect his and others' cultural authority, warned in the *Wall Street Journal* that "the greatest threat to the humanities lies within," a threat made by academic leftists who refused to use their texts and teaching for the goal of "spiritual refinement and spiritual elevation"; rather, this fifth column of experts expressed "perverse embarrassment . . . about the achievements of our civilization."[79] Within the bureaucratic halls of the shattered humanities, Bennett continued, "there seems to be competition for complete unintelligibility," as "self-isolating vocabularies . . . abound within subdisciplines."[80] Like Bate, Bennett targeted "deconstruction" as symptom and cause of the humanities' fragmentation, of its decline, for its confusedness and desolated jargon "denies that there are texts at all," and "if there are no texts, there are no great texts, and no argument for reading."[81] In other words, because deconstruction demolished "the text" and, as the study of "great works" was vital for cultivating students' appreciation of timeless, commonly held knowledge, virtues, ethics, morals, and visions for society, deconstruction contributed to the neglect of "the intellectual, moral and political traditions of our civilization," helping erase the purpose of the university itself.[82]

Then René Wellek, emeritus at Yale, donned his humanist mail and shield in a 1983 issue of the *New Criterion*, a journal established a year earlier "to be a kind of National Redoubt of High Culture" that protected readers from "the insidious assault on mind that was one of the most repulsive features of the radical movement of the sixties."[83] In his essay, Wellek bemoaned that "some of the recent developments [in literary theory] in their extreme skepticism and even nihilism" threatened to "destroy literary studies from the inside," to "'deconstruct' as they say, all literary study, interrupt tradition, dismantle an edifice built by the efforts of generations of scholars and students."[84] That Wellek's article prominently arrived in the public sphere while de Man lay dying underlined the pedagogical and intellectual dangers that literary humanists like Wellek believed deconstruction posed. It also foregrounded the degree to which the Yale School and cultural conservatives were talking past each other. Miller recalled: "As de Man himself put it one of the last times I saw him, a few days before his death, 'the stakes are enormous.' He was speaking, first and immediately, of a deplorably ignorant and malicious essay by René Wellek in the *New Criterion* accusing de Man and others of 'Destroying Literary Studies.' A copy was on de Man's bedside table with a friendly inscription from Wellek."[85]

While nonacademic articles spread mistranslations of deconstructive technicians' ideas, academia was treated to *The Yale Critics: Deconstruction in America* (1983), a collection of essays that situated the works of Bloom, de Man, Hartman, and Miller in relation to one another and Derrida.[86]

This volume and a smattering of more popular publications had prompted Derrida's allies Suzanne Gearhart and David Carroll to ask him to use his three March 1984 lectures on de Man to clarify "deconstruction in America."[87] Instead of directly responding to this appeal, Derrida subversively replied to the request's literariness, and his answer, including what he thought of his part in the American institution of deconstruction, was circuitous, if not willfully evasive. "I must," Derrida explained that April in Miami, "avoid that question . . . in a manner that is . . . altogether as deliberate, as thought-out, as analytical as possible."[88] To "define these words," Derrida insisted during his first lecture in March, "to make 'deconstruction in America' a theme of the object of an exhaustive definition is precisely, by definition, what defines the enemy of deconstruction."[89] For Derrida, Western metaphysics was deconstruction's adversary, and this way of thinking, by valorizing particular interpretations of "deconstruction in America," constructed hierarchical oppositions that marginalized unexpected or conflicting meanings of "deconstruction" "in" "America," obscuring the unending (de)construction in/of these words. Playfully emphasizing what "we have learned from 'Deconstruction,'" for example that "'deconstruction' is not a proper name, nor is America the proper name of deconstruction," Derrida then proposed that "deconstruction and America are two open sets which intersect partially according to an allegorico-metonymic figure."[90] "In this fiction of truth," a fiction that resembled de Man's influential 1973 rhetorical reading of Proust, Derrida coyly continued, "'America' would be the title of a new novel on the history of deconstruction and the deconstruction of history."[91] Derrida's great postmodern American novel would tell the story of deconstruction *and* this story's subversion of itself. Though the chance for Derrida to answer Gearhart and Carroll's question again arose in his second March lecture—he noted that "the thread of memory could orient us in Paul de Man's thought and guide us during our passage [through] the thread of 'deconstruction in America'"—Derrida followed only narrative slivers.[92] In April at Miami, Derrida explained: "I think New Criticism . . . was one of the premises preparing the way for deconstruction," but added that he was "incompetent to talk about . . . the relatively recent history of literary studies in America."[93]

De Man's death presented Derrida with opportunities—at Yale, in Miami, and at Cornell—to intervene in rapidly settling views about "deconstruction in America," yet Derrida kept weaving his sophisticated deconstructive texts instead. Derrida only wanted, he stated in Miami, to "increase the points of entry" into the issues.[94] Even as it solicited new readers, however, Derrida's unique approach led him to cede public ground; others defined deconstruction for him. He even tiptoed around the recent debate about his own work between Rudolphe Gasché, who popularized the view that American literary critics domesticated Derrida's philosophy, and Suanne Gearhart, who described the difference between Derrida and de Man in terms that were primarily linguistic.[95] Derrida's "nonintervention" did correspond to the Yale School's general habit of not clarifying its American institution of deconstruction: de Man, Hartman, and Miller, in their own ways, interpreted texts' rhetorical dimensions as guaranteeing the misreading of said texts, which meant that they would never fully enter into debates on "deconstruction in America" or whether they "deviated" from or "diluted" Derrida's project; they let a thousand interpretations bloom. "I have," de Man once noted with "ironic and moving pseudo-resignation" to Barbara Johnson, "all the fewer illusions about the possibility of countering these aberrations [about deconstruction] since such an expectation would go against the drift of my own readings."[96] From a de Manian perspective, what better way indeed to honor the call of literary language than to permit dis-figurations of one's own work?

Miller, however, had always been more willing to advocate on behalf of deconstruction, and he responded to the attacks. Following a series of 1984 and 1985 reports on the state of higher education sponsored by independent foundations, educational organizations, and Reagan's government that identified an escalating "crisis of the humanities," and amid the growing chorus of conservatives' objections to how academics' overspecialization had destroyed (literary) culture and prohibited the cultivation of opinion and taste, Miller adjusted his rhetorical response to the literary imperative.[97] In 1985, he gave several papers at UC-Irvine on how literary language in the novels of George Eliot, Henry James, and Anthony Trollope as well as the writings of Walter Benjamin, de Man, and Kant, demanded ethical decisions. "By 'the ethics of reading,'" Miller lectured, "I mean that aspect of the act of reading in which there is a response to the text that is both necessitated, in the sense that it is a response to an irresistible demand, and free, in the sense that I must take responsibility for my response and for the further effects, 'interpersonal,' institutional, social, political, or historical, of my act of reading."[98] For example, according to Miller, a "respect" achieved through "the consciousness or the submission of will" grounded the metaphysical thesis of Kant's *Grundlegung zur Metaphysik der Sitten* (1785), which aspired to expose the fundamental principle of moral law.[99] However, in an ostensibly marginal footnote, Kant defined "respect" as "an object neither of inclination nor of fear, though it has something analogous to both."[100] An act of literary language, Kant's "respect" was an undecidable, a choice *and* a command that deconstructively subverted the subject's willing "respect." Existing in the fleeting moment of defining it, Kant's "respect" was an instance of ethics, a textual performance, that, though bearing little resemblance to moral philosophers' categorizations, defenses, or endorsements of concepts of right and wrong behavior, was part of Miller's rhetorical response to the blame placed on deconstruction for the declining status of literary studies.

If "deconstructionism" was increasingly portrayed outside the university as a perverse project of academic specialists that posed a grave threat to the humanities' hallowed history and aims, members of the semidefunct Yale School were seen by many inside academe as leading experts in the field of literary theory whose presence on campus could add intellectual firepower and heft to any humanities discipline. Murray Krieger and dean of the School of Humanities William Lillyman thought as much, and, in the summer of 1985, began to court Miller and Derrida, reasoning that UC-Irvine was the next logical home for deconstruction. Krieger and Lillyman could marshal a good deal of evidence. In part due to the legacy of Krieger and Adams's School of Criticism and Theory, the university had become known for both enjoying the most diverse concentration of "critical theorists" in the world and having institutionalized theory in unheard-of ways. UC-Irvine's graduate students in English and comp lit, for example, could actually have a PhD concentration in critical theory. During the late 1970s, such courses included General Introduction to the Problems of Literary Theory and Its Methods, and History of the Problems of Theory.[101] Additionally, a focused research program in contemporary critical theory was created for faculty who specialized in this area. By contrast, a graduate student in Yale English could still earn a doctorate without taking a single theory course or being examined on it. Simply put, UC-Irvine's support for the kinds of specialized work that Miller dedicated himself to far outshone Yale's.

Miller deliberated the feasibility of operationalizing deconstruction on the West Coast. Remuneration was of course important. UC-Irvine offered him one of its highest-ever salaries ($91,000, even though housing and supporting luminous denizens like Miller meant pulling an ever-larger cut from dwindling resources for the humanities). Miller, though, was more concerned with how the move would affect his research. In a September 1985 letter to Wolfgang Iser, a reader-response theorist who had been recruited to UC-Irvine, Miller expressed his excitement at the possibility of working at "Irvine with you, Murray, [French philosopher Jean-François] Lyotard, the younger people already there, to which may possibly be added Derrida (for five weeks a year)."[102] In a letter to Derrida, Miller also mentioned the new research possibilities, the funding available at UC-Irvine, and "whether there is not occurring now a general shift of intellectual activity to the West Coast and whether both of us might not have a greater effect for 'deconstruction in America' out there than in spending another decade at Yale."[103] "Yale will always be Yale," Miller mused, "but I wonder if we have done about as much as can be done there for the moment. Certainly Paul thought so, and spoke in his last months of how he had thought he could make a real change at Yale but 'had not made a dent' in the place."[104] With de Man gone, junior faculty—Ellen S. Burt and Kevin Newmark in French, Andrzej Warminski in Comp Lit—once under his protection could no longer be ensured support, or, more importantly, tenure.[105] Nevertheless, while UC-Irvine seemed poised to open the next chapter in the institution of deconstruction in America, Miller worried about "the quality of graduate students who might be attracted to Irvine as compared to the Yale ones."[106] This was a nonissue, Krieger assured Miller, as the university was attracting some of the best doctoral students in the country interested in critical theory in general and literary theory and criticism in particular. UC-Irvine was to be a (literary) theorist's paradise.

Convincing Derrida to transfer was another matter. Miller explained to Lillyman that the French philosopher's own uneasiness must be allayed and his unique demands met. When Miller discussed with Lillyman the terms of UC-Irvine's proposal to Miller and Derrida's wish to continue "the public forum he has for one of his three seminars a week at Yale, that is, a format in which students and colleagues from all over, not just from Yale, [were] welcome," Lillyman asked if there was anything that he might miss from Yale.[107] Miller emphasized how much he valued Derrida as a colleague. "We'll hire him," said Lillyman outright. "How much does he make?" Miller told him, and Lillyman countered: "We can increase that by 50%."[108] Miller thought Lillyman was just "talking through his hat," but, in a week, a contract arrived for Derrida at a "greatly increased salary and as a permanent tenured off-scale (above the normal salary rankings) full distinguished professor third-time appointee in 'Humanities'"—Derrida would share his position with Lyotard (fall) and Iser (winter) to satisfy administrators—"with joint appointments all around, even in the philosophy department."[109] Derrida and Miller accepted.

Derrida's new appointment at UC-Irvine changed not only his orientation to the American institution of deconstruction but also his relationship to the institutions in which he worked. With his expertise extending into every humanities department, Derrida could deliver his anti-metaphysical project, his specialized vocabulary, across disciplines, possibly achieving Krieger's earlier hope of "unifying" humanistic dis-

course. His lectures in English at UC-Irvine in fact helped attract over-
flow crowds, and crammed material usually taught over the course of ten
traditional weeks into an astoundingly short five. At the same time, the
brevity of Derrida's required stay on campus permitted him to increase the
number and frequency of his talks on national and international lecture
and conference circuits, keeping him and his deconstruction before legions of fans desirous of his textual acumen.[110] And, lastly, Derrida's tenure
guaranteed him a professional stability that he had never enjoyed at Yale.
Every academic year, de Man and Miller had trudged into the provost's
office to plead, "Could Yale please appoint [Derrida] for another year as a
'lecturer without permanent appointment' for a six week visit to give the
equivalent of a semester of graduate seminars?"[111] After de Man's death,
Miller conducted this campaign more or less singlehandedly.

When Derrida and Miller joined UC-Irvine's community of humanist
experts, their arrival strengthened the reputation of the university's English and Comp Lit Department, its School of Humanities, and its immi-
nent Critical Theory Institute. UC-Irvine's chancellor Daniel G. Aldrich
declared after Miller's hire: "With the addition of J. Hillis Miller to our
already strong program in literary criticism, our School of Humanities
will command even closer attention in academic circles."[112] "It is a ter-
rible loss for Yale," Krieger explained, "but an absolute breakthrough for
Irvine. With him and others who will follow, Irvine should be the best
place anywhere for literary criticism."[113] Other members of UC-Irvine's literature departments concurred: "As one Irvine professor (who requested
anonymity) sees it, Miller's appointment means that Irvine can now boast
of a recognized 'world-class program' in critical theory while the Yale English department will be banished to the 'dustbin of history.'"[114] Indeed,
before Michael Holquist returned to Yale in 1986, colleagues warned him
that the university "was a 'wasteland' and the Yale literary community was
'devastated.'"[115] In certain corners, there was undisguised relief that Yale's
hegemony had finally ended. Some in the younger professional cohorts
resented having been shut out of the action—jobs, prestige, funding, and
so on—and, to them, the Yale School embodied that generation of postwar critics who hogged the support for literary studies and the humanities that remained. Eager for new ideas in New Haven, others considered
deconstructionists' move to UC-Irvine as evidence that the movement
was clearly exhausted: "In retort [to the abovementioned Irvine profes-
sor], a Yale professor sniffed (likewise not for attribution): 'When we're
done with (a movement) here, it is exported to the provinces.'"[116] Soon
new protocols and expectations emerged in Yale English, Comp Lit, and
French. The Yale School disbanded; the institution of deconstruction at
UC-Irvine had begun.[117]

Cracks in the Deconstructive Bulwark

In his 1986 address as the newly elected president of the Modern Language Association, J. Hillis Miller tried to right the literary-critical ship of state, observing the recent recoil from using the science of rhetorical reading to answer the literary imperative: "Literary study in the past few years has undergone a sudden, almost universal turn away from theory in the sense of an orientation toward language as such and has made a corresponding turn toward history, culture, society, politics, institutions, class and gender conditions, the social context, the material base."[118] "How many," Miller asked the professional body, "symposia, conferences, scholarly convention sessions, courses, books and new journals have had the word *history, politics, society* or *culture* in their titles?"[119] American critics' theoretical approaches were undeniably changing and multiplying, informed by the critical vocabularies of New Historicism, Marxism, feminism, postcolonialism, and cultural materialism. Either wholly rejecting deconstruction or splitting the difference between it and sociohistorical approaches to texts, this turn from language to history without rhetoric overlapped with confused and confusing diagnoses of the contemporary academy, often made by mobilizing nationalist myths of "common sense" to defend an ostensible Anglo-American (literary) humanist heritage and tradition. Phrase-mongering by the popular press about deconstruction's part in all this muddied the waters. Even a relatively fair profile of the Yale critics in a February 1986 *New York Times Magazine* article suggested the untoward, with British Marxist critic Terry Eagleton quoted as describing "academic deconstructionists" as only "engaged [in] 'a mirror-image of orthodox academic competition.'"[120] "As for the political right," the *Times Magazine* author pronounced, "it's probably safe to say that deconstruction drives neoconservatives mad."[121] English professor Peter Shaw "roused [an] audience at New York University to lusty approval when he warned that deconstruction and other post-structuralist excesses were demolishing traditional values and meanings."[122]

Speaking different languages and operating at cross-purposes, generalist defenders of literary humanism, regularly deploying lurid turns of phrase about the looming cultural catastrophe, and politically radical advocates of sociohistorical perspectives, made for an unusual alliance against deconstructionists. Nonetheless, these strange bedfellows shared an interest in history, and this concern traversed a new concentration across the North Atlantic world on memory, place, and heritage. In 1982, American historian Yosef Yerushalmi asked why it was "that while memory of the past was always a central component of Jewish experience, the historian was not its primary custodian."[123] A year later, French historian

Pierre Nora, with the bicentennial of the French Revolution approaching, coined his concept of "lieu de mémoire," a site of memory, which became the organizing idea of his massive four-volume project on the history and culture of the French nation. Three years later, French filmmaker Claude Lanzmann released *Shoah* (1985); in this documentary about the Holocaust, the past leapt into the present through interviews with witnesses and visits to crime scenes. President Reagan's May 1985 trip to the cemetery at Bitburg, West Germany, intended to commemorate the end of World War II in Europe four decades earlier, became an explosive political event; the graveyard contained plots for members of the Waffen-SS. The following year, the *Historikerstreit*, a debate in West German newspapers set right-wing against left-wing intellectuals over the singularity and moral significance of the Holocaust and the effects of remembrance of the Nazi past on German identity.

This broad transatlantic attention to memory, place, and heritage collided with deconstruction. *L'affaire Heidegger* in France was sparked in October 1987 by the publication of Victor Farias's book, which offered readers a wealth of documentary evidence of Heidegger's engagement with the Nazi regime.[124] "Heil Heidegger!" screamed the headline in Parisian daily *Libération*, while the German social historian Hugo Ott observed: "In France a sky has fallen in—*the sky of the philosophers*."[125] The headlines and statements were sensational, but French philosophers of the 1960s, like Derrida, *had* dazzlingly repurposed German philosophical texts—from Hegel's, Marx's, and Nietzsche's to Husserl's and, yes, Heidegger's—within the discursive and institutional limitations of their own intellectual communities. It was not entirely inappropriate, then, for articles in not only *Libération* but *Le Monde* and *El Pais* to pull Derrida into the ensuing polemics. The preface to Farias's book suggested that, "for numerous scholars, [Heidegger's] thinking has *an effect of the obvious* that no other philosophy has been able to achieve in France, with the exception of Marxism. [Heidegger's] Ontology culminates in a methodical *deconstruction* of metaphysics as such."[126] Though Heidegger's philosophy was not quite as evident to the postwar generation of French scholars as Farias wished, Heidegger himself did acknowledge to a former student that his notion of historicity, which developed out of his attempt to destroy the metaphysical dichotomies that shaped historical study and which was central to his comprehensive analysis of *Dasein* in *Being and Time* (1927), formed the basis for his political commitment to the Nazi regime.[127] This fact and others seemed to validate charges that "French Heideggerians" wanted at all costs to avoid the dreadful implications that Heidegger's legitimation of Nazism had for their work. A sizable portion of American academic humanists also long harbored suspicions about

Heidegger and the Heideggerian influence, though these misgivings were partly a function of how neatly "Heidegger" fit Anglo-American preju- dices, themselves resulting from belief in the myth of a "commonsense" culture that wisely sidestepped either histrionic, irrational quests for metaphysical truths or overly technical and obscurantist language. The knee-jerk reaction to a certain German philosopher who did both found its way into the 1986 *New York Times Magazine* profile of the Yale crit- ics, where "Yale scholar-critic of 18th-century English literature and the modern novel" Martin Price flatly stated that his "gut feeling is not to trust anyone who has read Heidegger."[128]

Derrida in fact also found Heidegger suspect, yet his suspicion never resulted in complete rejection; he long read Heidegger as an intellectual progenitor who deconstructively gave with one hand what he took away with the other. In the published version of a talk he gave at a March 1987 conference in Paris that spoke to Heidegger's engagement with National Socialism, Derrida used his technique and language of deconstruction to foreground the trajectory of the word "spirit" in Heidegger's writings, showing that Heidegger, despite his intent to destroy Western metaphys- ics, reproduced metaphysics' privileging of the self-presence of mean- ing.[129] "At the moment when [Heidegger's] discourse situates itself in a spectacular fashion in the camp of Nazism," Derrida summarized in a 1987 interview, "Heidegger takes up again the word 'spirit,' whose avoidance he had prescribed [in his earlier texts]; he removes the quotation marks with which he had surrounded it. He limits the deconstructive movement that he had begun earlier. He maintains a voluntarist and metaphysical discourse upon which he will later cast suspicion."[130] In *Being and Time*, Derrida stressed, Heidegger had vigilantly bracketed the word "spirit" because he recognized that it constructed an onto-theological hierarchy between transcendent and material that he had aimed to demolish so as to unconceal Being before intellection, prior to differentiation into ontic knowledge. After he aligned himself with the Nazi cause, however, Hei- degger dropped his scare quotes, employing "spirit" to denote the will of Hitler and Hitler's alignment of the *Volk* with the truth of Being. By transforming the destruction of the ontological difference between Being and being into a project of human intention, of Hitler's and the Germans' will, Heidegger, from 1934 to 1945, voluntarily entangled himself and his philosophy in both metaphysics and National Socialism.

That Derrida's deconstruction modified Heidegger's "antihumanist" philosophy had, since the late 1970s, provided pretext for Derrida's crit- ics to paint him as morally dubious. The "nouveaux philosophes," a faction of young, fashionable, and media-savvy French intellectuals, polemically and publicly maintained that a straight line could be drawn from Western philosophical texts, especially of the Marxist-Hegelian tradition, to the Soviet gulags; for these new philosophers, the soixante-huitards, Derrida included, claimed to subvert totalizing philosophies but really legitimated them.[131] Thus, when Derrida, in the 1987 interview, explained that his goal was to undermine the metaphysical opposition between Nazism and anti-Nazism, the trap was sprung; this was damning evidence. For Derrida, though, a metaphysical (and ahistorical) manner of thinking based on the will organized liberalism as much as fascism. When Heidegger praised "the freedom of spirit" in his *rektoratsrede*, his "celebration . . . resembles other European discourses (spiritualist, religious, humanist) which are generally opposed to Nazism."[132] However much Derrida underscored the "complex and unstable knot which [he] tr[ied] to untangle by recognizing the threads common to Nazism and to anti-Nazism," his suggestion that Nazism resembled discourses that resisted Nazism added credence to accusations that his deconstructive philosophy was strictly antihumanist, with no link to and therefore no sense of social or historical responsibility.[133] Derrida asserted that he wanted to be taken as a political thinker—after decades of compulsively complicating political references in his teachings and texts—yet this was a quite difficult proposition to accept, except for those already on board.

While *l'affaire Heidegger* gave legible warning signs, Derrida and his fellow travelers in America were to be blindsided by the next hurricane of mistranslations, resentments, and moral condemnations that "history" was soon to unleash on them. In 1986, Ortwin de Graef, a doctoral student at the Katholieke Universiteit Leuven in Belgium, had stumbled upon several of young de Man's literary reviews and reports of cultural events in *Het Vlaamsche Land*, a Flemish journal founded in January 1941 that received German financial backing and was considered the unofficial organ of DeVlag, a Flemish nationalist group that collaborated with the Nazis. In articles he wrote in 1942, de Man advocated for the creation of a new Europe, defended literature as aesthetic experience, and stressed, in language that echoed that of the Nazi regime, that an artist could unearth a creative vision in "great" cultures, such as that of Germany. De Graef proposed, in November 1986, an article on his findings to *Yale French Studies*; editors never responded. Six months later, de Graef excavated more from the archives: 169 articles, with similar themes, published between December 24, 1940, and November 28, 1942, in *Le Soir*, the largest Francophone Belgian daily newspaper and, when staffed by notorious collaborationists during the war, known as *Le Soir Volé* (The stolen evening). At an August 1987 conference in Antwerp, de Graef informed Samuel Weber, a former student and colleague of de Man, and Gayatri Spivak of his discovery. Upon returning to America, Weber told Derrida. Though at first skeptical of de Graef's intent and findings, Derrida contacted the doctoral student, who, mindful that he was, in Derrida's words, "handling a dangerous and spectacular explosive," sent Derrida copies of twenty-five of de Man's overtly pro-Nazi political articles.[134]

The foundations of the American institution of deconstruction were about to shake, with pressure already mounting; from earlier self-anointed protectors of traditional literary studies to cultural conservatives, the chorus emphatically prescribing a course correction of humanities education hit its crescendo.[135] William Bennett expanded his defense of cultural hierarchies to condemn multicultural curricula, which, he argued, resulted in the "dumbing-down of America." Protecting the value-laden oppositions between high and low, Euro-American and non-Western art, Nobel Prize winner Saul Bellow testily asked in a 1988 interview: "Who is the Tolstoy of the Zulus? The Proust of the Papuans? I'd be happy to read them."[136] In a slim 1987 volume, educator E. D. Hirsch Jr. civilly maintained that a nation required a common cultural vocabulary and that public schools should teach it.[137] The same year, Allan Bloom, in a best seller, compared the intellectual culture of the failed Weimar Republic to that of the United States and maintained that the relativism of modern liberal philosophy, by freeing students from moral obligations and diminishing their minds, had ruined the university. "Comparative literature," which Bloom offered as exemplifying this unprincipled relativism, "has now fallen largely into the hands of a group of professors who are influenced by the . . . Parisian Heideggerians, in particular Derrida, Foucault, and Barthes. The school is called Deconstructionism."[138] If concerned citizens still entertained doubts about which sixties-inspired school of specialized thought was most responsible for corrupting youth and destroying humanistic education, then they weren't paying attention.

And in the coming months, the history with(out) rhetoric prompted by the discovery de Man's *Le Soir* articles verified so much of what so many long believed, for both deconstructionists and their avowed enemies. But before such corroboration, Derrida circulated copies of and guided a discussion on de Man's *Le Soir* articles at a September 1987 conference at the University of Alabama in Tuscaloosa. Friends and allies were stunned. Largely containing commentary and reviews of unexceptional books from a Nazi-certified list, de Man's *Le Soir* contributions showed signs of sympathies for Flemish national aspirations and resentment toward France's cultural hegemony. Charitably read, the young de Man—misled by the Nazis' appropriation of the "Idea of Europe" to nominally preserve national traditions under German protection—was most interested in literary aesthetics; he often focused on the orderly development of literary genres and national traditions. Yet de Man had also contributed to a full page of anti-Semitic propaganda titled "The Jews and Us: The Cultural Aspects" in the March 4, 1941, issue. His chilling article, "Les Juifs dans la littérature actuelle," denied that Jews exercised a strong influence on European civilization, claiming that foreign intrusions, including *l'ingérence sémite*, kept it uncontaminated and healthy. It would, in fact, make no difference to literature, de Man terrifyingly claimed, if the Jews were sent to a "colony" isolated from Europe. De Man's cultural program in *Le Soir* advanced a "humanism" alright, a grotesque and racist one. Some shocked conference attendees in Alabama convinced Derrida, against his inclinations, to delay publication of de Man's writings: they could not be taken at face value and needed to be carefully parsed by a deconstructionist expert.

The discovery could not be contained. By way of the telephone game and the distribution of a few xeroxed pages, the news quickly spread, sending a shudder through the professoriate. And when the front page of the *New York Times* forced the rumor to the surface on December 1, 1987—"Yale Scholar's Articles Found in Nazi Paper"—"history" came in like a wrecking ball on the entire edifice of deconstruction.[139] Certain neo-orthodox literature professors at Yale indulged in schadenfreude; most were simply aghast. What *did* that flicker in de Man's eye conceal? Was he high priest or high charlatan? Journalists wrote up salacious stories, implying that all or most of de Man's *Le Soir* articles were explicitly anti-Semitic or supported Nazi propaganda and that de Man cultivated his postmodern deconstructive expertise to avoid responsibility for his repressed past. Here, for a readership primed for at least a half decade, was the culprit, the cultural saboteur: Paul de Man, an internationalist former Nazi sympathizer from heretical Yale. His concentration on the mechanical (nonhuman) linguistic conflicts of texts destroyed our common American culture, defiling literary education, especially the kind he himself saw, he wrote in 1982, as established by the "screen of received ideas" that circulated as "humanistic knowledge" and delivered in the language of moral fury and religiosity.[140]

Angry readers yearning to identify *the* nihilistic hyperspecialist who drove humanism out of higher education and demonstrate where the academization of literary studies had finally led need to have looked no further than a January 9, 1988, article in the *Nation* by Jon Wiener, a professor of American history at UC-Irvine.[141] Wiener cast de Man as "an academic Waldheim," referring to former secretary general of the United Nations Kurt Waldheim, whose service in the Wehrmacht had similarly been unearthed.[142] What's more, Wiener intimated, de Man's friends and allies appeared to have more to hide, as the delayed publication of de Man's articles and the editorial decision by deconstructionists to leave many untranslated were "an exercise in 'damage control.'"[143] For the sake of history and the humanities, Wiener implied, deconstructionists should be held publicly accountable. (Wiener also drew attention to the fact that de Man had brought German literary historian and theorist Hans Robert Jauss, who "is now known to have served in the SS," to Yale as a guest lecturer in the mid-1970s.)[144] American poet David Lehman, in a February 15, 1988, article in *Newsweek*, followed suit, reporting that "de Man expressed a virulent strain of anti-Semitism" in his wartime articles, that "deconstruction" was "hostile to the very principles of Western thought," and that "one Ivy League professor gleefully exclaim[ed], 'deconstruction turned out to be the thousand-year Reich that lasted 12 years.'"[145] Lehman's article also included a photo of de Man alongside a photo of marching Nazi stormtroopers. The danger that deconstructionists posed for humanity and the humanities was obvious.

Many on the inside of the deconstructive linguistic community viewed these swift condemnations as part of an extensive, multipronged metaphysical resistance to the desacralizing efforts of deconstruction. In a March 1988 letter to UC-Irvine colleagues, J. Hillis Miller explained his belief that newspaper and magazine articles' "real target" was not "de Man's early writings or his personality, but the type of work with which his name is associated, that is, so-called 'deconstruction,' and, beyond that, literary theory generally."[146] For Miller, it was not merely that the often-made accusations that deconstruction and literary theory caused the "crisis of the humanities" set the stage for the hostility toward de Man. No, these charges against de Man were made on behalf of the broader onto-theological opposition to the subversive effects of much advanced humanities work, work often undertaken by literary theorists and critics and the academic left, work that de Man the rigorous rhetorical reader had become a symbol of. Whether or not one accepts Miller's interpretation, the ease with which de Man and deconstruction were portrayed as enemies of "Western civilization" and the literary humanism that was to protect such a cultural heritage (now flushed out of the ivory tower) was surely in part due to deconstructionists' refusal, as Edward Said noted to *Newsweek*, to summarize the meaning of deconstruction or de Man's wartime articles. Werner Hamacher of Johns Hopkins flatly stated to Wiener: "I don't think this is a matter for journalists and newspapers."[147] Alice Kaplan, Professor of French at Yale, later recalled: "The de Manians said: 'This is a non-event; the revelation is a pure rhetorical construction, perpetrated by the media.'"[148] Yes, this *was* an institution trained to enjoy—with *jouissance*—spending a week rhetorically reading one sentence; one could imagine them spending a year on one of de Man's *Le Soir* articles. Regardless, dyed-in-the-wool deconstructionists' commitment to using their specialized vocabulary made translators of their critical projects sorely needed and sorely absent after the *New York Times* broke the news. Lacking those translations, popular publications had a field day, portraying the writings of de Man and anyone linked to him as they wished.

In fact, if not for de Man's reputation and influence among the highly specialized sector of the American academic humanistic workforce devoted to literary theory, his wartime articles might have come to light years before. Georges Poulet, a colleague of J. Hillis Miller's at Hopkins in the mid-1950s and of de Man's at the University of Zürich during the 1960s, was brother to Robert Poulet, a Belgian collaborator whose death sentence, in 1945, was commuted to exile. Georges likely knew about de Man's collaboration and could have raised the subject to American colleagues.[149] And, amazingly, in 1982, while conducting research for his book *Les métamorphoses de Tintin* (1984) on Hergé, another Belgian who wrote for *Le Soir Volé*, Jean-Marie Apostolidès, professor of French literature at Stanford University, discovered copies of de Man's articles in Harvard's Widener library. Apostolidès saw de Man as "a secondary figure in literary criticism and contemporary thought," but shared his findings with Jeffrey Mehlman, who earned his PhD from Yale French and worked with de Man in the early 1970s.[150] Mehlman straightaway comprehended the implications of Apostolidès's discovery and encouraged him to publish something on them. Not wondering about the reasons for Mehlman's reluctance to reveal de Man's writings himself—Mehlman had a complex connection to the institution of deconstruction—Apostolidès then mentioned the articles to Barbara Johnson. According to Apostolidès, though, "she paid little attention: history didn't interest her."[151] That Johnson and allies, even wavering ones like Mehlman, shunned the existence of de Man's articles indicates how much their "antihistorical" deconstructive disposition—their privileging of literary language as prior to and essential to (historical) discourse—facilitated de Man's "concealment" of his past. For, in America, de Man was tight-lipped, never offering any information on his Belgian life, and, in several instances, misled or lied when given the opportunity. His former Cornell student Juliet Flower MacCannell asked de Man what he "did during the war," and he answered, she told *Newsweek*, that he "went to England and worked as a translator."[152] When Thomas Keenan, a graduate student of de Man's at Yale, requested from de Man a complete list of his published works, de Man claimed he had a bad memory and had forgotten all that he wrote. When Geoffrey Hartman asked him why his bibliography listed "no significant essay before 1953," de Man tersely replied: "Nothing but journalism."[153]

De Man's pattern of evasion assumed a slightly different shape with Derrida, possibly owing to the nature of their intellectual friendship, in which they both spoke slightly different dialects of the deconstructive language and each saw the other as a true equal. During a conversation in the late 1970s, de Man hinted to Derrida that the protagonist in Henri Thomas's novel *Le Parjure* (1964)—initially titled *Hölderlin in America*—was modeled on him. "It's less flattering," de Man said of that original title in a 1977 letter to Derrida, "but much more truthful."[154] Intrigued at the suggestion that de Man was a "poet of the gods" in America, Derrida, in the spring of 1981, read *Le Parjure* and quickly wrote to de Man about Thomas's roman à clef: "I can't tell you any more, but all the same I can't remain silent about the fact that reading *The Liar* . . . has made a great impression on me, even overwhelmed me, has in any case roused deep echoes in me, 'unheimlich,' in other words with and without surprise. But I'm already saying too much."[155] Though de Man, as Derrida's biographer has noted, seems to have never replied to Derrida's letter, he did mention to Derrida that he perceived how much unstated autobiographical issues shaped Derrida's *Glas* (1974) and *The Post Card* (1980). Those two books, broadly received upon their translations into English as examples of Derrida's focus on a text's "literary practice," were allusively written with personal references and textual games that subverted the metaphysical fiction/fact opposition. "There are some books by you," Derrida recalled de Man telling him, "that I don't want to discuss with you. I won't even mention them to you."[156] Was this de Man's way of saying that he wanted to discuss neither the tacit autobiographical nature of Derrida's texts nor how his own personal history seeped into his writings? Whatever the answer to that question, a writer-journalist in August 1988 would unearth yet more about de Man's sordid past that mirrored the plot of Thomas's novel. Like Stéphane Chalier, *Le Parjure*'s main character, de Man was at one point bigamous (in 1948 he abandoned his first wife and two children in Europe), conducted questionable business practices (he borrowed and never repaid money to start a fine art book series, bankrupting his extended family), and was a petty liar and cheat (he failed to pay for an apartment he rented in 1953 while teaching at Bard College).[157] After de Graef's discovery, de Man's friends and colleagues as much as his skeptics justifiably asked the same question that Chalier coyly asked readers: "*What was known about his years before America?*"[158]

Despite de Man's evasions and allusions, his past was not very difficult to determine. Born on December 6, 1919, to a prosperous and well-connected family that was patriotically Flemish but also cosmopolitan, Paul Adolph Michel de Man was the nephew of Hendrik de Man, who had once led the Belgian Workers' Party. In 1983, de Man's onetime student Stanley Corngold, professor of German and comp lit at Princeton University, observed (in a footnote) that Hendrik de Man had "retired from public life" in 1941 after deciding "that the Socialist movement unavoidably participated in the decadence of the capitalist world order, and the best the responsible individual could do was cultivate his garden."[159] But that was not nearly the extent of Hendrik de Man's "intellectually and politically picaresque career," as Barbara Johnson later put it.[160] Hendrik had become a star among socialists after the publication of his 1927 book in which he argued against Marxist orthodoxy, which stressed the economic determination of ideas, that socialism must grapple with individuals' philosophies and goals as well as the cultural and sociopolitical differences that divided nations. Hendrik's celebrity, however, could not prevent the disillusionment and policy delays that marked his political fortunes as a Belgian government minister. Following the German invasion of Belgium in May 1940, Hendrik issued a "Manifesto" that dissolved the BWP and encouraged members to peacefully surrender and accommodate Hitler's policies. Nazism, he hoped, might evolve into true National Socialism. When Belgian ministers fled to establish a government in exile, Hendrik became de facto prime minister and advised, in June 1940, King Leopold III and his fellow Belgians that "for the working classes and for socialism, this collapse of a decrepit world is, far from a disaster, a deliverance."[161] Yet Flemish Nazi collaborators and the Nazi authorities quickly came to distrust the nonconformist Hendrik, banning him from giving public speeches after Easter 1941. He spent the next years in Paris, fleeing to Switzerland when the Allies invaded Normandy. In 1946, a Belgian military tribunal convicted Hendrik in absentia of treason. Seven years later, Hendrik, in exile, was killed in his car by a train; his son believed it suicide.

The chronicle of Paul de Man's Belgian life was relatively straightforward, yet still raised countless questions. Why collaborate? What was Hendrik's role? How did de Man's wartime experiences relate to his postwar existence and writings? The *capo di tutti capi* of the Hermeneutical Mafia left little to help answer these questions. Alice Kaplan reflected in 1993 that "everyone at Yale knew" about de Man's uncle and believed that Paul "had freed himself from an embarrassing episode of family history . . . by coming to the United States."[162] If that was the case, then did *Yale* prevent the outing of de Man's "open secret"? There *were* occasions when de Man alluded to his uncle's crime and fate. In the early 1980s, comp lit professor Dan Latimer mentioned to de Man that, "if one considered the historical context and the tragic pressures to which Hendrik de Man was subjected, one would see how utterly facile it is now to condemn him from our safe historical vantage-point." "To this," Latimer recalled, "de Man replied: 'He had plenty to be ashamed of, all right.'"[163] Just what de Man meant was unclear, never forthright about his past, even with Derrida.

And yet it was to the philosopher that the agony of responding to "Paul de Man's War" now so publicly and painfully fell.[164]

The Necessary Discord of Deconstruction

Whatever Derrida wrote in his spring 1988 *Critical Inquiry* seventy-two-page cri de coeur would garner attention, with elated enemies on all sides, and charges against deconstruction of nihilism, antihumanism, authoritarianism, and, of course, Nazism hanging in the air. Derrida understandably felt besieged, but his practiced mode of giving (deconstructively) complex answers to questions about "deconstruction in America," his work's relation to that of his friend de Man's, and Heidegger's entanglement with Nazism did not help his cause; Derrida never provided the clarity that readers needed in order to receive his response in *Critical Inquiry* without prejudice. And from the perspective of nondeconstructionists who conceived of history without rhetoric, Derrida's interpretations of de Man's postwar silence about his past as virtuous and his wartime articles as subversive of Nazi ideology simply confirmed that Derrida and deconstruction in toto were incapable of dealing with history as such, history qua history. However, this understanding of Derrida's reading of de Man's "war" in part mistranslated Derrida's reading of what were for him the historical conflicts of de Man's life and work. Derrida's deconstructive response to literature was only an idiom of his more fundamental concentration on the deconstruction of the onto-theological opposition between temporality and historicity. The reception of Derrida's work in the United States, though, tended to overlook how this key ingredient made his deconstruction differ from the other dialects spoken in the American institution of deconstruction; they ranged from Bloom's psychoanalytically informed attention to rhetorical refractions to Felman's rhetoricization of Lacan's psychoanalytic theories to de Man's ascetic concentration on texts' rhetorical dimensions. Nonspecialists heard only one deconstructive language, and that added yet another confusing element to the entire de Man Affair. Derrida's deconstructive narrative of de Man's "war" in his *Critical Inquiry* article provoked calls for nonrhetorical interpretations of de Man's writings and his life story. And Derrida's highly personal deconstructions of de Man beckoned yet more controversy. Persuading nonrhetorical readers? Derrida never stood much of a chance.

His prose style was somewhat to blame. As in his 1984 tribute to de Man, Derrida only obliquely explained that he was writing a deconstructive history. "Why," Derrida asked at the start of his essay, "do I now underscore that expression: *what is happening*? Because for me [the "revelation" about de Man] belongs to the order of the absolutely unforeseeable, which is always the condition of any event. Even when it seems to go back to a buried past, what comes about always comes from the future."[165] For Derrida, the apparent re-presentation of the past was a metaphysical illusion, and this illusion of presence, of access to a transcendental signified, masked the deferred and differentiated traces that constituted the past. In contrast, Derrida's future-oriented deconstructive history aimed to subvert metaphysics' privileging of the present, a valorization that constructed hierarchical oppositions that readers used to erase the conflicts of de Man's life and work. In fact, Derrida explained later in his essay, de Man himself had warned against the metaphysical confidences of "history." Derrida reported that, in his 1978 reading of Shelley's *The Triumph of Life*, de Man claimed that "reading as disfiguration, to the very extent that it resists [metaphysical] historicism, turns out to be historically more reliable than the products of historical archeology" and cautioned against "nihilistic allegories" that reduced "what 'always again demands to be read.'"[166] For Derrida, de Man's rhetorical readings of Shelley (and Rousseau) provided examples of how to deconstructively interpret de Man, A to Z. But to the unversed or unsympathetic, Derrida's opening section likely only seemed to prepare the way for the delivery of an anti-historical and exculpatory reading of de Man.

Derrida first composed his deconstructive narrative with de Man's thirty-five years of postwar silence. Derrida was unaware, he wrote, of the "dark time spent between 1940–42 by the Paul de Man [he] later read, knew, admired, loved."[167] In keeping with his commitment to undermine ahistorical metaphysical illusions of presence, however, Derrida highlighted evidence to subvert the onto-theological dualism between de Man's silence and the ways de Man could be read as having openly spoken about his past. De Man's silence "was not absolute," Derrida wrote, but "publicly broken on at least one occasion."[168] With a long quote from his taped remarks given in September in Tuscaloosa, Derrida explained: "In 1955, while de Man was at Harvard, there was an anonymous denunciation concerning his activity in Belgium during the war. And de Man explained himself at that moment, in a letter . . . to [Harvard's] Head of the Society of Fellows."[169] In it, de Man clarified that, "during the German occupation, in 1940–42, he maintained a literary column, but when the pressure of German censorship became too much . . . he ceased writing and did what decency demanded that he do."[170] Thus, Derrida claimed, de Man's silence "cannot be understood in the sense of a dissimulation."[171] Having posited a dichotomy between de Man's total silence and his open acknowledgment of his wartime activities, though, Derrida then offered a third interpretive option that historically disrupted that ahistorical opposition: de

Man, Derrida suggested, *did* speak to him about his wartime activities, but implicitly, indirectly: "At moments I say to myself: he supposed perhaps that I knew . . . And perhaps in effect I did know it in an obscure way."[172] According to Derrida, de Man's postwar writings were the best place to hear de Man's thoughts about his wartime activities and his struggle with his decision to stay silent. "He did the right thing," Derrida concluded, "by leaving us . . . an ordeal, the summons to a work of reading."[173] For Derrida, his and others' historical obligation was to write a deconstructive history that subverted the metaphysical faith in the re-presentation of the past, "interminabl[y]" producing conflicting readings of de Man's decades of silence and of his writings, with their concealed commentary.[174]

The American reception of Derrida's deconstruction prepared a discursive machine through which his interpretation of de Man's silence was fed. Ready to see deconstruction as a reading method that separated the text from context and history, many *Critical Inquiry* respondents read Derrida's deconstructive article as a transparent defense of de Man. In his *Critical Inquiry* response to Derrida, Cornell professor of German W. Wolfgang Holdheim, who spent the years of the German occupation in the Low Countries, argued that Derrida's "comments on de Man's persistent silence about his past" were "implausible and self-defeating"; Derrida, Holdheim wrote, "manage[d] to interpret de Man's silence as a virtue and a necessity."[175] Jon Wiener concurred, suggesting in his *Critical Inquiry* article that Derrida's explanation dismissed his friend's questionable behavior. "One of [de Man's] students," Wiener wrote, "reported that when asked about his past, de Man lied. Derrida was aware of this evidence when he wrote his essay" but ignored it.[176] And, Wiener maintained, Derrida's suggestion that "de Man 'did the right thing' when he hid the truth about his past" was "a morally bankrupt argument," "minimiz[ing] the extent of the problem de Man's actions pose."[177] In the eyes of Wiener and others, de Man's 1955 letter to Harvard administrators downplayed his involvement with *Le Soir* and conveniently passed over his work for *Het Vlaamsche Land* and *Bibliographie Deschenne*, the bulletin of a publishing house also under German control that he wrote for until March 1943. Moreover, de Man's Harvard letter that Derrida claimed at Tuscaloosa was a "public act" was really private, likely seen only by the director of the Society of Fellows.[178] "If Paul de Man had wanted to," Wiener argued, "he could have found a way during his adult life to explain what he had done and what he thought about it."[179] Deaf to Derrida's reading of de Man's public silence as a responsible deconstructive act, respondents heard only an unethical denial, a brazen attempt to protect a dead friend.

While Derrida's deconstructive narrative of de Man's silence was controversial, his deconstruction of de Man's *Le Soir* articles—especially de Man's chilling "Les Juifs dans la littérature actuelle"—would prove his most scandalous. Derrida conceded that de Man's *Le Soir* articles were clearly full of repugnant passages trafficking in racist and nationalist stereotypes, and therefore aligned and complicit with the official discourse of the German occupation: *"On the one hand*, [the] . . . *dominant* effect [of "Les Juifs" went] unquestionably in the direction of the worst."[180] De Man "describes the traits of what . . . are 'degenerate and decadent, because enjuivés ["enjewished"]' cultural phenomena . . . ; he mentions the 'important role' that the Jews have played in 'the phony and disordered existence of Europe since 1920.' He has recourse . . . to the stereotypical description of the 'Jewish spirit': 'cerebralness,' 'capacity for assimilating doctrines while maintaining a certain coldness in the face of them.' He notes that 'Jewish writers have always remained in the second rank.'"[181] Derrida also agonizingly highlighted de Man's "solution to the Jewish problem": "the creation of a Jewish colony isolated from Europe."[182]

But to write his deconstructive history, Derrida expertly extracted evidence from de Man's text that clashed with this text's apparent representation of the past. *"On the other hand* and *first of all*," Derrida stressed, "the primary, declared, and underscored intention" of "Les Juifs" was "an indictment of 'vulgar anti-Semitism.'"[183] Though "condemn[ing] vulgar antisemitism may leave one to understand that there is a distinguished antisemitism in whose name the vulgar variety is put down," de Man did not make this claim.[184] Consequently, Derrida underscored, "the phrase can also mean something else, and this reading can always contaminate the other in a clandestine fashion: to condemn 'vulgar antisemitism,' *especially if one makes no mention of the other kind,* is to condemn antisemitism itself *inasmuch as* it is vulgar, always and essentially vulgar."[185] For Derrida, the seeming implausibility of this second reading of "vulgar antisemitism" resulted from the value-laden hierarchy constructed by metaphysics' privileging of the self-presence of meaning and repression of deviant, aberrant meanings. But for Derrida, being a responsible and historically minded reader required identification of the repressed meaning of de Man's thesis against "vulgar antisemitism." "One ought not," Derrida insisted, "condemn these sentences . . . without examining everything that remains readable in a text one can judge to be disastrous." Thus, Derrida mined de Man's article for counterarguments against the official ideology of the German occupation. "It is not," he wrote, "particularly conformist to denounce anti-Semitism . . . at that moment, in that place."[186] "If de Man's article is necessarily contaminated by the forms of vulgar antisemitism that frame it [de Man's text was surrounded on the *Le Soir* page by anti-Semitic articles], *these coincide . . . in their vocabulary and logic . . .*

with the very thing that de Man accuses, as if his article were denouncing the neighboring articles."[187] While the last paragraph, "the only one that can be suspected of antisemitism," could have been doctored by editorial interference, Derrida's anti-anti-Semitic de Man had the courage to suggest that "Gide, Kafka, Lawrence, Hemingway, surrealism, futurism" were "already canonical: they belong to tradition, they have 'orthodox ancestors.'"[188] By placing these authors firmly inside the European tradition, Derrida's deconstructive de Man "reinscribes all of these 'accursed ones' in the then protective legitimacy of the canon and in the great literary family," mocking, in that ironic manner peculiar to de Man, the authorized language of the German occupation that cast these modernist writers and artists as "Degenerate Art."[189] For Derrida, then, the reader who possessed courage—the daring, the skill, the "cerebralness" that de Man ascribed to the "Jewish Spirit" in his article—might deconstructively respond to de Man's text's undermining of the metaphysical illusion of the past's representation to foreground de Man's article as an anticonformist "war" against the disturbing background that de Man was hired to endorse.[190]

It's worth mentioning here that Derrida (and later several other allies) neglected to engage de Man's *second* anti-Semitic article: "Blik op de huidige Duitse Roman Literatuur," published on August 20, 1942, in *Het Vlaamsche Land*.[191] In this essay, which appeared over a year following his anti-Semitic *Le Soir* article and fifteen days after the first train of Belgian Jews arrived at Auschwitz, de Man postulated a split in German literature, one that any novice deconstructionist would recognize as a violent hierarchical opposition, into two cultural groups. By producing a cerebral art, a "forced, caricatured representation of reality," based on "abstract principles," de Man proclaimed, the first group was in "an open conflict with the proper traditions of German art."[192] De Man branded the first faction as an "aberrant fashion," as "ontaarding," a Dutch translation of the German "*Entartung*," a word reserved for degenerate art and largely identified with non-Aryans.[193] "Mainly non-Germans, and in specific Jews," de Man wrote, "went in this direction."[194] De Man's second cultural group, primarily Germans and their Belgian supporters, upheld the proper character of German art. The existence of this article problematized the singular example that de Man's colleagues often used—Hartman would write of "an anti-Semitic piece," the "one" article that "engaged explicitly with the ideology of anti-Semitism."[195] To be fair, Derrida was unaware of de Man's second anti-Semitic article when he wrote his *Critical Inquiry* essay, but he did not take the opportunity to revise his deconstructive history for publication in *Responses* (1989), a volume of essays devoted to de Man's wartime writings. In 1990, Derrida even pondered whether he was "right" to suggest that de Man's *Le Soir* article was "unforgivable."[196]

For nonrhetorical readers of Derrida's 1988 interpretation of de Man, the American institution of deconstruction had cracked under the weight of history. Willing to protect de Man at any cost, Derrida spoke the language of excuse, with manipulative wordplay that proved the anti-historical nature of deconstruction. In their joint *Critical Inquiry* response, professor of American literature John Brenkman—who, in 1979, revised Derridean and de Manian deconstruction on Marxist and psychological grounds—and professor of English Jules David Law saw Derrida's readings of de Man's *Le Soir* articles, especially "Les Juifs," as preposterous.[197] "Try as he can," Brenkman and Law wrote, "Derrida cannot make de Man's first two paragraphs," which contain de Man's thesis against "vulgar anti-semitism," "sound anything more than ambiguous at best."[198] And Derrida's application of his second reading of de Man's thesis to the remaining paragraphs of "Les Juifs" was a "blatant misreading" which ignored—and here the pull of history without rhetoric exerted itself—that "the controlling paragraph . . . is more plausibly the final one" which "envision[ed] the forced removal of Jews from Europe."[199] Holdheim agreed, arguing that universal solvent Derrida "ma[de] the text say something other than what it says" by "employ[ing] . . . the age-old salami technique, which consists in cutting off slice after slice until the sausage has totally disappeared."[200] For respondents, then, Derrida couldn't pun his way out of de Man's articles' correspondence with their principal historical context; only a perverse reading could turn de Man's complicity into a resistance to all notions of anti-Semitism. Further, as commentators stressed, de Man's first *Le Soir* article appeared approximately two months after the German military command in Belgium outlawed all Jews from civil service. Though it is possible that de Man, following his uncle's directives, embraced fascism because he could reconcile his elitism and "refined antisemitism" with Nazi dogma, he appeared to have ignored the Nazis' crimes for a paycheck and the requirements of fatherhood (his articles appeared almost a month before the birth of his first son, Hendrik).[201]

Of course, a decoder ring for nondeconstructive readers of Derrida's *Critical Inquiry* article never materialized during the de Man Affair. Either unable or unwilling to see the different shades of deconstruction, respondents could decipher neither when Derrida deviated from his own typical deconstruction nor how his deconstruction differed from de Man's.[202] Derrida's reading of "Paul de Man's War" actually diverged from his own canonical statements in the late 1960s and early 1970s about what his deconstructive reading practice entailed. Orthodox Derrida, for example, would have generated some third interpretive route—such as a neologism—that straddled and therefore undermined the metaphysical binary between de Man's collaboration with and courageous defiance of

Nazi ideology. Derrida instead left readers with a sort of de Manian "undecidable": two incompatible readings that subverted each other. Unlike de Man might have, however, Derrida did not attribute de Man's wartime texts to the mechanical operations of language but to de Man the person, albeit a Derridean deconstructive notion of personhood. Also distinct from de Man's rhetorical reading was that Derrida linked and then undermined the "inner" text to the "outer" (con)text. For Derrida, de Man's texts' "internal" contradictions depended on accounting for the "external" dominant "extra"-textual milieu, with both being parts of the general text that composed the world. Respondents' claims that Derrida used an interpretive strategy at odds with what they understood as deconstruction was accurate—"Derrida's appeal to context and to authorial intention," Wiener wrote, "constitutes an abandonment of the deconstructive method"— but for the wrong reasons.[203] It was in fact de Man who had argued that the use of sociohistorical references distracted readers from the difficult labor of rhetorically responding to the literary imperative.

Though speaking the same specialized lexicon, deconstructionists also seemed to not notice, or at least tactfully passed over, Derrida's methodological departure. They instead expressed a range of responses to Derrida's reading of de Man's *Le Soir* articles, making Derrida's attempt to employ his deconstructive history to set the parameters for interpreting de Man not wholly successful. J. Hillis Miller, like Derrida, rhetorically engaged de Man's *Le Soir* articles, detecting traces in these texts of the ironic teacher, reader, and friend he knew. "I do think," he wrote, "it is a case of 'one [*sic*] the one hand,' and on the other. . . . In fact [he] in subtle and not so subtle [ways] attacks the Nazi line consistently, however ineffectively."[204] Rather surprisingly, though, a number of deconstructionists implicitly employed history without rhetoric to interpret Derrida's reading of de Man as having snuck ideological contraband into *Le Soir*'s pages. For them, the dominant context of de Man's writings rendered Derrida's interpretation unpersuasive. In an open letter to Derrida published in 1990, David Carroll, one of Derrida's earliest supporters in America, wondered why Derrida "assume[d] the worst of what [de Man] had written and in a sense assume[d] responsibility for it."[205] Carroll explained to Derrida: "I admire the courage of your text, the risks you took in it," but "you deemphasize, cover over, even smother, the worst aspects of [de Man's anti-Semitic] article, the very things you have admitted are 'disastrous' and 'unbearable.'"[206] Derrida believed Carroll "incapable of reading him," and their friendship soured for a time.[207] Others in the deconstructive discursive community cautiously disagreed with Derrida. In a February 1988 letter to the *London Review of Books*, Christopher Norris wrote: "It may be overgenerous to suggest, as some have done, that de Man was conduct-

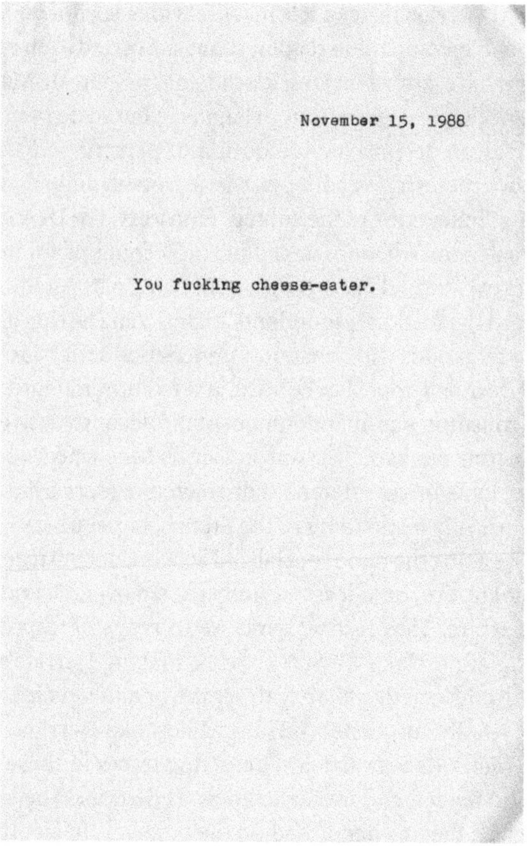

November 15, 1988

You fucking cheese-eater.

FIGURE 5.2 An anonymous note sent to J. Hillis Miller during the de Man Affair (Courtesy of J. Hillis Miller)

ing a kind of cryptic resistance campaign through these writings."[208] In 1989, Barbara Johnson found no relief in Derrida's argument that "de Man wants especially to propose a thesis on literature [in his most disturbing *Le Soir* article] that visibly interests him more . . . than either anti-Semitism or the Jews." "If there had not been people who, without any particular personal anti-Semitism, found the idea of deportation *reasonable*, there could have been no Holocaust," Johnson concluded.[209] Even if he snuck subversive messages into his article, even if he was more concerned with advancing a thesis about literature as Derrida argued, de Man gave voice to the Nazis' eliminationist program. De Man's ironically delivered dissident message served the Nazi regime.

Some deconstructionists sympathetically listened to Derrida's deconstructions of de Man; they agreed that de Man ought not be put on trial in absentia and understood and appreciated that Derrida aimed to intervene in explosive conversations about his friend. Yet like most nonrhetorical readers, many deconstructionists seem to have missed the degree to which Derrida wrote his deconstructive history to respond not only to the supposed re-presentation of the past but also "the present": fellow academics who had either acted as or combined forces with journalists to dismiss de Man and deconstruction. While the scandal was breaking, in fact, Derrida encouraged fellow deconstructionists to contest the incendiary charges and circulated a petition against the press coverage. As he indirectly explained in his *Critical Inquiry* article, for Derrida, the metaphysics of presence attempted to reduce de Man to one meaning, because it required readers to identify, expel, and then move on from what threatened metaphysics: de Man and deconstruction. That Derrida's reading of de Man deconstructively intervened in "the present" explains why Derrida railed against "the sensationalist flurry of hatred" in the *New York Times* and criticized Jon Wiener for his "stream of calumny or slanderous insinuation" about de Man and "deconstruction and its 'politics'" in the *Nation*.[210] Hence, too, Derrida's—seemingly unhinged—drawing of an equivalence between hostile critics of de Man and the Nazis: "To judge, to condemn the work of the man on the basis of what was a brief episode, to call for . . . censuring or burning his books is to reproduce the exterminating gesture."[211] By deconstructively reading Western metaphysics' control of the text, Derrida suggested, readers could "avoid reproducing . . . the *logic* of the discourse thus incriminated."[212] In part due to the confusion about the differences between Derrida's anti-metaphysical project and de Man's science of rhetorical reading, however, *Critical Inquiry* respondents read Derrida's "rules" for reading de Man—guidelines that more or less advocated the adoption of Derrida's deconstructive stance—as established out of blind loyalty to his friend. Derrida's outrageous demands, again, demonstrated to nondeconstructionists that the purported rigor of deconstruction, once confronted with base reality (history without rhetoric), collapsed into willful manipulation. Derrida was seen as simply protecting *his* "present": his intellectual empire.

Not unlike nonrhetorical readers, several prominent deconstructionists themselves did not deconstructively historicize the present, instead writing conversion narratives of de Man's pre- and postwar life and work. These narratives also failed to heed Derrida's "rules" for reading de Man, "rules" that called for deconstructively responding to any account of de Man's political conversion. Derrida, for instance, had warned against claiming either "everything derives from" the "early writings" or that there was "no relation, [a] sealed frontier between . . . the two moments of de Man's history and work";[213] the former constructed a hierarchy that reduced de Man to his collaboration, while the latter erected an opposition of or separation between de Man's pre- and postwar lives and words. Governed by metaphysical dualisms, these interpretations, for Derrida, ignored how, after de Man broke "with his past of 1940–42," he "never ceased reflecting on and interpreting this past," a self-reflexive reading that "proceeded with other *ruptures, divergences, displacements.*"[214] Derrida wanted others to institute a sound deconstructive history that stressed the differences and dislocations of "the present," not the binary oppositions upon which conversion narratives are based.

In a February 1988 essay, Christopher Norris, who recently completed a manuscript on de Man's political relevance, proposed that de Man developed a form of ideology critique in his postwar work that unmasked the dangers posed by the philosophy of language, custom, and organic national culture that he endorsed in his collaborationist articles. While cautioning against narratives that present a total and thus metaphysical vision of de Man's life and work, Norris's story was, still, one of conversion: horrified at the mistakes of his youth, de Man progressively worked from writing apolitical essays of the 1950s and 1960s—essays that engagé critics like Frank Lentricchia felt were heavily stacked against Marxist readings of texts—to his last essays on how a text's rhetorical elements subverted the symbolist aesthetics that underwrote philosophical systems and inspired literary nationalisms, the most extreme form of which was Nazis' cultural program; Joseph Goebbels saw politics as the ultimate art form, the symbol of the German nation, for example. The author de Man most opposed with his pedagogical-intellectual project in America, Norris concluded, was none other than his former self.[215] In a similar vein, Werner Hamacher, in a February 1988 article, submitted that de Man's postwar essays were a "*Trauerarbeit,*" a "work of mourning," a term used during the "*Historikerstreit*" in West Germany to denote the process of coming to terms with the Nazi past.[216] And Jonathan Culler suggested in his response to Derrida's essay, the only one Derrida felt "an honest reading," that "de Man's critique of the aesthetic ideology now resonates also as a critique of the fascist tendencies he had known."[217]

That deconstructionists viewed de Man's late work as an authoritative analysis of the dangers of intertwining politics and aesthetics illustrates an effect that the academization of literary studies had on American intellectual life. Lindsay Waters, de Man's editor at the University of Minnesota Press, suggested that "many of de Man's students" were attracted to de Man because "his thought [w]as a meditation on, around, and about literature and politics."[218] But de Man's politics were unintelligible to the engaged yet nonspecialized reader who upon hearing that de Man's late work was a political endeavor might have brandished a Marxist pamphlet or a midcentury essay by the New York Intellectuals as better examples of work that trenchantly analyzed the link between literature and politics. De Man himself in fact apparently enjoyed his reputation of being apolitical. The Yale community, Alice Kaplan recalled, believed "the pure intellectual had found his true home in the American University, where parties and politics didn't matter."[219] On the other hand, in addition to unfinished articles on Marx, Adorno, Althusser, and other Marxist thinkers as well as his series of seminars on aesthetic theory at Yale and the SCT, de Man certainly offered evidence, not so much of conversion as of development: "I don't think I ever was away from [political and ideological] problems, but they were always uppermost in my mind," he explained in a late interview. "I was able to progress from purely linguistic analysis to questions which are really already of a political and ideological nature. So that now I feel to do it a little more openly, though in a very different way than what generally passes as 'critique of ideology.'"[220] While the political valence of de Man's 1970s and early 1980s rhetorical readings was perhaps legible after the revelations, nondeconstructionists wondered most about de Man's 1950s and 1960s writings, which used the thematic vocabulary of consciousness and temporality to develop ways of reading literature as critiques of metaphysical truths and ideals. Was de Man silent about his work's political character and its relationship to his collaboration because, as Derrida submitted, de Man "chose not to take it on himself to provoke, during his life, this spectacular and painful discussion?"[221] To what extent was this discussion potentially excruciating and of an enormous magnitude partly because it would have prompted a collision between academics and nonacademics, specialists and nonspecialists, views of the relationship between politics and aesthetics?

Though not alone in translating his interpretation for a broader audience, Geoffrey Hartman perhaps most proficiently and most visibly undermined received wisdom about his friend's politics. In a March 1988 *New Republic* article, Hartman, like Norris, suggested that de Man over time grasped the nature of his errors.[222] Speaking with authority as a friend, a professional, and a refugee from Europe, Hartman argued that de Man's "turn from the politics of culture [in his wartime pieces] to the language of art [in his postwar literary criticisms] was not an escape into, but an escape out of, aestheticism: a disenchantment with that fatal aestheticizing [onto-theologizing] of politics, blatant in his own early writings, that gave fascism its false brilliance."[223] For example, when de Man in a 1983 lecture spoke of "killing the original" and "of the essential failure" of translation—a synonym for conversion—Hartman maintained that he was referring to the "mediated and compromised idiom of his early, journalistic writings."[224] "In light of what we now know, [de Man's] [mature] work appears more and more as a deepening reflection on the rhetoric of totalitarianism."[225] Even de Man's insistence on the impersonal operations of language, Hartman argued, implied that de Man considered his political error universal and therefore potentially repeatable, by anyone anywhere and anytime. In a fashion he admitted was foreign to de Man but characteristic of his lifelong interest in psychology, Hartman concluded that "de Man's critique of every tendency to totalize literature or language, to see unity where there is no unity, looks like a belated, but still powerful, act of conscience."[226]

Like Hartman, Miller considered de Man and the time that the friends spent together in a nonrhetorical manner, and, like Hartman, Miller's reflections illuminate how the de Man Affair might have been a tempest in a postmodern teapot for nonacademics, but for either members or opponents of the American institution of deconstruction it was of the highest political import. In a 1988 open letter to Jon Wiener that aligned to an extent with Derrida's "rule" for interpreting de Man, Miller reflected that, after "reading these newly discovered 'early writings,'" he understood what was "potentially at stake politically in what might appear to be merely 'academic' questions." Miller recalled "the urgency with which de Man advised me, the first time we met, in 1966 [sic], not to read the later Heidegger but to go back to *Sein und Zeit* [*Being and Time*] . . . , or the equal urgency with which he vigorously put in question, at a conference that took place in Zürich about 1969 [sic], some ideas I proposed in a paper about the organic development of the novel toward greater and greater sophistication and complexity."[227] For Miller, de Man's advice—steer clear of later Heidegger, who succumbed to metaphysical readings of poets; beware the philosophy of organicism, in which art over time accumulated cultural and transcendent truths—did not simply reflect de Man's personal preferences or theoretical interests. De Man's advice, Miller now interpreted, indicated his anguished struggle to develop a way of reading that pinpointed where and how he had made his earlier political errors *and* the implications this expert approach had for preventing the dangerous meshing of politics and aesthetics.

Pre–de Man Affair murmurings that deconstruction was haunted by the specter of World War II suddenly became dominant discourse. Already, in 1984, Terry Eagleton curiously remarked that "behind the . . . Yale School would seem to loom . . . [the] shadow of the holocaust. Harold Bloom is a Jew, Geoffrey Hartman is of central European Jewish provenance; de Man's uncle . . . was politically involved in the Second World War period."[228] The European connection was reinforced in a 1986 article by Jeffrey Mehlman. In it, Mehlman knitted a speculative web, as Martin Jay summarized, "about the putative links between the American reception of deconstruction . . . and the forgetting of Franco-German collaboration during the Second World War."[229] Acknowledging that he took "a few particularly vigorous intertextual leaps" to substantiate his claim, Mehlman concluded that readers should "imagine Derrida's opus as the textual instantiation of the amnesty or radical forgetting" of collaboration that characterized writings on postwar French politics.[230] The essay not only caused a falling out between Mehlman and Derrida but also served as an example of how the truncation and distortion of quotes and complex arguments contributed to the din of the de Man Affair. For instance: in his 1988 *Nation* article, Jon Wiener summarized Mehlman as arguing that there were "even grounds for viewing the whole of deconstruction as a vast amnesty project for the politics of collaboration during World War II." Editors removed the word "speculative" between "even" and "grounds," making Mehlman's argument conclusive and damning.[231] They did so for sensationalist purposes while mobilizing the binary between defenders of Western humanism and the deconstructionists, the former possessing a positive politics, the latter a negative one.

The cacophony of interpretive struggle, often between rhetorical and nonrhetorical approaches, in the wake of Derrida's deconstructive history of de Man raged loudest in spring of 1988. History qua history, for many, defined the meaning of de Man's texts. In a March issue of the *London Review of Books*, Wolfgang Holdheim criticized Christopher Norris's "historical approach" to "de Man's historical experience" as "not historical enough."[232] For Holdheim, "[de Man] must have been permanently traumatized" after the "atrocious revelations [of the Holocaust] that flooded us in 1945." *This* ordeal was "the ultimate historical and biographical ground of those stubborn presuppositions that pervade de Man's later work."[233] And in late March 1988, American historian Richard King suggested that "textualists" like Norris "will never acknowledge" that "we haven't understood a text fully, even if such an understanding implies that we can never get it all right since the text undermines its own efforts at coherence, if we haven't tried to understand the conditions of its coming into existence."[234] For King, the disruptive figural power of texts could not wholly override historical discourse, a discourse that could reasonably presume access to an author's mental or inner states. "If [completely understanding a text] involves using 'putative psychobiographical content,' so be it," King wrote.[235] Appearances to the contrary, not every rhetorical reader in the deconstructive camp eschewed the use of psychobiographical content to interpret their former colleague's life and writings.

In the midst of her project on trauma and testimony, Shoshana Felman psychoanalytically rhetoricized what she saw as de Man's literary imperative following his collaboration. In the 1989 issue of *Critical Inquiry*, she interpreted de Man's choice to work for *Le Soir* as the consequence of his being "captivated by the Nazis' seeming revolutionary promise."[236] After the Nazis exerted more control over newspapers, radio broadcasts, and public speech as well as after the news of the Nazis' extermination of Jews, however, Felman imagined that de Man recognized his error. He resigned from *Le Soir*, having only published one anti-Semitic article (she may or may not have been aware of his second one); de Man was then fired from the publishing house he worked for and translated Herman Melville's *Moby Dick* (1851) into Flemish for the remainder of the war. For Felman, de Man's post–*Le Soir* eleven-year break from writing was evidence of his deconstructive response to the hierarchic difference between himself and Melville's most famous text. De Man's subversion of the critic/text binary, for Felman, signaled the first instance of his postcollaborationist reading strategy. For, after finishing his translation of *Moby Dick*, Felman observed, de Man abandoned his wife and children to obsessively hunt, like Ahab, his own white whale; de Man's postwar silence was a "substitute for committing suicide" that marked his pursuit of Moby Dick: how to "wake up," how to break from the past and expose and analyze the cultural and artistic forms that caused his political error.[237] Felman also read de Man as deconstructively responding to Melville's Ishmael. Like the narrator of *Moby Dick*, de Man came to possess a "doubleness of vision" that allowed him to see "the bankruptcy of all conventional historical divisions and the blurring of boundaries."[238] The postwar de Man comprehended that any separation of (his) prewar and (his) postwar periods was illusory *and* that texts' subversions of themselves, including historical narratives, would always undermine any such split; de Man's wartime error of marrying politics and aesthetics was, for Felman, therefore hardly personal and hardly in the past but, as Hartman also argued, one potentially committed by everyone—here and now—due to the nature of consciousness and the machinelike power of language. Like a Hermes who tells us what and how to read his texts, de Man (in his postwar criticisms) cataloged as much as performed this doubleness of vision that exposed (and repeated) the universal error. As the Proust quote that served as the epigraph to de Man's first book reads, "Cette perpetualle erreur, qui est précisément la vie."[239]

Key support for Felman's psychoanalytically rhetoricized interpretation of de Man's literary conversion and then postwar literary performance of his doubleness of vision was de Man's 1979 reading of Rousseau's *The Confessions*. Felman argued that de Man's interpretation of Rousseau shows his understanding that any error may be justified in a confessional narrative because, as he wrote, "the experience always exists simultaneously as fictional discourse and as empirical event."[240] This predicament "makes it possible to excuse the bleakest of crimes."[241] Likewise, Hartman suggested that de Man's refusal to confess was because he came to see that the text's rhetorical dimensions—its doubleness—prohibited any unproblematic communication: "Even to say, quite simply, 'I was young, I made a mistake, I've changed my mind' remains blind if it overlooks the narrative shape of this or any confession."[242] This reading of de Man's implicit confession of his refusal to confess was perhaps best articulated by Ortwin de Graef. De Man's reading of Rousseau, he highlighted, pivoted on a mistranslation of Rousseau's line "I ought not fear to excuse myself." That de Man, fluent in French, rendered the sentence as if Rousseau *did* fear to excuse himself raised, once more, the question of de Man's intentions.[243] Did de Man "impersonify" himself, as Hartman later suggested, through Rousseau?[244] Perhaps de Man took the Roman saying *vox audita perit, littera scripta manet* as his mantra and acted accordingly. As compelling as the idea of de Man's confession of his nonconfession may have been to Felman and others, however, nondeconstructionists wouldn't hear atonement written between the lines. His whirlpool of lies drowned all exculpatory rhetoric.

It is unquestionably difficult, as Frank Lentricchia suggested to the *Nation*, to consider passages like de Man's reading of Rousseau without contemplating his human-all-too-human burden of guilty memory.[245] He may have wanted to be baptized in the River Lethe, but history qua history seemed to have enduringly hurt him. De Man's three decades of silence about his collaboration suggested he understood that a public admission of guilt would not only have irreparably damaged his professional life, as Derrida suggested in his *Critical Inquiry* article, but also likely have resulted in a break with friends, many of whom were Jewish, including Derrida (who experienced the anti-Semitic laws under the Vichy regime), Hartman (who fled to England from the Nazi regime), and Felman (who was born in Israel). This probable mixture of fear, pain, and guilt, nonetheless, made Felman's task of convincing nonrhetorical readers to accept the parallels she deconstructively described between de Man and Primo Levi and then Walter Benjamin a hard sell.[246] For Felman argued that de Man's rhetorical readings were similar to Primo Levi's account of the year he spent as a prisoner in the Auschwitz extermination camp in Nazi-occupied Poland. De Man, Felman wrote, "inscribe[d] the testimony of the muted witness and . . . address[ed] the lesson of historical events, not . . . as a cover-up or a dissimulation of the past, but as an ongoing, active *transformation of the very act of bearing witness*."[247] Allegories of the impossibility of witnessing the union between form and content, the sensuous and conceptual, the rhetorical and grammatical, de Man's postwar writings recorded and enacted his/the inability to repair the irreparable after the Holocaust. But Felman went even further with this line of argument. For Felman, "both de Man and [German Jewish philosopher] Benjamin experience[d]" the war "essentially as a mistake, ... as a historical misreading that leads both men to a misguided action."[248] Though Benjamin "dies as a consequence of his misreading the war"—he committed suicide on the French-Spanish border while escaping from the Nazis—de Man "survive[d] ... and construct[ed] his later life as a relentless struggle with the powers of historical deception." The fact that de Man devoted his last recorded lectures to Benjamin and the question of (mis)translation—as noted, a synonym for conversion—adds a certain validity to the parallel Felman drew.[249] Still, as Robert Holub stressed, Benjamin was a victim of a regime dedicated to exterminating the Jewish population of Europe.[250] Political questions might have been uppermost in de Man's mind after his "historical misreading," but most were unwilling to go as far as Felman. Deconstructing the metaphysical hierarchical opposition between de Man's verbal silence and written texts was one thing; the difference between de Man and Jewish figures was quite another.

(No) Last Words

By 1989, sheer fatigue over the de Man Affair set in among academics and journalists, with deconstruction, detached from its association with the Yale School and launched onto the national stage as a clear and present danger to Western civilization and humanistic education, becoming a subdued postmodern bugbear. Part of the initial outrage to the de Man case stemmed from expectations left over from the first half of the twentieth century that literary intellectuals could and should publicly provide judgments of taste and character and deliver a comprehensible understanding of the connections between politics and aesthetics. Because of their intellectual commitments, deconstructionists never fully met these expectations. These expectations nonetheless survived, even if having been largely forced outside the academy by the 1980s, partly by the convergence of economizing and the demands placed on the postwar academic humanist, both of which contributed to the fierce competition and the intense specialization it fostered that complex reading techniques like deconstruction epitomized. The expert vocabulary of deconstructionists was almost bound to eventually collide with the vocabulary of public discourse, which mobilized a general humanist perspective and all those interpretive categories that deconstructionists questioned. The case was closed, and the final verdict was that deconstruction was destruction, and all that jargon had been but a sham.

Within the American institution of deconstruction, though, the processing of de Man's past was far from over. There were no last words, and the discourse continued, generating turmoil still. "In certain ways, we never got over it," American professor of philosophy Avital Ronell reflected in 2003.[251] Hartman recalled in 2007 that during an "otherwise amiable conversation [with Derrida] at lunch in a favorite Paris hotel" sometime after the affair, he expressed doubt about Derrida's deconstructive reading of de Man's articles; Derrida, Hartman remembered, "may not have entirely forgiven me for questioning."[252] (Derrida, however, admitted in his *Critical Inquiry* essay that "sometimes a murmur of protest [against his own speculations about de Man's silence] stirs in me.")[253] While Hartman confronted Derrida in person, Harold Bloom seemed to have done so by proxy; he was likely the off-the-record critic who told the *Nation* that he was "shocked that there is a symposium" on de Man's articles. "We are discussing the butchery of the Belgian Jewish community."[254] Also, for Bloom, de Man's wartime actions were a question of personal conscience and ought not be the subject of petition drives. Bloom had lost family members in the Holocaust; rhetorically reading these serious issues was, for him, intolerable.

Yet Bloom's friendship with "Über-reader" de Man had always been complicated.[255] "The best critic and best human being I've known in my life," he said of de Man in 1985.[256] Bloom, however, perhaps knew more about his friend than he publicly disclosed. In 1989, Cynthia Chase, professor of French at Cornell, recounted that Bloom told her that de Man confessed to Bloom in 1970 during the interview process for de Man's position at Yale, even offering Bloom copies of his *Le Soir* writings. Bloom refused to read them, including the "one" that "was 'patently anti-Semitic.'"[257] "My God!," Bloom exclaimed when Chase told him the news in 1987, "I knew it. He told me. He was a baby; it was the poppa and the uncle." Bloom later denied Chase's story, averring instead that "Paul twice seemed to begin to want to say something to me, and before he had actually elucidated it he ceased." "Puzzled," Bloom assumed that some obscure past wrongdoing disturbed de Man.[258] "De Man," Bloom claimed, "never intimated that he had written anything anti-Semitic. It was only retrospectively that I realized what he meant."[259] What Bloom knew and when remain open questions, though Bloom's theory of poetic influence could be fruitfully applied to de Man's postwar situation, with de Man's deconstructive writings rhetorically refracting his debts to his youthful textual errors. Maybe this all accounts for Bloom's intensely focused and productive agonistic intellectual friendship with de Man.[260] Perhaps, as Blake wrote, "Opposition is true friendship."[261]

The unsolved interpretive mystery remained: Was de Man a master illusionist? Hartman reflected decades later that "de Man's silence about his past together with his antipsychologistic stance produced . . . an aporia

FIGURE 5.3 Harold Bloom at Yale, likely in the 1990s (Courtesy of Office of Public Affairs, Yale University, Photographs of Individuals [RU 686]; Manuscripts and Archives, Yale University Library)

or undecidable: precisely the fact that we cannot tell whether there was an intentional deception."[262] All of de Man's later writings produce this irresolution. "Blind, or was it blind, to the possibility of being rebiographied and so, however apparently impersonal, diminishing the intellectual pressure [on the text] he himself helped to impose. Did he deceive us or did he merely deceive himself? Is it in the nature of the intellect, when unconditionally followed through, to create this more than literary irony?"[263] A de Manian rhetorical history of de Man might meditate on the network of undecidables—the paradoxes and contradictions—that constituted his text and, as unsatisfying as that would likely be to nonrhetorical readers, leave it at that. For Hartman, however, it was as if de Man's unceasing examination of the uncontrollable power of rhetoric resulted in his performing and embodying his own post-Romantic predicament. De Man seemed to have made his scholarly—thus ostensibly objective—life revolve around his painful personal seduction by Romantic ideology, an ideology that led him to surrender to the fascist revolution, to yoke aesthetics and politics together.[264] Consider merely de Man's late interest in the impossibility of isolating autobiography as a genre, which he identified with prosopopoeia, "the master trope of poetic discourse" that describes the delusory tendency to bestow the gift of speech on an absent or deceased person, or an abstraction or inanimate object.[265]

The de Man Affair also raised many questions about the possibilities and limits of deconstruction itself. Are certain texts more appropriate to rhetorically read than others? The texts of popular culture appear within bounds, but racist writings like de Man's in *Le Soir* and *Het Vlaamsche Land*? These texts in fact seem to be ideal evidence that the desacralization (or deconstruction) of metaphysical dualisms had frontiers that Derridean "freeplay" could not undermine. But a de Manian rhetoricized response rang hollow as well. Alice Kaplan recalled that de Man once explained to her and other Yale graduate students the nature of the *"mise en abîme* . . . by describing a cocoa can with a girl on it holding a cocoa can with a girl on it holding a cocoa can. When does it stop? There are problems, concluded de Man, with trying to represent reality."[266] However true this may be, for many humanists, no textual problem represented how much deconstruction caused/contributed to the crisis of the humanities and destroyed literary education more than deconstructionists' attempted subversions of the signified reality that de Man's anti-Semitic articles carved at its joints. "Deconstruction gave us a sensitivity to language," Kaplan reflected, though "the rigor about language constrained our imagination."[267] To what extent should the meticulous attention to a text's rhetorical dimensions take precedence over understanding how a text references "history"? Is this a metaphysical trap, a dichotomy that falsely prevents infinitely descending into mise en abymes? Should one try to find a middle ground between the social and the figural forces of the text? Our difficulty in answering these questions points to how much deconstruction has heightened our awareness of the problem of reading.

With these and other questions unanswered—perhaps unanswerable— and amid the shift in the focus of critical discussions and approaches since the mid-1980s, the enthusiasm in the American academy for deconstructive criticism waned considerably. The Arnoldian view of poetry as "criticism of life," that quaint relic of the past, was by and large already pushed out of literary studies, but now so was the complex archformalist criticism practiced by de Man. The return of and to "history" accelerated by the de Man Affair, however, contributed not only to the marginalization of de Man's work but the obscuring of the Yale settings that instituted deconstruction in America as well. Ironically enough, another factor that underwrote this obfuscation was Derrida's continually rising star in the firmament of "French theory." By the late 1980s, Derrida's teachings had spread far beyond the constrained world of Yale Comp Lit—the word "deconstruction" had even become part of the Anglophone vernacular. A State Department official could speak of a blueprint for the "deconstruction" of a portion of the US embassy in Moscow, and, in 1988, English author and academic Malcolm Bradbury sent up Derrida's work in *My Strange Quest for Mensonge: Structuralism's Hidden Hero* ("mensonge" means a lie, as in a fib, in French).[268] Playing with the popular view that Derrida asserted language was a self-enclosed structure that never signified reality outside itself, Bradbury's story was a fictional biography of a philosopher who insisted that he "has never been known to anyone, even his closest friends, that he is no one, has achieved nothing, and does not exist. In short he has claimed to be a totally absent absence."[269] The same year as *Mensonge*'s publication, the Museum of Modern Art in New York City held a "deconstructivist architecture" exhibition. "Despite their radical appearance," museumgoers were told, the architects' projects were united, as they used "essentially traditional forms that have been subverted or displaced."[270] A word and concept no one person or group could claim to possess or own, "deconstruction" was now employed to denote a host of activities or procedures, from "analysis" to soft "historicizing." Deconstruction itself underwent deconstruction in the last decades of the twentieth century, becoming a kind of floating signifier, its recontextualizations ever proliferating its uses, depositing layers of meanings that largely concealed the sites of its American institution.

EPILOGUE

Don't Dream It's Over

Even after the revolutions in Poland and Hungary and the fall of the Berlin Wall in November 1989, not many foresaw the collapse, in late 1991, of the Union of Soviet Socialist Republics. Soon, President George H. W. Bush would proclaim the advent of a new world order. Many commentators enthusiastically embraced America's new supersovereignty. In 1992, political scientist Francis Fukuyama, who had briefly pursued graduate studies in Yale Comp Lit during the late 1970s ("deconstruction . . . was total bullshit," he came to believe), hypothesized that, with the conclusion of the struggle between communism and capitalism, "history" in the Hegelian sense had concluded; the victory of Western-style liberal democracy marked "the end point of mankind's ideological evolution."[1] Absent a counterpoint as much as a counterweight, cheerleaders of capitalism took their cues, building what George Monbiot has called "a self-serving racket," a political program that enacted policies—such as slashing taxes, deregulating and deunionizing what they could, outsourcing and offshoring what they could not—that favored the wealthy and large corporations.[2] In the previous decade, Americans referred to these policies as "Reaganism," the British "Thatcherism," in the global South "neocolonialism." But the end of the Cold War offered new opportunities to push these agendas. And by the turn of the twenty-first century, with the power of organizations free from the checks and controls of democracy, like the IMF, World Bank, and WTO, growing in tandem with the recalibration of domestic policies to market principles, the American welfare state and its compromise with capital was, for all intents and purposes, placed on life support.

During the last decades of the twentieth century, neoliberals' decades-in-the-making orientation of social and cultural life to corporate and financial interests greatly transformed state flagship and midtier universities. To be sure, market values always permeated the public university;

higher education has always been occupied with business interests, and an unsullied, sublime moment of "the life of the mind" there never was. But, if, as Geoffrey Galt Harpham has argued, the humanities "portray a 'dream of America,'" in that "they represent an aspiration of Americans since the first days of the Republic for a state so secure and prosperous that people could enjoy and appreciate culture for its own sake," then such a dream has very nearly ended for the non-elite.[3] Beginning in the late 1970s, the economistic view of human development increasingly marginalized the notion that colleges and universities should primarily aim to foster human growth by cultivating the appreciation of culture.[4] Certainly, many fought for the idea that state-funded higher education, and humanities departments in particular, should do precisely that. Yet as "the great decompression" proceeded at an accelerating clip during the 1990s and 2000s, the sheer power and all-encompassing presence of the neoliberal logic of the student-customer removed such an idea from public consideration, profoundly contributing to the disassembling of the networks and communities that instituted creative—that is, primarily noneconomic— endeavors in higher education.[5] Many Americans' state-subsidized visions of a "dream of America" were no more.

The situation at private institutions has not been as dire, though financial interests and the model of corporate governance have affected elite colleges and universities. At Yale, the humanities suffered displacement. When Michael Holquist returned to the university in 1986, "the 120 junior and senior class majors currently enrolled [in the literature major] represented not only an all-time high in enrollment, but some of the best students on campus as well." In 1985, "half of the majors graduating did so with distinction: four of the ten Mellon Fellowships awarded to Yale undergraduates . . . went to students in the Literature Major: two others were awarded a Marshall and a Clare-Mellon Fellowship for study in England."[6] Following this high point in the mid-1980s, when it was the second most popular major in Yale College, English saw a shift away from its central position in Yale's ecosystem.[7] At many other colleges and universities, the proportion of majors has fallen in every humanities field, with English and history at half pre–Great Recession peaks. This across-the-board plunge has everything to do with the effects of neoliberal rationality on administrators *and* students: in 1970, 70 percent of freshmen believed higher education should help "develop a meaningful philosophy of life"; about 40 percent felt an "essential" or "very important" purpose of education was to "make more money."[8] By the mid-1980s, while federal student aid suffered deep cuts and spending on higher education was slashed about 25 percent, these percentages flipped; since the Great Recession, "two-thirds of 14 to 23-year-old students" state that they "want a degree to provide financial security."[9]

Long gone is much of the support for the policies that underwrote and the many voices that cheered on the massification of higher education and its academic revolution; with all that went so many research and travel grants, grand international conferences, eminent visiting professorships, and tenure-track positions. In the 1960s, this enthusiasm for tertiary education and a rise in the status and funding of the hard sciences motivated academic humanists to justify the mission of their disciplines and the soundness of their research and teaching; the resultant search for analytically rigorous approaches helped generate the interpretive methodologies known later as "theory." In literary studies the New Critics offered their eminently teachable formalism during the 1940s and 1950s, while vanguard critics in the 1960s navigated the professional routes paved by the academic revolution to subvert established literary-critical practice to institute protodeconstruction in America. Homegrown networks intersected with the peculiar politics and departmental cultures at Yale in the 1970s to produce a uniquely rigorous and ironic defense of literary studies. Under different circumstances, this reflexive interpretive science that responded to the paradoxes of literature might never have happened at Yale or, had it happened, would have assumed a vastly different form on pages and in classrooms. It was the local idiosyncrasies at the university that informed Harold Bloom, Paul de Man, Geoffrey Hartman, and J. Hillis Miller's pedagogical-intellectual project, instituting deconstruction in America. These peculiarities included the legacy of literary humanism, which harmonized with Yale's self-conception as defender of religious and cultural hierarchies; the middecade departures of New Critics from Yale English; the retirement of René Wellek, which helped de Man embed his science of rhetorical reading in Comp Lit; the number of like-minded critics gathered in Yale literature departments; and the favorable conditions nurtured in the literature major for teaching deconstruction to undergraduates. Even during crises of the mid-1970s, de Man, Hartman, and Miller, thanks largely to their positions within the academy, were able to coordinate their research and teaching agendas. In 2002, Jonathan Culler expressed his hope that "at some point Yale will once again be the focal point of what is new and outrageous in literary studies."[10] Perhaps that is possible, but it's important to understand how Yale's "golden years" were predicated on the school's earlier centrality to literary studies as well as the substantial financial support and cultural value assigned to the humanities there and elsewhere.

While de Man and colleagues' responses to the rhetorical dimensions of texts challenged conventional literary-critical praxis, the feminist un-earthing of the deconstructive figural power of literature undertaken by Barbara Johnson, Shoshana Felman, Margaret Ferguson, Margaret Homans, and others not only contested pseudogenderless styles of in-terpretation but also effectuated and extended the reach of the American institution of deconstruction. De Man never fully got around to explor-ing the political and ideological consequences of texts; Johnson and her colleagues surely and rigorously did. These Brides of Deconstruction and Criticism, by the late 1970s, offered a novel vision of "America," one that subverted patterns of female effacement and marginalization as well as the ostensibly timeless gendered and sexual hierarchical oppositions that organized texts, curricula, and culture, advancing the humanistic possi-bilities of deconstruction. Johnson and company did so by exploiting the possibilities offered at Yale and domestic cultural traditions to cultivate their pedagogical-intellectual endeavors. With their expanded science of rhetorical reading, the Brides not only combated but also drew from the university's self-image, entrenched biases and prejudice, and second-wave feminists' curricula as well as the politics of the women's and gay libera-tion movements.[11] And the techniques of reading developed by feminist deconstructionists have played a meaningful role in the fights for gay, lesbian, and transgender rights. The work done and disseminated by the Brides is prime evidence that humanistic scholarship has mattered and can change national conversations and views.

Most deconstructionists and rhetorically inclined associates—really, even their detractors—were either members of the baby boom genera-tion or Generation X, for whom the worth of literature and the criticism devoted to it, not to mention humanistic learning more broadly, were in many respects self-evident. But the neoliberal conquest of higher education—and American culture—placed such indisputability in ques-tion; literary education does not hold the cultural value it once did. Bloom and Hartman occasionally addressed this transformation and students' desertion of literary studies for other disciplines and professions. Sound-ing suspiciously like New Critics and literary humanists whom he battled in the 1960s and 1970s, Bloom mustered a passionate defense of the West-ern canon against the "School of Resentment," a group that included aca-demic Marxists, feminists, and New Historicists, whom he felt injected political motives into their readings of texts instead of imparting the pure, self-sufficient aesthetics of literary value to readers and students.[12] Bloom's frustrations and anger may have been derived from his own "dis-turbing recognition" that "the faith in the Western literary canon . . . as a way of interpreting and so entering 'America' no longer exists."[13] His epic triumphs against his Yale critical fathers for admission to "America" meant little, it seemed, to the very culture that he envisioned through the poems of "strong poets." In his characteristically measured way, Hartman worried as well about the changing status of literary education and the text's autonomy. Expressing regret about his part in the reception of the deconstructive enterprise as a license to apply rhetorical reading to manipulate all discourse, Hartman worked to convince his colleagues of the importance of restoring "literature's specificity as a focus for thinking about culture," using William Wordsworth's "attempt to envision a modern culture that would not break with a rural sensibility . . . to relate poetry to politics in a consequent manner."[14] Try as they might, however, Hartman and Bloom could not reverse large-scale intellectual trends that read literature as a social document, subordinating the literary text to extratextual concerns and interests.

Hartman and Bloom remained members of the Yale establishment until their deaths in 2016 and 2019, respectively, but Derrida, a humanities professor at UC-Irvine, roamed widely. To the surprise of many Americans habituated to viewing Derrida's work solely as a philosophical response to literature, Derrida devoted considerable attention during the remaining seventeen years of his life to issues buried in the textual mix: politics, law, and ethics. Derrideans continue to debate the extent to which the de Man Affair drove the philosopher's "turn." For, against the repeated charge that (his) deconstruction was a set of arguments about language, an aestheticizing apolitical and ahistorical literary theory, Derrida, in 1989, provocatively argued that "deconstruction" was "justice," as "deconstruction" communicated the law while also subverting and reinventing it, all the while engaging the uniqueness and singularity of the situation or context.[15] Derrida's arguments were unsatisfying to those who wanted a politics that would fundamentally transform the world rather than produce deferred differences of meaning. Sympathetic left-liberal professors and students, though, welcomed Derrida's shift in emphasis. Part of Derrida's success in this respect was timing. With the end of the Cold War, which had helped tilt the very idea of "philosophy" toward a socially detached conception of truth, language, and method, the stigma against nonanalytic philosophy in America lessened. Derrida's turn was also well staged vis-à-vis the rise of cultural studies. While Bloom and Hartman defended the uniqueness of literature and how its surprising rhetorical power exceeded sociohistorical contextualization, Derrida's deconstruction became part of the interpretive toolkit of cultural critics of various stripes.

In the 1990s, Derrida's foregrounding of political, legal, and ethical topics won him newer and ever-larger audiences; soon, an all-purpose Derridean "deconstructo-speak" was the lingua franca in American humanities departments. But even as this was occurring, those sympathetic to his deconstructive readings and teachings were becoming increasingly concerned with neoliberal policies of privatization and marketization that unequally distributed basic resources and public goods, such as education, energy, land, medical care, and water. That is not to say that Derrida avoided pressing social problems; not only did Derrida's political engagement stretch back to the beginning of his career in France, but, in 1993, around the time when an anti-Marxist *Stimmung* reached a fever pitch in Europe and America, he defiantly conjured the specter of Marx in a lecture that formed the basis of *Spectres de Marx* (1993).[16] Responding to Fukuyama's summoning of the spirit of Alexandre Kojève, who, during the 1930s, developed Hegel's philosophy of the "end of history" and initiated a mode of "existential Marxism" that marked generations of French philosophers, Derrida probed the deconstructive legacy of Marxism for a post-Marxist world plagued by unemployment, homelessness, arms sales, atomic weaponry, ethnic wars, and America's unipolar status. Derrida also predicted the deconstructive formation of a new International.[17] Still, his deconstructive response to a metaphysical reading of texts was seen by many as failing to offer concrete solutions for immediate and global problems, climate change being just one. It was the very notion of the "concrete," of the self-possession or presence of meaning, that Derrida had, since the 1960s, placed in his deconstructive sights. To look to Derrida for simple answers was a fool's errand. In the infamous 2004 *New York Times* obituary for Derrida, the philosopher was portrayed as "notoriously difficult," "the personification of a French school of thinking" that "many Americans . . . felt was undermining many of the traditional standards of classical education."[18] Derrida's work evoked resentment, which further signaled its relevance. For why lace your obit with such sourness if not because Derrida's deconstruction still gets under your skin?

Even death couldn't put to rest the institution of American deconstruction. The de Manian discipline of rhetorical reading was in eclipse, as his absence from a best-selling literary theory anthology (1998) testified.[19] Nevertheless, de Man's former students and colleagues as well as younger scholars continued to mine his writings. For these devotees, de Man was a conceptual rhetorician of the highest order, his readings of texts a fount of interpretive insights that could be extended from de Man's original emphasis on literary language to the inhuman forces of our world. For example, in a 2012 volume, J. Hillis Miller argued that, because de Man showed how and when language was "a machine that, performatively, *verspricht (sich)*, falsely promises and contradicts itself at the same time," his texts help identify such "fallacious assumptions . . . that we ought just to get finance capitalism back on track and all will be well, or that global climate change might be reversed with some carbon cap laws, or that the humanities can be returned to their former glory."[20] It is not, Miller claimed, that de Man's writings aid in the complete debunking of such claims, nor that de Man's texts assist in reversing disasters. Rather, de Man's writings help readers "know what is happening," which is "better" than blundering around with the false hope of restoration or restitution. In the same volume, Claire Colebrook likewise suggested that contemporary horizons make de Man's work pertinent, as his highlighting of the linguistic struggles between a text's rhetorical and grammatical elements explains the workings of false narratives, including those about the 2008 financial crisis, globalization, and terrorism, and they gesture to the dimensions of unimaginable catastrophes like nuclear war and climate change.[21] Among a small cohort of humanities scholars at least, de Man inspires still. His interpretive approach to European philosophers' and poets' post-Romantic literary predicament is seen by some as a comprehensive reflexive science of interpretation that might help us tackle our own dilemmas.

The end of the East and West Coast institutions of deconstruction did not and will not mean the end of deconstructive activity in America. A look at not simply the syllabus of an undergraduate humanities course but also the news surely disabuses us of the notion that this intellectual endeavor was ephemeral, while, in the cultural landscape, deconstruction (at least in name) continues to be put to diverse uses: there's deconstruction and drugs, style, fiction, love, the postcolonial, psychoanalysis, technology, and so on. True, to a certain extent, this anecdotal side of deconstruction suggests a synergy between deconstruction and the cultural logic of late capitalism, an association that Derrida never denied.[22] Yet how uncanny is it that the postmodern stance of ironic detachment, of going "meta," so widely used to hawk commercial products, to some degree mirrors de Manian or Derridean readings? This intersection reveals the unexpected manners in which and places where deconstruction resonates and saturates. But beyond explaining deconstruction as a way of thinking and being, or as a force in American intellectual life, the story of deconstruction is one of a particular moment of opportunity in higher education. And this intellectual history of the American institution of deconstruction has aimed to illustrate how local traditions, distinctive networks, and curious personalities offered a dynamic place for culture to flourish and in turn be venerated and challenged.

Regardless of whether deconstructive theory and practice are compelling, the fact is that neoliberal logic continues to be the greatest threat to higher education. There has certainly been progress in some arenas—very importantly in terms of inclusion in the academy of underrepresented groups. But the overall erosion of the "dream of America" in universities has pushed the long-standing crisis of the humanities to the point of not-so-slow demolition, for both students and teachers. Tuition costs have skyrocketed, and students suffer from practically insurmountable debt. Meanwhile, politicians and administrators searching for the lowest costs and cheapest wages have reorganized the college experience and the academic work force. The latter now comprises hundreds of thousands of exploited part-time teachers for whom the professional life enjoyed during and shortly after the academic revolution is out of reach; a blessed few thousand tenured full professors, with endowed chairs, titles, and access to fellowships and grants, rest atop a pyramid of exploitation that they themselves wish was not the reality in which they partake. From a certain angle, the culture wars of the 1990s were but an epiphenomenon of this neoliberal triumph, for the true bogeyman dismantling the humanities was not deconstruction or French theory or feminist theory or relativism or revision of the canon but the hypercapitalist ethos boosted by the political right.

Without concentrated and concrete efforts to address the present state of higher education, humanities departments will shrink to minuscule dimensions. The narcissism of small differences among humanists means nothing when the humanities don't exist. Yet calls for more "theory" to revitalize humanists' teaching and research programs are misguided. In May 2018, several esteemed American historians issued a manifesto that argued for historians to finally embrace "theory" in order to transcend the discipline's "eighteenth century origins as an empiricist enterprise."[23] This request ignores the massive erosion of the financial and cultural support for the intellectual communities interested in this kind of work. The call for historians—and humanities scholars generally—to participate in some sort of "theory revolt" is slightly embarrassing when only those who enjoy security and comfort could ever participate in it. Now as we face a global pandemic, such stability is at ever-greater risk. Absent the recognition of and concerted pushback against the neoliberal hell in which we live, work, and learn, the development, proliferation, and employment of new and exciting theoretical perspectives and vocabularies will be impotent; the notion that these can then be used in classrooms is a dream in itself. Surely, if the Johns Hopkins Humanities Center recently had to change its name to the Department of Comparative Thought and Literature and scale back the scope of its mission after fifty years, then one can only imagine the pressures at lower-ranked and underfunded schools. The exact toll of "perma-austerity" cannot be known.[24] But a generation (or two) has already been robbed of opportunities to realize their creative potential that the dream machines of the humanities offer. Material and cultural reinvestment is urgent; it is necessary.

ACKNOWLEDGMENTS

Like the story this book tells, my intellectual formation occurred largely thanks to institutions of higher education and the individuals who inhabit them. At Wheaton College in Massachusetts, I belonged to a motley crew of kindred spirits, always eager to explore ideas' histories and consequences. I am indebted to those dear friends who gave me community. My liberal arts experience was foundational—and it was at Wheaton that I first heard of "deconstruction." But at the University of Maine I learned what it means to be a historian. There, parts of the project that became this book began. My adviser Michael Lang was a role model for how to think historically about ideas. Thank you, Michael, for trusting me with a folder of photocopied documents from the de Man Affair.

Set adrift after the 2008 financial crisis, like so many others of my generation, I started the life of a full-time adjunct. I detest and resent the conditions that facilitate such exploitation. Yet during that time, at Eastern Maine Community College, I enjoyed some of my most meaningful relationships with students. This book is as much about teaching as it is about scholarship, and I am grateful for the students I've taught, especially at EMCC, my teaching birthplace.

Entering the University of Wisconsin–Madison's PhD program with no funding package was a leap of faith, and I am thankful for each assistantship, scholarship, and fellowship that I received from the university and the History Department. The contingent institutional support was necessary for survival, but it was the people who truly sustained me. To name only some of those I owe my gratitude: Leslie Abadie, Rudy Koshar, Tony Michels, Adam Nelson, and friends Brad Baranowski, Meggan Bilotte, Aaron Dowdall, Daniel Hummel, Rivka Maizlish, Nick Strohl, and Kevin Walters. During arduous graduate school years, I received intellectual inspiration and nourishment from the Always Already Metaphysical Club and the Coalition of the Writing II.

I didn't know what I would need from an adviser when I entered my doctoral program, and it is providence that I was Jennifer Ratner-Rosenhagen's student. She has always encouraged me to think big and to put my work in conversation with as many people and groups as possible. She also set the highest professional and intellectual expectations and continues to inspire me to strive to meet them.

A six-month stay in 2014 in Leuven, funded by the Belgian American Educational Foundation and my great-aunt Vincenza Landino, allowed me to pursue research on Paul de Man in Belgium. Ortwin de Graef and Tom Toremans introduced me to the vibrant Department of Literary Studies at Katholieke Universiteit Leuven, while Jan Vanvelk gave me a crash course in Belgian culture and became a treasured friend.

During the research for this project, countless individuals assisted with sections, chapters even, which might otherwise have gone unwritten. Michael Holquist shared several retrospective essays and reflected on his teaching; Harold Bloom and Geoffrey Hartman entrusted me with their personal stories and insights; Patricia de Man provided incredible photographs of her father; J. Hillis Miller offered access to his archive at UC-Irvine and discussions at his home in Maine; and Haun Saussy gave me his graduate school lecture notes. This list could happily go on. Later, I feared that being an academic based in China whose work spans the North Atlantic intellectual world might cut me off from certain resources. Thankfully, Michael Lotstein and staff at Yale University and Jackson Bui and others at UC-Irvine ensured such worries were unfounded.

I am grateful for Andrew Hartman's and Kevin Schultz's shepherding of my project to the University of Chicago Press; Andrew's advice and solidarity continue to help me navigate the sea of uncertainty that is the contemporary academy. Anonymous readers made enormously appreciated suggestions about the book's content and form. I'm grateful to the many people at the press who have worked on this project; special thanks to Susannah Engstrom for her patience and help keeping me organized and on schedule, and to Christine Schwab for her careful attention to the manuscript in its final stages. I am deeply thankful to my editor, Timothy Mennel, who believed in this project, and whose encouragement and gentle criticisms came at the right moments. Tim also takes his authors—homesick and otherwise—to minor league ballgames, a memorable expression of his kindness.

While this book may have been designed in America, it was assembled in China. Academic exile from my country could have been this project's death knell, but the Chinese University of Hong Kong, Shenzhen, offered stability when other institutions could not or would not, helping ease the sting of displacement and giving me the peace of mind to complete the book. Of special note at CUHK-SZ were Wendong Cui, who warmly welcomed me to the newly built university; Lucas Scripter, who helped me think through issues that haunt my research still; and Yin Meng, who somehow found every article or book I needed. From afar, Vaneesa Cook read my manuscript and gave frank, invaluable feedback.

Family members also contributed to this project at key points and in key ways. Anni Outinen-Jones unhesitatingly assisted in the recovery of computer files (years of archival work almost lost to the ether); Jonathan and Susan Katz opened their home to me during my visits to Yale. The writing of this book came on the heels of a difficult final year of the doctoral program. My parents did not question my choices and my path at that time. Instead, they were truly supportive. Although it might seem like a small thing, Mom and Dad have also regularly sent me transpacific shipments of books, which have been as crucial for my well-being as for my work.

And yet it was at times so very difficult to continue this project. Though there were memorable acts of support that helped me endure the years of study, research, and writing that went into this book, there were painful moments and periods when I sought acceptance and assistance but did not receive it. "Had I but time," as Hamlet cried, "O, I could tell you—But let it be."

Above all, two loved ones gave me strength to follow through: Oliver, you were born when this project was just an amorphous, nascent thought; I now complete it as you enter middle school. Your zest for life always challenges my self-doubt. You have faced big changes with courage and an open heart, and witnessing that has helped to fuel me during difficult times. I often think about what the future will bring for you and your generation, and I hope we don't fail you. Laura, because I trust your insights and judgments so deeply, I've wanted you to be my first and last reader of all things. In this way, you contributed directly to this book. And I cannot express how grateful I am for your love. For years on end, you have remained unwavering in your support of my dreams. Thank you.

NOTES

Introduction

1. René Wellek, "Destroying Literary Studies," *New Criterion*, December 1, 1983, 1.

2. William Bennett, "The Shattered Humanities," *Wall Street Journal*, December 31, 1982, 10.

3. Kenneth L. Woodward et al., "A New Look at Literary Criticism," *Newsweek*, June 22, 1981, 80–83, 80.

4. Allan Bloom, *The Closing of the American Mind: How Higher Education Has Failed Democracy and Impoverished the Souls of Today's Students* (New York: Simon and Schuster, 1987), 379.

5. Camille Paglia, "Junk Bonds and Corporate Raiders: Academe in the Hour of the Wolf," *Arion: A Journal of Humanities and the Classics* 1:2 (1991): 196; Paglia, "Ninnies, Pedants, Tyrants and Other Academics," *New York Times Magazine*, May 5, 1991, 32.

6. Works on deconstruction that have deployed a "history of ideas" approach, a narrative mode that reads texts in relation to prior texts and thus only infrequently in relation to events contiguous with the production and reception of these texts, include Jonathan Culler, *On Deconstruction: Theory and Criticism after Structuralism* (Ithaca, NY: Cornell University Press, 1982); Frank Lentricchia, *After the New Criticism* (Chicago: University of Chicago Press, 1980); Christopher Norris, *Deconstruction: Theory and Practice* (New York: Methuen, 1982); Vincent Leitch, *Deconstructive Criticism: An Advanced Introduction* (New York: Columbia University Press, 1982); and Michael Ryan, *Marxism and Deconstruction: A Critical Articulation* (Baltimore: Johns Hopkins University Press, 1982). A second group of works, which has avoided the "history of ideas" approach, either has a too restricted temporal scope and/or has insufficiently considered the institution of deconstruction in America. See François Cusset, *French Theory: How Foucault, Derrida, Deleuze, & Co. Transformed the Intellectual Life of the United States*, trans. Jeff Fort (Minneapolis: University of Minnesota Press, 2008); Jonathan Arac, Wlad Godzich, and Wallace Martin, eds., *The Yale Critics: Deconstruction in America* (Minneapolis:

University of Minnesota Press, 1983); Peter C. Herman, ed., *Historicizing Theory* (Albany: SUNY Press, 2004), 69–98, 99–112, 209–34.

7. The body of scholarship on "French theory," a problematic term used to describe the multiplicity of interpretive positions associated with French structuralism, poststructuralism, and postmodernism, has often focused on the stakes in French but not American intellectual/academic life. Political sociologist Niilo Kauppi in his *French Intellectual Nobility: Institutional and Symbolic Transformations in the Post-Sartrian Era* (Albany: SUNY Press, 1996) provided an analysis of "the sociohistorical conditions for the production of theory in the French intellectual field in the post-Sartrian era." For historical studies on this topic, see Edward Baring, *The Young Derrida and French Philosophy, 1945–1968* (Cambridge: Cambridge University Press, 2011); Julian Bourg, ed., *After the Deluge: New Perspectives on the Intellectual and Cultural History of Postwar France* (Lanham, MD: Lexington Books, 2004); Bourg, *From Revolution to Ethics: May 1968 and Contemporary French Thought* (Montreal: McGill–Queen's University Press, 2007); Tamara Chaplin, *Turning On the Mind: French Philosophers on Television* (Chicago: University of Chicago Press, 2007). A notable exception to the scholarly tendency to tell European origin stories and synoptic histories is Jason Demers's book *The American Politics of French Theory: Derrida, Deleuze, Guattari, and Foucault in Translation* (Toronto: University of Toronto Press, 2019). Though Demers examines the American places, writers, and events that inspired French thinkers from around 1968–78 to employ a political prism to reinterpret contemporary philosophy, he still treats theory as a European provenance and influence. For an incisive argument about how "French Theory is a 'hard case' for historians," see Warren Breckman, "Times of Theory: On Writing the History of French Theory," *Journal of the History of Ideas* 71:3 (2010): 339–61, particularly 360–61.

8. See Cusset's preface to the English edition of *French Theory*, xiv. There, he read the cross-cultural links between American politics and French ideas as a chain of mistranslations; and "what got lost in translation" according to Cusset, Warren Breckman has observed, "was the highly politicized impulse of French writers like Derrida, Deleuze, and Foucault within a French intellectual context that was . . . still shaped by the critique of capitalism and shadowed by Marxism." For Breckman's assessment of Cusset's *French Theory*, see "Times of Theory," 343.

9. Woodward et al., "A New Look at Literary Criticism," 83.

10. See Rodolphe Gasché, *The Tain of the Mirror: Derrida and the Philosophy of Reflection* (Cambridge, MA: Harvard University Press, 1986), 1–4.

11. For examples of those who emphasized continuity between the New Criticism and not only deconstruction but other so-called poststructuralist approaches, see Lentricchia, *After the New Criticism*; Gerald Graff, *Literature against Itself: Literary Ideas in Modern Society* (Chicago: University of Chicago Press, 1979); Norris, *Deconstruction*. Scholarship that portrayed deconstruction as a radical departure from established critical practice includes Jonathan Culler, *The Pursuit of Signs: Semiotics, Literature, Deconstruction* (Ithaca, NY: Cornell University Press, 1981), especially chapter 1, "Beyond Interpretation," 3–17.

12. A useful summary of mass media representations of deconstruction was given by Herman Rapaport. See Herman Rapaport, "Demonizing Deconstruction: Walter Jackson Bate, René Wellek, and David Lehman," in *The Theory Mess: Deconstruction in Eclipse* (New York: Columbia University Press, 2001), 27–34.

13. Matthew Arnold, *Culture and Anarchy and Other Writings*, ed. Stefan Collini (Cambridge: Cambridge University Press, 1993), 79.

14. The 1987 discovery of de Man's writings prompted an avalanche of hostile articles—even a few books. For the latter, see David Lehman, *Signs of the Times: Deconstruction and the Fall of Paul de Man* (New York: Poseidon, 1991), and the more recent Evelyn Barish, *The Double Life of Paul de Man* (New York: Liveright, 2014).

15. Jonathan Culler, *Framing the Sign: Criticism and Its Institutions* (Norman: University of Oklahoma Press, 1988), 15. Culler has used the term "poststructuralism" rather than "postmodernism." In the popular imagination, the two terms themselves are conflated.

16. For an early historical depiction of "deconstruction" and other key developments in architecture, literary theory, painting, and philosophy as expressions of a 1970s postmodernist consciousness, see J. David Hoeveler Jr.'s *The Postmodernist Turn: American Thought and Culture in the 1970s* (Boston: Twayne, 1996), 15–34.

17. See Daniel T. Rodgers, *Age of Fracture* (Cambridge, MA: Harvard University Press, 2011), 158–59.

18. Warren Breckman has argued that one of the reasons that French theory—including deconstruction—is difficult to historicize is because of "the resistance of its major figures to the kinds of techniques whereby historians customarily historicize their subjects." See Breckman, 361. Derrida, Breckman has also insightfully observed, responded to a request in 2000 to reflect on the history of theory by stressing that, while there was "the Americanization of a certain deconstruction," deconstruction resisted being either the subject or the object of historicization. See Jacques Derrida, "Deconstructions: The Im-possible," in *French Theory in America*, ed. Slyvère Lotringer and Sande Cohen (New York: Routledge, 2001), 13. Breckman's point about Derrida's resistance to historians' narratives is important. Derrida's underlining to American interlocutors that (his) deconstruction subverted narrativization not only began in the early 1980s but also—partly because he outlived many of his contemporaries, partly because of his academic celebrity—significantly affected historical portrayals of deconstruction during the 1990s and 2000s. See this book's epilogue for more on this topic.

19. This has been noted by Jonathan Culler, preface to *On Deconstruction*, i.

20. Quoted in Culler, preface to *On Deconstruction*, i. Lee Jenkins, "With No. 754, Bonds Moves to 1 Away from Record," *New York Times*, July 25, 2007. Woody Allen, *Deconstructing Harry*, DVD, 1997.

21. Anders Behring Breivik, "2083: A European Declaration of Independence," 34, 35.

22. Philip Rucker and Robert Costa, "Bannon Vows a Daily Fight for 'Deconstruction of the Administrative State,'" *Washington Post*, February 24, 2017.

23. W. H. Auden, "For Sigmund Freud," *Kenyon Review* 2:1 (Winter 1940): 33.

24. Mark Currie, *The Invention of Deconstruction* (New York: Palgrave Macmillan, 2013), 37.

25. Marc Redfield, *Theory at Yale: The Strange Case of Deconstruction in America (Lit Z)* (New York: Fordham University Press, 2015).

26. This book's approach draws inspiration from the work of Michel Foucault; see "Nietzsche, Genealogy, History," in *The Foucault Reader*, ed. Paul Rabinow (New York: Pantheon, 1984), 80, 86.

27. For an example of a transnational intellectual and cultural history that does *not* do this but deconstructs the notion of a national origin of a thinker and his or her ideas, see Jennifer Ratner-Rosenhagen, *American Nietzsche: A History of an Icon and His Ideas* (Chicago: University of Chicago Press, 2012). *American Nietzsche* is one of a number of books published over the last decade or so that have explored the American reception of European thinkers. This scholarship includes Martin Woessner's *Heidegger in America* (Cambridge: Cambridge University Press, 2011) and Drew Maciag's *Edmund Burke in America: The Contested Career of the Father of Modern Conservatism* (Ithaca, NY: Cornell University Press, 2013).

28. During the 1990s and 2000s, American historians began to debunk the conventional narrative about "American exceptionalism," about the nation's unique character, that John Lewis Gaddis and his generation infused into their Cold War historiography. A groundbreaking work in the demystification of American exceptionalism is John Bender, *A Nation among Nations* (New York: Hill & Wang, 2006).

29. The "American institution" of deconstruction is therefore not about how exceptional or unique—terms freighted with moral value—the institution of deconstruction in America was, but rather about the particularities and peculiarities of this institutionalization.

30. Richard Rorty announced the "linguistic turn" in 1967 chiefly in reference to language philosophy in the tradition from Wittgenstein and Carnap. Richard M. Rorty, ed., *The Linguistic Turn: Essays in Philosophical Method* (Chicago: University of Chicago Press, 1967). See also Kerwin Lee Klein, *From History to Theory* (Berkeley: University of California Press, 2011), 11, 15, 60–63; Judith Surkis, "When Was the Linguistic Turn? A Genealogy," *American Historical Review* 117 (2012): 702–3, 722.

31. For an exploration of the desacralization of academic culture during the middle decades of the last century, see David A. Hollinger, *Science, Jews, and Secular Culture: Studies in Mid-Twentieth Century American Intellectual History* (Princeton, NJ: Princeton University Press, 1996).

32. Michael Holquist, "Literature after 'X,'" *New Journal*, December 6, 1986, 44.

33. See Hollinger, *Science, Jews, and Secular Culture*, 4, 6–7.

34. For a discourse highly influential in the nonacademic world that blamed the sixties for value relativism in American culture and the abandonment of the "structure of rational inquiry" and the search for truth in the nation's universities, see the chapters "Culture" and "Values" for the former and "The Sixties" for the latter, in Bloom, *The Closing of the American Mind*, 185–93, 194–216, 313–35.

35. Christopher Jencks and David Riesman, *The Academic Revolution* (Garden City, NY: Doubleday, 1968). Burton J. Bledstein argued that, since the mid-

nineteenth century, the university helped forge attitudes among Americans about specialization, mobility, merit, and achievement; together, these attitudes produced the "culture of professionalism." See Burton J. Bledstein, *The Culture of Professionalism: The Middle Class and the Development of Higher Education in America* (New York: Norton, 1978). The academic revolution could be understood as an extension of the "culture of professionalism."

36. Douglas Heath, review of *The Academic Revolution*, by Christopher Jencks and David Riesman, *Political Science Quarterly* 86:2 (1971): 308.

37. Culler, *Framing the Sign*, 23.

38. See Mark Jancovich, *The Cultural Politics of the New Criticism* (Cambridge: Cambridge University Press, 1993).

39. W. K. Wimsatt, "Poetry and Christian Thinking," in *The Verbal Icon: Studies in the Meaning of Poetry* (Lexington: University Press of Kentucky, 1954), 267.

40. For an investigation of such sixties activism at the University of Texas and its relation to state politics of the 1960s and national politics of the 1970s, see Doug Rossinow, *The Politics of Authenticity: Liberalism, Christianity and the New Left in America* (New York: Columbia University Press, 1998).

41. On occasion, the deconstructive confederation has been deemed to also encompass a faction of critics—Paul Bové, Joseph Riddel, and William V. Spanos—identified since the mid-1970s with the journal *Boundary 2*.

42. Winkler was not a "Bride" per se, though certainly an ally.

43. See Bruno Perreau, *Queer Theory: The French Response* (Stanford, CA: Stanford University Press, 2016).

44. Grant Webster, *The Republic of Letters: A History of Postwar American Literary Opinion* (Baltimore: Johns Hopkins University Press, 1979), 105.

45. John Adams to Abigail Adams, May 12, 1780, quoted in Fred R. Shapiro, ed., *The Yale Book of Quotations* (New Haven, CT: Yale University Press, 2006), 5.

46. A note on this book's scope: even the chronicler most sensitive to the spirit of deconstructionist thought could not examine every warp and weft of the Yale School members' and associates' texts and teachings in a single volume, nor is it feasible to completely examine the influence of de Man and company. This might disappoint those looking for such comprehensiveness; those intimately familiar with the Yale School's work may lament this or that absent theme, significance, or point. The author fully acknowledges that other configurations and readings of the Yale School members' and allies' teachings and texts are not simply possible but can and should be written.

Chapter One

1. Geoffrey Hartman, "Structuralism: The Anglo-American Adventure," *Yale French Studies* 36/37 (1966): 148.

2. Herbert Muschamp, "Paul Rudolph Is Dead at 78; Modernist Architect of the 60's," *New York Times*, August 9, 1997.

3. "The War against the War," *Time*, May 18, 1970.

4. Ellen Katz, "May Day—What Happened?," *New Journal*, February 2, 1990, 7.

5. Joseph B. Treaster, "Brewster Doubts Fair Black Trials," *New York Times*, April 25, 1970.

6. The scholarship on the radical politics of the sixties on university campuses is vast. In addition to the Rossinow text cited above, see Matthew Levin, *Cold War University: Madison and the New Left in the Sixties* (Madison: University of Wisconsin Press, 2013).

7. Wimsatt's Yale paper became an article, "Day of the Leopards," delivered to the First Annual Congress for the Arts, Religion and Culture at the Museum of Modern Art in New York City on February 3, 1968, and published in *Ventures, Magazine of the Yale Graduate School* 9:2 (Fall 1969).

8. For an intellectual history of the great books idea see Tim Lacy, *The Dream of a Democratic Culture: Mortimer J. Adler and the Great Books Idea* (New York: Palgrave Macmillan, 2013).

9. This phrase is used to reference the approach advocated by Cleanth Brooks. See *The Norton Anthology of Theory and Criticism* (New York: Norton, 2010), 1214.

10. The subversion of hierarchical distinctions between the high arts and popular culture in the lit major paralleled approaches developed and used in American studies.

11. François Cusset mistakenly described the lit major as a program "designed for graduate students." See Cusset, *French Theory*, 114.

12. In popular narratives, deconstruction in America is said to have begun at Yale and then disseminated to less prominent universities. The campus peace movement, it has been shown, took the opposite direction, starting at state universities and spreading to larger prominent colleges. See Kenneth Heineman, *Campus Wars: The Peace Movement at American State Universities in the Vietnam Era* (New York: New York University Press, 1993).

13. "Raucous," when understood, of course, in the context of the parameters of an academic meeting. The MLA protest is therefore an example of how the radical sixties sometimes directly intruded on what was intended to be a quiet affair.

14. Florence Howe, Frederick C. Crews, Louis Kampf, Noam Chomsky, Paul Lauter, and Richard Ohmann, "Reforming the MLA: Letter to the Editor," *New York Review of Books*, December 19, 1968. Louis Kampf and Paul Lauter, eds., *Politics of Literature: Dissenting Essays on the Teaching of English* (New York: Pantheon, 1970).

15. Roger L. Geiger, "Demography and Curriculum: The Humanities and Higher Education from the 1950s through the 1980s," in *The Humanities and the Dynamics of Inclusion since World War II*, ed. David A. Hollinger (Baltimore: Johns Hopkins University Press, 2006), 50–72, 66.

16. See Mark Grief, *The Age of the Crisis of Man: Thought and Fiction in America, 1933–1973* (Princeton, NJ: Princeton University Press, 2015).

17. Peter Brooks, *The Novel of Worldliness: Crébillon, Marivaux, Laclos, Stendhal* (Princeton, NJ: Princeton University Press, 1969), 4.

18. Ibid., 5.

19. Howard Felperin, *In Another Life: The Decline and Fall of the Humanities through the Eyes of an Ivy-League Jew* (Bloomington, IN: AuthorHouse, 2014), 39.

20. William Swartz, "Literature X: Trailblazing Course Set for Next Year," *Yale Daily News* 93, February 24, 1970, 1. See Alvin Kernan's remembrances of the GI Bill in Kernan, *In Plato's Cave* (New Haven, CT: Yale University Press, 2000), 2–3, 81. The 1969 Yale meeting on literary education also included Adam Parry, chair of Classics, who played an important role in discussions before dying in a motorcycle accident in Germany in 1971.

21. For an exploration of Ferdinand de Saussure's intellectual influence on structuralism, see François Dosse, *History of Structuralism: The Rising Sign 1954–1966* (Minneapolis: University of Minnesota Press, 1998), 1:45.

22. Jean Cohen, *La structure du langage poétique* (Paris: Flammarion, 1966), 193.

23. Peter Brooks, "Man and His Fictions: One Approach to the Teaching of Literature," *College English* 35:1 (1973): 42. See Serge Boubrovsky and Tzvetan Todorov, eds., *L'enseignement de la littéraire* (Paris: Plon, 1971), 590–91.

24. Cleanth Brooks, "The Language of Paradox," in *The Well Wrought Urn: Studies in the Structure of Poetry* (New York: Harcourt, 1956), 3–21.

25. Roman Jakobson quoted in Boris Eichenbaum, "The Formal Method," in *Literary Theory: An Anthology*, ed. Julie Rivkin and Michael Ryan, 2nd ed. (Malden, MA: Blackwell: 2004), 7; emphasis added.

26. See Paul de Man, "The Rhetoric of Blindness: Jacques Derrida's Reading of Rousseau," in *Blindness and Insight: Essays in the Rhetoric of Contemporary Criticism*, rev. ed. (Minneapolis: University of Minnesota Press, 1983), 102–41.

27. René Wellek, "The Name and Nature of Comparative Literature," in *Discriminations: Further Concepts of Criticism* (New Haven, CT: Yale University Press, 1970), 4.

28. Wellek quoted in Brooks, "Man and His Fictions," 42.

29. Kernan, *In Plato's Cave*, 189–90. Kernan's scholarship included his groundbreaking *The Plot of Satire* (New Haven, CT: Yale University Press, 1965).

30. Kernan, *In Plato's Cave*, 190.

31. Ibid.

32. Michael Holquist, "Literature X," *Yale Alumni Magazine* 37:6 (March 1974): 10–15, 10.

33. "Proposed Program in Literature for Yale College," RU 126, 1983-A-051, Box 14, Folder 166, Records of Dean Howard Taft, Yale College Records of the Dean 1969–1973, Yale University Archive (YUA).

34. Michael Holquist, interview by Gregory Jones-Katz, August 21, 2014. Holquist, "Literature X," 11.

35. Brooks, "Man and His Fictions," 40–41.

36. Ibid.

37. David Todd, "Faculty Consolidates Computer Sciences, Passes Literature," *Yale Daily News* 98, February 27, 1970, 1.

38. Brooks, "Man and His Fictions," 41.

39. Ibid.

40. See Alvin Toffler, *Future Shock* (New York: Random House, 1970).

41. Holquist, interview by Gregory Jones-Katz, August 21, 2014.

42. William Fields, "Symphony Concert 'Remarkable,'" *Yale Daily News* 53, November 25, 1969, 4, 3.

43. William Blake also espoused a radical politics of the French Revolution. William Wordsworth, "The Tables Turned; An Evening Scene, On the Same Subject," in *The Miscellaneous Poems of William Wordsworth* (London: Longman, Hurst, Rees, Orme, and Brown, 1820), 77.

44. T. S. Eliot, "The Function of Criticism," in *Selected Prose of T. S. Eliot*, ed. Frank Kermode (London: Faber and Faber, 1975), 69.

45. Quoted in René Wellek, "The Attack on Literature," *American Scholar* 42:1 (Winter 1972–73): 27.

46. W. K. Wimsatt, *Days of the Leopards: Essays in Defense of Poems* (New Haven, CT: Yale University Press, 1976), xii.

47. Mark Royden Winchell, *Cleanth Brooks and the Rise of Modern Criticism* (Charlottesville: University Press of Virginia, 1996), 365–66.

48. Holquist, "Literature X," 12.

49. Brooks, "Man and His Fictions," 42.

50. Laura R. Cohen, "Literature X—World Premiere," *Yale Daily News* 91, February 22, 1971, 5.

51. Kernan and Holquist quoted in Cohen, "Literature X," 5.

52. Brian McHale, "1966 Nervous Breakdown; or, When Did Postmodernism Begin?," *Modern Language Quarterly* 69:3 (2008): 408.

53. Brooks, "Man and His Fictions," 43n4.

54. Kernan quoted in Cohen, "Literature X," 5.

55. Ibid.

56. Ibid.

57. Holquist, "Literature X," 10–11.

58. Alvin B. Kernan, introduction to Alvin B. Kernan, Peter Brooks, and J. Michael Holquist, *Man and His Fictions: An Introduction to Fiction-Making, Its Forms and Uses* (New York: Harcourt Brace Jovanovich, 1973), 4.

59. Ibid., 7.

60. Holquist, "Literature X," 12.

61. Ibid.

62. Cohen, "Literature X," 5.

63. "Proposed Program in Literature for Yale College," 2.

64. These modern texts are, of course, "ordinary" to us; for that time, Lit X's architects' choice to include them in the curriculum was considered by some to be improper.

65. Cohen, "Literature X," 5.

66. Kernan, Brooks, and Holquist, *Man and His Fictions*, 4.

67. Holquist, "Literature X," 13.

68. Peter Brooks and Michael Holquist to Robert L. Jackson and Victor Erlich,

March 15, 1972, RU 126, 1983-A-051, Box 14, Folder 167, Records of Dean Howard Taft, YUA.

69. Cohen, "Literature X," 5. Brooks, "Man and His Fictions," 43.

70. Brooks, "Man and His Fictions," 43.

71. Ibid.

72. Kernan, Brooks, and Holquist, *Man and His Fictions*, 10.

73. Brooks, "Man and His Fictions," 45.

74. Alain Robbe-Grillet, *Pour un nouveau roman* (Paris: Minuit, 1963), 47.

75. Kernan, Brooks, and Holquist, *Man and His Fictions*, 9–10.

76. Ibid., 188.

77. Ibid., 238–39.

78. Ibid., 307.

79. Brooks, "Man and His Fictions," 46. Kernan, Brooks, and Holquist, *Man and His Fictions*, 9.

80. J. Hillis Miller, interview by Gregory Jones-Katz, October 15, 2014.

81. Holquist taught a course on utopias with Todorov in 1967 at Yale. See Vladimir Propp, *Morphology of the Folktale* (Austin: University of Texas Press, 1968). Tzvetan Todorov, *Poetics of Prose* (Ithaca, NY: Cornell University Press, 1977). Peter Brooks, "Constructing Narrative: An Interview with Peter Brooks," in *Psychoanalysis and Storytelling* (Oxford: Blackwell, 1994), 103–5.

82. Brooks, "Man and His Fictions," 46.

83. Kernan, Brooks, and Holquist, *Man and His Fictions*, 307–11.

84. Kernan, introduction to Kernan, Brooks, and Holquist, *Man and His Fictions*, 4.

85. Kernan, Brooks, and Holquist, *Man and His Fictions*, 414.

86. Brooks, "Man and His Fictions," 46.

87. "Proposed Program in Literature for Yale College."

88. Jack H. Morgan, ed., "Literature X," *Yale Course Critique, 1972* (New Haven, CT: Yale Daily News, 1972), 92.

89. Ibid.

90. Ibid.

91. Quoted in Holquist, "Literature X," 14.

92. Morgan, "Literature X," 92.

93. Cohen, "Literature X," 5.

94. Kernan, *In Plato's Cave*, 191.

95. Holquist, "Literature after 'X,'" 45.

96. Kernan, *In Plato's Cave*, 191. Clive Barnes, "Heller's 'We Bombed in New Haven' Opens," *New York Times*, October 17, 1968. Holquist, "Literature after 'X,'" 4.

97. Quoted in Kernan, *In Plato's Cave*, 191.

98. Peter Demetz to Horace Taft, May 26, 1972, RU 126, 1983-A-051, Box 14, Folder 166, Yale College Records of the Dean 1969–1973, YUA.

99. Ibid.

100. Holquist, "Literature X," 10.

101. "Development of the Literature Major," RU 126, 1984-A-030, I, Box 30,

Folder 429, Yale College Records of the Dean 1969–1973, YUA, 1. See Reed to Horace Taft, May 22, 1972, Box 30, Folder 43, Yale College Records of the Dean 1969–1973, YUA.

102. Ibid.

103. Ibid.

104. Yale's American Studies Department could have been another candidate.

105. Quoted in Bruce Kuklick, "Philosophy at Yale in the Century after Darwin," *History of Philosophy Quarterly* 21 (2004): 333.

106. Ibid., 332.

107. Horace Taft to Alvin Kernan, January 14, 1973, Box 30, Folder 43, Yale College Records of the Dean 1969–1973, YUA.

108. Alvin Kernan to Horace Taft, January 5, 1972, RU 126, 1983-A-051, Box 14, Folder 166, Yale College Records of the Dean 1969–1973, YUA.

109. "Pamphlet on the Literature Major," RU 126, 1983-A-051, Box 30, Folder 429, Records of Dean Howard Taft, Yale College Records of the Dean 1969–1973, YUA.

110. Jerome J. Politt to Horace Taft, undated, Box 14, Folder 166, Yale College Records of the Dean, (RU 126) 1983-A-051, 1; Holquist, "Literature X," 13.

111. William K. Simpson to Alvin Kernan, April 19, 1972, Box 14, Folder 166, Yale College Records of the Dean (RU 126) 1983-A-051, YUA.

112. John W. Hall to Alvin Kernan, March 6, 1972, Box 14, Folder 166, Yale College Records of the Dean (RU 126) 1983-A-051. Janny Scott, "John W. Hall, Historian of Japan, Dies at 81," *New York Times*, October 27, 1997.

113. David Hollinger, "The Disciplines and the Identity Debates, 1970–1995," in *American Academic Culture in Transformation: Fifty Years, Four Disciplines*, ed. Stephen Bender and Carl E. Schorske (Princeton, NJ: Princeton University Press, 1998), 359.

114. Brooks, "Man and His Fictions," 48.

115. Peter Brooks, "Funding Proposal for the Literature Major," June 20, 1975, RU 126, 1984-A-030, Box 30, Folder 429, Yale College Records of the Dean 1969–1973, YUA.

116. Christopher H. Foreman, "Erich Segal: Does He Have a Choice?," *Harvard Crimson*, May 9, 1972.

117. Trudeau quoted in Mark Blankenship, "Erich Segal's Yale Story," *Yale Alumni Magazine*, March/April 2010.

118. Alvin Kernan to Horace Taft, May 12, 1972, RU 126, 1983-A-051, Box 14, Folder 166, Yale College Records of the Dean 1969–1973, YUA.

119. Holquist, "Literature X," 13–14.

120. Holquist, "Literature after 'X,'" 45.

121. Holquist, "Literature X," 14.

122. Ibid.

123. Brooks, "Man and His Fictions," 48.

124. Holquist, "Literature after 'X,'" 45.

125. Holquist, "Literature X," 14.

126. Quoted in ibid., 10.

127. Holquist contributed an article to the 1967 *Yale French Studies* special issue titled "Literature and Revolution" (the issue's title in homage to Leon Trotsky's famous work). Michael Holquist, "The Mayakovsky Problem," *Yale French Studies* 39 (1967): 126–36. Holquist, interview by Gregory Jones-Katz, September 7, 2014.

128. "Proposed Program in Literature for Yale College," 1. Lionel Trilling, *Mind in the Modern World* (New York: Viking, 1972), 18. For Trilling, a sure sign of the profession's chaos was that the modernist literary canon, which he and other critics celebrated but a decade earlier, had been subjected to skeptical scrutiny by a younger generation.

129. Not all of these left-wingers were Lit X enthusiasts; Jeffrey Mehlman recollected that he, as a graduate student in Yale's French Department, viewed Lit X as an "exercise in rightwing anarchism." Jeffrey Mehlman, interview by Gregory Jones-Katz, August 15, 2015.

130. Quoted in Holquist, "Literature X," 14.

131. Quoted in ibid., 15.

132. Brooks, "Man and His Fictions," 48.

133. Robert M. Thomas Jr., "René Wellek, 92, a Professor of Comparative Literature, Dies," *New York Times*, November 16, 1995.

134. Thomas Greene, "Versions of a Discipline," in *Building a Profession: Autobiographical Perspectives on the History of Comparative Literature in the United States*, ed. Lionel Gossman and Mihai Spaiosu (Albany: SUNY Press, 1994), 40.

135. René Wellek, "Literary Theory, Criticism, and History," in *English Studies Today*, ed. G. A. Bonnard (Bern: Francke Verlag, 1961), 62.

136. Ibid., 65. See also Todd, "Faculty Consolidates Computer Sciences, Passes Literature X," 1.

137. René Wellek, *A History of Modern Criticism, 1750–1950*, vol. 3, *The Age of Transition* (New Haven, CT: Yale University Press, 1965), vi–vii.

138. René Wellek, "Literary History," in *Literary Scholarship: Its Aims and Methods*, ed. Norman Foerster (Chapel Hill: University of North Carolina Press, 1941), 109.

139. René Wellek, "Memories of the Profession," in *Building a Profession*, 10.

140. René Wellek, "Comparative Literature Today," in *Discriminations*, 48.

141. René Wellek to Robert L. Jackson, March 14, 1972, RU 126, 1983-A-051, Box 14, Folder 166, Yale College Records of the Dean 1969–1973, YUA. Wellek's opposition to Lit X was long running: "I long ago wrote a strong letter to Kernan with the same purport, and I have again reasserted my point of view in a letter to Mr. Peter Brooks."

142. Holquist, interview by Gregory Jones-Katz, August 21, 2014.

143. René Wellek, "Some Principles of Criticism," in Wellek, George Steiner, and Richard Hoggart, *The Critical Moment: Essays on the Nature of Literature* (New York: McGraw-Hill, 1964), 40.

144. J. Hillis Miller, email correspondence with Gregory Jones-Katz, August 15, 2014.

145. René Wellek, "The Crisis in Comparative Literature," in *Concepts of Criticism*, ed. Stephen Nichols Jr. (New Haven, CT: Yale University Press, 1963), 290.

146. Wellek to Jackson, March 14, 1972.

147. Alexander M. Shenker to Horace Taft, February 28, 1972, Box 14, Folder 166, Yale College Records of the Dean (RU 126) 1983-A-051, YUA.

148. Robert L. Jackson and Victor Erlich to Horace Taft, March 6, 1972, RU 126, 1983-A-051, Box 14, Folder 167, Yale College Records of the Dean 1969–1973, YUA. Jackson and Erlich's views were originally expressed in a letter, now lost, to Kernan in 1969. Wellek's letter to Kernan expressing his opposition to the establishment of the literature major and solidarity with Professor Jackson's views is no longer extant.

149. Marissa Brostoff, "Victor Erlich, 93, Scholar of Russian Literature," *Forward*, December 5, 2007.

150. For a history of Russian formalism, see Victor Erlich, "Russian Formalism," *Journal of the History of Ideas* 34 (1973): 627–38. Erlich, *Russian Formalism: History— Doctrine* (The Hague: Mouton, 1955).

151. Quoted in Jackson and Erlich to Taft, March 6, 1972, 2.

152. Ibid., 3.

153. Ibid., 2.

154. Ibid.

155. Ibid., 3.

156. Ibid.

157. Brooks and Holquist to Jackson and Erlich, March 15, 1972.

158. Chet Cobb, "Faculty Approves Lit Major," *Yale Daily News* 121, April 21, 1972, 3.

159. Holquist, interview by Gregory Jones-Katz, September 7, 2014.

160. Holquist, "Literature X," 14; Holquist, "Literature after 'X,'" 5. Brooks, "Man and His Fictions," 48.

161. "Notes 20 April 1972, Faculty Meeting," RU 126, 1985-A-014, Box 15, Folder 268, 1.

162. Peter Brooks, interview by Gregory Jones-Katz, September 7, 2014.

163. Holquist, "Literature X," 14–15. Holquist, interview by Gregory Jones-Katz, September 7, 2014.

164. Peter Brooks to Horace Taft, July 3, 1975, RU 126, Box 30, Folder 429, Yale College Records of the Dean 1969–1973, YUA.

165. Brooks, "Man and His Fictions," 48.

166. "Proposal to the Pew Charitable Trusts," RU 126, Box 30, Folder 429, Yale College Records of the Dean 1969–1973, YUA.

167. "Pamphlet on the Literature Major."

168. Holquist, "Literature X," 15.

169. Ibid.

170. Ibid.

171. Peter Brooks, "Constructing Narrative," 104.

172. Peter Steiner, "Michael Holquist (1935–2016)," *Slavic and East European Journal* 60:3 (2016): 536.

173. Kernan, *In Plato's Cave*, 157. Kernan's views about Lit X seem to have foreshadowed the canon wars of the 1980s and 1990s.

174. Holquist, "Literature after 'X,'" 45.

Chapter Two

1. See Carl Schorske, "The New Rigorism in the Human Sciences," *Daedalus* 216:1 (1997): 289–309.

2. John Kenneth Galbraith famously used the term "the affluent society" in 1958 to denote how America had become wealthy in the private but not the public sector during the postwar period, leading to, among other issues, poverty and economic inequality. Galbraith, *The Affluent Society* (Boston: Houghton Mifflin Harcourt, 1958).

3. Louis Menand, "Demise of Disciplinary Authority," in *What's Happened to the Humanities?*, ed. Alvin Kernan (Princeton, NJ: Princeton University Press, 1997), 213.

4. P. Metzger, "The Academic Profession in the United States," in *The Academic Profession: National, Disciplinary, and Institutional Settings*, ed. Burton R. Clark (Berkeley: University of California Press, 1987), 124. See Roger L. Geiger, *American Higher Education since World War II: A History* (Princeton, NJ: Princeton University Press, 2019), particularly 4–16 on the GI Bill and 91–119 on the dominance of the university in American society.

5. See Gerald Graff, *Professing Literature: An Institutional History* (Chicago: University of Chicago Press, 1987), 121–26. Joseph North explores the temporary truce between literary scholars and literary critics during the middle decades of the twentieth century in *Literary Criticism: A Concise Political History* (Cambridge, MA: Harvard University Press, 2017).

6. The New Critics extended the work done by English critics I. A. Richards and William Empson during the 1920s and 1930s. See I. A. Richards, *Principles of Literary Criticism* (London: Routledge & Kegan Paul, 1924) and William Empson, *Seven Types of Ambiguity* (New York: New Directions, 1930). For a compelling case that the New Critics' emphasis on the text itself obscured the politically progressive aspects and evacuated the psychological interests of Richards's work, see North, *Literary Criticism*.

7. Cleanth Brooks Jr. and Robert Penn Warren, *Understanding Poetry: An Anthology for College Students* (New York: Henry Holt, 1938).

8. Brooks saw the poems of metaphysical poet John Donne as models of how to effectively use conceits. And, according to Murray Krieger, "one might think of the method of the New Criticism as the canonization of Donne's 'The Canonization.' That poem served as the master-text (or perhaps as the metatext) for at least two generations of New Critics." See Murray Krieger, "My Travels with the Aesthetic,"

in *Revenge of the Aesthetic: The Place of Literature in Theory Today*, ed. Michael P. Clark (Berkeley: University of California Press, 2000), 216.

9. Brooks and Warren, *Understanding Poetry*, 219–20.

10. Quoted in Catherine Gallagher, "The History of Literary Criticism," in *American Academic Culture in Transformation*, 153.

11. John Crowe Ransom, "Criticism, Inc.," *Virginia Quarterly Review* 13 (1937): 586–87.

12. W. K. Wimsatt Jr. and M. C. Beardsley, "The Intentional Fallacy," *Sewanee Review* 54:3 (1946): 471.

13. W. K. Wimsatt Jr. and M. C. Beardsley, "The Affective Fallacy," *Sewanee Review* 57:1 (1949): 31.

14. See W. K. Wimsatt Jr. and Cleanth Brooks Jr., *Literary Criticism: A Short History* (New York: Knopf, 1957).

15. Webster, *The Republic of Letters*, 177.

16. Jacques Ehrmann, "Discussion Highlights Selected from the Deliberations of the Colloquium on Literary Criticism Held at Yale University, March 25–27, 1965," November 23, 1964, Box 26, Folder 21, Colloquium on Literary Criticism Yale University 1964–1965, J. Hillis Miller Papers, UC-Irvine, hereafter JHM Papers, 6.

17. Imre Salusinszky, "Barbara Johnson," in *Criticism in Society: Interview with Jacques Derrida, Northrop Frye, Harold Bloom, Geoffrey Hartman, Frank Kermode, Edward Said, Barbara Johnson, Frank Lentricchia, and J. Hillis Miller*, ed. Imre Salusinszky (New York: Routledge, 1987), 156.

18. See Jacques Ehrmann, "Introduction," *Yale French Studies* 36/37 (1966): 5–9.

19. This colleague was Peter Brooks. See Peter Brooks in "The Following Tributes Were Offered at the Memorial Service for Paul de Man Held at the Yale University Art Gallery on January 18, 1984," *Yale French Studies* 69 (1985): 4–5.

20. Paul de Man, "The Return to Philology," in *The Resistance to Theory* (Minneapolis: University of Minnesota Press, 1986), 24.

21. William H. Pritchard, "Teaching: Reuben A. Brower," *American Scholar* 54:2 (1985): 239–47.

22. See Paul de Man, "L'Impasse de la critique formaliste," *Critique* 109 (1956): 438–500, reprinted as "The Dead-End of Formalist Criticism," in *Blindness and Insight*, 229–45.

23. M. H. Abrams, *The Mirror and the Lamp: Romantic Theory and the Critical Tradition* (London: Oxford University Press, 1953).

24. Paul de Man, "Structure intentionnelle de l'image romantique," *Revue international de philosophie* 51 (1960): 68–84.

25. M. H. Abrams, "Structure and Style in the Greater Romantic Lyric," in *From Sensibility to Romanticism: Essays Presented to F. A. Pottle*, ed. F. W. Hilles and Harold Bloom (New York: Oxford University Press, 1965), 551.

26. De Man, "Structure intentionnelle de l'image romantique," 82; author's translation.

27. Ibid., 81; author's translation.

28. Jacques Ehrmann to Participants in the Colloquium on Literary Criticism,

October 29, 1964, Box 26, Folder 21, Colloquium on Literary Criticism Yale University 1964–1965, JHM Papers; Paul de Man, "György Lukács's *Theory of the Novel*," *Modern Language Notes* 81:5 (1966): 527–34.

29. De Man, "György Lukács's *Theory of the Novel*," 529.

30. Ibid., 530, 531.

31. Ibid., 531.

32. Ibid., 533.

33. Ibid., 532, 534.

34. J. Hillis Miller, interview by Gregory Jones-Katz, August 23, 2019.

35. See Georges Poulet, "Phenomenology of Reading," *New Literary History* 1:1 (1969): 53–68.

36. J. Hillis Miller, "Constantly Contingent: An Interview with J. Hillis Miller," by Gregory Jones-Katz, *Derrida Today* 8:1 (2015): 50.

37. J. Hillis Miller, *Charles Dickens: The World of His Novels* (Cambridge, MA: Harvard University Press, 1958).

38. Ibid., viii.

39. Ehrmann, "Discussion Highlights," 5.

40. De Man, "György Lukács's *Theory of the Novel*," 534.

41. Ehrmann, "Discussion Highlights," 5. De Man also suggests Miller "go back to the example [he] gave in [his] paper of Proust's discussion of discontinuous time in the *Education Sentimentale*—a correct view. Or to [Gaston] Bachelard's critique of [Henri] Bergson in *La dialectique de la durée*."

42. Jacques Derrida, "Heidegger, the Philosophers' Hell," in *Points . . . : Interviews, 1974–1994*, ed. Elisabeth Weber (Stanford, CA: Stanford University Press, 1995), 181–90.

43. Martin Heidegger, "The Self-Assertion of the German University," trans. K. Harries, *Review of Metaphysics* 38:3 (1985): 467–502.

44. Martin Heidegger, *Being and Time*, trans. Joan Stambaugh (Albany: SUNY Press, 1996), 1.

45. Martin Heidegger, *An Introduction to Metaphysics*, trans. R. Manheim (New Haven, CT: Yale University Press, 1959), 199. The recent publication of Heidegger's notebooks, written between 1931 and 1941, has again instigated intense debate about the relationship of his Nazism, particularly his anti-Semitism, to his philosophical project. See Martin Heidegger, *Ponderings II–VI: Black Notebooks, 1931–1938*, trans. Richard Rojcewicz (Bloomington: Indiana University Press, 2016); Richard Wolin, "On Heidegger's Antisemitism: The Peter Trawny Affair," *Antisemitism Studies* 1:2 (2017): 245–79.

46. For a reception history of Heidegger's philosophy in America, see Martin Woessner's *Heidegger in America*. John McCumber has investigated how "the political pressures of the McCarthy era might have skewed the development" of American philosophy in *Time in the Ditch: American Philosophy and the McCarthy Era* (Evanston, IL: Northwestern University Press, 2001), quote on xvii.

47. Jack Foley, "Paul de Man and the Cornell Demaniacs," *E-Ratio Editions*, no. 14 (2011): 15, http://www.eratiopostmodernpoetry.com/issue14.html.

48. Ehrmann, "Discussion Highlights," 5.

49. Paul de Man, "Les exégèses de Hölderlin par Martin Heidegger," review of Else Buddeberg's "Heidegger und die Dichtung Hölderlin, Rilke," *Deutsche Vierteljahrsschrift für Literaturwissenschaft und Geistesgeschichte* 26:4 (1952): 293–330; de Man, "Beda Alleman's *Hölderlin und Heidegger* (1954)," *Critique* 12:100–101 (1955): 800–819.

50. De Man, "Heidegger's Exegeses of Hölderlin," in *Blindness and Insight*, 250.

51. Ibid., 254–55.

52. Ibid., 250.

53. Ibid., 259.

54. J. Hillis Miller, *The Disappearance of God: Five Nineteenth-Century Writers* (Cambridge, MA: Harvard University Press, 1962); Miller, *Poets of Reality: Six Twentieth-Century Writers* (Cambridge, MA: Harvard University Press, 1965).

55. Miller, *Poets of Reality*, 10.

56. J. Hillis Miller, "Tales out of (the Yale) School," in *Theoretical Schools and Circles in the Twentieth-Century Humanities: Literary Theory, History, Philosophy*, ed. Marina Grishakova and Silvi Salupere (New York: Routledge, 2015), 118.

57. Ibid.

58. Geoffrey Hartman, *A Scholar's Tale: Intellectual Journey of a Displaced Child of Europe* (New York: Fordham University Press, 2007), 9.

59. Ibid., 166.

60. Geoffrey Hartman, *The Unmediated Vision: An Interpretation of Wordsworth, Hopkins, Rilke, and Valéry* (New York: Harcourt, Brace and World, 1954), 128–29.

61. Hartman, *A Scholar's Tale*, 10.

62. Hartman, *The Unmediated Vision*, x.

63. Hartman, *A Scholar's Tale*, 168.

64. Miller, "Constantly Contingent," 62.

65. See Geoffrey Hartman, "Romanticism and 'Anti-Self-Consciousness,'" *Centennial Review* 6:4 (1962): 553–65.

66. Hartman, *A Scholar's Tale*, 29.

67. Ibid., 77.

68. Stanley Corngold, "Remembering Paul de Man: An Epoch in the History of Comparative Literature," in *Building a Profession*, 183.

69. Paul de Man, "Heaven and Earth in Wordsworth and Hölderlin," in *Romanticism and Contemporary Criticism: The Gauss Seminar and Other Papers*, ed. E. S. Burt, Kevin Newmark, and Andrzej Warminski (Baltimore: Johns Hopkins University Press, 1993).

70. Ibid., 138.

71. Geoffrey Hartman, interview by Gregory Jones-Katz, June 15, 2014.

72. Geoffrey Hartman, *Wordsworth's Poetry, 1787–1814* (New Haven, CT: Yale University Press, 1963), 17.

73. De Man, "Heaven and Earth in Wordsworth and Hölderlin," 138.

74. Ibid.

75. Ibid., 145.

76. Ibid., 146.

77. Ibid.

78. Geoffrey Hartman, "Beyond Formalism," unpublished manuscript, Box 26, Folder 21, Colloquium on Literary Criticism Yale University 1964–1965, JHM Papers, 1. Hartman's contribution was published as "Beyond Formalism," *Modern Language Notes* 81:5 (1966): 542–56.

79. Hartman, "Beyond Formalism" (ms), 1–2.

80. Ibid., 1.

81. Ibid.

82. Ibid., 2.

83. T. S. Eliot saw James as a case of an artist whose mind, "so fine that no idea could violate it," was immune to the corrosive dangers of self-consciousness. See T. S. Eliot, "In Memory of Henry James," in *The Complete Prose of T. S. Eliot: The Critical Edition*, vol. 1, *Apprentice Years, 1905–1918*, ed. Ronald Schuchard and Jewel Spears Brooker (Baltimore: Johns Hopkins University Press, 2014), 650.

84. Hartman, "Beyond Formalism" (ms), 1. See Georges Poulet, *Études sur le temps humain*, vol. 3, *Le point de départ* (Paris: Plon, 1964).

85. Hartman, "Beyond Formalism" (ms), 12, 13.

86. Ibid., 13.

87. Ibid., 15, 16.

88. De Man quoted in Ehrmann, "Discussion Highlights," 6.

89. Ibid.

90. Hartman, "Beyond Formalism" (ms), 17.

91. Ehrmann, "Discussion Highlights," 6.

92. Ibid.

93. J. Hillis Miller, "The Literary Criticism of Georges Poulet," *Modern Language Notes* 78:5 (1963): 474.

94. Ehrmann, "Discussion Highlights," 7.

95. Ibid.

96. Maurice Merleau-Ponty, "Concerning Marxism," in *Sense and Nonsense*, trans. Hubert L. Dreyfus and Patricia A. Dreyfus (Evanston, IL: Northwestern University Press, 1964), 121. The original in French was published in 1946, but quotations in the text are from this translation.

97. Maurice Merleau-Ponty, *Humanism and Terror: An Essay on the Communist Problem*, trans. John O'Neill (Boston: Beacon, 1969), 153. The original in French was published in 1947, but quotations in the text are from this translation.

98. Ibid., 130.

99. Ehrmann, "Discussion Highlights," 8.

100. Ibid.

101. Ibid.

102. Ibid.

103. Ibid., 7.

104. J. Hillis Miller, "The Antitheses of Criticism: Reflections on the Yale Colloquium," *Modern Language Notes* 81:5 (1966): 557–71.

105. Ibid., 557.

106. Ibid.

107. Ibid., 558.

108. Ibid., 559.

109. Ibid.

110. Jacques Ehrmann to J. Hillis Miller, March 20, Box 26, Folder 21, Colloquium on Literary Criticism Yale University 1964–1965, JHM Papers; Miller, "The Antitheses of Criticism," 557.

111. "Request for Grant Action," Ford Foundation Grants, FA732D, Reel 1452, Report 06600108, Ford Foundation Archive, 10.

112. Stuart W. Leslie, "Richard Macksey and the Humanities Center," *Modern Language Notes* 134:5 (2019): 931.

113. "Request for Grant Action," 5.

114. Richard Macksey, "Anniversary Reflections," in *The Structuralist Controversy: The Languages of Criticism and the Sciences of Man*, rev. ed., ed. Richard Macksey and Eugenio Donato (Baltimore: Johns Hopkins University Press, 2007), xi.

115. Greg Barnhisel, *Cold War Modernists: Art, Literature, and American Cultural Diplomacy* (New York: Columbia University Press, 2015), 184.

116. "A Structuralist Institute at the Johns Hopkins University: A Proposal to the Ford Foundation: Humanities & Arts Division, October 1965," Ford Foundation Grants, FA732D, Reel 1452, Report 06600108, Ford Foundation Archive, 2.

117. Macksey, "Anniversary Reflections," xii.

118. R. S. Crane, "History versus Criticism in the Study of Literature," reprinted in *The Languages of Criticism and the Structure of Poetry* (Toronto: University of Toronto Press, 1953), 13.

119. Ibid.

120. Webster, *The Republic of Letters*, 120.

121. Macksey, "Anniversary Reflections," xii.

122. "Hopkins and the Development of American Criticism," Ford Foundation Grants, FA723D, Reel 1453, Report 06600108, Ford Foundation Archive, 13.

123. A. O. Lovejoy, *The Great Chain of Being: A Study of the History of an Idea* (1936; repr., New York: Harper Torchbooks, 1960), 7.

124. See A. O. Lovejoy, "On the Discrimination of Romanticisms," *PMLA* 39 (1924): 229–53. René Wellek famously responded to Lovejoy's slicing and dicing of "Romanticism" with a defense of literary periods as evaluative categories and a reaffirmation of cultural periods as discrete entities. See René Wellek, "The Concept of 'Romanticism' in Literary History II: The Unity of European Romanticism," *Comparative Literature* 2 (1949): 147–72.

125. "Grant Acceptance Letters," Ford Foundation Grants, FA723D, Reel 1453, Report 06600108, Ford Foundation Archive, 5.

126. "A Structuralist Institute at the Johns Hopkins University," 17–18.

127. Quoted in Leslie, "Richard Macksey and the Humanities Center," 931. Richard Macksey, "Letter to Ryerson," July 27, 1965, Johns Hopkins University Archive, Box 5, Macksey Papers, 08-09.01, Macksey Promotions.

128. "A Structuralist Institute at the Johns Hopkins University," 3.

129. Ibid., 4, 3.

130. Ibid., 4.

131. Ibid., 13–15, 2.

132. "Narrative Report," Ford Foundation Grants, FA723D, Reel 1453, Report 06600108, Ford Foundation Archive, 3.

133. Charles Morazé, "Literary Invention," in *The Structuralist Controversy*, 25, 26, 28, 29.

134. Roland Barthes, "To Write: An Intransitive Verb?," in *The Structuralist Controversy*, 134–45; Tzvetan Todorov, "Language and Literature," in *The Structuralist Controversy*, 125–33.

135. See Benoît Peeters, *Derrida: A Biography*, trans. Andrew Brown (Cambridge: Polity, 2013), 59–79.

136. Jacques Derrida, *Edmund Husserl's Origin of Geometry: An Introduction*, trans. John O. Leavey (Lincoln: University of Nebraska Press, 1989).

137. Ibid., 77.

138. Ibid., 50, 78, 79.

139. Ibid., 86, 87, 92.

140. Ibid., 102, 118.

141. Ibid., 152.

142. Jacques Derrida, *Of Grammatology*, trans. Gayatri Chakravorty Spivak (Baltimore: Johns Hopkins University Press, 1976), 158.

143. Jacques Derrida, *Heidegger: The Question of Being and History*, trans. Thomas Dutoit (Chicago: University of Chicago Press, 2016), 15. For the first monograph on this topic, see Sean Gaston, *Jacques Derrida and the Challenge of History* (London: Rowman and Littlefield, 2019).

144. Derrida, *Heidegger*, 138. See also Martin Heidegger, *Being and Time*, trans. John Macquarrie and Edward Robinson (New York: Harper and Row, 1961), 78.

145. Derrida, *Heidegger*, 92, 133, 153.

146. Ibid., 155.

147. Ibid., 138.

148. Ibid.

149. Ibid., 224; emphasis added.

150. "A Structuralist Institute at the Johns Hopkins University," 1.

151. Jacques Derrida, "Structure, Sign and Play in the Discourse of the Human Sciences," in *The Structuralist Controversy*, 252.

152. Ibid., 253.

153. Ibid.

154. Ibid., 254.

155. Jacques Derrida, "Discussion," in *The Structuralist Controversy*, 270–71.

156. Miller, "Tales out of (the Yale) School," 118.

157. Jean Rousset, *Forme et signification: Essais sur les structures littéraires, de Corneille à Claudel* (Paris: Corti, 1963); Jacques Derrida, "Force and Signification," in *Writing and Difference*, trans. Alan Bass (Chicago: University of Chicago Press, 1978), 3–30.

158. Rousset, *Forme et signification*, i; author's translation.

159. Derrida, "Force and Signification," 4, 15, 13–14.

160. Ibid., 16.

161. Ibid., 4–5.

162. Ibid., 19.

163. Ibid.

164. Ibid., 16. Rodolphe Gasché, *Deconstruction, Its Force, Its Violence: Together with "Have We Done with the Empire of Judgment?"* (Albany: SUNY Press, 2016), 9.

165. Neil Hertz, interview by Gregory Jones-Katz, June 15, 2014.

166. This was "a text then little read," Derrida recalled. Jacques Derrida, *Memoires for Paul de Man*, trans. Cecile Lindsay, Jonathan Culler, Eduardo Cadava, and Peggy Kamuf (New York: Columbia University Press, 1986), 127.

167. Paul de Man, "An Interview with Paul de Man," by Stefano Rosso, *Critical Inquiry* 12:4 (1986): 791. De Man was not the only one who detected this uncanny intersection. Samuel Weber, then writing his dissertation at Cornell under de Man, attested that "it rapidly seemed to me that Derrida was doing what Paul de Man was trying to do." Quoted in Peeters, *Derrida*, 181.

168. Paul de Man, "Rhétorique de la cécité: Derrida lecteur de Rousseau," *Poétique* 4 (1970): 445–75. De Man, "The Rhetoric of Blindness: Jacques Derrida's Reading of Rousseau," in *Blindness and Insight*, 102–41. See Peeters, *Derrida*, 557n41.

169. Derrida, *Memoires for Paul de Man*, 127.

170. De Man, "The Rhetoric of Blindness," 114. Jean Starobinski, *Jean-Jacques Rousseau: La transparence et l'obstacle* (Paris: Plon, 1957).

171. De Man, "The Rhetoric of Blindness," 115.

172. Ibid., 116, 114, 113.

173. Ibid., 114, 115.

174. Derrida, *Of Grammatology*, 235.

175. De Man, "The Rhetoric of Blindness," 115.

176. Ibid., 135.

177. Ibid., 119.

178. Ibid., 136.

179. Ibid., 139.

180. Ibid., 141; emphasis added.

181. Ibid.

182. Ibid., 138, 138–39.

183. "A Structuralist Institute at the Johns Hopkins University," 17, 18.

184. See Hartman, *A Scholar's Tale*, 5, 184n19.

185. Geoffrey Hartman, "Structuralism: The Anglo-American Adventure," *Yale French Studies* 36/37 (1966): 152.

186. Marshall McLuhan, *Understanding Media: The Extensions of Man* (New York: Signet, 1964).

187. Hartman, "Structuralism," 152, 154. This article's argument provoked W. K. Wimsatt to accuse Hartman and others of "battering the [literary] object." See the beginning of chapter 1.

188. Ibid., 155.

189. Northrup Frye, *The Anatomy of Criticism: Four Essays* (Princeton, NJ: Princeton University Press, 1957), 350, 352.

190. Hartman, "Structuralism," 161.

191. Ibid., 154.

192. Ibid.

193. Kafka quoted in ibid., 167.

194. Ibid., 167.

195. Morton W. Bloomfield, "Thoughts on the Topic (Languages of the Humanistic Studies)," May 4–7, 1968, La Jolla, California, Box 26, Folder 24, Conference on the Languages of the Humanistic Study 1968, JHM Papers, 1–2, 3.

196. Leslie, "Richard Macksey and the Humanities Center," 930.

197. "The Continuing Seminars," Ford Foundation Grants, FA723D, Reel 1453, Report 06600108, Ford Foundation Archive, 11.

198. Derrida, general introduction to *Heidegger*, x.

199. See Peeters, *Derrida*, 193–94. Derek Attridge, "The First Session," in *Acts of Literature*, by Jacques Derrida, ed. Derek Attridge (New York: Routledge, 1992), 110.

200. Jacques Derrida, "The Double Session," in *Dissemination*, trans. Barbara Johnson (Chicago: University of Chicago Press, 1983), 187.

201. See Barbara Johnson, translator's introduction to *Dissemination*, xxiv.

202. Derrida, "The Double Session," 206.

203. Ibid., 229, 245–46.

204. Ibid., 210, 206.

205. See Catherine Clément to Jacques Derrida, quoted in Peeters, *Derrida*, 208.

206. Peeters, *Derrida*, 201.

207. J. Hillis Miller, "Memorandum, Conference on the Languages of the Humanistic Studies," May 4–7, 1968, La Jolla, California, Box 26, Folder 24, JHM Papers, 6.

208. Ibid., 4, 5, 6.

209. Ibid., 1.

210. Ibid., 7.

211. Ibid.

212. Ibid., 8.

213. Ibid.

214. Geoffrey Hartman, "Memorandum, Conference on the Languages of the Humanistic Studies," May 4–7, 1968, La Jolla, California, Box 26, Folder 25, JHM Papers, 1.

215. Ibid.

216. Ibid., 2.

217. Ibid.

218. Ibid., 5.

219. Leslie, "Richard Macksey and the Humanities Center," 926.

220. Paul de Man, "Form and Intent in the American New Criticism," in *Blindness and Insight*, 21. De Man translated and revised this article from the original "New

324 * Notes to Pages 114–121

criticism et nouvelle critique," *Preuves* 16:188 (October 1966): 29–37. De Man, "Acknowledgments," in *Blindness and Insight*, xiii.

221. De Man, "Form and Intent in the American New Criticism," 22.

222. Ibid., 31–32.

223. Peeters, *Derrida*, 181.

224. Miller, "Tales out of (the Yale) School," 119.

225. "Narrative Report: The Languages of Criticism and the Sciences of Man: Les Langages Critiques et Les Sciences de L'Homme 1966–68," Ford Foundation Grant No. 66-108, Ford Foundation Archive, 12.

226. Paul de Man, "Introduction," De Man Introduction to 1968 Zurich Conference, Box 39, Folder 7, Paul de Man's Wartime Writings 1942–1988, JHM Papers, 5.

227. Ibid., 6.

228. Charles S. Singleton, preface to *Interpretation: Theory and Practice* (Baltimore: Johns Hopkins University Press, 1969), v.

229. De Man, foreword to revised edition of *Blindness and Insight*, xii.

230. Jonathan Freedman, *The Temple of Culture: Assimilation and Anti-Semitism in Literary Anglo-America* (Oxford: Oxford University Press, 2000), 23; Paul de Man, "The Rhetoric of Temporality," in *Interpretation: Theory and Practice*, 174.

231. De Man, "The Rhetoric of Temporality," 191.

232. Ibid., 203.

233. "Continuing Seminars and Related Events," Ford Foundation Grant No. 66-108, Ford Foundation Archive, 48. Peeters, *Derrida*, 202. Jacques Derrida, "The Ends of Man," *Philosophy and Phenomenological Research* 30:1 (1969): 34.

234. Derrida, "The Ends of Man," 48.

235. Ibid., 45.

236. Ibid., 48, 56.

237. J. Hillis Miller to Jacques Derrida, June 2, 1969, Box 3, Folder 42, Derrida 1971–2001, JHM Papers, Critical Theory Archive, 1.

238. J. Hillis Miller to Paul de Man, June 2, 1969, Box 3, Folder 42, Derrida 1971–2001, JHM Papers, Critical Theory Archive, 1.

239. Morton W. Bloomfield and Stephen R. Graubard to Northrop Frye, December 23, 1968, RS105_nfrye_Box 65, Folder 02, conference correspondence, Northrop Frye Archives, E. J. Pratt Library at Victoria University, 1.

240. Stephen R. Graubard, "Preface to the Issue 'Theory in Humanistic Studies,'" *Daedalus* 99 (1970): vi, v.

241. Ibid., vi.

242. Geoffrey Hartman, "Toward Literary History," *Daedalus* 99 (1970): 364.

243. Ibid., 355.

244. Ibid., 369.

245. Ibid.

246. Paul de Man, "Literary History and Literary Modernity," *Daedalus* 99 (1970): 384–404.

247. Ibid., 392, 399–400.

248. Ibid., 400.

249. Ibid.

250. Ibid., 403.

251. J. Hillis Miller, "Williams' 'Spring and All' and the Progress of Poetry," *Daedalus* 99 (1970): 416.

252. Ibid., 429.

253. Ibid., 417.

254. Ibid., 427.

255. Ibid., 419.

256. Ibid., 429.

257. Ibid.

258. Ibid., 429, 430.

259. These journals included *New Literary History* (1969), *Diacritics* (1971), *Feminist Studies* (1972), *Critical Inquiry* (1974), and *Social Text* (1979). Jeffrey Williams, "The Brief, Wondrous Life of the Theory Journal," *Chronicle Review*, October 16, 2011.

Chapter Three

1. Edward W. Said, "Two without a Context," *New York Times Book Review*, December 10, 1972, 4–5, 12.

2. William H. Pritchard, "The Hermeneutical Mafia or, After Strange Gods at Yale," *Hudson Review* 28:4 (1975–76): 601.

3. See also Gerald Graff, "Fear and Trembling at Yale," *American Scholar* 46:4 (1977): 467–78; Richard Poirier, "The Fate of Reading," *New York Review of Books*, April 20, 1975, BR6.

4. The Yale group was not alone in this endeavor. Stateside, Kenneth Burke had been working in the field of rhetorical literary criticism for several decades; in France, Tzvetan Todorov and Gérard Genette were leaders in the field.

5. Neil Gross, *Richard Rorty: The Making of an American Philosopher* (Chicago: University of Chicago Press, 2008), 284. See Schorske, "The New Rigorism in the Human Sciences," 301. See also David Bromwich, "The Cost of Professionalism in the Humanities," in *Learned Societies and the Evolution of the Disciplines*, American Council of Learned Societies (ACLS) Occasional Paper no. 5 (New York, 1988), 9–16. For how methods in literary studies were scientistic during this period, see Wallace Martin, "Criticism in the Academy," in *The Cambridge History of Literary Criticism*, ed. A. Walton Litz, Louis Menand, and Laurence Rainey, vol. 7, *Modernism and the New Criticism* (Cambridge: Cambridge University Press, 2000), 269–321.

6. Yale had a tradition and a position of leadership in the academic study of religions.

7. Freedman, *The Temple of Culture*, 184.

8. Felperin, *In Another Life*, 62.

9. Evelyn Barish, *The Double Life of Paul de Man* (New York: Liveright, 2014), 433.

10. De Man, *Blindness and Insight*.

11. Yale College Catalog quoted in Roberto González Echevarría, *Love and the Law in Cervantes* (New Haven, CT: Yale University Press, 2005), xiii.

12. Kernan, *In Plato's Cave*, 197.

13. Paul de Man, "Genesis and Genealogy in Nietzsche's *The Birth of Tragedy*," *Diacritics* 2:3 (1972): 44–53.

14. Ibid., 45.

15. Ibid., 46.

16. Paul de Man, Box 15, Folder 20, Rousseau and Nietzsche, Teaching Notes circa 1971–1972, Paul de Man Papers, Special Collections and Archives, Critical Theory Archive, UC-Irvine, hereafter PDM Papers; De Man, Box 11, Folder 11, Nietzsche (Yale), PDM Papers, 1–13.

17. De Man, "Genesis and Genealogy," 52.

18. Ibid., 49.

19. De Man, Box 15, Folder 20, Rousseau and Nietzsche, Teaching Notes circa 1971–1972, PDM Papers.

20. De Man, "Genesis and Genealogy," 48.

21. Salusinszky, "Barbara Johnson," 156.

22. Ibid.

23. Ibid., 157. The first part of this quotation is from Nietzsche, quoted from *The Portable Nietzsche*, ed. and trans. Walter Kaufmann (New York: Penguin, 1976), 44. The second Johnson quotes in the interview.

24. Felperin, *In Another Life*, 62.

25. Nietzsche quoted in Harold Bloom, *The Anxiety of Influence: A Theory of Poetry*, 2nd ed. (New York: Oxford University Press, 1997), 49.

26. Harold Bloom, *Shelley's Mythmaking* (New Haven, CT: Yale University Press, 1959).

27. Percy Shelley, *The Masque of Anarchy: A Poem* (London: Edward Moxon, 1832), 47.

28. Harold Bloom, *The Visionary Company: A Reading of English Romantic Poetry* (New York: Doubleday, 1961).

29. *The Complete Poetry and Prose of William Blake*, rev. ed., ed. David V. Endman, commentary by Harold Bloom (New York: Anchor Books, 1988), 153.

30. Harold Bloom, "The Internalization of Quest-Romance," *Yale Review* 58:4 (Summer 1969): 526–36.

31. Harold Bloom, *The Western Canon: The Books and School of the Ages* (New York: Riverhead Books, 1995), 483.

32. Tom Shadwell, "The Wasteland of New Criticism," *Yale Daily News* 99, February 25, 1959, 2.

33. Timothy T. Yates, ed., "English 45b," *Yale Course Critique, 1967* (New Haven, CT: Yale Daily News, 1967), 61.

34. Michael Angelo Baris and Hunter Morrison., eds., "English 45b," *Yale Course Critique, 1968* (New Haven, CT: Yale Daily News, 1968), 66.

35. Felperin, *In Another Life*, 7.

36. Quoted in Felperin, *In Another Life*, 7.

37. Geoffrey Hartman, "A Life of Learning: Charles Homer Haskins Lecture for 2000," ACLS Occasional Paper no. 46 (New York, 2000), 13.

38. See Paul de Man, "The Crisis of Contemporary Criticism," *Arion: A Journal of Humanities and the Classics* 6:1 (1967): 38–57.

39. Jacques Ehrmann, "The Death of Literature," *New Literary History* 3:1 (1971): 32, 41n5.

40. Ibid., 43; emphasis in original.

41. Newton Garver, preface to *Speech and Phenomena, and Other Essays on Husserl's Theory of Signs*, by Jacques Derrida, trans. David B. Allison (Evanston, IL: Northwestern University Press, 1973), ix–xxix.

42. See Jean-Philippe Mathy, *French Resistance: The French-American Culture Wars* (Minneapolis: University of Minnesota Press, 2000), 2.

43. See Currie, *The Invention of Deconstruction*, 39, 38. De Man, "Genesis and Genealogy," 45.

44. Alexander Gelley, "Form as Force," review of *De la grammatologie*, by Jacques Derrida, *Diacritics* 2:1 (1972): 9.

45. Currie, *The Invention of Deconstruction*, 81–107.

46. Frederic Jameson, *Postmodernism, or, The Cultural Logic of Late Capitalism* (London: Verso, 1991), 91.

47. See Elisabeth Roudinesco, "Lacan and Derrida in the History of Psychoanalysis," *Journal of European Psychoanalysis* 2 (Fall 1995–Winter 1996): 91–106.

48. Jacques Lacan, *Écrits: The First Complete Edition in English*, trans. Bruce Fink (New York: Norton, 2006), 6–48.

49. Ibid., 16.

50. Ibid., 17.

51. Ibid., 30.

52. Jacques Derrida, "The Purveyor of Truth," *Yale French Studies* 52 (1975): 31–113.

53. Ibid., 50.

54. Jacques Derrida, "Positions," in *Positions*, trans. Alan Bass (Chicago: University of Chicago Press, 1981), 69.

55. Charles Singleton, quoted in Leslie, "Richard Macksey and the Humanities Center," 936; Charles Singleton to Lincoln Gordon, January 22, 1980, Johns Hopkins University Archive, RG02.001. Box 32, Office of the Provost, Series 9, f., Humanities Center, 1969–1971.

56. Leslie, "Richard Macksey and the Humanities Center," 936.

57. J. Hillis Miller, "Tradition and Difference," *Diacritics* 2:4 (Winter 1972): 6–13, 8.

58. Miller, "Constantly Contingent," 59.

59. Ibid.

60. J. Hillis Miller, Box 30, Folder 42, English 48b: "The Language of Poetry 1973–1974," JHM Papers.

61. Wald Godzich, "Paul de Man and the Perils of Intelligence," in *The Culture of Literacy* (Cambridge, MA: Harvard University Press, 1994), 134. Paul de Man, "Semiology and Rhetoric," *Diacritics* 3:3 (1973): 27–33, 27.

62. De Man, "Semiology and Rhetoric," *Diacritics*, 28.

63. W. B. Yeats, *The Collected Poems of W. B. Yeats*, ed. Richard J. Finneran (New York: Palgrave Macmillan, 1989), 217.

64. De Man, "Semiology and Rhetoric," *Diacritics*, 30.

65. Ibid., 32.

66. Ibid., 30.

67. Paul de Man, "Semiology and Rhetoric," in *Allegories of Reading: Figural Language in Rousseau, Nietzsche, Rilke, and Proust* (New Haven, CT: Yale University Press, 1979), 14.

68. De Man, "Semiology and Rhetoric," *Diacritics*, 31.

69. Ibid.

70. Quoted in ibid., 31.

71. De Man, "Semiology and Rhetoric," in *Allegories of Reading*, 66.

72. De Man, "Semiology and Rhetoric," *Diacritics*, 31.

73. See Cleanth Brooks's discussion of metaphor in his pioneering essay, "Irony as a Principle of Structure," reprinted in *Literary Opinion in America*, 3rd ed., ed. Morton Dauwen Zabel (New York: Harper and Row, 1962), 729–41.

74. Some of de Man's graduate students read his deconstructive intervention into the inside/outside metaphor as a statement against the American military presence in Vietnam. See Corngold, "Remembering Paul de Man," 188.

75. J. Hillis Miller to Harold Bloom, August 10, 1973, Box 24, Folder 22, JHM Papers.

76. T. S. Eliot, "Tradition and Individual Talent," in *Selected Essays 1917–1932* (New York: Harcourt, Brace and Company, 1932), 7. Bloom, *The Anxiety of Influence*, 30.

77. Paul de Man, "Review of Harold Bloom's *Anxiety of Influence*," *Comparative Literature* 26:3 (1974): 269.

78. Geoffrey Hartman, "War in Heaven," *Diacritics* 3:1 (Spring 1973): 28.

79. Ibid.

80. Ibid.

81. Ibid.

82. Miller to Bloom, August 10, 1973.

83. Paul de Man to J. Hillis Miller, August 26, 1973, Box 12, Folder 9, Correspondence, PDM Papers, 1.

84. Felperin quoted in Kim Rogal, "The Politics of Poetics," *Yale Daily News* 101, March 6, 1974, 9.

85. Other professors who either retired or left Yale English included Maynard Mack, Alvin Kernan, Charles Prouty, E. Talbot Donaldson, and Richard Sewall.

86. Hartman, "A Life of Learning," 10. See W. K. Wimsatt, "The Concrete Universal," in *The Verbal Icon*, 69–83.

87. Cleanth Brooks, *Modern Poetry and the Tradition* (Chapel Hill: University of North Carolina Press, 1939).

88. Hartman, "A Life of Learning," 46, 17. Imre Salusinszky, "Harold Bloom," in *Criticism in Society*, 61. For more on Jews at Yale, see Dan A. Oren, *Joining the Club: A History of Jews and Yale* (New Haven, CT: Yale University Press, 1985). "Frederic

Pottle, Yale's senior Romanticist, kept the flame alive in his cool, scientific way," Hartman recalled in "A Life of Learning," 13.

89. This is not to say that other Jewish critics at Yale completely shied away from the topic. Charles Feidelson Jr., the first tenured Jewish scholar in the department, subtly worked against the conflation of Christianity and criticism by revising, in a 1948 book, scholars' inclinations to magnify the symbol to metaphysical proportions and tell stories of American literature that justified the American self in Puritan identities and practices. See Barbara Foley, "From New Criticism to Deconstruction: The Example of Charles Feidelson's 'Symbolism and American Literature,'" *American Quarterly* 36 (1984): 44–70. Jewish American Stanley Fish, a graduate student in Yale English during the late 1950s and early 1960s, should be included in any larger study on this topic, as his "Reader Response" approach to literature deliberately broke with the New Critical tradition of his mentors Cleanth Brooks and W. K. Wimsatt. Hartman, as a graduate student, delivered a talk titled "Darkness and the Absence of the Soul in Hebrew Liturgy" at the Hillel Graduate Society and in the 1960s performed self-guided readings in the Jewish tradition and "[h]ere and there smuggle[d] a poem by Judah Halevi or a Biblical source into [his] classes." "U-Notes," *Yale Daily News* 76, October 8, 1955, 4; Hartman, "A Life of Learning," 8. The most famous member of the first generation of Jews to earn a tenured position in English literature in the Ivy League was Lionel Trilling. He began his career writing essays and fictions in the pages of *Menorah* from 1925 to 1931, and, in 1932, became the first Jew taken on as an instructor by Columbia's English Department; in 1948, he became the university's first Jewish full professor in English. Other Jews would follow in Trilling's footsteps. See Susanne Klingenstein, *Jews in the American Academy, 1900–1940: The Dynamics of Intellectual Assimilation* (Syracuse, NY: Syracuse University Press, 1998), 137.

90. See Hollinger, *Science, Jews, and Secular Culture*, particularly chapter 2, 17–41.

91. Rogal, "The Politics of Poetics," 9.

92. See one such response in Bernard S. Adams, "Liberal Education and the 'New Vocationalism,'" *Liberal Education* 61:3 (1975): 339–48.

93. David E. Eisenbud, ed., "English," *Yale Course Critique, 1975* (New Haven, CT: Yale Daily News, 1975), 73e.

94. Miller quoted in Rogal, "The Politics of Poetics," 9.

95. Faulkner quoted in ibid.

96. "Brewster Names Hartman to Plan Humanities Council," *Yale Daily News* 104, March 6, 1973, 3.

97. Rogal, "The Politics of Poetics," 9.

98. Ibid.

99. Geoffrey Hartman, "The Interpreter: A Self-Analysis," *New Literary History* 4 (Winter 1973): 213–27.

100. Ibid., 213.

101. Ibid., 226.

102. Hartman, "A Life of Learning," 10.

103. Hartman, *A Scholar's Tale*, 74, 79.

104. Derrida, *Glas*, trans. John P. Leavey Jr. and Richard Rand (Lincoln: University of Nebraska Press, 1986).

105. Hartman, *A Scholar's Tale*, 69.

106. Hartman, "Monsieur Texte: On Jacques Derrida, His *Glas*," *Georgia Review* 29:4 (Winter 1975): 759–97, 773.

107. Jean Genet, *Funeral Rights*, trans. Bernard Frechtman (New York: Grove, 1994), 157.

108. Hartman, "Monsieur Texte"; Geoffrey Hartman, "Monsieur Texte II: Epiphany in Echoland," *Georgia Review* 30:1 (Spring 1976): 169–204.

109. Hartman, "Monsieur Texte," 763, 775.

110. Hartman, "Monsieur Texte II," 177.

111. Hartman, "Monsieur Texte," 782, 784.

112. Hartman partly corrected such a view in "Literary Criticism and Its Discontents," *Critical Inquiry* 3:2 (1976): 203–20.

113. Hartman, "Monsieur Texte II," 177.

114. Hartman, "Monsieur Texte," 784.

115. Hartman, "A Life of Learning," 8.

116. Hartman, introduction to *Saving the Text: Literature/Derrida/Philosophy* (Baltimore: Johns Hopkins University Press, 1981), xxii. Hartman, *A Scholar's Tale*, 72. The "temples" are in reference to Paul Valéry's "logocentric vision."

117. Hartman, *A Scholar's Tale*, 70.

118. Hartman, "Monsieur Texte II," 189. Hartman, "Monsieur Texte," 779. Hartman, "A Life of Learning," 8.

119. Hartman, *A Scholar's Tale*, 75.

120. Hartman, "A Life of Learning," 8. Donoghue quoted in Geoffrey Hartman, "Tea and Totality: The Demand of Theory on Critical Style," in *Minor Prophesies: The Literary Essay in the Culture Wars* (Cambridge, MA: Harvard University Press, 1991), 59.

121. Culler quoted in Rogal, "The Politics of Poetics," 8.

122. "Bloom Fills DeVane Seat," *Yale Daily News* 106, March 14, 1974, 2.

123. Wlad Godzich, "Harold Bloom as Rhetorician," *Centrum: Working Papers of the Minnesota Center for Advanced Studies in Language, Style, and Literary Theory* 6:2 (1978): 43.

124. Harold Bloom, *A Map of Misreading* (Oxford: Oxford University Press, 1975), 149.

125. Harold Bloom, *Kabbalah and Criticism* (New York: Seabury, 1975), 66.

126. Ibid., 16, 37, 46.

127. Ibid., 64.

128. Ibid., 67.

129. J. Hillis Miller, "Stevens' Rock and Criticism as a Cure II," *Georgia Review* 30:2 (1976): 339.

130. Harold Bloom to J. Hillis Miller, August 17, 1974, Box 24, Folder 1, 1956–1977 Correspondence, JHM Papers.

131. Harold Bloom, "Emerson and Ammons: A Coda," *Diacritics* 3:4 (1973): 45.

132. Harold Bloom to J. Hillis Miller, undated, Box 31, Folder 26, JHM Papers, 1.

133. Bloom, "Emerson and Ammons," 46. See also Bloom, *Wallace Stevens: The Poems of Our Climate* (Ithaca, NY: Cornell University Press, 1980), 161.

134. Harold Bloom to J. Hillis Miller, undated, Box 31, Folder 26, JHM Papers, 1.

135. Leslie Brisman, *Milton's Poetry of Choice and Its Romantic Heirs* (Ithaca, NY: Cornell University Press, 1973); Howard Felperin, *Shakespearean Romance* (Princeton, NJ: Princeton University Press, 1972).

136. Harold Bloom to J. Hillis Miller, August 17, 1974, Box 31, Folder 26, JHM Papers, UC-Irvine, 1.

137. See Freedman, *The Temple of Culture*, 20.

138. Paul de Man to Jacques Derrida, April 28, 1974, quoted in Peeters, *Derrida*, 272.

139. Richard Rand quoted in Peeters, *Derrida*, 281.

140. See Jeffrey Mehlman, *Adventures in the French Trade: Fragments toward a Life* (Stanford, CA: Stanford University Press, 2010), 75.

141. The topics of these seminars included debt, signature, countersignature, proper names, and death.

142. Jacques Derrida, *Signéponge/Signsponge*, trans. Richard Rand (New York: Columbia University Press, 1984), Rand on front flap. See also Derrida's comments on 116.

143. Richard Rand, introduction to *Signéponge/Signsponge*, x. Francis Ponge, "Fable," in *Tome premier* (Paris: Gallimard, 1965), 144.

144. Rand, "Greenwood," in *Signéponge/Signsponge*, ix.

145. Derrida quoted in Peeters, *Derrida*, 279.

146. Ibid.

147. See René Wellek, "The Crisis of Comparative Literature," in *Concepts of Criticism*, ed. Stephen G. Nichols Jr. (New Haven, CT: Yale University Press, 1963), 283.

148. For a compelling consideration of Derrida's 1975 ENS seminar and an argument of how it served as the "matrix" of Derrida's deconstruction, see Francesco Vitale, *Biodeconstruction: Jacques Derrida and the Life Sciences*, trans. Mauro Senatore (Albany: SUNY Press, 2018), 2.

149. Jonathan Culler, *Structuralist Poetics: Structuralism, Linguistics and the Study of Literature* (Ithaca, NY: Cornell University Press, 1975), specifically chapter 10, 281–96.

150. Mehlman, *Adventures in the French Trade*, 75–76.

151. Paul De Man to Jacques Derrida, quoted in Peeters, *Derrida*, 273.

152. J. Hillis Miller, Box 1, Folder 8, 1975 I Notebook, JHM Papers.

153. Ibid.

154. J. Hillis Miller, "Ariadne's Thread: Repetition and the Narrative Line," *Critical Inquiry* 3:1 (1976): 57–77.

155. Miller, "Stevens' Rock and Criticism as a Cure II," 335, 338.

156. J. Hillis Miller, Box 1, Folder 8, 1975 I Notebook, JHM Papers.

157. J. Hillis Miller, "The Year's Books: On Literary Criticism," *New Republic*, November 29, 1975, 30–33, 33.

158. Ibid., 33.

159. Poirier, "The Fate of Reading."

160. Pritchard, "The Hermeneutical Mafia," 601.

161. Ibid., 602; see also 602n2.

162. Hartman, "Literary Criticism and Its Discontents," 203.

163. Paul de Man, Box 12, Folder 8, Rhetorical Readings (Yale); Irony (Yale) 1975–1976, PDM Papers.

164. Originally published as Jacques Derrida, "La mythologie blanche: La métaphore dans le texte philosophique," *Poétique* 5 (1971): 1–51.

165. Jacques Derrida, "White Mythology: Metaphor in the Text of Philosophy," *New Literary History* 6 (Autumn 1974): 11.

166. Jacques Derrida, "Freud and the Scene of Writing," *Yale French Studies* 48 (1972): 86.

167. De Man, Box 12, Folder 8, Rhetorical Readings (Yale); Irony (Yale) 1975–1976, PDM Papers, 14. Derrida, "White Mythology," 11. See also Derrida, "Freud and the Scene of Writing," 75.

168. Paul de Man, "Political Allegory in Rousseau," *Critical Inquiry* 2:4 (1976): 674. De Man, "Allegory of Reading (*Profession de foi*)," in *Allegories of Reading*, 245.

169. Paul de Man, notebook, Box 12, Folder 8, Rhetorical Readings (Yale); Irony (Yale) 1975–1976, PDM Papers.

170. De Man quoted in *Allegory and Representation*, ed. Stephen J. Greenblatt (Baltimore: Johns Hopkins University Press, 1981), viii.

171. Geoffrey Hartman, "Paul de Man, Fascism, and Deconstruction: Blindness and Insight," *New Republic*, March 7, 1988, 30.

172. De Man, preface to *Allegories of Reading*, x.

173. Miller, in a fashion similar to de Man, contested works of deconstruction that used the historical category of modernism. See J. Hillis Miller, "Deconstructing the Deconstructors," *Diacritics* 5 (1975): 24–31.

174. T. S. Eliot, "Dante," in *Selected Essays* (New York: Harcourt, Brace, 1950), 231, note to section 2.

175. Cleanth Brooks, "Keats's Sylvan Historian: History without Footnotes," *Sewanee Review* 52:1 (1944): 91.

176. Geoffrey Hartman, "History-Writing as Answerable Style," *New Literary History* 2:1 (Autumn 1970): 74.

177. Hartman, "Polemical Memoir," in *A Critic's Journey: Literary Reflections, 1958–1998* (New Haven, CT: Yale University Press, 1999), xxiii.

178. Judy Wurtzel, class assignment for J. Hillis Miller, Box 31, Folder 11, Literature 120a, JHM Papers.

179. Juliet Guichon, class assignment for J. Hillis Miller, Box 31, Folder 6, Literature 120a, Narrative Forms 1979–1984, JHM Papers.

180. Ashley Curtis, class assignment for J. Hillis Miller, Box 31, Folder 7, Literature 120a Narrative Forms 1979–1984, JHM Papers.

181. Bill Jewett, "Closure in Literary Criticism: A Parable," Box 31, Folder 6, Literature 120a, Narrative Forms 1979–1984, JHM Papers.

182. Ibid.

183. Ibid.

184. "Literature Y: Syllabus," Box 31, Folder 7, Literature 120 Narrative Forms 1979–1984, JHM Papers, 1–4. "Literature 300: Syllabus," Box 31, Folder 7, Literature 120 Narrative Forms 1979–1984, JHM Papers.

185. "Literature Y: Syllabus," Box 31, Folder 7, Literature 120 Narrative Forms 1979–1984, JHM Papers, 1–4. "Literature 300: Syllabus," Box 31, Folder 7, Literature 120 Narrative Forms 1979–1984, JHM Papers. Paul de Man, "Rhetorical Readings, Lit Z (130b) (Yale) 1981," PDM Papers. De Man, "Semiology and Rhetoric," *Diacritics*, 32.

186. Minutes: Governing Board of the Literature Major, May 6, 1974, accession 051, Box 50, Folder 167, Yale College Records of the Dean 1969–1973, YUA.

187. Paul de Man and Geoffrey Hartman, "Curriculum for Lit Z Proposal (1975)," Box 15, Folder 23, "Lit Z," drafts of proposal to create Yale undergraduate literature course, PDM Papers.

188. Ibid., n. 1.

189. See Paul de Man, "Interview with Robert Moynihan (1984)," in *The Paul de Man Notebooks*, ed. Martin McQuillan (Edinburgh: Edinburgh University Press, 2014), 162.

190. Paul de Man, notebook, Box 13, Folder 2, Lit Z (Yale) 1977, PDM Papers.

191. Ibid.

192. Paul De Man and Geoffrey Hartman, "Exercise II 'Science' and 'Art' in Nietzsche's *Truth and Falsity in an Ultramoral Sense*," Box 14, Folder 2, Lit Z (Yale) 1977, PDM Papers.

193. Ibid.

194. Paul de Man, notebook, Box 13, Folder 2, Lit Z (Yale) 1977, PDM Papers.

195. Paul de Man, notebook, Box 14, Folder 2, Lit 130b (Lit Z), with J. Hillis Miller (Yale); Hegel (Yale) 1979–1980, PDM Papers.

196. Percy Bysshe Shelley, *The Major Works Including Poetry, Prose, and Drama*, ed. Zachary Leader and Michael O'Neill (Oxford: Oxford University Press, 2003; reissued 2009), 614.

197. Paul de Man, "Rousseau and English Romanticism" (1978), in *The Paul de Man Notebooks*, 115–16.

198. Paul de Man, notebook, Box 14, Folder 2, Lit 130b (Lit Z), with J. Hillis Miller (Yale); Hegel (Yale) 1979–1980, PDM Papers; emphasis added.

199. Ibid.

200. Ibid.

201. Incorrectly filed: Carl Goldfarb, "'The Wild Swans at Coole,' 'Leda and the Swan' and 'Coole Park and Ballylee, 1931'; a Toehold in Yeats's Poetry," Box 31, Folder 12, Literature 130b Reading and Rhetorical Structures, JHM Papers, 1.

202. Ibid.

203. Ibid.

204. Ibid., 7.

205. Ibid.

206. Ibid., 7–8.

207. Ibid., 8.

208. Andrej Warminski, "Interview: Deconstruction at Yale," by Stuart Barnett, in *Material Inscriptions: Rhetorical Reading in Practice and Theory* (Edinburgh: Edinburgh University Press, 2013), 220.

209. Peter Brooks, "Aesthetics and Ideology: What Happened to Poetics?," *Critical Inquiry* 20:3 (1994): 512.

210. Denis Donoghue, "Deconstructing Deconstruction," *New York Review of Books* 27:10 (June 12, 1980), 41.

211. Woodward et al., "A New Look at Literary Criticism," 80.

212. Donald Reiman, letter to the editor, *Times Literary Supplement*, February 18, 1983.

213. See Hayden White, *Metahistory: Historical Imagination in Nineteenth-Century Europe* (Baltimore: Johns Hopkins University Press, 1973). J. Hillis Miller, "Beginning with a Text: Review of *Beginnings: Intention and Method* by Edward W. Said," *Diacritics* 6:3 (1976): 2–7, at 7.

214. Wayne Booth, "'Preserving the Exemplar': Or, How Not to Dig Our Own Graves," *Critical Inquiry* 2:3 (1976): 423.

215. See Wayne Booth, "M. H. Abrams: Historian as Critic, Critic as Pluralist," *Critical Inquiry* 2:3 (1976): 444.

216. M. H. Abrams, "The Limits of Pluralism: The Deconstructive Angel," Box 24, Folder 25, Critical Inquiry 1976–1977, JHM Papers, 14.

217. See Currie, *The Invention of Deconstruction*, 46.

218. Miller, "The Critic as Host," *Critical Inquiry* 3:3 (1977): 446–47.

219. Ibid., 447.

220. Abrams, "The Limits of Pluralism," 5.

221. David Bevington to J. Hillis Miller, December 30, 1977, Box 24, Folder 25, Critical Inquiry 1976–1977, JHM Papers.

222. Paul de Man, "Self (*Pygmalion*)," in *Allegories of Reading*, 176.

223. John Locke, "Essay on Human Understanding," in *The Works of John Locke*, 9 vols. (London, 1824), 2:27; emphasis added.

224. Ibid., 2:17.

225. Paul de Man, notebook, Box 12, Folder 10, NEH Seminar (Yale) 1976, PDM Papers. See Paul de Man, "The Epistemology of Metaphor," *Critical Inquiry* 5:1 (1978): 13–30.

226. Paul de Man, "NEH Seminar 1981," Box 14, Folder 6, PDM Papers; De Man, "Rhetorical Readings: Director: Paul de Man, Yale University," in *The Paul de Man Notebooks*, 253.

227. De Man, "Director's Report on Rhetorical Readings (1982): Director: Paul de Man," in *The Paul de Man Notebooks*, 256.

228. Paul de Man, "An Interview with Paul de Man," by Rosso, 789. Students in Europe, de Man explained, "were mostly destined to teaching in secondary school." He also tellingly reflected that "the situation of teaching in Europe . . . is of course much closer to ideological and political questions, while on the contrary, in the States, one is much closer to professional questions." Ibid., 789, 788.

229. Barbara Johnson, "Art for Something's Sake," *Journal of Aesthetic Education* 36:3 (2002): 29.

230. Salusinszky, "Barbara Johnson," 161.

231. Warminski, "Interview," 220.

232. Paul de Man, "Introduction to *Studies in Romanticism*," in "The Rhetoric of Romanticism," special issue, *Studies in Romanticism* 18:4 (1979): 495–99.

233. Ibid., 498.

234. Ibid.

235. Timothy Bahti, "Figures of Interpretation, the Interpretation of Figures: A Reading of Wordsworth's 'Dream of the Arab,'" *Studies in Romanticism* 18:4 (1979): 625.

236. Salusinszky, "Harold Bloom," 67.

237. Heather Mac Donald, "Down and Out with Paul de Man," in *Why I Turned Right: Leading Baby Boom Conservatives Chronicle Their Political Journeys*, ed. Mary Eberstadt (New York: Threshold Editions, 2007), 116.

238. Hartman quoted in Peeters, *Derrida*, 328.

239. De Man quoted in ibid., 295.

240. Lentricchia, *After the New Criticism*, 317.

241. See Richard Rorty, "Transcendental Arguments, Self-Reference, and Pragmatism," in *Transcendental Arguments and Science: Essays in Epistemology*, ed. Peter Bieri, Rolf P. Hortsman, and Lorenz Krüger (Dordrecht: D. Reidel, 1979), 77–104.

242. John R. Searle, "Reiterating the Differences: A Reply to Derrida," in *Glyph: Johns Hopkins Textual Studies*, ed. Henry Sussman and Samuel Weber (Baltimore: Johns Hopkins University Press, 1977), 198–208; Derrida returned the volley, arguing that Searle's unwitting repetition of Derrida's earlier explanations of Austin's unintentional subversion of the metaphysical dichotomy between serious and nonserious communication enacted deconstruction. The *Glyph* confrontation conferred a kind of celebrity upon Derrida in American literary studies, but it "increased tensions with proponents of analytic philosophy" and united Derrida's enemies, those defenders of good sense, precisely the kind of reasoning Derrida read as self-deconstructing. Derrida, "Limited Inc a b c . . . ," in *Glyph: Johns Hopkins Textual Studies 2*, trans. Samuel Weber (Baltimore: Johns Hopkins University Press, 1977), 162–254. Peeters, *Derrida*, 327. Also coming from the analytic philosophical perspective was John Ellis, who launched a critique of Derrida's philosophical project in the late 1980s. See John M. Ellis, *Against Deconstruction* (Princeton, NJ: Princeton University Press, 1989).

243. De Man to Ellen Graham, November 1979, Box 19, Folder 7, 1979 November–December, PDM Papers.

244. Jacques Derrida, "Who or What Is Compared? The Concept of Comparative Literature and the Theoretical Problems of Translation," trans. Eric Prenowitz, *Discourse* 30:1 and 2 (2008): 22.

245. Ibid., 23, 24.

246. Ibid., 33.

247. Ibid., 34.

248. Ibid.

249. Ibid., 39, 50.

250. Ibid., 46, 47.

251. Paul de Man, notebook, Box 14, Folder 4, Hegel and English Romanticism, with Hartman (Yale) 1980, PDM Papers.

252. Ibid.

253. Ibid.

254. Paul de Man, "Sign and Symbol in Hegel's 'Aesthetics,'" *Critical Inquiry* 8:4 (1982): 775, 769.

255. De Man, notebook, Box 14, Folder 4, Hegel and English Romanticism, with Hartman (Yale) 1980, PDM Papers. The work de Man referenced is Wordsworth's "Ode: Intimations of Immortality from Recollections of Early Childhood."

256. Geoffrey Hartman, "From the Sublime to the Hermeneutic," in *The Fate of Reading and Other Essays* (Chicago: University of Chicago Press, 1975), 118; initially published as "The Sublime and the Hermeneutic," in *Mouvements premiers: Etudes critiques offertes à Georges Poulet* (Paris: Corti, 1972), 149–57.

257. De Man, notebook, Box 14, Folder 4, Hegel and English Romanticism, with Hartman (Yale) 1980, PDM Papers.

258. Justus George Lawler to J. Hillis Miller, August 25, 1977, Box 24, Folder 25, Critical Inquiry 1976–1977, JHM Papers.

259. Salusinszky, "Harold Bloom," 68.

260. Ibid.

261. Imre Salusinszky, "Geoffrey Hartman," in *Criticism in Society*, 81.

262. Geoffrey Hartman, preface to *Deconstruction and Criticism*, by Harold Bloom et al. (New York: Seabury, 1979), vii.

263. Ibid., viii.

264. Ibid., ix.

265. Hartman and Bloom were more concerned with literary texts' psychological provenance.

266. Jacques Derrida, "Living On: Border Lines," in Bloom et al., *Deconstruction and Criticism*, 89n1, 80n1, 90n1.

267. Ibid., 146, 99n1; see also 122.

268. Harold Bloom, "The Breaking of Form," in Bloom et al., *Deconstruction and Criticism*, 1.

269. Ibid., 14, 16.

270. Ibid., 3; emphasis added.

271. Paul de Man, "Shelley Disfigured," in Bloom et al., *Deconstruction and Criticism*, 40, 41.

272. Ibid., 49.

273. Ibid., 56.

274. Ibid., 46.

275. Helen Vendler, "Presidential Address, 1980," *PMLA* 96:3 (1981): 344.

276. Josué Harari, *Textual Strategies: Perspectives in Post-Structuralist Criticism* (Ithaca, NY: Cornell University Press, 1979), 68–69.

277. Salusinszky, "Barbara Johnson," 161.

278. See Paul de Man, "Autobiography as De-facement," *Modern Language Notes* 94:5 (1979): 919–30.

279. Michael P. Clark, introduction to *Revenge of the Aesthetic*, 2.

280. Salusinszky, "Barbara Johnson," 167.

281. See Geoffrey Hartman, ed., *Psychoanalysis and the Question of the Text* (Baltimore: Johns Hopkins University Press, 1978).

282. See Alexander Freer, "Faith in Reading: Revisiting the Midrash-Theory Connection," *Paragraph* 39:3 (2016): 335–57.

283. Hartman, "Polemical Memoir," xxvii; Hartman, "A Life of Learning," 18.

284. Hartman, "A Life of Learning," 19. See also Hartman's contribution to Bloom et al., *Deconstruction and Criticism*.

285. Salusinszky, "Harold Bloom," 51.

286. See Harold Bloom, *Agon: Towards a Theory of Revisionism* (Oxford: Oxford University Press, 1982); Bloom, *The Breaking of the Vessels* (Chicago: University of Chicago Press, 1982).

Chapter Four

1. Barbara Johnson, "Gender Theory and the Yale School," *Genre* 17:1–2 (Summer 1984): 101–12, 101.

2. Woodward et al., "A New Look at Literary Criticism," 83.

3. Culler, *On Deconstruction*, 43–64; Shoshana Felman, *La folie et la chose littéraire* (Paris: Seuil, 1978), 2.

4. Johnson, "Gender Theory and the Yale School," 101.

5. Richard Rorty, *Achieving Our Country: Leftist Thought in Twentieth-Century America* (Cambridge, MA: Harvard University Press, 1998), 80.

6. In contrast, see Andrew Hartman's sweeping narrative in *A History of the Culture Wars: A War for the Soul of America* (Chicago: University of Chicago Press, 2015), 134–70.

7. David A. Hollinger, introduction to *The Humanities and the Dynamics of Inclusion since World War II*, 2–3.

8. For a persuasive argument that cultural studies in America was indebted not only to post-sixties identity politics but also to American studies, see David R. Shumway, "The Sixties, the New Left, and the Emergence of Cultural Studies in the United States," in *Historicizing Theory*, 235–54.

9. Rosalind Rosenberg, "Women in the Humanities: Taking Their Place," in *The Humanities and the Dynamics of Inclusion since World War II*, 249.

10. Ibid., 248.

11. Ibid., 258, 257.

12. "Women's Studies," *Newsweek*, October 26, 1970, 61.

13. Lora H. Robinson, "The Emergence of Women's Courses in Higher Education," *Research Currents ERIC Higher Education* (September 1972): 1. See Tamar Berkowitz, ed., *Who's Who and Where in Women's Studies* (Old Westbury, NY: Feminist Press, 1974).

14. Rosenberg, "Women in the Humanities," 257. See Marilyn Jacoby Boxer,

When Women Ask the Questions: Creating Women's Studies in America (Baltimore: Johns Hopkins University Press, 1998), 7–24; Roberta Salper, "San Diego State 1970: The Initial Year of the Nation's First Women's Studies Program," *Feminist Studies* 37:3 (Fall 2011): 656–82.

15. Jonathan Lear, "How Yale Selected Her First Coeds," *New York Times Magazine*, April 13, 1969, 72, 76.

16. Mary B. Arnstein, chairman, Report to the President from the University Committee on the Education of Women, 1973–1974, July 1, 1974, Records of President Brewster, MS-6-778, ACCN II, Box 258, Folder 11, Manuscripts and Archives at Yale University. Amy Vita Kesselman, "Women's Liberation and the Left in New Haven, Connecticut, 1968–1972," *Radical History Review* 81 (Fall 2001): 17.

17. Julien Dedman, *The Rape of Yale: How a Great University Went Wrong* (Southport, CT: Southport Productions, 1969), 11.

18. Elga Wasserman to Kingman Brewster, May 11, 1970, Records of President Brewster, RU 11 Manuscripts and Archives at Yale University, Box 60, Folder 13, "Coeducation 1969–70," 1–5.

19. Marcia Graham Synnott, *Student Diversity at the Big Three: Changes at Harvard, Yale, and Princeton since the 1920s* (New Brunswick, NJ: Transaction, 2013), 140.

20. Ibid. "A Report to Yale Corporation by the Yale Undergraduate Women's Caucus," Box 16, Folder 7, Papers of Catherine A. MacKinnon 1946–2009, Schlesinger Library, Radcliffe Institute, Harvard University, Cambridge, MA, 1.

21. See "A Report to the President from the Committee on the Status of Professional Women at Yale," May 1971, 3, 15, http://wff.yale.edu/sites/default/files/files/1971_A_Report_to_the_PresidentProfWomen.pdf; Mary B. Arnstein, chairman, "Report: Correspondence from Barbara Deinhardt, Administrative Assistant to Elga Wasserman, re: 'Women's Studies,'" July 14, 1972, Women's and Gender Studies Files (WGSF), Manuscripts and Archives at Yale University.

22. "A Report to the Yale Corporation from the Yale Undergraduate Women's Caucus (1977)," Manuscripts and Archives, Yale University, New Haven, CT, 5.

23. Ibid.

24. Nan Robertson, "Betty Friedan Ushers in a 'Second Stage,'" *New York Times*, October 19, 1981. Freidan's course served as a testing ground for Friedan's *The Second Stage* (New York: Summit Books, 1981). Rosenberg, "Women in the Humanities," 257.

25. David A. Hollinger, "The Disciplines and the Identity Debates," in *American Academic Culture in Transformation*, 362–63.

26. Catherine MacKinnon, Memo to the Committee on the Education of Women, re "Notes Toward an Argument for Women's Studies," November 1, 1978, WGSF, Box 16, Folder 7, 1. Katherine Kennedy, "The Emerging Women Series of the New Haven Socialist/Feminist Women's Group," Box 16, Folder 6, Papers of Catherine A. MacKinnon 1946–2009, Schlesinger Library, Radcliffe Institute, Harvard University.

27. Kirsten E. Lodal, "Engendering an Intellectual Space: The Development

of Women's Studies at Yale University 1969–2001" (unpublished senior essay, Yale University, 2001), 17.

28. Catherine MacKinnon, "Feminism and Humanism: An Introduction to Women's Studies, Original Proposal for Syllabus, 1976–1977," Box 16, Folder 7, 1; MacKinnon to the Rescorla Committee, April 12, 1976, Box 16, Folder 8, Papers of Catherine A. MacKinnon 1946–2009, Schlesinger Library, Radcliffe Institute, Harvard University, 3.

29. Carol Mostow quoted in Lodal, "Engendering an Intellectual Space," 18.

30. Catherine MacKinnon, *Sexual Harassment of Working Women: A Case of Sex Discrimination* (New Haven, CT: Yale University Press, 1979), 1.

31. See Mary Rowe, "Saturn's Rings: A Study of the Minutiae of Sexism Which Maintain Discrimination and Inhibit Affirmative Action Results in Corporations and Non-Profit Institutions," in *Graduate and Professional Education of Women: Proceedings of AAUW Conference Held at the AAUW Educational Center, May 9–10, 1974* (Washington, DC: American Association of University Women, 1974), 1–9.

32. The 1978 summer term had a total enrollment of 119 men and women. See "Yale College Summer Term 28 May to 15 August: Plan Ahead," *Yale Daily News* A, November 16, 1977, 19. See Suzanne Koven and Robin Wharton, eds., "Lit 80-20a: Sexual Politics in Literature," *Yale Course Critique, 1977* (New Haven, CT: Yale Daily News, 1977), 130.

33. Faye Crosby, "The Denial of Personal Discrimination," *American Behavioral Scientist* 27:3 (January 1984): 371–86.

34. Nancy Cott, *The Bonds of Womanhood: "Women's Sphere" in New England, 1780–1835* (New Haven, CT: Yale University Press, 1977). See also Louise A. Tilly and Joan W. Scott, *Women, Work, and Family* (New York: Routledge, 1978).

35. "A Report to the Yale Corporation from the Yale Undergraduate Women's Caucus (1977)," 13; Jason Friedman, "Gay Alumni Form Organizations, Plan GLAD Panel," *Yale Daily News* 109, April 4, 1984, 3; Jack Winkler, "Gardens of Nymphs: Public and Private in Sappho's Lyrics," *Women's Studies: An Interdisciplinary Journal* 8:1–2 (Spring/Summer 1981): 83.

36. Koven and Wharton, "Lit 80-20a: Sexual Politics in Literature," 130. Mary Ellman, *Thinking about Women* (New York: Harcourt, Brace and World, 1968). Kate Millet, *Sexual Politics* (New York: Doubleday, 1970). Patricia Meyer Spacks, *The Female Imagination: A Literary and Psychological Investigation of Women's Writing* (New York: Knopf, 1975). Ellen Moer, *Literary Women: The Great Writers* (New York: Doubleday, 1976). Elaine Showalter, "Literary Criticisms," *Signs* 1:1 (Fall 1975): 435–60. Showalter, *A Literature of Their Own: British Women Novelists from Bronte to Lessing* (Princeton, NJ: Princeton University Press, 1977).

37. Koven and Wharton, "Lit 80-20a: Sexual Politics in Literature," 130.

38. "A Report to the Yale Corporation from the Yale Undergraduate Women's Caucus (1977)," 14, 12, emphasis added; Mary Ressler, "Women's Caucus Sharpens Focus," *Yale Daily News* 38, November 9, 1977.

39. Kernan, Brooks, and Holquist, *Man and His Fictions*, 520–22; Kernan, *In Plato's Cave*, 191.

40. For Johnson's recollection of her time at Yale, see Salusinszky, "Barbara Johnson," 156–57.

41. Barbara Johnson, "The Critical Difference: Review of S/Z by Roland Barthes," *Diacritics* 8:2 (Summer 1978): 4.

42. Ibid.

43. Ibid., 3.

44. Ibid., 8.

45. Ibid., 3.

46. Ibid.

47. See de Man, "Semiology and Rhetoric," in *Allegories of Reading*, 17.

48. Suzanne Bernard, *Le poème en prose de Baudelaire jusqu'à nos jours* (Paris: Librairie Nizet, 1959), 13; author's translation.

49. Barbara Johnson, "Le lyrisme et son double," in *Défigurations du langage poétique: La seconde révolution baudelairienne* (Paris: Flammarion, 1979), 76; author's translation.

50. Johnson, *Défigurations*, 37; author's translation.

51. Culler, *On Deconstruction*, 228n1.

52. Derrida, "Les fins de l'homme," in *Marges de la philosophie* (Paris: Minuit, 1972), 124–64. Barbara Johnson, "Le dernier homme," in *Les fins de l'homme: A partir du travail de Jacques Derrida*, ed. Philippe Lacoue-Labarthe and Jean-Luc Nancy (Paris: Galilée, 1981), 259, 265.

53. "Literature 120a: Narrative Forms," Syllabus Fall 1980, Box 31, Folder 6, Literature 120a Narrative Forms 1979–1984, JHM Papers, 1.

54. "Literature 120a: Narrative Forms," Syllabus Fall 1979, Box 31, Folder 8, Literature 120a Narrative Forms 1979–1984, JHM Papers, 1.

55. "Literature 120," Paper Topics, Fall 1980, Box 31, Folder 9, JHM Papers, 1.

56. Margaret Homans, "Studies in the Feminine Poetic Imagination: Dorothy Wordsworth, Emily Brontë, and Emily Dickinson" (PhD diss., Yale University, 1978), 1.

57. Ibid., 1.

58. Margaret Homans, *Bearing the Word: Language and Female Experience in Nineteenth-Century Women's Writings* (Chicago: University of Chicago Press, 1986), xii.

59. Ibid., 29.

60. Ibid., 29, 30.

61. Harold Bloom, "Frankenstein, or the New Prometheus," *Partisan Review* 32:4 (Fall 1965): 613, 614; Bloom, "Afterword," in Mary W. Shelley, *Frankenstein, or, The Modern Prometheus* (New York: Signet / New American Library, 1965).

62. Harold Bloom to J. Hillis Miller, August 27, 1974, Box 31, Folder 26, JHM Papers, Critical Theory Archive, UC-Irvine Libraries Special Collections, 4. See Ellen Moer's 1973 discussion of *Frankenstein* in the *New York Review of Books* and her 1976 *Literary Women*, which included her interpretation of the novel as an example of the "Female Gothic" and which helped to elevate Mary Shelley's status. Ellen Moers, "Female Gothic," in *Literary Women*, 90–98. See also Marc A. Rubenstein, "'My

Accursed Origin': The Search for the Mother in *Frankenstein*," *Studies in Romanticism* 15:2 (Spring 1976): 165–94; Sandra Gilbert, "Horror's Twin: Mary Shelley's Monstrous Eve," *Feminist Studies* 4:2 (Summer 1978): 48–73.

63. Yale professor of English Howard Felperin considered the new "feminist way of thinking" as merely "a new politics of unearned entitlement" that replaced "an older politics of unearned preferment." See Felperin, *In Another Life*, 82. To be fair, Bloom mentored the students he felt no other faculty member at Yale could. He, for example, enthusiastically directed Camille Paglia's dissertation on sexual deviance in ancient and modern art.

64. Rosenberg, "Women in the Humanities," 255.

65. Sandra Gilbert and Susan Gubar, *The Madwoman in the Attic: The Woman Writer and the Nineteenth-Century Literary Imagination* (New Haven, CT: Yale University Press, 1979).

66. Ibid., 17.

67. Marjorie Garber, a Shakespearean scholar, earned her doctorate in English from Yale in 1969 and was assistant professor there until 1979, when she accepted a full professorship at Haverford College; Garber moved to Harvard in 1981. Her first book, *Dream in Shakespeare* (1974), was nominally deconstructive, in that she largely used Freudian theory.

68. Mary Poovey, "A Science of the Specific: An Interview with Mary Poovey," by Caroline Arni and Mischa Suter, *Historische Anthropologie Jahrgang* 3 (2016): 432–44, 432, 443.

69. Mary Poovey, "My Hideous Progeny: Mary Shelley and the Feminization of Romanticism," *PMLA* 95:3 (Spring 1980): 332, 338.

70. François Rigolot, review of *Father Figures: Genealogy and Narrative Structure in Rabelais*, by Carla Freccero, *Modern Philology* 91:4 (1994): 482.

71. Margaret W. Ferguson, *Trials of Desire: Renaissance Defenses of Poetry* (New Haven, CT: Yale University Press, 1983), 20. Ferguson, "The Exile's Defense: DuBellay's *La Deffense* et illustration de la langue françoyse," *PMLA* 32:2 (1978): 275.

72. Thomas M. Greene, *The Light in Troy: Imitation and Discovery in Renaissance Poetry* (New Haven, CT: Yale University Press, 1982), 195–96.

73. Miller, "Tales out of (the Yale) School," 116. See also Shoshana Felman, *La "folie" dans l'oeuvre Romanesque de Stendhal* (Paris: Corti, 1971).

74. Jacques Lacan, "God and the Jouissance of Women," in *Feminine Sexuality: Jacques Lacan and the École Freudienne*, ed. Juliet Mitchell and Jacqueline Rose (New York: Norton, 1983), 144.

75. Quoted in Peter L. Rudnytsky, *Rescuing Psychoanalysis from Freud and Other Essays in Re-vision* (London: Karnac Books, 2011), 153.

76. Phyllis Chesler, *Women and Madness* (Garden City, NY: Doubleday, 1972); Luce Irigaray, *Speculum de l'autre femme* (Paris: Minuit, 1974). Shoshana Felman, "Women and Madness: The Critical Phallacy," *Diacritics* 5:4 (1975): 10.

77. Felman, "Women and Madness," 10.

78. Ibid.

79. Hélène Cixous, "The Laugh of the Medusa," trans. Keith Cohen and Paula Cohen, *Signs* 1:4 (1976): 875–93, 881.

80. See Elaine Marks and Isabelle de Courtivron, eds., *New French Feminisms: An Anthology* (Amherst: University of Massachusetts Press, 1980).

81. Bina Freiwald, "The Problem of Trans-lation: Reading French Feminisms," *Traduire la théorie* 4:2 (1991): 60–61.

82. Shoshana Felman, "To Open the Question," *Yale French Studies* 55/56 (1977): 5–10, 7.

83. Ibid.

84. Shoshana Felman, "Turning the Screw of Interpretation," in "Literature and Psychoanalysis: The Question of Reading, Otherwise," special issue, *Yale French Studies* 55/56 (1977): 196.

85. Barbara Johnson, "The Frame of Reference: Poe, Lacan, Derrida," *Yale French Studies* 55/56 (1977): 465.

86. Ibid., 464.

87. Ibid., 464, 465, 464.

88. Jacques Derrida, *The Post Card: From Socrates to Freud and Beyond*, trans. Alan Bass (Chicago: University of Chicago Press, 1987), 150–51.

89. Dennis Williams, Marsha Zabarsky, and Dianne H. McDonald, "Out of the Academic Ghetto," *Newsweek*, October 31, 1983, 86.

90. Kellie Bean, *Post-Backlash Feminism: Women and the Media since Reagan-Bush* (Jefferson, NC: McFarland, 2007), 18.

91. Judith Berman Brandenburg, quoted in "Yale to Offer BA in Women's Studies: Becomes 2nd Ivy League School to Offer a Major—Will Begin in 1982," *New York Times*, November 22, 1981.

92. Eve Kosofsky Sedgwick, "Sedgwick Sense and Sensibility: An Interview with Eve Kosofsky Sedgwick," by Mark Kerr and Kristin O'Rourke, *Thresholds: Viewing Culture* 9 (1994), http://nideffer.net/proj/Tvc/interviews/20.Tvc.v9.intrvws.Sedg.html.

93. Eve Kosofsky Sedgwick, "The Coherence of Gothic Conventions" (PhD diss., Yale University, 1975).

94. "Life of Eve Kosofsky Sedgwick," http://evekosofskysedgwick.net/biography/biography.html, accessed February 27, 2020.

95. Eve Kosofsky Sedgwick, "The Character in the Veil: Imagery of the Surface in the Gothic Novel," *PMLA* 96:2 (1981): 259.

96. "Life of Eve Kosofsky Sedgwick."

97. Colette Gaudin, Mary Jean Green, Lynn Anthony Higgins, Marianne Hirsch, Vivian Kogan, Claudia Reeder, and Nancy Vickers, introduction to *Feminist Readings: French Texts / American Contexts*, ed. Gaudin et al., special issue, *Yale French Studies* 62 (1981): 2–18, 2.

98. Ibid.

99. Ibid., 11.

100. Ibid., 5.

101. Elizabeth Abel, "Editor's Introduction," *Critical Inquiry* 8:2 (1981): 173. The original context of this sentence appeared in Barbara Johnson, *The Critical Differ-*

ence: Essays in the Contemporary Rhetoric of Reading (Baltimore: Johns Hopkins University Press, 1980), 284.

102. Barbara Johnson quoted in Abel, "Editor's Introduction," 173.

103. Jane Gallop, *Around 1981: Academic Feminist Literary Theory* (New York: Routledge, 1992), 15.

104. Barbara Johnson, "My Monster / My Self," *Diacritics* 12:2 (1982): 2–10.

105. Ibid., 4.

106. Ibid., 5.

107. Quoted in ibid., 2, 5.

108. Ibid.

109. Ibid., 4.

110. Gallop, *Around 1981*, 244.

111. Ibid.; emphasis added.

112. See Jacques Lacan, *Écrits: A Selection*, trans. Alan Sheridan (London: Tavistock, 1977), 158.

113. Johnson, "My Monster / My Self," 3.

114. See Gayatri Chakravorty Spivak, "Finding Feminist Readings: Dante-Yeats," *Social Text* (Fall 1980): 73–87.

115. Elaine Showalter, "Women's Space: Writing the History of Feminist Criticism," *Tulsa Studies in Women's Literature* 3:1/2 (1984): 38; Gayatri Chakravorty Spivak, "Displacement and the Discourse of Women," in *Displacement: Derrida and After*, ed. Mark Krupnick (Bloomington: Indiana University Press, 1983); Christopher Norris, *Deconstruction: Theory and Practice* (London: Methuen, 1982), 71.

116. Gayatri Chakravorty Spivak, "French Feminism in an International Frame," *Yale French Studies* 62 (Summer 1981): 154–84. Spivak, "Displacement and the Discourse of Women," 173, 233.

117. Spivak, "'Draupadi' by Mahasveta Devi," *Critical Inquiry* 8:2 (Winter 1981): 381.

118. Ibid., 383.

119. Spivak, "Can the Subaltern Speak?," in *Marxism and the Interpretation of Culture*, ed. Cary Nelson and Lawrence Grossberg (London: Macmillan, 1988), 280–81.

120. Gayatri Chakravorty Spivak, "The Great Wheel: Stages in the Personality of Yeats's Lyric Speak" (PhD diss., Cornell University, 1967); Spivak, *Myself Must I Remake: The Life and Poetry of W. B. Yeats* (New York: Cromwell, 1974).

121. Gayatri Chakravorty Spivak, translator's preface to Derrida, *Of Grammatology*, ix–xc.

122. Ibid., lxxxvii.

123. See Spivak, "Preface: Reading *De la Grammatologie*," in *Reading Derrida's Of Grammatology*, ed. Sean Gaston and Ian Maclachlan (London: Continuum, 2011), xxx.

124. Spivak, translator's preface, lxxxvii.

125. Paul de Man, letter of recommendation for John Simon Guggenheim Foundation Memorial Foundation, Box 16, Folder 5, 1971, PDM Papers, UC-Irvine.

126. Ibid.

127. Spivak, translator's preface, liii.

128. Derrida, *Of Grammatology*, 158.

129. See Toril Moi, *Sexual/Textual Politics* (London: Methuen, 1985).

130. See Shoshana Felman, "Education and Crisis, or the Vicissitudes of Teaching," *American Imago* 48:1 (1991): 473–95; Shoshana Felman and Dori Laub, *Testimony: Crisis of Witnessing in Literature, Psychoanalysis, and History* (London: Routledge, 1992). See Steven Weine, "Testimony in New Haven," in *Testimony after Catastrophe: Narrating the Traumas of Political Violence* (Evanston, IL: Northwestern University Press, 2006), 32.

131. Barbara Johnson, "Metaphor, Metonymy and Voice in Zora Neale Hurston's *Their Eyes Were Watching God*," in *A World of Difference* (Baltimore: Johns Hopkins University Press, 1987), 212, 165.

132. Ibid., 218. See also Henry Louis Gates Jr., "Zora Neale Hurston and the Speakerly Text," in *The Signifying Monkey: A Theory of African American Literary Criticism* (New York: Oxford University Press, 1988), 184–232.

133. See bell hooks, *Ain't I a Woman? Black Women and Feminism* (London: South End, 1981). Cherríe Moraga and Gloria Anzaldúa, "Introduction, 1981," in *This Bridge Called My Back: Writings by Radical Women of Color*, ed. Moraga and Anzaldúa (Watertown, MA: Persephone, 1981), xliii.

134. Johnson, "Gender Theory and the Yale School," 102.

135. Ibid.

136. "WGSS at Yale: Reflections, Celebrations, and Visions," Yale University, Women's, Gender, and Sexuality Studies, https://wgss.yale.edu/about, accessed December 4, 2020.

137. Johnson, "Gender Theory and the Yale School," 101. Paul de Man was originally scheduled to speak on the topic of deconstruction and genre theory. After his death, Johnson was invited to take his place; it was an ironic and fitting substitution, as Johnson's talk deconstructively placed what was apparently marginal—"sexual difference in the Yale School"—as in fact central.

138. Johnson, "Gender Theory and the Yale School," in *A World of Difference*, 37.

139. Ibid.

140. Ibid., 35, 36, 35.

141. Paul de Man, "Epistemology of Metaphor," 15. Quoted in Johnson, "Gender Theory and the Yale School," in *A World of Difference*, 37, 38.

142. Johnson, "Gender Theory and the Yale School," in *A World of Difference*, 39.

143. Ibid., 41.

144. Ibid., 41, 40. See also Johnson, "Gender Theory and the Yale School," 102.

145. Mary Wilson Carpenter, introduction to *A Life with Mary Shelley*, by Barbara Johnson (Stanford, CA: Stanford University Press, 2014), xxi.

146. "Boston Area Colloquium on Feminist Theory," Northeastern University Center for Humanities, 1982–1985, http://jwa.org/sites/jwa.org/files/jwa04la.pdf.

147. Ibid.

148. Eve Kosofsky Sedgwick, "Homophobia, Misogyny and Capital: The Example of 'Our Mutual Friend,'" *Raritan* 2 (1983): 126–51.

149. Sedgwick, "Sedgwick Sense and Sensibility."

150. Eve Kosofsky Sedgwick, *Between Men: English Literature and Male Homosocial Desire* (New York: Columbia University Press, 1985), 92.

151. Ibid., 95.

152. Ibid., 16.

153. "Life of Eve Kosofsky Sedgwick."

154. Eve Kosofsky Sedgwick, "Jane Austen and the Masturbating Girl," *Critical Inquiry* 17:4 (Summer 1991): 819, 833, 821n8.

155. Sedgwick, "Queer and Now," in *Tendencies* (London: Routledge, 1994), 15, 14.

156. Eve Kosofsky Sedgwick, *Epistemology of the Closet* (Berkeley: University of California Press, 1990), 1.

157. Ibid., 93.

158. Judith Butler, "Preface to the Paperback Edition," in *Subjects of Desire: Hegelian Reflections in Twentieth-Century France* (1987; repr., New York: Columbia University Press, 1999), xiii.

159. Judith Butler, "Sex and Gender in Simone de Beauvoir's *Second Sex*," *Yale French Studies* 72 (Winter 1986): 35–49, 48.

160. Judith Butler, "Performative Act and Gender Constitution: An Essay in Phenomenology and Feminist Theory," *Theatre Journal* 40:4 (1988): 523.

161. Judith Butler, *Gender Trouble: Feminism and the Subversion of Identity* (1990; repr., New York: Routledge, 2010), 187.

162. Geoffrey Hartman to Murray Krieger, Box 70, Folder 7, Brochures and Publicity, 1986–1992, Dartmouth, Murray Krieger Papers, Critical Theory Archive, UC-Irvine, 1.

163. Hartman, *A Scholar's Tale*, 98.

164. George Will, "Literary Politics," *Newsweek*, April 22, 1991, 72.

165. Hartman, *A Scholar's Tale*, 99–100. Spivak's lecture was published as Gayatri Chakravorty Spivak, "Displacement and the Discourse of Women," in *Displacement: Derrida and After*.

166. Quoted in Derrida, "The Double Session," in *Dissemination*, 213.

167. Quoted in ibid., 201.

168. Ibid., 225.

169. Ibid., 213.

170. Spivak, "Displacement and the Discourse of Women," 175.

171. See Marjorie Garber, "The Insincerity of Women," in *Desire in the Renaissance: Psychoanalysis and Literature*, ed. Valeria Finucci and Regina Schwartz (Princeton, NJ: Princeton University Press, 1994), 19–38.

172. Judith Newton and Nancy Hoffman, "Preface," *Feminist Studies* 14:1 (1988): 1, 3.

173. Joan W. Scott, "Deconstructing Equality-versus-Difference: Or, the Uses of Poststructuralist Theory for Feminism," *Feminist Studies* 14:1 (1988): 43.

174. Ibid.

175. Ibid., 47.

176. Ibid., 47–48, 44.

177. See "Criticism, Feminism, and the Institution," in *The Post-Colonial Critic: Interviews, Strategies, Dialogues*, ed. Sarah Harasym (New York: Routledge, 1990), 1–16, particularly 10–11.

178. Scott, "Deconstructing Equality-versus-Difference," 38.

179. Ibid., 42.

180. Zillah R. Eisenstein, *The Female Body and the Law* (Berkeley: University of California Press, 1988), 110.

181. Scott, "Deconstructing Equality-versus-Difference," 42.

182. Ibid., 46.

183. Ibid.

184. Eisenstein, *The Female Body and the Law*, 163.

185. Johnson, "Gender Theory and the Yale School," in *A World of Difference*, 32.

Chapter Five

1. Paul de Man, "The Resistance to Theory," *Yale French Studies* 63 (1982): 3, 12.

2. Ibid., 13.

3. Ibid., 20.

4. See Fredric Jameson, *The Political Unconscious: Narrative as a Socially Symbolic Act* (Ithaca, NY: Cornell University Press, 1981).

5. See David Simpson, "Literary Criticism and the Return to 'History,'" *Critical Inquiry* 14:4 (1988): 721–22.

6. "Yale Scholar's Articles Found in Pro-Nazi Paper," *New York Times*, December 1, 1987. Andrew Hartman has offered an interpretation of the "so-called de Man affair" as a battle in the "culture wars" about whether "the United States [could] have a national purpose in the absence of foundational principles." See Andrew Hartman, *A History of the Culture Wars*, 141.

7. George Scialabba, *What Are Intellectuals Good For?* (Boston: Pressed Wafer, 2009), 23. For a classic history about how the reorganization of cities and the growth of the university contributed to the decline and disappearance of the "public intellectual," see Russell Jacoby, *The Last Intellectuals: American Culture in the Age of Academe* (New York: Basic Books, 1987). Burton J. Bledstein has explored how "the university not only segregated ideas from the public, intellectual segregation occurred with the development of each new department in the university." See Bledstein, *The Culture of Professionalism*, 327–28.

8. John Aubrey Douglas, *The California Idea and American Higher Education: 1850 to the 1960 Master Plan* (Stanford, CA: Stanford University Press, 2000).

9. Hazard Adams, *Critical Theory since Plato* (New York: Harcourt Brace Jovanovich, 1971).

10. Hazard Adams to Barbara B. Smith, August 2, 1976, Box 70, Folder 2, Brochures and Publicity (1977), Murray Krieger Papers, 1.

11. "Professional Notes and Comment," *PMLA* 90:5 (1975): 945.

12. See Judith Olson, "Literary Theory More Critical," Box 70, Folder 1, Brochures and Publicity (1976), Murray Krieger Papers, 1. Alex Wood, "Public Informa-

tion Office, University of California, Irvine, Literary Criticism Grant," August 26, 1975, Box 70, Folder 1, Brochures and Publicity (1976), Murray Krieger Papers, 1. Murray Krieger and Hazard Adams, "Renewal NEH Application," Box 65, Folder 6, NEH Sit, Murray Krieger Papers, Visit Agenda and Documents (July 1976), Murray Krieger Papers, 2. Krieger and Adams, untitled paper, Box 70, Folder 2, Brochures and Publicity (1977), Murray Krieger Papers, 1.

13. "For the last forum," 1976, Box 70, Folder 8, Colloquia (1976), Murray Krieger Papers, 1.

14. "Some Questions for 'The Last Forum,'" Box 70, Folder 8, Colloquia (1976), Murray Krieger Papers, 1.

15. Murray Krieger, "Literature vs. Ecriture: Constructions and Deconstructions in Recent Critical Theory," Box 70, Folder 14, Colloquia Papers (1977), Murray Krieger Papers, 1, 2, 4.

16. Murray Krieger, "Issues for Final Meeting, August 2, 1978," Box 70, Folder 10, SCT Colloquium (1978), Murray Krieger Papers, 1.

17. Murray Krieger, "Poetic Presence and Illusion: Renaissance Theory and the Duplicity of Metaphor," *Critical Inquiry* 5:4 (1979): 597–619.

18. Stephen G. Nichols, "Pictures of Poetry in Marot's *Épigrammes*," in *Revenge of the Aesthetic*, 93.

19. Woodward et al., "A New Look at Literary Criticism," 80.

20. "School of Criticism and Theory to Hold Symposium at NU, May 8–9," *Northwestern University News*, April 13, 1981, Box 70, Folder 5, Brochures and Publicity (1981), Murray Krieger Papers, 1.

21. Wolfgang Iser, "The Current Situation of Literary Theory: Key Concepts and the Imaginary," *New Literary History* 11:1 (1979): 1.

22. Murray Krieger, "Questions Submitted for Final Colloquium," Box 70, Folder 12, Colloquia (1981), Murray Krieger Papers, 1–2.

23. Prospectus and Application, Summer 1982, Box 70, Folder 6, Brochures and Publicity: Northwestern (1982–1985), Murray Krieger Papers, 1.

24. PDM Papers, Box 14, Folder 7, School of Criticism seminar Kant and Schiller, 1.

25. Ibid., 2.

26. Ibid.

27. Geoffrey Hartman in "The Following Tributes Were Offered at the Memorial Service for Paul de Man Held at the Yale University Art Gallery on January 18, 1984," *Yale French Studies* 69 (1985): 7.

28. J. Hillis Miller, *Fiction and Repetition: Seven English Novels* (Cambridge, MA: Harvard University Press, 1982), 16, 6, 9.

29. "The Figure in the Carpet" is a term, first used by Henry James in his 1869 short story of the same name, to denote the "clue" to deciphering an author's work.

30. Miller, *Fiction and Repetition*, 40.

31. Ibid., 52, 67, 70.

32. J. Hillis Miller to A. Bartlett Giamatti, November 28, 1982, Box 24, Folder 28, Emory and FU Offers 1982, JHM Papers, 1.

33. Ibid.

34. J. Hillis Miller to Dr. Charles F. Sidman, dean, November 23, 1982, Box 24, Folder 28, Emory and FU Offers 1982, JHM Papers, 1.

35. J Hillis Miller at de Man Seminar, Box 49, Folder 31, Paul de Man 1982–1996, JHM Papers.

36. "Seminar on 'Aesthetic Theory from Kant to Hegel,' Yale University, Fall Semester, 1982," compiled from the lecture notes of Roger Blood, Cathy Caruth, and Suzanne Roos, *The Paul de Man Notebooks*, 262.

37. Ibid.

38. Ibid., 260.

39. Ibid., 259.

40. Ibid., 266.

41. Ibid., 262.

42. Ibid., 262–63.

43. Ibid., 268.

44. Ibid., 267.

45. Ibid.

46. Ibid., 267–68.

47. Ibid., 268, 266.

48. Ibid., 270.

49. Ibid., 268.

50. Ibid., 266, 269.

51. Ibid., 262, 279.

52. Miller notes from de Man seminar, Aesthetic Theory from Kant to Hegel Fall Semester 1982, Box 49, Folder 21, Paul de Man 1982–1996, JHM Papers.

53. Ibid.

54. Paul de Man, notes on Theory of Rhetoric in the 18th and 20th centuries (Yale 1983), Box 14, Folder 8, PDM Papers, 1.

55. Haun Saussy, interview by Gregory Jones-Katz, March 20, 2014.

56. For an analysis of the iconography of critical theory, including its various uses during the de Man Affair, see Jerome Christensen, "From Rhetoric to Corporate Populism: A Romantic Critique of the Academy in an Age of High Gossip," *Critical Inquiry* 16:2 (1990): 438–65.

57. Hartman in "The Following Tributes," 6.

58. Derrida, "Translations of Pages 13–16 and 17–21," *Yale French Studies* 1986 (69): 323, 334. See de Man's comment, in "Lyric and Modernity" (1969), on Mallarmé's "Tombeu de Verlaine" that "Like all true poets, Verlaine is a poet of death, but death for Mallarmé means precisely the discontinuity between the personal self and the voice that speaks in the poetry from the bank of the river, beyond death." Paul de Man, "Lyric and Modernity," in *Blindness and Insight*, 181.

59. Shoshana Felman in "The Following Tributes," 8.

60. Barbara Johnson in "The Following Tributes," 10.

61. Johnson in "The Following Tributes," 10; E. S. Burt in "The Following Tributes," 11.

62. Felperin, *In Another Life*, 64.

63. Jacques Derrida, "Mnemosyne," in *Memoires for Paul de Man*, 3.

64. Ibid.

65. Ibid.

66. Jacques Derrida, "The Art of Mémoires," in *Memoires for Paul de Man*, 48.

67. Ibid., 56.

68. Jacques Derrida, "Acts," in *Memoires for Paul de Man*, 145. See Paul De Man, "Promises (Social Contract)," in *Allegories of Reading*, 270.

69. De Man himself disavowed the competition as to whether "deconstruction" derived from his work or Derrida's. "I consciously came across 'deconstruction' for the first time in the writings of Jacques Derrida." See preface to de Man, *Allegories of Reading*, x.

70. Jacques Derrida, "Psyche: Inventions of the Other," in *Psyche: Inventions of the Other*, ed. Peggy Kamuf and Elizabeth Rottenberg (Stanford, CA: Stanford University Press, 2007), 1:8.

71. Ibid., 1:11, 8.

72. Ibid., 1:16–19.

73. Jacques Derrida, "The Art of Mémoires," in *Memoires for Paul de Man*, 58.

74. Walter Jackson Bate, "The Crisis in English Studies," *Harvard Magazine*, September–October 1982, 46.

75. Ibid., 52.

76. Ibid.

77. Ibid., 47.

78. Ibid., 53.

79. William J. Bennett, "The Shattered Humanities," *Wall Street Journal*, December 31, 1982, 10.

80. Ibid.

81. Ibid.

82. Ibid.

83. John Ganz, "The Decline of *The New Criterion*," *Baffler*, January 10, 2018, https://thebaffler.com/latest/decline-of-the-new-criterion-ganz.

84. René Wellek "Destroying Literary Studies," *New Criterion* 2:4 (December 1983): 2, 8.

85. J. Hillis Miller, March 27, 1988, Box 39, Folder 7, Paul de Man's Writings 1942–1988, JHM Papers.

86. Jonathan Arac, Wlad Godzich, and Wallace Martin, eds., *The Yale Critics: Deconstruction in America* (Minneapolis: University of Minnesota Press, 1983).

87. Derrida, "Mnemosyne," 17.

88. Jacques Derrida, "Deconstruction in America: An Interview with Jacques Derrida," *Critical Exchange* 17 (Winter 1985): 2.

89. Derrida, "Mnemosyne," 17.

90. Ibid., 18.

91. Ibid.

92. Ibid., 48.

93. Derrida, "Deconstruction in America," 9.

94. Ibid.

95. Rudolphe Gasché, "Deconstruction as Criticism," *Glyph* 6 (1979): 177–216; "'Setzung' and 'Übersetzung': Notes on Paul de Man," review of *Allegories of Reading*, by Paul de Man, *Diacritics* 11:4 (1981): 36–57; Suzanne Gearhart, "Philosophy *before* Literature: Deconstruction, Historicity, and the Work of Paul de Man," *Diacritics* 13:4 (Winter 1983): 63–81.

96. Johnson in "The Following Tributes," 10.

97. See *The Conditions of Excellence in American Higher Education* (Washington, DC: National Institute of Education, 1984); William J. Bennett, *To Reclaim a Legacy: A Report on the Humanities in Higher Education* (Washington, DC: National Endowment for the Humanities, 1984); *Integrity in the College Curriculum* (Washington, DC: Association for American Colleges, 1985); and Ernest L. Boyer, *College: The Undergraduate Experience in America* (New York: Harper and Row, 1986).

98. J. Hillis Miller, *The Ethics of Reading: Kant, de Man, Eliot, Trollope, James, and Benjamin* (New York: Columbia University Press, 1987), 43.

99. Immanuel Kant quoted in Miller, *The Ethics of Reading*, 17.

100. Ibid.

101. Murray Krieger and Hazard Adams, "Ph.D. Concentration in Critical Theory," Box 70, Folder 2, Brochures and Publicity (1977), Murray Krieger Papers.

102. J. Hillis Miller to Wolfgang Iser, August 20, 1985, Box 24, Folder 29, Irvine Offer 1985–1986, JHM Papers, UC-Irvine, 1.

103. J. Hillis Miller to Jacques Derrida, August 20, 1985, Box 24, Folder 29, Irvine Offer 1985–1986, JHM Papers, UC-Irvine, 1.

104. Ibid.

105. Warminski, "Interview," 229.

106. Miller to Derrida, August 20, 1985, 1.

107. Miller, "Constantly Contingent," 65.

108. Ibid.

109. Ibid., 45.

110. David R. Shumway, "The Star System in Literary Studies," in *The Institution of Literature*, ed. Jeffrey J. Williams (Albany: SUNY Press, 2002), 173–202.

111. Miller, "Constantly Contingent," 65.

112. Aldrich quoted in Phil Sneiderman, "Yale Literary Prof. Lured Away to UCI," *Orange Coast Daily Pilot*, February 2, 1986.

113. Quoted in Sneiderman, "Yale Literary Prof. Lured Away to UCI."

114. Quoted in Lynn Smith, "UCI Will Try Deconstructing with Yale Critic," *Los Angeles Times*, March 9, 1986, 1.

115. Holquist, "Literature after 'X,'" 45.

116. Smith, "UCI Will Try Deconstructing with Yale Critic."

117. Ellen S. Burt and Andrej Warminski would also come to call UC-Irvine their institutional home.

118. J. Hillis Miller, "Presidential Address 1986: The Triumph of Theory, the Resistance to Reading, and the Question of the Material Base," *PMLA* 102 (1987):

283. Not all either were convinced of or wanted this apparent "triumph of theory." Four years before Miller's address, literary critics Walter Benn Michaels and Steven Knapp proclaimed that "theory is not just another name for practice." "Our thesis has been that no one can reach a position outside practice, that theorists should stop trying and that theoretical enterprise come to an end." Walter Benn Michaels and Steven Knapp, "Against Theory," *Critical Inquiry* 8:4 (1982): 742.

119. Miller, "Presidential Address 1986," 282–83.

120. Colin Campbell, "The Tyranny of the Yale Critics," *New York Times Magazine*, February 9, 1986, sect. 6, p. 20.

121. Ibid.

122. Ibid.

123. Yosef Hayim Yerushalmi, "Prologue to the Original Edition," in *Zakhor: Jewish History and Jewish Memory* (Seattle: University of Washington Press, 1982), xxxiii.

124. Victor Farias, *Heidegger et le Nazisme* (Paris: Galilée, 1987).

125. Robert Maggiori, "Heil Heidegger," *Libération*, October 16, 1987. Hugo Ott, "Wege und Abwege: Zu Victor Farias' kritischer Heidegger-Studi," *Neue Zücher Zeitung* 275 (November 27, 1987): 67.

126. Quoted in Derrida, "Heidegger, the Philosophers' Hell," in *Points . . . : Interviews*, 187.

127. For work on the German precursors of so-called French theory (stretching back to the eighteenth century), see Andrew Bowie, *From Romanticism to Critical Theory: The Philosophy of German Literary Theory* (New York: Routledge, 1997); and Azade Seyhan, *Representation and Its Discontents: The Critical Legacy of German Romanticism* (Berkeley: University of California Press, 1991). Alan Schrift has explored some of the intellectual roots of French theory in the work of an earlier generation of French philosophers, including Maurice Merleau-Ponty, Georges Canguilhem, Gaston Bachelard, and Jean Cavaillès. See Alan Schrift, "Is There Such a Thing as 'French Philosophy'? Or Why Do We Read the French So Badly?," in *After the Deluge*, 30–31.

128. Martin Price quoted in Campbell, "The Tyranny of the Yale Critics."

129. In February 1988 in Heidelberg, Germany, Derrida also discussed the political implications of Heidegger's philosophy, this time with Hans-Georg Gadamer and Philippe Lacoue-Labarthe. See Jacques Derrida, Hans-Georg Gadamer, and Philippe Lacoue-Labarthe, *Heidegger, Philosophy, and Politics: The Heidelberg Conference*, ed. Mireille Calle-Gruber, trans. Jeff Fort (New York: Fordham University Press, 2016).

130. Derrida, "Heidegger, the Philosophers' Hell," 185.

131. See Chaplin, *Turning On the Mind*.

132. Heidegger quoted in Derrida, "Heidegger, the Philosophers' Hell," 185.

133. Ibid.

134. Derrida, "Like the Sound Deep Within a Shell: Paul de Man's War," *Critical Inquiry* 14:2 (1988): 597.

135. See Richard Wolin, "Preface to the MIT Press Edition," in *The Heidegger*

Controversy: A Critical Reader, ed. Richard Wolin (Cambridge, MA: MIT Press, 1993), xi.

136. Saul Bellow quoted in James Atlas, "Chicago's Grumpy Guru: Best-Selling Professor Allan Bloom and the Chicago Intellectuals," *New York Times Magazine*, January 3, 1988.

137. E. D. Hirsch Jr., *Cultural Literacy: What Every American Needs to Know* (Boston: Houghton Mifflin, 1987).

138. Bloom, *The Closing of the American Mind*, 379.

139. "Yale Scholar Wrote for Pro-Nazi Paper," *New York Times*, December 1, 1987.

140. Paul de Man, "The Return to Philology," in *The Resistance to Theory*, 23.

141. Jon Wiener, "Deconstructing de Man," *Nation* 246:1 (January 9, 1988): 22–24.

142. Ibid., 22.

143. Ibid.

144. Ibid.

145. David Lehman, "Deconstructing de Man's Life: An Academic Idol Falls into Disgrace," *Newsweek*, February 15, 1988, 63–65.

146. J. Hillis Miller to Marilyn Moriarty and Lara Ruffolo, March 20, 1988, Box 39, Folder 7, Paul de Man's Writings 1942–1988, JHM Papers.

147. Quoted in Wiener, "Deconstructing de Man," 24.

148. Alice Kaplan, *French Lessons: A Memoir* (Chicago: University of Chicago Press, 1993), 167.

149. Peeters, *Derrida*, 393.

150. Quoted in Peeters, *Derrida*, 392.

151. Ibid.

152. Juliet Flower MacCannell quoted in Jon Wiener, "The Responsibilities of Friendship: Jacques Derrida on Paul de Man's Collaboration," *Critical Inquiry* 15:4 (1989): 800.

153. Hartman, *A Scholar's Tale*, 83.

154. Quoted in Peeters, *Derrida*, 328.

155. Derrida quoted in Peeters, *Derrida*, 328.

156. Derrida quoted in ibid., 398.

157. See James Atlas, "The Case of Paul de Man," *New York Times Magazine*, August 28, 1988, 36.

158. Quoted in Jacques Derrida, "'Le Parjure,' Perhaps: Storytelling and Lying ('Abrupt Breaches of Syntax')," in *Without Alibi* (Stanford, CA: Stanford University Press, 2000), 184.

159. Peter Dodge, *A Documentary Study of Hendrik de Man, Socialist Critic of Marxism* (Princeton, NJ: Princeton University Press, 1979), 16, quoted in Stanley Corngold, "Error in Paul de Man," *Critical Inquiry* 8:3 (1982): 489.

160. Barbara Johnson, preface to *A World of Difference*, xiii.

161. Henri de Man, "Manifeste aux membres du Parti Ouvrier Belge," in Dodge, *A Documentary Study of Hendrik de Man*, 326–28.

162. Kaplan, *French Lessons*, 161.

163. Dan Latimer, *London Review of Books*, May 5, 1988.

164. Derrida, "Paul de Man's War," 590–652.

165. Ibid., 593.

166. Paul de Man, "Shelley Disfigured," in *Rhetoric of Romanticism* (New York: Columbia University Press, 1984), 123, quoted in Derrida, "Paul de Man's War," 642.

167. Derrida, "Paul de Man's War," 597.

168. Ibid., 637.

169. Ibid., 636.

170. Ibid., 637.

171. Ibid.

172. Ibid., 639.

173. Ibid.

174. Ibid.

175. W. Wolfgang Holdheim, "Jacques Derrida's Apologia," *Critical Inquiry* 15:4 (1989): 793.

176. This student was Juliet Flower MacCannell, referenced in Jon Wiener, "The Responsibilities of Friendship," 799.

177. Wiener, "The Responsibilities of Friendship," 799.

178. Derrida, "Paul de Man's War," 636.

179. Wiener, "The Responsibilities of Friendship," 799.

180. Derrida, "Paul de Man's War," 623.

181. Ibid., 622.

182. Ibid., 631.

183. Ibid., 623, 624, 623.

184. Ibid., 624.

185. Ibid., 624–25.

186. Ibid., 625.

187. Ibid., 625–26.

188. Ibid., 629, 628.

189. Ibid., 628.

190. Ibid., 623.

191. Paul de Man, "Menschen en Boeken: Blik op de huidige Duitse Roman Literatuur," *Het Vlaamsche Land*, August 20, 1942, in *Wartime Journalism, 1939–1943*, trans. Ortwin de Graef, ed. Werner Hamacher, Neil Hertz, and Thomas Keenan (Lincoln: University of Nebraska Press, 1988), 323–24.

192. Paul de Man, "People and Books: A View on Contemporary German Fiction," *Het Vlaamsche Land*, August 20, 1942, in *Wartime Journalism, 1939–1943*, 325–26.

193. Ibid.

194. Ibid. See the discussion of this article in Robert C. Holub, *Crossing Borders: Reception Theory, Poststructuralism, Deconstruction* (Madison: University of Wisconsin Press, 1992), 155.

195. Hartman, "Paul de Man, Fascism, and Deconstruction," 26. Hartman did, nevertheless, note "prejudicial reference[s] to Jews by de Man." See ibid., 27.

196. Quoted in Peeters, *Derrida*, 399. See Derrida, "Paul de Man's War," 623. See also John Brenkman's contribution, "Fascist Commitments," in *Responses: On Paul de Man's Wartime Journalism*, ed. Werner Hamacher, Neil Hertz, and Thomas Keenan (Lincoln: University of Nebraska Press, 1989), especially 33–34.

197. John Brenkman, "Deconstruction and the Social Text," *Social Text* 1 (1979): 186–88.

198. John Brenkman and Jules David Law, "Resetting the Agenda," *Critical Inquiry* 15:4 (1989): 809.

199. Ibid.

200. Holdheim, "Jacques Derrida's Apologia," 789.

201. Brenkman and Law, "Resetting the Agenda," 809; Holdheim, "Jacques Derrida's Apologia," 792; Wiener, "The Responsibilities of Friendship," 797.

202. Dominick LaCapra suggested that "transferential relations between [Derrida] and de Man" perhaps accounted for the "apologetic tendencies" of Derrida's response. See Dominick LaCapra, "The Personal, the Political and the Textual: Paul de Man as Object of Transference," *History and Memory* 4:1 (1992): 27.

203. Wiener, "The Responsibilities of Friendship," 799.

204. J. Hillis Miller, Box 39, Folder 7, Paul de Man's Writings 1942–1988, JHM Papers. Consider also Fredric Jameson's approach to de Man's wartime journalism. Jameson, as LaCapra has noted, attempted to perform the "curious feat of intertextual[ly] one-up[ping]" Derrida's essay: he suggested that de Man's article "was actually telling 'garden-variety anti-Semites' that they would 'be better advised to stop talking about the Jews altogether and to cultivate [their] own garden.'" Jameson cited in LaCapra, "The Personal, the Political and the Textual," 28.

205. David Carroll, "The Sorrow and the Pity of Friendship and Politics: An Open Letter to Jacques Derrida," unpublished, UC-Irvine Archives. A version of this letter was published as "The Temptation of Fascism and the Question of Literature: Justice, Sorrow, and Political Error (an Open Letter to Jacques Derrida)," *Cultural Critique* 15 (Spring 1990): 39–81.

206. Carroll, "The Temptation of Fascism," 76, 68.

207. Peeters, *Derrida*, 396.

208. Christopher Norris, "Paul de Man's Past," *London Review of Books* 10:3 (February 4, 1988): 7–11.

209. Johnson, "Preface to the Paperback Edition," in *A World of Difference*, xv–xvi.

210. Derrida, "Paul de Man's War," 591, 647n1.

211. Ibid., 651.

212. Ibid., 645.

213. Ibid., 640, 641.

214. Ibid., 648.

215. See Norris, "Paul de Man's Past," 7–11.

216. Werner Hamacher, "Fortgesetzte Trauerarbeit: Paul de Mans komplizierte Strategie: Eine Erwiderung," *Frankfurter Allgemeine Zeitung*, February 24, 1988. Similarly, Eric Santner suggested in 1990 that de Man "sought to *displace* and *disperse* the particular, historical tasks of mourning which for him, as is now known,

were substantial and complex, with what might be called structural mourning, that is, mourning for those 'catastrophes' that are inseparable from being-in-language." Eric Santner, *Stranded Objects: Mourning, Memory, and Film in Postwar Germany* (Ithaca, NY: Cornell University Press, 1990), 29.

217. Jacques Derrida, "Biodegradables: Seven Diary Fragments," *Critical Inquiry* 15:4 (1989): 822; Jonathan Culler, "'Paul de Man's War' and the Aesthetic Ideology," *Critical Inquiry* 15:4 (1989): 780.

218. Lindsay Waters, "Paul de Man: A Sketch of Two Generations," in *Responses*, 402.

219. Kaplan, *French Lessons*, 161.

220. Paul de Man, "An Interview with Paul de Man," by Stefano Rosso, in *The Resistance to Theory*, 121.

221. Derrida, "Paul de Man's War," 639.

222. Hartman, "Paul de Man, Fascism, and Deconstruction," 27–31.

223. Ibid., 31.

224. Ibid., 30.

225. Ibid., 31.

226. Ibid.

227. J. Hillis Miller, "Open Letter to Jon Wiener," Box 39, Folder 7, Paul de Man's Writings 1942–1988, JHM Papers, 12.

228. Terry Eagleton, *The Function of Criticism* (London: Verso, 1984), 100–101.

229. Martin Jay, "The Descent of de Man," *Salmagundi*, no. 78/79 (1988): 22.

230. Jeffrey Mehlman, "Writing and Deference: The Politics of Literary Adulation," *Representations* 15 (1985): 12. For a polemical interpretation of postwar intellectual politics in France, one that foregrounds its historicist and violent tendencies, see Tony Judt, *Past Imperfect: French Intellectuals, 1944–1956* (Berkeley: University of California Press, 1992).

231. See Mehlman, *Adventures in the French Trade*, 78.

232. Wolfgang Holdheim, "Letter to the Editor," *London Review of Books* 10:6 (March 17, 1988): 4.

233. Ibid.

234. Richard King, "Fateful Swerve," *London Review of Books* 10:7 (March 31, 1988).

235. Ibid.

236. Shoshana Felman, "Paul de Man's Silence," *Critical Inquiry* 15:4 (1989): 710.

237. Ibid., 717, 707.

238. Ibid., 719.

239. De Man, *Blindness and Insight* (New York: Oxford University Press, 1971).

240. De Man, "Excuses (Confessions)," in *Allegories of Reading*, 293.

241. Ibid.

242. Hartman, "Paul de Man, Fascism, and Deconstruction," 30.

243. Ortwin de Graef, "Silence to Be Observed: A Trial for Paul de Man's Inexcusable Confessions," in *(Dis)continuities: Essays on Paul de Man*, ed. Luc Herman, Kris Humbeeck, and Geert Lernout (Amsterdam: Rodopi, 1989), 61.

244. Hartman, *A Scholar's Tale*, 49.

245. Wiener, "Deconstructing de Man," 24.

246. Richard Rand, however, asked, "Are not . . . Paul de Man and his deconstruction somehow overwhelmingly Jewish—as Jewish as anyone, perhaps, in our multi-national 1980's, can be?" See Richard Rand, *"Rigor Vitae,"* in *Responses,* 354.

247. Felman, "Paul de Man's Silence," 722.

248. Ibid., 737.

249. See Paul de Man, "Conclusions: Walter Benjamin's 'Task of the Translator,'" in *The Resistance to Theory,* 73–105.

250. Holub, *Crossing Borders.*

251. Quoted in Michael Payne and John Schad, eds., *Life. After. Theory: Jacques Derrida, Toril Moi, Frank Kermode and Christopher Norris* (New York: Bloomsbury Academic, 2003), 175.

252. Hartman, *A Scholar's Tale,* 77, 76.

253. Derrida, "Paul de Man's War," 639.

254. Quoted in Wiener, "Deconstructing de Man," 24.

255. Bloom dedicated *A Map of Misreading* (1975) to de Man; he also announced the appearance of "a new mythic being—clearly implied by Paul de Man in particular—the reader as Overman, the *Überleser.*" Bloom, *A Map of Misreading,* 5.

256. Salusinszky, "Harold Bloom," 67.

257. Atlas, "The Case of Paul de Man," 36.

258. Cynthia Chase, "Trappings of an Education," in *Responses,* 78n20.

259. Quoted in Atlas, "The Case of Paul de Man," 36.

260. For his part, Derrida went to his go-to response: accusing the unidentified *Nation* source of acting more reprehensibly than de Man had because the source aimed to shut down debate, an effort, for Derrida, that metaphysically endeavored to end deconstruction. Not coincidentally, this disagreement seems to have effectively finished Derrida and Bloom's friendship.

261. William Blake, *The Marriage of Heaven and Hell* (Oxford: Oxford University Press, 1975), xxv.

262. Hartman, *A Scholar's Tale,* 88.

263. Ibid.

264. For the author's consideration of how the unrepresented presence of de Man's past might have shaped his life and work, see "The Riddle of Paul de Man," *Intellectual History Review* 20:2 (2010): 253–71.

265. Paul de Man, "Hypogram and Inscription: Michael Riffaterre's Poetics of Reading," *Diacritics* 11:4 (1981): 33. See also de Man, "Autobiography as Defacement," 919–30.

266. Kaplan, *French Lessons,* 150.

267. Ibid., 172.

268. Malcolm Bradbury, *My Strange Quest for Mensonge: Structuralism's Hidden Hero* (New York: Penguin, 1988).

269. Ibid., 26.

270. "The Museum of Modern Art: Deconstructivist Architecture," pamphlet, June 1988, 3.

Epilogue

1. Francis Fukuyama, "What Follows the End of History? Identity Politics," interview by Evan Goldstein, *Chronicle Review*, August 27, 2018, https://www.chronicle.com/article/What-Follows-the-End-of/244369. Francis Fukuyama's statement about "history" comes from a 1989 article, "The End of History?," which then served as the "distant origins" of a later volume. See Francis Fukuyama, "The End of History?," *National Interest* 16 (Summer 1989): 3; *The End of History and the Last Man* (New York: Free Press, 1992), xi.

2. George Monbiot, "Neoliberalism—the Ideology at the Root of All Our Problems," *Guardian*, April 15, 2016, https://www.theguardian.com/books/2016/apr/15/neoliberalism-ideology-problem-george-monbiot.

3. Geoffrey Galt Harpham, *The Humanities and the Dream of America* (Chicago: University of Chicago Press, 2011), cover.

4. See Christopher Newfield, *Unmaking the Public University: The Forty-Year Assault on the Middle Class* (Cambridge, MA: Harvard University Press, 2008).

5. Claudia Goldin and Robert A. Margo, "The Great Compression: The Wage Structure in the United States at Mid-Century," *Quarterly Journal of Economics* 107 (1992): 1–34; John D. Donahue, *The Warping of Government Work* (Cambridge, MA: Harvard University Press, 2008), 180.

6. Holquist, "Literature after 'X,'" 46.

7. See Beverly Waters, "A Yale Book of Numbers, 1976–2000," Yale Reference Series, August 2001, https://oir.yale.edu/sites/default/files/pierson_update_1976-2000.pdf.

8. Alexander W. Astin, Sarah A. Parrot, William S. Korn, and Linda J. Sax, *The American Freshman: Thirty Year Trends, 1966–1996* (Los Angeles: Higher Education Research Institute, 1997), 12, 13.

9. Jeffrey J. Selingo, "College Students Say They Want a Degree for a Job. Are They Getting What They Want?," *Washington Post*, September 1, 2018, https://www.washingtonpost.com/news/grade-point/wp/2018/09/01/college-students-say-they-want-a-degree-for-a-job-are-they-getting-what-they-want.

10. Jonathan Culler, "The Return to Philology," *Journal of Aesthetic Education* 36:3 (2002): 12.

11. For an exploration of how the anti-gay-marriage movement in France portrayed "gender theory" as imported from America and contaminating the gender roles of the "French nation," see Perreau, *Queer Theory*.

12. See Bloom, *The Western Canon*.

13. Freedman, *The Temple of Culture*, 215.

14. Geoffrey Hartman, introduction to *The Fateful Question of Culture* (New York: Columbia University Press, 1997), 2. Hartman, "A Life of Learning," 11.

15. Jacques Derrida, "Force of Law: The 'Mystical Foundation of Authority,'" *Cardozo Law Review* 11 (1990): 919–1046.

16. Jacques Derrida, *Spectres de Marx*, trans. Peggy Kamuf (Paris: Galilée, 1993; repr., New York: Routledge, 1994).

17. For more on Kojève's influence, see Ethan Kleinberg, *Generation Existential: Heidegger's Philosophy in France, 1927–1961* (Ithaca, NY: Cornell University Press, 2005), particularly 49–83.

18. Jonathan Kandall, "Jacques Derrida, Abstruse Theorist, Dies at 74," *New York Times*, October 10, 2004.

19. See Julie Rivkin and Michael Ryan, eds., *Literary Theory: An Anthology*, 2nd ed. (Oxford: Blackwell, 1998).

20. J. Hillis Miller, "Paul de Man at Work: In These Bad Days, What Good Is an Archive?," in *Theory and the Disappearing Future: On de Man, on Benjamin*, by Tom Cohen, Claire Colebrook, and J. Hillis Miller (London: Routledge, 2012), 87.

21. Claire Colebrook, introduction to *Theory and the Disappearing Future*, 19, 21, 16.

22. Frederic Jameson explored this connection in his *Postmodernism, or, The Cultural Logic of Late Capitalism*.

23. Ethan Kleinberg, Joan Wallach Scott, and Gary Wilder, "Theses on Theory and History," May 2018, http://theoryrevolt.com/.

24. Christopher Newfield coined the term "perma-austerity"; see, for example, Christopher Newfield, "The Higher Ed Austerity Deal Is Falling Apart," *Inside Higher Ed*, January 12, 2015.

INDEX